QUASI-CONSTITUTIONAL LAWS OF CANADA

Quasi-constitutional Laws of Canada

JOHN HELIS

IRWIN LAW

Published in 2018 by

Irwin Law Inc
Suite 206, 14 Duncan Street
Toronto, Ontario
M5H 3G8
www.irwinlaw.com

ISBN: 978-1-55221-494-7 e-book ISBN: 978-1-55221-495-4

Printed and bound by CPI Group (UK) Ltd, Croydon, CR0 4YY

Library and Archives Canada Cataloguing in Publication

Helis, John, author
Quasi-constitutional laws of Canada / John Helis.

Includes bibliographical references and index.
Issued in print and electronic formats.
ISBN 978-1-55221-494-7 (softcover).—ISBN 978-1-55221-495-4 (PDF)

1. Law—Canada—Interpretation and construction. 2. Constitutional law—Canada. 3. Civil rights—Canada. I. Title.

KE482.S84H45 2018	349.71	C2018-904067-X
KF425.H45 2018		C2018-904068-8

Canada

Ontario
Ontario Media Development Corporation
Société de développement de l'Industrie des médias de l'Ontario

To my wife Isabelle, who is my greatest inspiration. I could not have done it without you. To my children, Theodore and Sophia, who have lived with this project their entire lives, and to my mother, for her love and support. Words cannot express how grateful I am to all of you.

Summary Table of Contents

Detailed Table of Contents

CHAPTER 2

The Broad, Liberal, and Purposive Interpretation of Quasi-constitutional Legislation 17

Foreword

Almost fifty years ago, the legal concept of *quasi-constitutionality* began to emerge in Canada. In a series of landmark judgments, the Supreme Court of Canada held that the *Canadian Bill of Rights, 1960*, an ordinary Act of Parliament, was not like other ordinary Acts of Parliament.[1] This statute held a special place, a kind of primacy, even a sense of supremacy, in relation to other statutes. Under orthodox assumptions about parliamentary sovereignty that prevailed in Canada and other common law parliamentary systems around the world, this was not supposed to be possible. Yes, *constitutional* statutes like the *British North America Act, 1867* (now the *Constitution Act, 1867*)[2] took primacy over ordinary statutes. However, the idea that sovereign legislatures — including Canadian federal and provincial legislatures, when acting within the bounds set by constitutional statutes — could enact super-statutes that somehow limited how law could be made in the future was an idea that lawyers and judges who were still trained in Victorian-era jurisprudence could not fathom. Yet, in the early 1970s, Canadian judges saw their way through the thicket of old theories about the nature of parliamentary authority and concluded that, in effect, not all statutes are born equal. Some statutes are so fundamental in the rights and values that they protect that

1 *Canadian Bill of Rights*, SC 1960, c 44. See, in particular, *R v Drybones*, [1970] SCR 282 and *R v Curr*, [1972] SCR 889.

2 (UK), 30 & 31 Vict, c 3, reprinted in RSC 1985, Appendix II, No 5.

they may be considered to be, using a term coined by the Chief Justice of Canada, Bora Laskin, *quasi-constitutional*.[3]

The idea of quasi-constitutionality has since extended to embrace a significant range of federal and provincial statutes — not just statutory bills of rights, but also statutes protecting human rights in the private sector, privacy rights, language rights, access to information, and even certain common law principles, like the right to one's good reputation. The result has been a revolution in the way that fundamental rights and values, statutes, and constitutional law are understood in Canada. Yet, the remarkable thing about this development is that it has gone largely unnoticed. It has been, to borrow an expression, a quiet revolution. Of course, practitioners and commentators who deal with specific statutory regimes have quickly adjusted, and, in the common law way, complex lines of caselaw have gradually emerged over the years that articulate the implications of quasi-constitutionality for particular contexts. In this sense, quasi-constitutionality has been noticed for a long time. However, the idea of quasi-constitutionality as a *general* principle of Canadian constitutionalism, one of the organizing principles that transcends specific statutory contexts to define the very character of law and rights in Canada, has been left largely unexplored and unexplained — until now.

With the publication of this book, John Helis provides us with the first sustained analysis of quasi-constitutionality as a central principle of Canadian public law. This is a significant achievement for at least four reasons. First, Dr Helis synthesizes a vast array of cases in an effort to show that judicial conclusions stretching across diverse legislative contexts manifest certain common normative assumptions. His study is thus exemplary of that style of legal exposition that combines attention to granular, doctrinal detail with an interpretive aspiration for broader, principled coherence.

Second, Dr Helis confronts the reality that the general principles that bring coherence to the law of quasi-constitutionality challenge received notions about Canadian constitutional and legal structure. They disrupt the images and categories of law that we have long accepted. They draw into question the simple picture of our legal system as a series of norms arranged in a linear and hierarchical fashion, with constitutional law at the top, ordinary statute law in the middle, and common law at the bottom. The concept of quasi-constitutionality is difficult to fit within this picture.

3 *Hogan v R*, [1975] 2 SCR 574 at 579.

One important difficulty in this respect is the orthodox view of parliamentary sovereignty. Each Parliament is sovereign and so no Parliament can bind its successors. Not only can one statute expressly repeal or modify any earlier statute, but a mere conflict between two statutes will mean that the later statute impliedly repeals the earlier statute — no matter how trivial the later one or how fundamental the earlier one. In explaining these points, the words of the great British constitutional scholar, Albert Venn Dicey, cast a long shadow over the idea of quasi-constitutionality: "Should the Dentists Act, 1878, unfortunately contravene the terms of the Act of Union" — the statute that unified Scotland and England as Great Britain and purported on its face to protect certain terms of the union — "the Act of Union would be *pro tanto* repealed."[4] It would not be long, however, before caselaw from the dominions challenged this view,[5] and British scholars would respond by making a minor amendment to the Diceyan conception of parliamentary sovereignty: one statute might impose on subsequent statutes a certain "manner and form" requirement to be met before the first statute could be repealed or modified; that, in other words, the rule of implied repeal would be replaced by a requirement of express repeal for certain statutes. In this way, all could be explained in a manner consistent with the traditional respect for parliamentary sovereignty and legislative intent that gives law its linear and hierarchical structure.

The third, and perhaps most far-reaching contribution that Dr. Helis makes in this book is his rejection of this explanation of quasi-constitutionality in favour of a much more profound reconsideration of constitutionalism within the common law tradition. Building upon caselaw in which judges have given certain statutes primacy over other statutes even in absence of explicit statutory language to this effect,[6] Dr Helis argues that quasi-constitutionality is explained not by reference to legislative intent about the *procedural* forms of lawmaking, but that it is to be understood through an interpretation that explains and justifies legislative intent alongside the special status that *substantive* principles of fundamental law have within the legal order. His approach breaks down

4 AV Dicey, *Introduction to the Study of the Law of the Constitution*, 8th ed (London: Macmillan, 1915) at 41.

5 *New South Wales v Trethowan*, [1932] AC 526 (JCPC).

6 *Insurance Corporation of British Columbia v Heerspink*, [1982] 2 SCR 145; *Winnipeg School Division No 1 v Craton*, [1985] 2 SCR 150.

barriers between constitutional and ordinary law and offers a more integrated or holistic reading of our legal system.

This is a challenging set of ideas important for broader debates about the nature of law and legality in Canada, but also in other common law jurisdictions. Indeed, the fourth contribution made by this book is its engagement with similar debates that are unfolding elsewhere. It brings a fresh *Canadian* perspective to questions about, for example, "constitutional statutes" in the United Kingdom or "super-statutes" in the United States, and it provides a further dimension to the ideas surrounding weak-form and strong-form judicial review and the notion of a distinctive Commonwealth style of constitutionalism that continues to evolve in the literature. This engagement with comparative law adds considerably to the richness of the book's insights.

Why was the concept of quasi-constitutionality marginalized for so long in Canada? The simple answer may be that a generation of lawyers and scholars have been, perhaps justifiably, dazzled by the bright lights of the *Canadian Charter of Rights and Freedoms*. However, a newer generation of lawyers and scholars are returning to neglected and larger questions of constitutional design and structure, including the reality that constitutionalism as a normative ideal manifests itself in our law at varied and integrated levels of legal discourse. Formal, entrenched constitutional law is just one of those levels — and perhaps, for the average person, not always the most important one. As Dr Helis emphasizes, quasi-constitutional law is often implemented at first instance by administrative officials and tribunals that are closer and more accessible to the people. This book makes broad claims about constitutional theory, but it never strays far from the day-to-day realities of the experience of the law. Dr Helis is to be commended for combining theory and practice within a compelling narrative that draws from the shadows and into the light important but neglected truths about the legal protection of fundamental rights and values in Canada.

Mark D Walters

Full professor, Faculty of Law, McGill University
FR Scott Professor of Public and Constitutional Law

Acknowledgements

I would like to express my gratitude to Mark Walters for his invaluable help in ensuring the success of this project. The completion of this book is in large measure a result of Professor Walters's guidance and mentorship. I am forever in his debt. I am thankful to the numerous people who provided feedback on early drafts of this work, including Matthew Lewans, Janet Hiebert, Tsvi Kahana, Lisa Kerr, Beverley Baines, and Jonathan Rose. A special thanks to Vincent Kazmierski, who encouraged me to pursue this project. Lastly, I gratefully acknowledge the financial support from the Social Sciences and Humanities Research Council (SSHRC).

CHAPTER 1

Introduction

A number of laws in Canada are referred to as quasi-constitutional by the courts in recognition of their importance. Quasi-constitutional laws consist of several federal and provincial statutes that were enacted through the regular legislative process, as well as one common law principle. They have received this label by the courts because they are of "fundamental importance,"[1] of "fundamental value in our society,"[2] and, indeed, "fundamental in the Canadian legal system."[3]

Quasi-constitutionality is a judicial designation. The term itself is not found anywhere in legislation or in the written Constitution. Rather, it is a judicial response to laws that have been "designed and adopted to perform a more fundamental role than ordinary statutes in this country."[4] This fundamental role has resulted in the Supreme Court of Canada declaring that quasi-constitutional laws, "save . . . constitutional laws, [are] more important than all others."[5]

As a consequence of their importance, the Supreme Court of Canada has held that quasi-constitutional laws "supersede all other laws when

1 *Hill v Church of Scientology of Toronto*, [1995] 2 SCR 1130 at para 120 [*Hill*].

2 *R v Osolin*, [1993] 4 SCR 595 at para 21.

3 *Lavigne v Canada (Office of the Commissioner of Official Languages)*, 2002 SCC 53 at para 24 [*Lavigne*].

4 *Law Society of Upper Canada v Skapinker*, [1984] 1 SCR 357 at para 10 [*Skapinker*].

5 *Insurance Corporation of British Columbia v Heerspink*, [1982] 2 SCR 145 at 158 [*Heerspink*].

conflict arises,"[6] that they should be interpreted in a broad, liberal, and purposive manner, and that they "may not be altered, amended, or repealed, nor may exceptions be created to . . . provisions, save by clear legislative pronouncement."[7]

Chief Justice Bora Laskin first coined the term "quasi-constitutional" in his dissenting decision in the 1974 case of *Hogan v R*, where he described the *Canadian Bill of Rights* as "a half-way house between a purely common law regime and a constitutional one."[8] This is significant because it appears to challenge the traditional perspective of Canadian law with its fixed hierarchy of legal norms that include, in descending importance, the Constitution, legislation, and the common law. Quasi-constitutionality as described by Laskin CJ does not fit neatly within this traditional perspective and hierarchy. The Supreme Court of Canada has continued to stress this middle-ground approach to quasi-constitutionality since the term was formulated, and quasi-constitutional laws have been described by the Court as "almost constitutional,"[9] as "not quite constitutional but certainly more than the ordinary,"[10] as "not a part of the Constitution of the country," but rather "somewhere between a statute and a constitutional instrument."[11] The Court has also referred to quasi-constitutional laws as being "closely linked to the values and rights set out in the Constitution, and this explains the quasi-constitutional status that this Court has recognized them as having."[12]

Interestingly, the Supreme Court of Canada chose the occasion presented in *Law Society of Upper Canada v Skapinker*, the first case involving the *Canadian Charter of Rights and Freedoms* to reach the Court, to explain the status of quasi-constitutionality as a category of law and its relationship to the Constitution. Justice Estey, writing for a unanimous Court, held that

> the *Canadian Bill of Rights* is, of course, in form, the same as any other statute of Parliament. It was designed and adopted to perform a more fundamental role than ordinary statutes in this country. It is, however,

6 *Ibid.*

7 *Winnipeg School Division No 1 v Craton*, [1985] 2 SCR 150 at 156 [*Craton*].

8 *Hogan v R*, [1975] 2 SCR 574 at 597; *Canadian Bill of Rights*, SC 1960, c 44.

9 *Robichaud v Canada (Treasury Board)*, [1987] 2 SCR 84 at para 13 [*Robichaud*].

10 *Ontario Human Rights Commission and O'Malley v Simpsons-Sears Ltd*, [1985] 2 SCR 536 at para 12 [*O'Malley*].

11 *Skapinker*, above note 4 at para 10.

12 *Lavigne*, above note 3 at para 25.

> not a part of the Constitution of the country. It stands, perhaps, somewhere between a statute and a constitutional instrument.[13]

Justice Estey's immediate purpose was to consider the Court's experience under the *Canadian Bill of Rights* as a starting point for the interpretation and application of the *Charter*, although ironically, in echoing the Court's pre-*Charter* decisions, he stressed quasi-constitutionality as a type of third category of law at a time when the Court could have abandoned this distinction in favour of the more authoritative *Charter*. The bold statements by Laskin CJ and Estey J remain valid as courts and administrative tribunals now routinely employ quasi-constitutionality to achieve rather remarkable results. Surprisingly, however, quasi-constitutionality has received limited attention in the literature, and few efforts at explaining its significance have been made.

The purpose of this book is to provide a broad overview of quasi-constitutionality, which considers its legal impact, its theoretical basis, and its historical development. At a theoretical level, quasi-constitutionality is a statutory and common law form of fundamental law with theoretical links to the underlying principles of the Constitution. This fundamental character results in a special approach to the interpretation and application of quasi-constitutional statutes, even vis-à-vis other laws, despite the fact that they are enacted through the regular legislative process. This approach includes two salient features that are rooted in statutory interpretation. First, the courts have adopted a broad, liberal, and purposive approach to the interpretation of quasi-constitutional statutes, which expands the rights these statutes protect. Second, quasi-constitutional statutes hold primacy and supersede regular statutes in the interpretive exercise. Primacy affects the interpretation of regular statutes, which must be interpreted in a manner that avoids conflict with quasi-constitutional statutes. Quasi-constitutional statutes are therefore not subject to the doctrine of implied repeal. They are always prioritized in the interpretive exercise over regular statutes. Most significantly, when a provision in a regular statute cannot be interpreted in a manner that avoids conflict with a quasi-constitutional one, a court or tribunal, in some instances, can declare the impugned provision inoperable or devise a comparable remedy. The primacy of quasi-constitutional legislation therefore provides a form of judicial review that is distinct from constitutional supremacy.

---

13 *Skapinker*, above note 4 at para 10; *Canadian Charter of Rights and Freedoms*, Part I of the *Constitution Act, 1982*, being Schedule B to the *Canada Act 1982* (UK), 1982, c 11.

A. LAWS DESIGNATED AS QUASI-CONSTITUTIONAL

Quasi-constitutional laws are comprised mostly of federal and provincial statutes, but a common law principle has also received this designation. The common thread among quasi-constitutional laws is that they are all rights-based regimes that cover the traditional civil liberties, the protection against discrimination, the right to privacy, the right to access government information, language rights, and the common law protection of a person's good reputation. The current laws recognized by the courts as quasi-constitutional can be grouped into six categories that correspond to the specific types of rights they uphold. Quasi-constitutionality, however, may not be a closed list; additional categories may eventually be recognized by the courts.

1) Statutes Upholding Civil Liberties

The first category of quasi-constitutional law comprises statutes that protect traditional civil liberties against the action of government. The *Canadian Bill of Rights*, which applies at the federal level, was the first statute categorized as quasi-constitutional by the Supreme Court of Canada. Initially there were provincial equivalents to the *Canadian Bill of Rights*, although only the *Alberta Bill of Rights* remains in force as a separate statute; elements of traditional civil liberties are, however, found in some provincial human rights statutes. Since the *Alberta Bill of Rights* resembles the *Canadian Bill of Rights*, the courts have adopted the same approach for its interpretation. Consequently, most of the focus on this category of quasi-constitutional law is on the *Canadian Bill of Rights*.

The jurisprudence under the *Canadian Bill of Rights* established one of the basic attributes of quasi-constitutionality that has been extended to other quasi-constitutional statutes. The primacy of quasi-constitutional legislation was established under the *Canadian Bill of Rights*, and the courts are to use the *Canadian Bill of Rights* as an interpretive tool to construe the other statutes in accordance with the rights that it enshrines. In the 1970 decision of *R v Drybones*,[14] the Supreme Court of Canada confirmed that courts can proceed to declare "inoperative" provisions in other statutes that conflict with the *Canadian Bill of Rights*.

---

14 [1970] SCR 282 [*Drybones*].

The Supreme Court of Canada, unfortunately, also adopted a restrictive approach to the interpretation of the *Canadian Bill of Rights*, which makes conflict with its terms exceedingly rare. This approach affected the future impact of the *Drybones* decision; it was also an impetus for a constitutionally entrenched bill of rights. Despite this setback, the experience under the *Canadian Bill of Rights* had two positive attributes in addition to establishing the primacy of quasi-constitutional legislation and the resulting declarations of inoperability. First, the Court made a concerted effort to avoid the shortcomings of the *Canadian Bill of Rights* by adopting a different approach to the interpretation of the *Charter* and other quasi-constitutional legislation, which, in all instances, are to be interpreted in a broad, liberal, and purposive manner. This expansive approach to the interpretation of other quasi-constitutional statutes when combined with the principle of primacy and declarations of inoperability arguably has resulted in the type of impact under human rights legislation initially hoped for under the *Canadian Bill of Rights*. Second, even though many of the rights contained in the *Canadian Bill of Rights* have been replicated in the *Charter*, the two that have not—namely, the right to the enjoyment of property and the right to a fair hearing for the determination of a person's rights and obligations—continue to apply and can have a significant impact.[15]

2) Human Rights Legislation

Much of the focus on quasi-constitutionality is in regard to federal, provincial, and territorial human rights statutes, the second category of quasi-constitutional law.[16] Despite the fact that some human rights statutes have incorporated elements of traditional civil liberties, their importance lies primarily with the protection against discrimination. Human

---

15 Lorne Sossin, "The Quasi-revival of the *Canadian Bill of Rights* and Its Implications for Administrative Law" (2004) 25 *Supreme Court Law Review* (2d) 191 at 192.

16 *Canadian Human Rights Act*, RSC 1985, c H-6; *Alberta Human Rights Act*, RSA 2000, c A-25.5; British Columbia *Human Rights Code*, RSBC 1996, c 210; *Saskatchewan Human Rights Code*, SS 1979, c S-24.1; Manitoba *Human Rights Code*, CCSM c H175; Ontario *Human Rights Code*, RSO 1990, c H.19; Quebec *Charter of Human Rights and Freedoms*, CQLR c C-12; New Brunswick *Human Rights Act*, RSNB 2011, c 171; Nova Scotia *Human Rights Act*, RSNS 1989, c 214; Prince Edward Island *Human Rights Act*, RSPEI 1988, c H-12; Newfoundland and Labrador *Human Rights Act, 2010*, SNL 2010, c H-13.1; Yukon *Human Rights Act*, RSY 2002, c 116; Northwest Territories *Human Rights Act*, SNWT 2002, c 18; Nunavut *Human Rights Act*, SNu 2003, c 12.

rights statutes are unlike bills of rights because they protect against discrimination as outlined in a defined list of grounds. These grounds extend to the actions of both governments and private actors in a limited number of social areas such as employment, services, and housing.

As quasi-constitutional legislation, human rights statutes have been recognized as holding primacy over all other enactments. Similar to the *Canadian Bill of Rights*, the primacy of human rights legislation ensures that other statutes are interpreted in a rights-protective manner. When such an interpretation is not possible, regular statutes that contain an irreconcilable conflict with human rights legislation can be declared inoperable, even in the absence of a primacy provision.

The special rules of interpretation applied to quasi-constitutional legislation were largely developed under human rights statutes. In a number of decisions, the Supreme Court of Canada confirmed that human rights statutes are to receive a broad, liberal, and purposive interpretation because of their fundamental and quasi-constitutional character.[17] This interpretive approach remedied the shortcomings of the Court's interpretation of the *Canadian Bill of Rights*.

3) Privacy Acts

Legislation protecting personal privacy is likewise recognized as quasi-constitutional in both the caselaw and the literature. There are two kinds of privacy statutes. The first "protect[s] the privacy of individuals with respect to personal information about themselves held by a government institution" and "provide[s] individuals with a right of access to that information."[18] The second protects personal privacy in the private sector and addresses the collection, use, and disclosure of personal information by commercial organizations.[19]

Examples of the first kind of privacy statute are the federal *Privacy Act* and provincial equivalents that protect the privacy of individuals in the way that government retains and discloses information. Such statutes

---

17 See, for example, *O'Malley*, above note 10; *Robichaud*, above note 9 at para 8; *New Brunswick (Human Rights Commission) v Potash Corporation of Saskatchewan Inc*, [2008] 2 SCR 604 at para 65. This is linked back to the *obiter* comments of Lamer J in *Heerspink*, above note 5.

18 *Dagg v Canada (Minister of Finance)*, [1997] 2 SCR 403 at para 64; *Englander v TELUS Communications Inc*, 2004 FCA 387 at para 37 [*Englander*].

19 *Englander*, *ibid* at para 38; *Mountain Province Diamonds Inc v De Beers Canada Inc*, 2014 ONSC 2026 at para 37 [*Mountain Province Diamonds Inc*].

have been recognized by the Supreme Court of Canada as holding quasi-constitutional status in several decisions.[20] Most provincial statutes combine the protection of privacy and the right to access government information in one statute.[21] These provincial statutes generally cover both the provincial and municipal government levels, with the exception of Ontario and Saskatchewan, which have separate statutes for the provincial and municipal levels.[22] This kind of privacy statute is recognized as quasi-constitutional, in part, because of the close connection of privacy to human rights legislation, as the protection of privacy at the federal level was initially found in the *Canadian Human Rights Act.* It is also due to what has been called its overall "quasi-constitutional mission," and its role "in the preservation of a free and democratic society."[23]

The second kind of privacy statute that applies to the private sector begins with the federal *Personal Information Protection and Electronic Documents Act*, or *PIPEDA*, which, the Ontario Court of Appeal explained, "applies across Canada unless it has been displaced by provincial legislation that the Governor-in-Council by order has declared is

---

20 *Lavigne*, above note 3 at paras 23–24; *Canada (Information Commissioner) v Canada (Commissioner of the Royal Canadian Mounted Police)*, 2003 SCC 8 at para 26; *Pro Swing Inc v Elta Golf Inc*, 2006 SCC 52; *HJ Heinz Co of Canada Ltd v Canada (Attorney General)*, 2006 SCC 13 at para 28. See also Ruth Sullivan, *Sullivan on the Construction of Statutes*, 5th ed (Markham, ON: LexisNexis, 2008) at 507.

21 Canada *Privacy Act*, RSC 1985, c P-21; Alberta *Freedom of Information and Protection of Privacy Act*, RSA 2000, c F-25; British Columbia *Freedom of Information and Protection of Privacy Act*, RSBC 1996, c 165; Manitoba *The Freedom of Information and Protection of Privacy Act*, CCSM c F175; Quebec *An Act respecting Access to Documents Held by Public Bodies and the Protection of Personal Information*, CQLR c A-2.1; New Brunswick *Right to Information and Protection of Privacy Act*, SNB 2009, c R-10.6; Nova Scotia *Freedom of Information and Protection of Privacy Act*, SNS 1993, c 5; Prince Edward Island *Freedom of Information and Protection of Privacy Act*, RSPEI 1988, c F-15.01; Newfoundland and Labrador *Access to Information and Protection of Privacy Act*, SNL 2002, c A-1.1; Yukon *Access to Information and Protection of Privacy Act*, RSY 2002, c 1; Northwest Territories *Access to Information and Protection of Privacy Act*, SNWT 1994, c 20; Nunavut *Access to Information and Protection of Privacy Act*, SNWT (Nu) 1994, c 20.

22 Saskatchewan's two statutes are *The Freedom of Information and Protection of Privacy Act*, SS 1990-91, c F-22.01, which applies at the provincial level of government, and *The Local Authority Freedom of Information and Protection of Privacy Act*, SS 1990-91, c L-27.1, which applies at the local municipal level. Similarly, Ontario has the *Freedom of Information and Protection of Privacy Act*, RSO 1990, c F.31, and the *Municipal Freedom of Information and Protection of Privacy Act*, RSO 1990, c M.56.

23 *Lavigne*, above note 3 at para 25. *Alberta (Information and Privacy Commissioner) v United Food and Commercial Workers, Local 401*, 2013 SCC 62 at para 19.

substantially similar to *PIPEDA*."[24] Three provinces have passed statutes recognized by federal regulation as being substantially similar to *PIPEDA*, which displace *PIPEDA* in those provinces except with respect to federal undertakings.[25] Four other provinces have passed legislation recognized under *PIPEDA* as protecting personal health information, which therefore allows *PIPEDA* to continue to apply with respect to other forms of personal information in the private sector.[26]

With the two kinds of privacy laws, every organization and business, both public and private, is now subject to privacy laws that address the collection, retention, and disclosure of personal information about identifiable persons.[27] The Supreme Court of Canada endorsed the quasi-constitutional status of the second category of privacy legislation in the 2013 case of *Alberta (Information and Privacy Commissioner) v United Food and Commercial Workers, Local 401*.[28]

4) Access-to-Information Legislation

The purpose of access-to-information legislation is to provide the public with a right to access records held by government institutions and to clearly outline any exceptions to this right.[29] The Supreme Court of Canada confirmed that access-to-information statutes are quasi-constitutional in the 2011 decision of *Canada (Information Commissioner)*

24 *Personal Information Protection and Electronic Documents Act*, SC 2000, c 5 [*PIPEDA*]; *Royal Bank of Canada v Trang*, 2014 ONCA 883 at para 11, rev'd 2016 SCC 50, but not on this point.

25 *Organizations in the Province of Alberta Exemption Order*, SOR/2004-219; *Personal Information Protection Act*, SA 2003, c P-6.5; *Organizations in the Province of British Columbia Exemption Order*, SOR/2004-220; *Personal Information Protection Act*, SBC 2003, c 63; *Organizations in the Province of Quebec Exemption Order*, SOR/2003-374; *An Act respecting the protection of personal information in the private sector*, CQLR c P-39.1.

26 *Personal Health Information Custodians in New Brunswick Exemption Order*, SOR/2011-265; *Personal Health Information Privacy and Access Act*, SNB 2009, c P-7.05; *Personal Health Information Custodians in Newfoundland and Labrador Exemption Order*, SI/2012-72; *Personal Health Information Act*, SNL 2008, c P-7.01; *Personal Health Information Custodians in Nova Scotia Exemption Order*, SOR/2016-62; *Personal Health Information Act*, SNS 2010, c 41; *Health Information Custodians in the Province of Ontario Exemption Order*, SOR/2005-399; *Personal Health Information Protection Act, 2004*, SO 2004, c 3.

27 Sandra M Anderson, "Alberta's Statutory Privacy Regime and Its Impact on the Workplace" (2006) 43 *Alberta Law Review* 647 at para 9.

28 Above note 23 at para 22. See also *Mountain Province Diamonds Inc*, above note 19 at para 37.

29 See, for example, the federal *Access to Information Act*, RSC 1985, c A-1, s 2(1).

v Canada (Minister of National Defence).[30] Leading up to this decision, the Court had previously concluded that the right to access government information embodies a "derivative right" of the freedom of expression.[31]

The Court stressed that special rules of construction apply to access-to-information legislation because of its quasi-constitutional nature. These rules require that the right to access "must be interpreted liberally, [and] exceptions to it must be interpreted narrowly."[32] Rather than containing the type of primacy provision typically found in human rights legislation, the federal *Access to Information Act* includes a schedule of provisions found in other statutes under which the general right to access is restricted.[33]

5) Language Rights Legislation

Statutes that designate English and French as official languages or that expand legislative, judicial, or government services in one of the official languages were expressly held as quasi-constitutional by the Supreme Court of Canada in the 2002 decision of *Lavigne v Canada (Office of the Commissioner of Official Languages)*. Prior to this decision, the Federal Court of Appeal recognized the federal *Official Languages Act* as quasi-constitutional in the 1991 decision of *Canada (Attorney General) v Viola*.[34] The rationale for the quasi-constitutional status of language rights statutes is that they reflect and are an extension of the language rights in the Constitution.[35] The courts have also confirmed that the language rights provisions in the *Criminal Code* hold quasi-constitutional status.[36]

In *R v Beaulac* the Supreme Court of Canada adopted a broad, liberal, and purposive interpretation of all language rights, which reversed a line

30 2011 SCC 25 at para 83 [*Canada (Information Commissioner)*].

31 *Ontario (Public Safety and Security) v Criminal Lawyers' Association*, 2010 SCC 23 at para 30.

32 *Canada (Information Commissioner)*, above note 30 at para 83.

33 *Access to Information Act*, above note 29, s 24(1), states: "The head of a government institution shall refuse to disclose any records requested under this Act that contains information the disclosure of which is restricted by or pursuant to any provision set out in schedule II."

34 *Lavigne*, above note 3 at para 22; *Canada (Attorney General) v Viola*, [1991] 1 FC 373 at para 16 (CA) [*Viola*].

35 *Lavigne*, above note 3 at para 23; *Viola*, *ibid*.

36 *Canada (Commissioner of Official Languages) v Canada (Department of Justice)*, 2001 FCT 239 at paras 139, 142, 182, 194, & 195. In reaching this conclusion, the Federal Court in this case relied on *R v Beaulac*, [1999] 1 SCR 768 [*Beaulac*]. See also *R v MacKenzie*, 2004 NSCA 10 at para 58.

of decisions that held that language rights should be interpreted with "restraint" because they are a product of "political compromise."[37] Moreover, like the other categories of quasi-constitutional laws, the Court confirmed that language rights statutes have primacy over other laws.[38]

6) The Protection of a Person's Good Reputation

The common law protection of a person's good reputation is related to the right to privacy and is observed in the context of defamation suits where it is balanced with the competing freedom of expression. In *Éditions Écosociété Inc v Banro Corp*, the Supreme Court of Canada cited its earlier decision of *Hill v Church of Scientology of Toronto* for the proposition that this common law right holds quasi-constitutional status because it "represents and reflects the innate dignity of the individual, a concept which underlies all *Charter* rights."[39]

B. THE OUTLINE

Since this book seeks to provide a broad overview of quasi-constitutionality in Canada, it necessarily considers why certain laws are designated as quasi-constitutional and the legal significance of this designation. It begins in Chapter 2 with the application of the broad, liberal, and purposive interpretation. Chapter 3 considers the effects of primacy and the influence of quasi-constitutional legislation over regular statutes. Given that the courts attribute quasi-constitutionality and the legal significance of this designation to the fundamental nature of rights, Chapter 4 engages with the theory underpinning quasi-constitutionality. Finally, Chapter 5 explores the development of quasi-constitutionality and its defining legal characteristics.

1) Chapter 2: A Broad, Liberal, and Purposive Interpretation of Quasi-constitutional Legislation

Chapter 2 examines the special rules of interpretation applied to quasi-constitutional legislation since the Supreme Court of Canada has confirmed

37 *Beaulac*, above note 36 at paras 16 and 24.
38 *Lavigne*, above note 3 at para 40.
39 *Éditions Écosociété Inc v Banro Corp*, 2012 SCC 18 at para 57, citing *Hill*, above note 1 at para 120.

that it "deserves a broad, liberal, and purposive interpretation befitting of this special status."[40] This approach is clearly articulated by the Court and is recognized in the literature on statutory interpretation. Far less studied is how this approach is routinely applied by courts and tribunals. This chapter, therefore, reviews its application to four of the five groups of quasi-constitutional statutes. The Court never endorsed a broad, liberal, and purposive approach to the interpretation of the *Canadian Bill of Rights*. Instead, it adopted a restrictive construction that is largely responsible for the weaknesses of this statute. In recognizing the weaknesses with the *Canadian Bill of Rights*, the Court adopted a more expansive approach to the interpretation of the other categories of quasi-constitutional statutes to advance rights.

This chapter moves beyond merely quoting the statements of the Supreme Court of Canada which establish the broad, liberal, and purposive interpretation of quasi-constitutional legislation. It considers the significant results achieved by lower courts, tribunals, and other administrative bodies that regularly interpret and apply these statutes. It also reviews the corresponding strict and narrow interpretation of limitations to rights found in quasi-constitutional statutes—for example, defences, exceptions, and exemptions—and how this similarly helps advance rights.

2) Chapter 3: The Primacy of Quasi-constitutional Legislation

The focus of Chapter 3 is on the primacy of quasi-constitutional legislation, which concerns the influence of quasi-constitutional legislation on the interpretation of regular statutes. Even though quasi-constitutional statutes were enacted through the regular legislative process, they have been assigned an elevated legal status over other statutes in the interpretive process, commonly referred to as "primacy." Quasi-constitutional statutes often contain a primacy provision, but courts have recognized this function even in the absence of an express provision due to the fundamental nature of rights.[41] This chapter is intended to provide a practical

40 *Canada (Canadian Human Rights Commission) v Canada (Attorney General)*, 2011 SCC 53 at para 62.

41 See, especially, *Heerspink*, above note 5; *Craton*, above note 7; *Canada (Attorney General) v Druken*, [1989] 2 FC 24 at para 7 (CA), aff'g (*sub nom Druken v Canada (Employment and Immigration Commission)*) (1987), 8 CHRR D/4379 (CHRT), leave to appeal to SCC refused, [1988] SCCA No 433. See also the dissenting reasons of Dickson CJ and Lamer J in *Bhinder and Canadian Human Rights Commission v Canadian National Railway Co*, [1985] 2 SCR 561 at paras 18–19, and the dissenting reasons of McLachlin J and

guide to the operation of primacy in cases before courts and tribunals. (More theoretical questions about this function are reserved for Chapter 4.)

The first step to primacy involves interpreting regular statutes in a manner that is consistent with the fundamental rights contained in quasi-constitutional legislation to avoid conflict. Although the primary role of primacy is to avoid conflict between statutes, a quasi-constitutional statute can also guide the interpretation of a regular statute in the absence of a conflict when it can be subject to two possible interpretations. Chapter 3 begins with the application of this interpretive function under the five categories of quasi-constitutional statutes and the results achieved by the courts and tribunals. This aspect of primacy bears some resemblance to the approach in other Commonwealth countries, where the courts lack jurisdiction to invalidate legislation and, instead, are mandated to interpret statutes in a rights-protective manner.

When a conflict between a regular statute and a quasi-constitutional one cannot be avoided through interpretation, a Canadian court or tribunal can proceed to the second step and declare the impugned provision in the regular statute inoperable or devise a comparable remedy. This approach is unlike other jurisdictions in the Commonwealth and offers only a limited comparison to the developments in the United Kingdom. First developed under the *Canadian Bill of Rights*, this remedy is increasingly being used under human rights legislation. In the human rights context, there must be a finding of discrimination under one of the grounds and in one of the social areas covered by human rights legislation, such as service or employment. Therefore, a statute cannot be directly challenged under human rights legislation as it can be under section 15(1) of the *Charter*; rather, a challenge requires, for example, a finding that a service scheme established by legislation is discriminatory. Although this remedy has not been explicitly endorsed by the courts under the other categories of quasi-constitutional legislation, it is not always necessary to declare a provision inoperable, particularly given the way some categories of quasi-constitutional statutes operate. The most obvious example is access-to-information legislation, where the right to access

---

L'Heureux-Dubé J in *Cooper v Canada (Human Rights Commission)*, [1996] 3 SCR 854 at para 100. This principle is also invoked by the Canadian Human Rights Tribunal. See, for example, *Canada (Attorney General) v Uzoaba*, [1995] 2 FCR 569 (TD); *Franke v Canada (Canadian Armed Forces)*, [1998] CHRD No 3 at paras 753–66, aff'd (*sub nom Canada (Canadian Human Rights Commission) v Canada (Canadian Armed Forces) (re Franke))*, [1999] 3 FC 653 (TD).

can be prioritized without declaring a competing confidentiality clause in a regular statute inoperable.

Despite this difference it is recognized that practical similarities exist between declarations of inoperability under quasi-constitutional human rights legislation and orders of invalidity under the Constitution when a law violates section 15(1) of the *Charter*. The inoperability of a statutory interpretation may not be as transformative of the law as its invalidity, yet in the circumstances of the immediate case, it provides a comparable remedy for the individual rights claimant, as the impugned provision is not applied. Accordingly, the courts have grappled with the question of whether a separate analytical framework should be maintained under human rights legislation in these types of cases in the form of the *prima facie* case, or whether the analysis should be based on or influenced by the approach adopted under section 15(1) of the *Charter*. The focus of this chapter is on presenting the framework as set out in the 2010 decision of the Ontario Court of Appeal in *Ontario (Director, Disability Support Program) v Tranchemontagne*, and how it is being applied by tribunals. (The developments leading up to this decision are reserved for Chapter 5.)[42]

3) Chapter 4: The Theory of Quasi-constitutionality

Chapter 4 examines the theoretical basis of quasi-constitutionality and its relationship to the Constitution. Despite the practical similarities between declarations of inoperability under quasi-constitutional legislation and orders of invalidity under the Constitution, the two are theoretically distinct. Most simply, inoperability, unlike invalidity, does not denote that the impugned provision was not legally enacted, but rather prioritizes the application of a quasi-constitutional right in the case of conflict with a provision in a regular statute. This distinction is equally relevant to the invalidity of a statutory provision because of its violation of a constitutional right, or because it contravened a constitutional or statutory manner and form provision.

Most important, while many quasi-constitutional statutes contain a primacy provision, the courts have recognized this function even in the absence of an express provision because of the fundamental nature of quasi-constitutional rights. The Supreme Court of Canada has confirmed the fundamental nature of quasi-constitutional laws in numerous decisions.

42 *Ontario (Director, Disability Support Program) v Tranchemontagne*, 2010 ONCA 593.

Indeed, it has gone as far as considering it as their "most important characteristic."[43] In doing so the Court is largely influenced by what can be referred to as the modern understanding of fundamental law, which associates the term with judicial review and a more onerous process for amendment and repeal than regular law. Yet, while the modern understanding of fundamental law provides a starting point for uncovering the theoretical basis of quasi-constitutionality, the methods of amendment and repeal and judicial review represent the results or consequences of the fundamental nature of quasi-constitutional law but not its basis. Instead, *fundamental* implies a link with the Constitution and the foundational principles that underpin it. The legislature can override primacy, amend, or outright repeal a quasi-constitutional statute, but because of its fundamental character, this cannot occur impliedly. Courts will recognize an abrogation of fundamental rights only when there is clear statutory language.[44]

The broad, liberal, and purposive interpretation was similarly adopted by courts because of the fundamental nature of quasi-constitutional legislation. Just as *Charter* rights have been "given a broad and generous interpretation so as to enhance and preserve the underlying rights,"[45] courts have held that this approach also applies to quasi-constitutional legislation.[46] The basis of this interpretive approach is more nuanced in the case of quasi-constitutionality because it is a statutory form of fundamental law. Specifically, courts can presume that the legislature intended to uphold fundamental quasi-constitutional rights over all other legislation during the interpretive exercise, but legislative intent also necessarily means that courts will depart from this interpretive approach when there is clear legislative language to the contrary.

4) Chapter 5: The Development of Quasi-constitutionality

Chapter 5 explores the development of the defining legal characteristics of quasi-constitutionality studied in chapters 2, 3, and 4, and how they were gradually extended to the six categories of quasi-constitutional laws.

---

43 *Tranchemontagne v Ontario (Director, Disability Support Program)*, 2006 SCC 14 at para 33.

44 *Craton*, above note 7.

45 *Fédération Franco-Ténoise v Canada (Attorney General)*, 2008 NWTCA 6 at para 60 [*Franco-Ténoise*]. The court cites the following cases for this principle: *Hunter v Southam Inc*, [1984] 2 SCR 145 at 156; *R v Big M Drug Mart Ltd*, [1985] 1 SCR 295 at 344; *United States of America v Cotroni*, [1989] 1 SCR 1469 at 1480.

46 *Franco-Ténoise*, above note 45; *Lavigne*, above note 3 at para 23.

The development of the characteristics of quasi-constitutionality reveals the interconnectedness of these rights and their relationship to the Constitution. The principles of primacy developed under the *Canadian Bill of Rights* as the first quasi-constitutional statute, but the Supreme Court of Canada's adoption of a restrictive interpretation made it rare for other statutes to be held in violation of its terms.

In view of this weakness, the Court adopted a more expansive interpretation of human rights legislation that created a significantly more robust rights regime, particularly when combined with primacy. When it first began interpreting the right to equality in section 15(1) of the *Charter*, the Court turned to its jurisprudence under human rights legislation for guidance. The Court's subsequent adoption of a more stringent test under section 15(1) of the *Charter* raised questions about the appropriate analysis to be adopted when a government service created by legislation is challenged under human rights legislation—an issue still in the process of being conclusively determined.

Privacy was first protected under human rights legislation but was subsequently paired with access-to-information regimes to properly account for the balancing of these two rights. The Court endorsed the interpretive principles developed under human rights legislation for privacy and access-to-information rights, it is important to note, because of their quasi-constitutional character.

Legislative language rights have been recognized as quasi-constitutional both for their early developments, which surpassed the original rudimentary constitutional protections, and for their reflection and extension of the language rights that were constitutionally entrenched in 1982. All language rights regimes, whether constitutional or quasi-constitutional, must be interpreted expansively in a broad, liberal, and purposive approach.

Finally, the common law protection of a person's good reputation displays the significance of quasi-constitutionality as it is a right to be balanced in a defamation suit with the constitutional freedom of expression in section 2(b) of the *Charter*.

CHAPTER 2

The Broad, Liberal, and Purposive Interpretation of Quasi-constitutional Legislation

The Supreme Court of Canada has developed a unique approach to the interpretation of quasi-constitutional legislation compared to regular statutes on the basis that "it is inappropriate to rely solely on a strictly grammatical analysis . . . [for] the interpretation of legislation which is constitutional or quasi-constitutional in nature."[1] As a result, the Court has repeatedly stated that quasi-constitutional laws must be given a broad, liberal, and purposive interpretation.

This chapter will explore the application of the broad, liberal, and purposive interpretation of quasi-constitutional legislation in order to reveal the concrete results achieved by courts and tribunals. A comprehensive review of this interpretive approach is necessary because it is a defining feature of quasi-constitutionality compared to regular legislation. The intention of this chapter is to display how this interpretive approach is applied in practice and how it significantly expands the rights contained in quasi-constitutional legislation. Doing this requires a more in-depth study than merely repeating the declarations by the Supreme Court of Canada on the broad, liberal, and purposive interpretation of quasi-constitutional legislation; it will necessarily involve considering

1 *Quebec (Commission des droits de la personne et des droits de la jeunesse) v Montréal (City); Quebec (Commission des droits de la personne et des droits de la jeunesse) v Boisbriand (City)*, 2000 SCC 27 at para 30 [*Boisbriand*]. This case was cited by McLachlin CJ in her dissent in *New Brunswick (Human Rights Commission) v Potash Corporation of Saskatchewan Inc*, 2008 SCC 45 at para 67 [*Potash*].

how this interpretive approach is implemented by the lower courts, tribunals, boards of inquiries, and the access and privacy commissioners that routinely administer these statutes.

This chapter begins by reviewing the process involved in the broad, liberal, and purposive interpretation, and then proceeds to the results achieved under four groups of quasi-constitutional statutes — namely, human rights legislation, access-to-information acts, privacy acts, and statutes providing language rights. It also considers how courts further advance rights through a narrow and restrictive interpretation of the defences, exceptions, exemptions, and other forms of limitation in quasi-constitutional legislation.

A. THE APPLICATION OF THE BROAD, LIBERAL, AND PURPOSIVE INTERPRETATION TO QUASI-CONSTITUTIONAL LEGISLATION

The broad, liberal, and purposive interpretation applies to all categories of quasi-constitutional statutes except the statutory bills of rights, which include the *Canadian Bill of Rights* and the *Alberta Bill of Rights*. It is most commonly used for the interpretation of human rights legislation. Chief Justice Antonio Lamer observed in *University of British Columbia v Berg* that "this Court has repeatedly stressed that a broad, liberal and purposive approach is appropriate to human rights legislation."[2] Justice Charron stated for a majority Court in *Canada (Information Commissioner) v Canada (Minister of National Defence)* that, "in order to create a meaningful right of access to government information, it should be given a broad and liberal interpretation."[3] Justice Gonthier, for a unanimous Court in *Lavigne v Canada (Office of the Commissioner of Official Languages)*, cited with approval a statement by Nöel J of the Federal Court that a "purposive approach to the interpretation of the *Privacy Act* is . . . justified by the statute's quasi-constitutional legislative roots,"[4] while Nöel J further

2 [1993] 2 SCR 353 at para 26 [*Berg*]. See also *Quebec (Commission des droits de la personne et des droits de la jeunesse) v Maksteel Québec Inc*, 2003 SCC 68 at para 10; Mélanie Samson, "Interprétation large et libérale et interprétation contextuelle : convergence ou divergence?" (2008) 49 *Les Cahiers de droit* 297 at para 6; Ruth Sullivan, *Sullivan on the Construction of Statutes*, 5th ed (Markham, ON: LexisNexis, 2008) at 497.

3 *Canada (Information Commissioner) v Canada (Minister of National Defence)*, 2011 SCC 25 at para 48 [*Canada (Information Commissioner)*].

4 *Lavigne v Canada (Office of the Commissioner of Official Languages)*, 2002 SCC 53 at para 24 [*Lavigne*], citing *Canada (Privacy Commissioner) v Canada (Labour Relations*

stressed that "[i]t is well established that the provisions of the *Access Act* and of the *Privacy Act* must be afforded a broad and purposive interpretation."[5] It has likewise been confirmed that "[o]fficial languages statutes are quasi-constitutional and are to be given a broad purposive interpretation to achieve the goal of fostering official languages."[6]

The broad, liberal, and purposive interpretation of quasi-constitutional legislation begins with a purposive analysis, which seeks to uncover the purpose or legislative intent behind the statute and then undertake an interpretation of its provisions that advances this overarching purpose. A purposive analysis does not automatically lead to a broad and liberal interpretation; however, it has been noted that "courts do often refer to them in tandem," which is certainly the case when it comes to interpreting quasi-constitutional legislation.[7] Courts have determined that the purpose of quasi-constitutional legislation is best advanced through a broad and liberal interpretation of the rights that they protect, and consequently also through a narrow and restrictive interpretation of exemptions and defences.[8]

1) A Purposive Analysis

A purposive analysis finds its roots in the modern principle of statutory interpretation, which, as Professor Ruth Sullivan explains, emphasizes

---

Board), [1996] FCJ No 1076 at para 47 (TD) [*Canada (Privacy Commissioner)*].

5 *Canada (Privacy Commissioner), ibid* at para 44.

6 *Fédération Franco-Ténoise v Canada (Attorney General)*, 2008 NWTCA 6 at para 60, leave to appeal to SCC refused (*sub nom Northwest Territories (Attorney General) v Fédération Franco-Ténoise*), [2008] SCCA No 432. The court of appeal for the Northwest Territories relied on decisions from the Supreme Court of Canada in support of this conclusion, including *R v Beaulac*, [1999] 1 SCR 768; *Jones v Attorney General of New Brunswick*, [1975] 2 SCR 182; *Quebec (Attorney General) v Blaikie (No 1)*, [1979] 2 SCR 1016; *Quebec (Attorney General) v Blaikie (No 2)*, [1981] 1 SCR 312; *Reference re Manitoba Language Rights*, [1985] 1 SCR 721; *Ford v Quebec (Attorney General)*, [1988] 2 SCR 712. See also *Lalonde v Ontario (Commission de restructuration des services de santé)*, [2001] OJ No 4767 at para 90 (CA) [*Lalonde*]; *Thibodeau v Air Canada* (2005), [2006] 2 FCR 70 at paras 45–46 (FC) [*Thibodeau*]; *Lavigne*, above note 4 at para 23; *Canada (Attorney General) v Viola*, [1991] 1 FC 373 at 386 (CA) [*Viola*].

7 Stéphane Beaulac, *Handbook on Statutory Interpretation: General Methodology, Canadian Charter and International Law* (Markham, ON: LexisNexis, 2008) at 218.

8 Wayne A MacKay, "Evolving Fundamental Principles and Merging Public Law Silos: The Reshaping of Canada's Constitutional Landscape" (2013) *Supreme Court Law Review* (2d) 83 at para 46.

the "complex, multi-dimensional character of statutory interpretation."[9] It was first formulated in Canada by Elmer Driedger in the mid-1970s:

> Today there is only one principle or approach, namely, the words of an Act are to be read in their entire context in their grammatical and ordinary sense harmoniously with the scheme of the Act, the object of the Act and the intention of Parliament.[10]

The modern principle has been declared to be the Supreme Court of Canada's preferred approach.[11] It is now "used in all areas of the law and, in fact, in all facets of legal interpretation."[12] This development is relatively recent — hence its designation as the modern principle, or modern approach. It stands in contrast to the plain meaning rule of statutory interpretation that requires a literal application of legislative provisions. Courts often seek to justify the use of a purposive analysis by identifying an ambiguity in the literal meaning of a statute; however, a purposive analysis is now recognized as justified in its own right.[13]

Professor Sullivan explains that courts determine legislative purpose either directly, through purpose statements and preambles, or indirectly, through a contextual reading of the legislation.[14] She ultimately expresses the view that preambles and purpose statements are "the most authoritative

9 Sullivan, above note 2 at 1.

10 Elmer A Driedger, *The Construction of Statutes* (Toronto: Butterworths, 1974) at 67. While Driedger formulated the modern principle in the first edition of *The Construction of Statutes*, Stéphane Beaulac and Pierre-André Côté note that courts usually cite the principle from the second edition. See Stéphane Beaulac & Pierre-André Côté, "Driedger's 'Modern Principle' at the Supreme Court of Canada: Interpretation, Justification, Legitimization" (2006) 40 *Revue juridique Thémis* 131 at para 2; Elmer A Driedger, *The Construction of Statutes*, 2d ed (Toronto: Butterworths, 1983) at 87.

11 *Re Rizzo & Rizzo Shoes Ltd*, [1998] 1 SCR 27 at para 21.

12 Beaulac & Côté, above note 10 at para 4.

13 Professor Sullivan states that "[m]odern courts do not need an excuse to consider the purpose of legislation. Today purposive analysis is a regular part of interpretation, to be relied on in every case, not just those in which there is ambiguity or absurdity." Sullivan, above note 2 at 257. Courts, however, still sometimes look for ambiguity to justify a purposive analysis, even in some instances with quasi-constitutional legislation. See, especially, *Bell Canada v Canadian Telephone Employees Association*, 2003 SCC 36 at para 26, cited in *Canada (Human Rights Commission) v Canadian Airlines International Ltd*, 2006 SCC 1 at para 15 [*Canadian Airlines International*]; *Athabasca Tribal Council v Amoco*, 1980 ABCA 141 at para 26, cited in *Re Prue*, [1984] AJ No 1006 at para 28 (QB); *Cormier v Alberta (Human Rights Commission)* (1984), 56 AR 351 at paras 45–47 [*Cormier*].

14 Sullivan, above note 2 at 269–71.

evidence of purpose,"[15] and, indeed, courts have declared that "[t]he use of the preamble of an act to fully grasp its purpose is a method that is without controversy."[16] This approach of searching for the legislative purpose directly or indirectly is regularly used by courts and tribunals. In *Ndem v General Accident Assurance Co of Canada*, for example, it was held that "[t]he presence of the preamble [in Ontario's quasi-constitutional *French Language Services Act*] makes it unnecessary to resort to the speculative method for ascertaining legislative purpose, that is, by drawing my own inferences after reading the legislation in context."[17]

Courts and tribunals therefore routinely cite from preambles and purpose statements in quasi-constitutional statutes when determining the legislative purpose. In the case of human rights legislation, this practice was first endorsed by the Supreme Court of Canada in *Ontario Human Rights Commission and O'Malley v Simpsons-Sears Ltd.*[18] It is best explained by the Ontario Human Rights Tribunal in *Addai v Toronto*:

> In addition to the specific provisions related to discrimination, the *Code* contains a preamble which reflects the kinds of experiences the legislation is directed at remedying. It speaks not just to equality in relation to the law, but also to the values of understanding, mutual respect and dignity and the necessity to ensure that every citizen has the opportunity to contribute fully to the community. The analysis of a claim of discrimination under the *Code* must be animated by these important principles.[19]

Courts likewise look to the purpose statements contained in access-to-information and privacy statutes. The purpose statement in the federal *Access to Information Act* states that "government information should be available to the public."[20] In *Rubin v Canada (Minister of Transport)*, the Federal Court of Appeal held that "Parliament has deemed it fit to include

15 *Ibid* at 271. Likewise, Kent Roach believes that preambles "can play a valuable role in describing the purposes of legislation and the deliberative processes and events that led to its enactment." Kent Roach, "The Uses and Audiences of Preambles in Legislation" (2001) 47 *McGill Law Journal* 129 at para 62.

16 *Bronskill v Canada (Canadian Heritage)*, [2013] 2 FCR 563 at para 20 (FC) [*Bronskill*], var'd 2012 FCA 250, leave to appeal to SCC refused, [2012] SCCA No 509.

17 [2000] OFSCID No 167 at para 37 [*Ndem*].

18 [1985] 2 SCR 536 at para 12 [*O'Malley*].

19 *Addai v Toronto (City)*, 2012 HRTO 2252 at para 46. See also *Attis v New Brunswick (School District 15)*, [1991] NBHRBID No 1 at para 57 [*Attis*]; *Pannu, Kang and Gill v Prestige Cab Ltd*, [1986] AJ No 1717 at para 8 (CA) [*Prestige Cab Ltd*].

20 *Access to Information Act*, RSC 1985, c A-1, s 2(1).

in the [*Access to Information*] Act a clause setting out the purpose of the Act. In my opinion, this is significant and should not be ignored."[21] In *Dagg v Canada (Minister of Finance)*, La Forest J considered the purpose of the federal *Privacy Act*, which he described as seeking to "protect the privacy of individuals with respect to personal information about themselves held by a government institution [and] provide individuals with a right of access to that information."[22]

Courts also begin their interpretation of language rights statutes by reviewing their preamble to establish purpose. In *Lalonde et al v Commission de restructuration des services de santé*, the Ontario Court of Appeal reviewed the preamble of Ontario's *French Language Services Act* and it described its purpose as "a statutory recognition of the cultural heritage of the French speaking population and a reflection of the Legislative Assembly's commitment to preserve that cultural heritage for future generations."[23] In considering the provincial government's decision to reduce significantly the services of the only French-language hospital in Ontario, the court found that "[i]t can hardly be said that the serious adverse effects of the Commission's directions are consistent with the purpose and objectives of the F.L.S.A."[24]

2) A Broad and Liberal Interpretation

After establishing the purpose of quasi-constitutional legislation, courts search for an interpretive approach that will advance its special nature. The roots of the special interpretive approach to human rights legislation are typically traced back to comments by Lamer J (later CJ) in *Insurance Corporation of British Columbia v Heerspink*, in which he referred to human rights statutes as "fundamental law" and "more important than all others."[25] Although *Heerspink* is often credited as the starting point for the adoption of the broad, liberal, and purposive interpretation of human rights legislation, the Supreme Court of Canada did not endorse this approach directly until three years later in *O'Malley*, where it rejected a narrow construction in favour of an interpretive approach in line with

21 *Rubin v Canada (Minister of Transport)*, [1997] FCJ No 1614 at para 18 (CA) [*Rubin*].

22 [1997] 2 SCR 403 at para 64 [*Dagg*].

23 *Lalonde*, above note 6 at para 145.

24 *Ibid* at para 163.

25 *Insurance Corporation of British Columbia v Heerspink*, [1982] 2 SCR 145 at 158 [*Heerspink*].

the special nature of human rights legislation. Justice McIntyre wrote for a unanimous Court in *O'Malley*:

> It is not, in my view, a sound approach to say that according to established rules of construction no broader meaning can be given to the *Code* than the narrowest interpretation of the words employed. The accepted rules of construction are flexible enough to enable the Court to recognize in the construction of a human rights code the special nature and purpose of the enactment (see Lamer J. in *Insurance Corporation of British Columbia v Heerspink* . . .), and give to it an interpretation which will advance its broad purposes. Legislation of this type is of a special nature, not quite constitutional but certainly more than the ordinary — and it is for the courts to seek out its purpose and give it effect.[26]

The Supreme Court of Canada has since recognized that "[n]arrow interpretations may sterilize human rights laws and defeat their very purpose,"[27] and as a result, courts are not to "inspect these statutes with a microscope,"[28] or approach them "in a niggardly fashion."[29] The courts continue to apply the broad, liberal, and purposive interpretation to human rights legislation devoutly since *Heerspink* and *O'Malley*.[30]

As noted above, the Supreme Court of Canada has held that access-to-information legislation "should be given a broad and liberal

---

26 *O'Malley*, above note 18 at para 12.

27 *Canadian Airlines International*, above note 13 at para 15. The Court of Appeal of Saskatchewan similarly emphasized that "[a] narrow restrictive interpretation which would defeat the purpose of the legislation, that is, the elimination of discrimination, should be avoided." *Canadian Odeon Theatres Ltd v Saskatchewan Human Rights Commission*, [1985] SJ No 268 at para 45 (CA), leave to appeal to SCC refused, [1985] SCCA No 129.

28 *Canada (Attorney General) v Rosin*, [1991] 1 FC 391 at para 16 (CA) [*Rosin*]. Cited with approval by Lamer CJ in *Berg*, above note 2 at para 32.

29 *Robichaud v Canada (Treasury Board)*, [1987] 2 SCR 84 at para 8 [*Robichaud*].

30 *CNR v Canada (Human Rights Commission)*, [1987] 1 SCR 1114 at para 24 [*CNR*]; *Vilven v Air Canada*, 2009 FC 367 at para 79; *Canada (Attorney General) v Mossop*, [1993] 1 SCR 554 at para 94; *Boisbriand*, above note 1 at para 30; *Gould v Yukon Order of Pioneers*, [1996] 1 SCR 571 at para 5 [*Gould*]; *Berg*, above note 2; *University of Alberta Non-Academic Staff Assn v University of Alberta*, [1997] AJ No 803 at para 70 (QB) [*University of Alberta Non-Academic Staff Assn*]; *Potash*, above note 1 at para 65; *British Columbia (Public Service Relations Commission) v British Columbia Government and Service Employees' Union (BCGSEU) (Meiorin Grievance)*, [1999] 3 SCR 3 at para 44 [*Meiorin Grievance*]; *Rosin*, above note 28 at para 15; *Béliveau St-Jacques v Fédération des employées et employés de services publics Inc*, [1996] 2 SCR 345 at para 116; *Augustus v Gosset*, [1996] 3 SCR 268 at para 59; *Canada (Canadian Human Rights Commission) v Canada (Attorney General)*, 2011 SCC 53 at para 62; Alan LW D'Silva, "Giving Effect to Human Rights Legislation: A Purposive Approach" (1991) 3 *Windsor Review of Legal and Social Issues* 45.

interpretation."[31] The same approach is taken with respect to privacy. In *Dagg* La Forest J noted that the interpretation of privacy acts should be based on the fact that the right to privacy is "deliberately broad," and on the "foundational position of privacy interests in our social and legal culture."[32]

Courts similarly seek out an interpretive approach for legislation providing language rights on the basis of its purpose and special nature. In *Lavigne* the Supreme Court of Canada cited with approval the following statement from the Federal Court of Appeal in *Canada (Attorney General) v Viola*:

> by virtue of its preamble, its purpose as defined in section 2 and its taking precedence over other statutes in accordance with subsection 82(1), it belongs to that privileged category of quasi-constitutional legislation which reflects "certain basic goals of our society" and must be so interpreted "as to advance the broad policy considerations underlying it.[33]

The Supreme Court then stated that "[t]he Federal Court was correct to recognize the special status of the *Official Languages Act*. The constitutional roots of that Act, and its crucial role in relation to bilingualism, justify that interpretation."[34]

The Supreme Court of Canada now fully endorses a broad, liberal, and purposive interpretation of language rights in contrast to a restrictive approach it previously adopted in a trilogy of cases decided in 1986.[35] In *R v Beaulac* Bastarache J wrote for the majority:

> Language rights must in all cases be interpreted purposively, in a manner consistent with the preservation and development of official language communities in Canada . . . To the extent that *Société des*

---

31 *Canada (Information Commissioner)*, above note 3 at para 48.

32 *Dagg*, above note 22 at para 69. Justice La Forest cited from *Canada (Information Commissioner) v Canada (Solicitor General)*, [1988] 3 FC 551 at 557 (TD) [*Canada (Solicitor General)*].

33 *Viola*, above note 6 at 386, cited in *Rogers v Canada (Correctional Service)*, [2001] 2 FCR 586 at para 59 (TD); *Fédération Franco-Ténoise v Canada (Attorney General)*, 2006 NWTSC 20 at para 125, leave to appeal to SCC refused, [2008] SCCA No 432.

34 *Lavigne*, above note 4 at para 23.

35 *MacDonald v City of Montreal*, [1986] 1 SCR 460; *Société des Acadiens du Nouveau-Brunswick Inc v Association of Parents for Fairness in Education*, [1986] 1 SCR 549; *Bilodeau v Manitoba (Attorney General)*, [1986] 1 SCR 449. For an overview of the trilogy and its aftermath, see Marc Cousineau, "Survol des droits linguistiques : enfin de vrais droits linguistiques au Canada" (2000) 32 *Ottawa Law Review* 117 at para 24.

> *Acadiens du Nouveau-Brunswick* . . . stands for a restrictive interpretation of language rights, it is to be rejected.[36]

The interpretive approach adopted by the Court in *Beaulac* and in subsequent decisions is viewed as having completely revolutionized language rights in Canada.[37] Moreover, this interpretive approach is applied universally among the language rights regimes contained in section 133 of the *Constitution Act, 1867*, the *Charter*, in federal and provincial language rights legislation, and the *Criminal Code*. In this respect, the language rights established under the *Criminal Code* have been recognized as quasi-constitutional in addition to the official languages legislation.[38]

It is important to acknowledge that the broad, liberal, and purposive interpretive approach was never applied to the statutory bills of rights. Despite some indications from the Supreme Court of Canada that it would interpret the *Canadian Bill of Rights* generously, such as in the 1976 case of *Miller and Cockriell v The Queen*, it did not. In that case, Laskin CJ stated it is the "duty of the Court not to whittle down the protections of the *Canadian Bill of Rights* by a narrow construction of what is a quasi-constitutional document."[39] Nonetheless, the Court interpreted the Bill narrowly and consequently restricted the scope of its enumerated rights. It adopted what has been described as a "frozen concept" of rights, whereby the Bill only protects rights as they existed in the common law when it was enacted in 1960.[40] Thus, when the Court endorsed a form

36 *R v Beaulac*, [1999] 1 SCR 768 at para 25 [*Beaulac*]. The Ontario Court of Appeal also stated, "[i]t is now clear . . . that this narrow and restrictive approach has been abandoned and that language rights are to be treated as fundamental human rights and accorded a generous interpretation by the courts." *Lalonde*, above note 6 at para 132.

37 Marc Cousineau writes: "Ces quatre décisions, *le Renvoi relatif à la sécession du Québec, R. c. Beaulac* et *Arsenault-Cameron c. Ile-du-Prince-Édouard* de la Cour suprême du Canada ainsi que *Lalonde c. Ontario (Commission de restructuration des services de santé)* de la Cour divisionnaire de l'Ontario, ont complètement révolutionné les droits linguistiques du Canada." Above note 35 at para 2. See also *Arsenault-Cameron v Prince Edward Island*, 2000 SCC 1 at para 27; *Lalonde*, above note 6.

38 *Canada (Commissioner of Official Languages) v Canada (Department of Justice)*, 2001 FCT 239 at paras 139, 142, 182, 194, & 195. In reaching this conclusion, the Federal Court in this case relied on *Beaulac*, above note 36. *Constitution Act, 1867* (UK), 30 & 31 Vict, c 3, reprinted in RSC 1985, App II, No 5; *Canadian Charter of Rights and Freedoms*, Part I of the *Constitution Act, 1982*, being Schedule B to the *Canada Act 1982* (UK), 1982, c 11 [*Charter*]; *Criminal Code*, RSC 1985, c C-46.

39 *Miller and Cockriell v The Queen*, [1977] 2 SCR 680 at 689–90. *Canadian Bill of Rights*, SC 1960, c 44.

40 Walter Tarnopolsky, "A New Bill of Rights in the Light of the Interpretation of the Present One by the Supreme Court of Canada" in Law Society of Upper Canada, ed,

of judicial review under the *Canadian Bill of Rights* in the 1969 decision of *R v Drybones*, whereby laws that contravened its provisions would be found to be inoperable, the continued impact of this decision was limited by the narrow construction of the enumerated rights in subsequent *Canadian Bill of Rights* cases. Practically, therefore, while the *Bill of Rights* could effectuate judicial review over other statutes, this occurred only in a limited number of cases because the rights that the Bill protects were construed narrowly. The effect of this interpretive approach has been called "disappointing to observers who had hoped that it would approach the *Bill* sympathetically, and interpret it liberally."[41] The same interpretive approach was applied to the *Alberta Bill of Rights* because the two statutes are virtually identical.[42]

This review displays the process by which quasi-constitutional statutes are interpreted broadly, liberally, and purposively. The remaining sections will consider the impact of this interpretive approach in both the determination of the scope of rights under quasi-constitutional legislation and the scope of exceptions and available defences.

B. A BROAD, LIBERAL, AND PURPOSIVE INTERPRETATION OF HUMAN RIGHTS LEGISLATION

The broad, liberal, and purposive interpretation of human rights legislation is well established. It can be traced back to the adoption of the concept of constructive discrimination as well as that of direct discrimination; it is also observed in efforts to interpret human rights legislation consistently throughout the country, despite minor differences in terminology. Some of the most significant results in the advancement of rights have occurred through a broad, liberal, and purposive interpretation of both the enumerated grounds of discrimination and the social areas covered by human rights legislation.

The Constitution and the Future of Canada (Toronto: R De Boo, 1978) 161 at 181–91.

41 Joel Bakan et al, eds, *Canadian Constitutional Law*, 4th ed (Toronto: Emond Montgomery, 2010) at 714.

42 *Lavallee v Alberta (Securities Commission)*, 2009 ABQB 17 at para 169, aff'd 2010 ABCA 48, leave to appeal to SCC refused, [2010] SCCA No 119.

1) Adverse Effect or Constructive Discrimination

O'Malley is not only the case where the Supreme Court of Canada endorsed the broad, liberal, and purposive interpretation of human rights legislation, but also the first decision from the Court to display the concrete legal impact of this interpretive approach. It does so through its adoption of the principle of adverse effect or constructive discrimination.[43] Up to the *O'Malley* decision, there was no explicit recognition from the Court that human rights legislation applies to anything other than direct discrimination. Direct discrimination occurs where there is a practice or rule in place that is discriminatory on its face. The motive or intention to discriminate is usually obvious in direct forms of discrimination, but in *O'Malley*, the Court clarified that a narrow construction of human rights legislation that requires a motive be proven would create "an insuperable barrier" — discrimination "would be easy to cloak in the formation of rules which, though imposing equal standards, could create . . . injustice and discrimination by the equal treatment of those who are unequal."[44]

The application of a broad, liberal, and purposive interpretation by the Court in *O'Malley* resulted in focus being placed on whether the policy has a discriminatory effect rather than on its motive. As McIntyre J explained for a unanimous Court:

> It is the result or the effect of the action complained of which is significant. If it does, in fact, cause discrimination; if its effect is to impose on one person or group of persons obligations, penalties, or restrictive conditions not imposed on other members of the community, it is discriminatory.[45]

Adverse effect or constructive discrimination therefore captures conduct or policies that appear neutral yet result in discrimination in practice. The Court in *O'Malley* relied on the American term "adverse effect discrimination," which was developed in the context of the *Civil Rights Act*. On this point McIntyre J stated:

> I am of the opinion that this Court may consider adverse effect discrimination as described in these reasons a contradiction of the terms of the *Code*. An employment rule honestly made for sound economic or business reasons, equally applicable to all to whom it is intended to

43 *O'Malley*, above note 18 at paras 15–16.

44 *Ibid* at para 14.

45 *Ibid* at para 12.

> apply, may yet be discriminatory if it affects a person or group of persons differently from others to whom it may apply.[46]

The adoption of the principle of adverse effect or constructive discrimination in *O'Malley* significantly increased the reach of human rights legislation. The impact has been described as having "very considerably expanded the scope of the rights . . . since a whole new range of fact situations beyond the explicit use of a prohibited ground are now subjected to assessment."[47]

Adverse effect or constructive discrimination can even be found in situations where the respondent's motivations are well intentioned but still result in discrimination in practice. This occurred in *Bhinder v Canadian National Railway*, which was decided by the Supreme Court of Canada in the same year as *O'Malley*. This case involved a Sikh who was banned from wearing his religious headdress while working because a policy by Canadian National Railway required the use of a hard hat.[48] As in *O'Malley*, the Court in *Bhinder* extended the application of the *Code* to adverse effect discrimination; it did, however, find the hard hat policy to be a *bona fide* occupational requirement. While human rights statutes now routinely contain provisions that extend protection to adverse effect or constructive discrimination the Court in *O'Malley* and *Bhinder* confirmed this effect through interpretation and without "express statutory support."[49]

---

46 *Ibid* at para 18.

47 Denise Réaume, "Defending the Human Rights Codes from the *Charter*" (2012) 9 *Journal of Law and Equality* 67 at para 48.

48 *Bhinder v Canadian National Railway Co*, [1985] 2 SCR 561 [*Bhinder*].

49 *O'Malley*, above note 18 at para 13. See also *Robichaud*, above note 29 at para 10; *Wiens v Inco Metals Co* (1988), 9 CHRR D/4795 (Ont Bd Inq). In *Wiens v Inco Metals Co*, a fetal protection policy that was adopted in good faith and with good intentions was found to discriminate constructively. An example of a human rights statute that expressly protects against constructive discrimination is the Ontario *Human Rights Code*, RSO 1990, c H.19, s 11(1):

> A right of a person under Part I is infringed where a requirement, qualification or factor exists that is not discrimination on a prohibited ground but that results in the exclusion, restriction or preference of a group of persons who are identified by a prohibited ground of discrimination and of whom the person is a member, except where, (a) the requirement, qualification or factor is reasonable and *bona fide* in the circumstances; or (b) it is declared in this Act, other than in section 17, that to discriminate because of such ground is not an infringement of a right. Alan D'Silva observes that *O'Malley* and *Bhinder* "made it clear that absent specific statutory language there is no requirement of proving intent in human rights cases." He also notes that the *Human Rights Code* was amended prior to the Supreme Court of Canada's decisions in *O'Malley* and *Bhinder* to include

2) A Uniform Interpretation of Human Rights Legislation

Due to the broad, liberal, and purposive interpretive approach, courts try to interpret quasi-constitutional statutes uniformly throughout the country despite minor differences in the statutes from one province to the next. Chief Justice Lamer described it in *Berg*:

> If human rights legislation is to be interpreted in a purposive manner, differences in wording between provinces should not obscure the essentially similar purposes of such provisions, unless the wording clearly evinces a different purpose on behalf of a particular provincial legislature.[50]

The Saskatchewan Court of Appeal relied on this principle in *Saskatchewan (Human Rights Commission) v Prince Albert Elks Club Inc* to interpret family status as a ground of discrimination consistent with the legislation in the rest of the country, despite obvious differences with the *Saskatchewan Human Rights Code*.[51] In this case a woman was dismissed from her job at a golf course because she married a man while he was serving a life sentence at the penitentiary for six counts of second-degree murder. Saskatchewan's *Code* defines marital status as a "state of being engaged to be married, married, single, separated, divorced, widowed or living in a common-law relationship," but unlike other statutes also provides that "a relationship with a particular person is not discrimination on the basis of marital status."[52] The case was initially dismissed by the Board of Inquiry as a result of this peculiar feature of the *Saskatchewan Human Rights Code*, as it was found that the dismissal was due to a particular person. The Court of Appeal disagreed and found that a broad, liberal, and purposive interpretation meant to "discourage discrimination" requires the provision to be interpreted consistently with other human rights instruments.[53] It achieved this by finding that her dismissal was not based on her marriage to her husband as an individual, but rather

---

"constructive discrimination," although these cases originated before its enactment. D'Silva, above note 30 at 49.

50 *Berg*, above note 2 at para 32. In *Okanagan Rainbow Coalition v Kelowna (City)*, 2000 BCHRT 21 at para 73 [*Okanagan Rainbow Coalition*], the British Columbia Human Rights Tribunal cited Lamer CJ in *Berg* and held that "I find the definitional differences between the human rights legislation in Ontario, New Brunswick and British Columbia to be of no consequence."

51 *Saskatchewan (Human Rights Commission) v Prince Albert Elks Club Inc*, 2002 SKCA 106 [*Prince Albert Elks Club Inc*].

52 *Saskatchewan Human Rights Code*, SS 1979, c S-24.1, s 2(i.01).

53 *Prince Albert Elks Club Inc*, above note 51 at para 20.

to his group characteristics as an inmate who was convicted of a serious offence.[54]

3) Interpreting the Grounds of Discrimination

The reach of human rights legislation has also been extended through a broad, liberal, and purposive interpretation of both the grounds of discrimination and the social areas where discrimination is prohibited. The protection against discrimination in human rights legislation is limited by both a list of enumerated grounds of discrimination that includes race, colour, place of origin, ethnicity, creed, sex, sexual orientation, age, marital status, family status, criminal record, and disability, as well as a defined group of social areas where discrimination is prohibited, such as employment, services, accommodations, vocational associations, and the formation of contracts. In *Berg* Lamer CJ observed that "the basic motivation behind such limiting words is clear: the legislature did not wish human rights legislation to regulate all of the private activities of its citizens."[55] However, the application of the broad, liberal, and purposive interpretation to the grounds of discrimination and the defined list of relationships has expanded the scope of protections under human rights legislation.

Human rights tribunals apply the broad, liberal, and purposive interpretation to the grounds of discrimination at the outset of a hearing by refusing to take an overly technical approach when considering whether the complainant has identified the correct ground of discrimination in the application. It is recognized that complainants are not "skilled pleaders" and therefore tribunals "should be reluctant to permit a case to turn on the language of the documents such as the complaint."[56] Tribunals instead focus on whether discrimination has been established in one or more of the grounds. They will not dismiss an application simply because discrimination is established at the hearing under a different ground from

---

54 *Ibid* at para 47. See also *Decision No 1529/04I2*, 2008 ONWSIAT 547 at para 35, where the Ontario Workplace Safety and Insurance Appeals Tribunal relied on decisions from other provinces in determining that employment insurance is a service, even though it recognized some differences in the statutory language on what constitutes a service.

55 *Berg*, above note 2 at para 9.

56 *Borho v Atco Lumber Company*, Report of a Board of Inquiry under the BC *Human Rights Code*, dated 30 April 1976 at 11; Ian A Hunter, "Human Rights Legislation in Canada: Its Origin, Development and Interpretation" (1976) 15 *University of Western Ontario Law Review* 24 at 53.

the one marked on the application. This principle was clearly articulated by the British Columbia Human Rights Tribunal:

> In conducting a hearing into a complaint before it, the Tribunal is required to determine whether, on the basis of the information before it, there has been discrimination contrary to the *Code*. It would not be in accordance with the public interest, or with the purposes of the *Code*, for the Tribunal to dismiss a complaint of discrimination before it because, although the complainant had established that discrimination had occurred, he or she had filed her complaint under the wrong area of discrimination. This would be an unduly technical approach, contrary both to the purposes of the *Code* and to the underlying nature of legislation such as the *Code*.
>
> In this regard, the Supreme Court of Canada has frequently noted that human rights legislation has a unique, quasi-constitutional nature and ought to be interpreted in a liberal and purposive manner in order to advance the broad policy considerations underlying it.[57]

Human rights tribunals thus allow for an application to be amended up to and during the hearing.[58]

The broad, liberal, and purposive approach has greatly expanded the scope of the enumerated grounds of discrimination by interpreting certain characteristics as falling within the scope of one of the grounds that a narrower interpretation would not have recognized. For example, Ontario's *Human Rights Code* does not explicitly prohibit discrimination on the basis of transgender; however, the Ontario Human Rights Tribunal concluded that it falls under discrimination on the basis of sex through a broad, liberal, and purposive interpretation in *Hogan v Ontario (Minister of Health and Long-Term Care)*. The tribunal reasoned

> that the construction of the terms sex and gender are flexible enough to enable it to conclude that transsexuals and the intersexed fall within the ground of sex to recognize the *Code*'s special nature and purpose of the enactment, and to give it an interpretation that advances its broad

---

57 *Stephenson v Sooke Lake Modular Home Co-operative Association (No 2)*, 2007 BCHRT 410 at paras 13–14.

58 *Patelas and Boyd v Pattinson*, 2010 BCHRT 181 at para 32; *Brar v British Columbia Veterinary Medical Assn*, 2007 BCHRT 445 at para 10; *Petterson and Poirier v Gorcak (No 3)*, 2009 BCHRT 439 at para 424.

> purposes to protect every person from unlawful discrimination on the ground of sex.[59]

Sex discrimination has also been expanded to include sexual harassment[60] and pregnancy[61] through the broad, liberal, and purposive interpretive approach. Despite the expansive interpretation of what constitutes discrimination on the basis of sex, human rights statutes are being amended to include gender expression and gender identity as grounds of discrimination.[62]

The application of the broad, liberal, and purposive approach has expanded the meaning of the grounds of marital status and family status. These grounds are not restricted to the ordinary and grammatical meaning of "distinctions based on the mere fact that the complainant has a certain type of marital or family status."[63] In *Health Sciences Assn of British Columbia v Campbell River and North Island Transition Society*, the British Columbia Court of Appeal suggested that family status as a prohibited ground of discrimination should not be interpreted too broadly because it could potentially cause "disruption and great mischief in the workplace." It thus found that a *prima facie* case is made out only "when a change in a term or condition of employment imposed by an employer results in serious interference with a substantial parental or other family duty or obligation of the employee."[64] The Canadian Human Rights

---

59 2006 HRTO 32 at para 127 [*Hogan*]. The Ontario Human Rights Commission first took the position that the ground of sex under human rights law could be interpreted to include the rights of transgender people in 1999. See Ontario Human Rights Commission, *Policy on Preventing Discrimination Because of Gender Identity and Gender Expression* (Toronto: Ontario Human Rights Commission, 2014) at para 10. See also *Waters v BC Medical Services Plan*, 2003 BCHRT 13 at paras 134–35; *Sheridan v Sanctuary Investments Ltd (No 3)* (1999), 33 CHRR D/467 (BCHRT); *Mamela v Vancouver Lesbian Connection*, [1999] BCHRTD No 51 at paras 92–94; *Ferris v OTEU*, [1999] BCHRTD No 55 at paras 82–83; *Montreuil v National Bank of Canada*, 2004 CHRT 7 at para 36.

60 *Janzen v Platy Enterprises Ltd*, [1989] 1 SCR 1252.

61 *Brooks v Canada Safeway Ltd*, [1989] 1 SCR 1219.

62 See, for example, *An Act to amend the Canadian Human Rights Act and the Criminal Code*, SC 2017, c 13, and *An Act to amend the Human Rights Code with Respect to Gender Identity and Gender Expression*, SO 2012, c 7, which added "gender expression and identity" as enumerated grounds of discrimination.

63 *Canada (Attorney General) v Johnstone*, 2014 FCA 110 at para 64 [*Johnstone*]; see also *B v Ontario (Human Rights Commission)*, 2002 SCC 66.

64 *Health Sciences Assn of British Columbia v Campbell River and North Island Transition Society*, 2004 BCCA 260 at paras 38–39 [*Campbell River*].

Tribunal explicitly rejected this restrictive approach in *Hoyt v Canadian National Railway*:

> With respect, I do not agree with the [British Columbia Court of Appeal's] analysis. Human rights codes, because of their status as 'fundamental law,' must be interpreted liberally so that they may better fulfill their objectives . . . It would, in my view, be inappropriate to select out one prohibited ground of discrimination for a more restrictive definition.[65]

In *Whyte v Canadian National Railway*, the Canadian Human Rights Tribunal compared differences between the *Campbell River* and *Hoyt* decisions and concluded:

> [T]aking into account the special nature and status of human rights legislation as a quasi-constitutional legislation, the Tribunal concludes that the interpretation and application of family status proposed in *Hoyt* is the proper one to adopt. As stated earlier, human rights legislation must be given a liberal and purposive interpretation, in which protected rights receive a broad interpretation, while exceptions and defenses are narrowly construed.[66]

In the 2014 decision of *Canada (Attorney General) v Johnstone*, Mainville J, of the Federal Court of Appeal, cited a long line of decisions finding that family status incorporates parental obligations such as childcare.[67]

Family status in the *Human Rights Code* of Ontario is defined as "the status of being in a parent and child relationship."[68] The Human

---

65 *Hoyt v Canadian National Railway*, [2006] CHRD No 33 at para 120 [*Hoyt*].

66 *Whyte v Canadian National Railway*, 2010 CHRT 22 at para 175 [*Whyte*].

67 *Johnstone*, above note 63 at para 59. See also the decision of Mainville J in *Canadian National Railway Co v Seeley*, 2014 FCA 111 at paras 63–71, in which Mainville J cited *Brown v Canada (Department of National Revenue)*, 1993 CanLII 683 (CHRT); *Hoyt*, above note 65; *Woiden v Lynn*, 2002 CanLII 8171 (CHRT); *Closs v Fulton Forwarders Incorporated and Stephen Fulton*, 2012 CHRT 30; *Richards v Canadian National Railway*, 2010 CHRT 24; *Whyte*, above note 66; *Seeley v Canadian National Railway*, 2010 CHRT 23; *Johnstone v Canada (Attorney General)*, 2007 FC 36; *Patterson v Canada (Revenue Agency)*, 2011 FC 1398 at paras 34–35; *Devaney v ZRV Holdings Limited and Zeidler Partnership Architects*, 2012 HRTO 1590; *Callaghan v 1059711 Ontario Inc*, 2012 HRTO 233; *McDonald v Mid-Huron Roofing*, 2009 HRTO 1306; *CD v Wal-Mart Canada Corp*, 2009 HRTO 801; *Canada Post Corp v Canadian Union of Postal Workers (Sommerville Grievance)* (2006), 156 LAC (4th) 109 (Can Lab Arb); *Ontario Public Service Employees Union v Ontario Public Service Staff Union (DeFreitas Grievance)*, [2005] OLAA No 396.

68 *Human Rights Code*, above note 49, s 10(1).

Rights Tribunal of Ontario has recognized that "the definition of family status may well extend to care relationships other than that between a biological/adoptive parent and child,"[69] and the Ontario Human Rights Commission's *Policy and Guidelines on Discrimination Because of Family Status* provides a particularly broad definition:

> The Commission has taken the position that the ground of family status includes care relationships between adult children and those who stand in parental relationship to them. For example, individuals providing eldercare for aging parents are protected from discrimination under the ground of family status. The protection extends to include anyone in a "parent type" of relationship with the caregiver. For example, a person providing eldercare to a grandparent who played a significant role in his or her upbringing may be protected under the ground of family status.[70]

Family status for the commission, therefore, does not rest on blood or adoptive ties, but rather on "relationships of care, responsibility and commitment that resemble a parent–child relationship."[71] In the 2015 case of *Canada (Attorney General) v Hicks*, the Federal Court, through the application of the broad, liberal, and purposive interpretation, also reached the conclusion that the "prohibited ground of discrimination of family status should encompass the eldercare obligation."[72]

Human rights legislation protects people against discrimination in employment on the ground of criminal conviction, and through a broad, liberal, and purposive interpretation, human rights tribunals have also held that the legislation protects people charged but not convicted.[73] The respondent in *Salter v Peace River South School District 59* argued that the ground of "criminal or summary conviction charge" should be interpreted narrowly and that the British Columbia Council of Human Rights erred in the earlier decision *Dore v Crown Tire Service Ltd* by holding that

---

69 *MF v Child and Family Service Timmins and District*, 2010 HRTO 18 at para 11.

70 Ontario Human Rights Commission, *Policy and Guidelines on Discrimination Because of Family Status* (Toronto: Ontario Human Rights Commission, 2007) at para 10.

71 *Ibid.*

72 *Canada (Attorney General) v Hicks*, 2015 FC 599 at para 70.

73 *Dore v Crown Tire Service Ltd* (1989), 10 CHRR D/5433 (BCCHR); *Salter v Peace River South School District 59*, [1989] BCCHRD No 6 at para 12 [*Salter*]; *BAO v New Westminster (City) Police Department*, [1989] BCCHRD No 25; *Muir v Emcon Services Inc*, [1991] BCCHRD No 22.

this ground also protects those that have been charged but not convicted of an offence. In rejecting this argument, the council stated:

> I am not persuaded by counsel's arguments in that regard. Counsel argued that the criminal conviction provision in section 8 of the *Human Rights Act* should be narrowly interpreted. This view appears to be inconsistent with the "purposive interpretation" adopted by the Courts and Tribunals in dealing with human rights legislation.[74]

This was extended further in *Clement v Jackson* to criminal acts that do not even result in charges being laid.[75] The complainant in that case was dismissed from her employment because she acknowledged that she was caught stealing from a previous employer but never charged. The British Columbia Human Rights Tribunal held that it would be an absurd result if the protection against discrimination extended to those charged or convicted of a criminal offence, but not to those where charges were never laid.[76]

The broad, liberal, and purposive interpretation has had a particularly significant effect on disability as a ground of discrimination. Courts and tribunals have acknowledged that their role is not "to attempt to outline a detailed list of physical disabilities," but rather to "analyze each situation on a case by case basis, in a liberal but judicious fashion."[77] This is not to suggest that this ground of discrimination differs from the other grounds on a theoretical level. Courts and tribunals have recognized that disability has characteristics similar to the other grounds of discrimination, "such as race, religion, creed, colour or ethnic origin."[78] However, in doing so, they have not restricted disability to conditions that render a person incapacitated or that have persistent symptoms. An overactive thyroid was held to be a disability in *Morrison v O'Leary Associates*, despite the fact it caused only a temporary physical disability. The Board of Inquiry reasoned that, "[a]lthough her symptoms were transitory, the Complainant's illness is a life long chronic ailment which is controlled or regulated through medication."[79] The Board of Inquiry also characterized this condition as one "which the general population does not suffer."[80]

---

74 *Salter*, above note 73 at para 11.

75 *Clement v Jackson*, 2006 BCHRT 411.

76 *Ibid* at para 18.

77 *Morrison v O'Leary Associates*, [1990] NSHRBID No 3 at para 61 [*Morrison*].

78 *Ibid* at para 55.

79 *Ibid* at para 60.

80 *Ibid*.

Tribunals are diligent to prevent expansion of the meaning of disability as an enumerated ground of discrimination to capture all ailments through the broad, liberal, and purposive interpretation. They want to avoid "trivializing the purposive nature" of human rights legislation.[81] In *Morrison*, the Nova Scotia Board of Inquiry noted that disability should be interpreted in light of "characteristics common to other protected categories in the Act such as race, religion, creed, colour or ethnic origin, namely that the person in this category can do nothing of his own volition to remove himself from the category."[82] Thus, the purpose of human rights legislation would be negated and not advanced if disability as a ground of discrimination is interpreted so broadly as to include characteristics that are not immutable.

Courts and tribunals have, therefore, been cautious not to expand the interpretation of disability to include conditions that are contrary to the purpose of human rights legislation. In *Ouimette v Lily Cup Ltd*, a board of inquiry rejected that the seasonal flu was a disability because this interpretation would run contrary to the very purpose behind Ontario's *Human Rights Code*. It is worth quoting the reasoning of the board on this point:

> . . . In my view, it would be wrong to attempt to stretch the meaning of illness under s. 9(b)(i) of the *Code* to include the flu. It would be wrong to do so, in part, because of the effect of such a construction on the high purpose otherwise achieved by the interpretation provision in protecting those who are actually or perceived to be materially impaired through illness. Where the *Code* calls for defined groups to be protected, the Commission would include literally everyone suffering from a few days' illness. I cannot accept that the intent of s. 9(b)(i) is to embrace such kinds of discrimination.[83]

Likewise, the British Columbia Council of Human Rights in *Nielson v Sandman Four Ltd* rejected the argument that a temporary inability to work from transitory sciatica constituted a disability under the province's *Human Rights Act*.[84] For this reason in determining that a thyroid condition was a disability in *Morrison*, the Nova Scotia Board of Inquiry was quick to point out that, while the "symptoms were transitory," the illness

81 *Ibid* at para 61.

82 *Ibid* at para 55.

83 *Ouimette v Lily Cups Ltd* (1990), 12 CHHR D/19 at D/33 (Ont Bd Inq).

84 *Nielson v Sandman Four Ltd*, [1986] BCCHRD No 4.

itself "is a life long chronic ailment . . . from which the general population does not suffer."[85]

Short of a constitutional challenge under section 15 of the *Charter*, as was the case in *Vriend v Alberta* where sexual orientation was read into Alberta's human rights legislation as a prohibited ground of discrimination, courts and tribunals cannot generate new grounds of discrimination.[86] However, similar results can be achieved through a broad, liberal, and purposive interpretation of the grounds of discrimination as in *Hogan* where transgender was interpreted to fall under sex as a prohibited ground. The Ontario Human Rights Tribunal in *Hogan* reasoned:

> Ontario is correct that, in this case, the Tribunal has no jurisdiction to read in new grounds into the *Code*. However, the Tribunal is required to interpret the *Code* in a broad and liberal manner that gives full effect to the broad policy of the *Code* and not be restrictive by giving a narrow interpretation to words used to express the protection, especially where doing so, would exclude any person.[87]

The tribunal in *Hogan* thus acknowledged that it lacks the jurisdiction to create new grounds of discrimination, but it proceeded to achieve substantively similar results through a broad, liberal, and purposive interpretation.

Courts and tribunals have further expanded the scope of the grounds of discrimination by establishing that they capture situations where a person does not possess the characteristics of one of the prohibited grounds but is perceived to. This is often called the "subjective component" of discrimination, which, as the British Columbia Court of Appeal explained, "focuses not on the actual characteristics of the person but on the attitudes, prejudices and stereotypes of others that impose limitations on that person's human dignity, respect and right to equality."[88] Justice Benoit, of the Quebec Superior Court, best described this in *Commission des droits de la personne du Québec v Ville de Laval*:

> When an employer refuses to hire someone because it considers the candidate's skin to be too brown, regardless of whether the candidate actually has brown skin or whether the employer subjectively perceives it as such, the employer has engaged in discriminatory practices on the

85 *Morrison*, above note 77 at para 60.

86 *Vriend v Alberta*, [1998] 1 SCR 493.

87 *Hogan*, above note 59 at para 123.

88 *School District No 44 (North Vancouver) v Jubran*, 2005 BCCA 201 at para 45, leave to appeal to SCC refused, [2005] SCCA No 260 [*Jubran*].

> basis of colour and it must then justify the exclusion as a requirement of the employment. Thus, whether the exclusion is based on race, colour, sex, sexual orientation, civil status, religion, political convictions, language, ethnic or national origin or social condition, discrimination exists whether the employer's identification of that race, colour, sex, or sexual orientation is objective or purely subjective.[89]

Courts adopted this notion of perceived, or subjective, discrimination in order to advance the purpose of human rights statutes, namely, to reduce discrimination.

In *Korthe v Hillstrom Oil Company Ltd*, the British Columbia Council of Human Rights applied this reasoning to a record of conviction as a prohibited ground of discrimination:

> Based on these decisions which hold that a broad and liberal interpretation must be given to the Act, I have no hesitation in holding that the Complainant can successfully advance a breach of s. 8 of the Act based on circumstances where she was terminated by her employer based on the erroneous presumption that she had been involved in some sort of illegal activity which was the subject of a criminal investigation.[90]

Similarly, in *School District No 44 (North Vancouver) v Jubran*, the British Columbia Court of Appeal held that a complainant in a case alleging discriminatory harassment on the basis of sexual orientation does not have to be homosexual.[91] It even went one step further and determined that the harassers did not have to have a subjective perception of the complainant as homosexual. The harassers said that they routinely use homophobic epithets with friends as a joke, not as an insult, and they argued they knew full well that the complainant was not homosexual. Regardless of whether they perceived the complainant to be homosexual, the court found that

> [t]he effect of their conduct, however, was the same whether or not they perceived Mr. Jubran to be homosexual. The homophobic taunts directed against Mr. Jubran attributed to him the negative perceptions, myths and stereotypes attributed to homosexuals.[92]

---

89 *Commission des droits de la personne du Québec v Ville de Laval*, [1983] CS 961 at 966 [*Laval*], cited by the Supreme Court of Canada in *Boisbriand*, above note 1 at para 56.

90 *Korthe v Hillstrom Oil Company Ltd*, [1997] BCCHRD No 37 at para 32.

91 *Jubran*, above note 88.

92 *Ibid* at para 47.

In the court of appeal's view, requiring the complainant to prove the subjective percepts of homosexuality on the part of the harassers would be equivalent to having to prove their intention to discriminate.[93]

When Benoit J described the subjective perception of the grounds of discrimination in the *Laval* case, he explicitly excluded its application to discrimination on the basis of disability on the rationale that "the ground of exclusion based on a person's handicap cannot be a matter of perception, since the *Charter* protects a person who is a handicapped person."[94] This understanding was characteristic of how courts viewed disability in some of the early jurisprudence. After reviewing the reasons of Benoit J, the Supreme Court of Canada explained: "case law from that period indicates that courts rejected subjective perception in the case of handicap, although they did take it into account when considering other grounds of discrimination."[95] Perception of disability is now enumerated as a prohibited ground of discrimination in several provincial and territorial human rights statutes, although even in jurisdictions where it is not, tribunals have held that it is prohibited through a broad, liberal, and purposive interpretation.[96]

Since the Supreme Court of Canada's decision in *Quebec (Commission des droits de la personne et des droits de la jeunesse) v Montréal (City); Quebec (Commission des droits de la personne et des droits de la jeunesse) v Boisbriand (City)*, there is no question that discrimination on the basis of disability can be interpreted with a subjective component — the perception of a disability that captures ailments which do not result in any limitation or functional disability. The Court held that

> a "handicap" may exist even without proof of physical limitations or the presence of an ailment. The "handicap" may be actual or perceived and, because the emphasis is on the effects of the distinction, exclusion or preference rather than the precise nature of the handicap, the cause and origin of the handicap are immaterial. Further, the *Charter* also

---

93 *Ibid* at para 50.

94 *Laval*, above note 89 at 966, cited in *Boisbriand*, above note 1 at para 57.

95 *Boisbriand*, *ibid* at para 58.

96 Ontario *Human Rights Code*, above note 49, s 10(3); *Human Rights Act*, SNWT 2002, c 18, s 55(2.1); *Human Rights Act, 2010*, SNL 2010, c H-13.1, s 9(3); *Human Rights Act*, S Nu 2003, c 12, s 1; *Human Rights Act*, RSNS 1989, c 214, s 3(1); *Boisbriand*, above note 1 at para 48.

> prohibits discrimination based on the actual or perceived possibility that an individual may develop a handicap in the future.[97]

Despite the significance of this case, the Supreme Court of Canada acknowledged that it was merely recognizing what it called "a clear trend" in the jurisprudence. It said, "courts have consistently recognized that discrimination based on 'handicap' includes a subjective component."[98]

The interpretation of disability with a subjective component has resulted in a considerable extension of rights as courts and tribunals have found a variety of conditions to constitute disabilities that do not result in functional limitations: these include congenital physical malformations, asthma, diabetes, speech impediments, obesity, acne, epilepsy, being HIV positive, being generally "unfit" on medical grounds, having narrowing in the lumbar spine, and "bubbles in the lungs."[99]

4) Interpreting the Social Areas in Human Rights Legislation: Employment

In addition to restricting discrimination to a defined list of grounds, human rights legislation in Canada does not extend to all social relationships; it is, rather, confined to a list of specific contexts, or social areas. Chief Justice Lamer in *Berg* explains that "the legislature has stated, through the limiting words . . . that some relationships will not be subject

---

97 *Ibid* at para 81.

98 *Ibid* at para 62. The Court referred to the following cases: *Québec (Commission des droits de la personne et des droits de la jeunesse) v Montréal (Communauté urbaine)* (1992), 16 CHRR D/141 (TDPQ); *Québec (Commission des droits de la personne et des droits de la jeunesse) v Lessard, Beaucage, Lemieux Inc* (1992), 19 CHRR D/441 (TDPQ); *Commission des droits de la personne du Québec v Montréal (Ville de)*, DTE 94T-600; *Commission des droits de la personne du Québec v Ville de Montréal*, [1994] RJQ 2097 (TDPQ).

99 *Boisbriand*, above note 1 at para 48; *Morrison*, above note 77 at para 61; *Biggs v Hudson*, [1988] BCCHRD No 22; *Labelle v Air Canada* (1983), 4 CHRR D/1311 (CHRT); *De Jong v Horlacher Holdings Ltd (cob "Family Tree Restaurant")*, [1989] BCCHRD No 13; *Matlock v Canora Holdings Ltd* (1983), 4 CHRR D/1576 (BC Bd Inq); *St Thomas v Canada (Canadian Armed Forces)*, [1991] CHRD No 3; *Davison v St Paul Lutheran Home of Melville, Saskatchewan* (1992), 15 CHRR D/81 (Sask Bd Inq); *Thwaites v Canada (Armed Forces)*, [1993] CHRD No 9; *Brideau v Air Canada* (1983), 4 CHRR D/1314 (CHRT); *Roy v BC Rail Ltd* (1987), 8 CHRR D/3646 (BCCHR); *Funk v Stowe-Woodward Inc* (1987), 8 CHRR D/4024 (BCCHR); *Bahlsen v Canada (Minister of Transport)*, [1997] 1 FC 800 (CA), leave to appeal to SCC refused, [1997] SCCA No 51; *Cinq-Mars v Transports Provost Inc* (1988), 9 CHRR D/4704 (CHRT); *Hajla v Well and Plaza Restaurant* (1987), 8 CHRR D/3879 (Ont Bd Inq).

to scrutiny under human rights legislation."[100] It has also been described to mean that the application of human rights legislation is limited to "particular areas of social life."[101] In contrast to the *Charter*, which applies to government action in "an unlimited variety of contexts in which the state asserts its authority," human rights legislation applies to both government and private actors but in a limited number of social areas.[102]

Although courts and tribunals have to remain mindful that human rights protections are limited to these social areas, through the application of the broad, liberal, and purposive interpretation, they have found a variety of relationships to fall within these areas that would not have been captured through a more restrictive interpretation. This is particularly the case in the areas of employment and services.

Most litigation under human rights legislation occurs in the area of employment, so it is not surprising that the scope of protection against discrimination in the area of employment has been a topic of extensive judicial consideration. The Supreme Court of Canada has held that courts and tribunals are to apply a broad, liberal, and purposive interpretation to employment as a social area covered by human rights legislation when determining the nature of the relationship between the parties.[103] As Ballance J, of the Supreme Court of British Columbia, described in the case of *HMTQ et al v Emergency Health Services Commission et al*:

> There can be no doubt that human rights legislation must be interpreted liberally and in a manner consistent with its underlying purposes and its quasi-constitutional status. The *Code* definition of "employment" can and should be interpreted generously and flexibly to further *Code* purposes and protect against or remedy acts of prohibited discrimination.[104]

---

100 *Berg*, above note 2 at para 27. Likewise, Clackson J, of the Alberta Court of Queen's Bench, explained that "[t]he Act does not contain a broad or blanket prohibition on discrimination. It does not say that no person shall discriminate. Rather, it prohibits those undertaking certain activities, from doing so in a discriminatory manner." *Lockerbie & Hole Industrial Inc v Alberta (Human Rights and Citizenship Commission, Director)*, 2009 ABQB 241 at para 21, aff'd 2011 ABCA 3 [*Lockerbie*].

101 Lesli Bisgould, "Twists and Turns and Seventeen Volumes of Evidence, or How Procedural Developments Might Have Influenced Substantive Human Rights Law" (2012) 9 *Journal of Law and Equality* 5 at para 27.

102 *Ibid.*

103 *McCormick v Fasken Martineau DuMoulin LLP*, 2014 SCC 39 at para 19 [*McCormick*].

104 *HMTQ et al v Emergency Health Services Commission et al*, 2007 BCSC 460 at para 152 [*HMTQ*].

This direction gives courts flexibility in the interpretive exercise, and they are not constrained by more restrictive interpretations found in other law areas that address employment relationships. For example, in *Robichaud v Canada (Treasury Board)*, in determining whether an employer was liable for the sexual harassment of an employee by a supervisor, the Supreme Court of Canada concluded that there was liability on the part of the employer without considering whether this liability was tort based or otherwise. Justice La Forest reasoned that the intention of the federal *Human Rights Act* is to hold employers liable for the discriminatory acts of their employees; it is not to be based on stricter notions of employer liability in the criminal or quasi-criminal context, or on vicarious liability under tort law.[105] More recently, in the 2017 decision of *British Columbia Human Rights Tribunal v Schrenk*, a majority Court asserted that human rights legislation is not limited to protecting employees against discriminatory harassment by their supervisors in the workplace, but "[r]ather, its protection extends to all employees who suffer discrimination with a sufficient connection to their employment context. This may include discrimination by their co-workers, even when those co-workers have a different employer."[106]

The most important result of this interpretive approach is that employment in the human rights context "has a broader meaning than is ascribed to it in employment law."[107] Courts have noted that human rights legislation often leaves the term "employment" general and undefined, while it is often very specifically defined in the employment or labour law context.[108] This means that courts and tribunals reject a rigid application of the traditional criteria of determining an employment relationship from the employment law and labour law contexts for its use in the human rights context.[109] Courts and tribunals will not rigidly apply the traditional tests for determining an employment relationship, although they will generally hold the relationship to be one of employment "if any of the traditional criteria relied upon to define employment in other legal contexts, are present."[110] Instead, they require a "consideration of factors

105 *Robichaud*, above note 29 at para 17.

106 *British Columbia Human Rights Tribunal v Schrenk*, 2017 SCC 62 at para 3.

107 *Vancouver Rape Relief Society v Nixon*, 2005 BCCA 601 at para 18, leave to appeal to SCC refused, [2006] SCCA No 365 [*Vancouver Rape Relief Society*].

108 *Rosin*, above note 28 at para 23; *Tulk v Newfoundland (Ministry of Health and Community Services)* (2002), 210 Nfld & PEIR 101 at para 15 (SCTD) [*Tulk*].

109 *Prestige Cab Ltd*, above note 19 at para 11.

110 *Lockerbie*, above note 100 at para 38.

that are well beyond what traditional common law perceptions of the employer–employee relationship might dictate."[111]

In *Cormier v Human Rights Commission*, the Alberta Court of the Queen's Bench reviewed a number of cases where the question of whether there was an employment relationship was considered under the common law of master and servant, labour relations, employment standards legislation, and tax law. It concluded that, in the human rights context, the term should advance the purpose of the statute and thus must be interpreted broadly, liberally, and purposively.[112]

The Supreme Court of Canada described the analysis as follows in the 2014 decision of *McCormick v Fasken Martineau DuMoulin:*

> Deciding who is in an employment relationship for purposes of the *Code* means, in essence, examining how two synergetic aspects function in an employment relationship: control exercised by an employer over working conditions and remuneration, and corresponding dependency on the part of a worker. In other words, the test is who is responsible for determining working conditions and financial benefits and to what extent does a worker have an influential say in those determinations? The more the work life of individuals is controlled, the greater their dependency and, consequently, their economic, social and psychological vulnerability in the workplace.[113]

The Supreme Court of British Columbia explained that "the intent behind such an expansive interpretation is to ensure that the person/entity committing the discrimination does not escape accountability for the discriminatory act by reason of some legalistic technicality based more on form than on substance."[114] The courts have therefore acknowledged that a broader analysis results in "finding employment relationships to exist in this context where in other contexts they might not have so found."[115]

The courts have interpreted the factors of control and remuneration much more expansively under human rights legislation. In *Canada (Attorney General) v Rosin*, the Federal Court of Appeal held that the elements of remuneration, control, and benefit meant that the Armed

111 *Reid v Vancouver Police Board*, 2005 BCCA 418 at para 41, leave to appeal to SCC refused, [2005] SCCA No 463.

112 *Cormier*, above note 13.

113 *McCormick*, above note 103 at para 23.

114 *HMTQ*, above note 104 at para 152.

115 *Rosin*, above note 28 at para 23.

Forces employed, in the context of the *Canadian Human Rights Act*, a cadet taking a parachuting course. These elements were only marginally present in *Rosin* and certainly not sufficiently enough to find employment in the employment law or labour law context. On the question of remuneration specifically, the Federal Court of Appeal explained that, "[n]ormally, for employment relations to exist, money is paid as wages to someone who works for the person who pays those wages, but in the human rights context the situation is much more flexible."[116]

This understanding has resulted in employment relationships being found in numerous cases in the human rights context where a salary was not paid directly by the respondent. In *Tulk*, the Newfoundland and Labrador Supreme Court found that there was an employment relationship between the complainant and the Ministry of Health and Community Services for the purposes of the *Human Rights Code* even though the complainant was directly hired as a personal care worker by an individual, not by the ministry. Among the factors that the court considered was the fact that the ministry provided the care recipient with the funds for the complainant's remuneration, and it "retained the right to withhold the funds . . . if they did not believe she was properly providing home care services."[117]

In *Prestige Cab Ltd*, a taxi company refused to allow members of the Sikh faith to drive cabs because a policy required drivers to be clean-shaven. The Alberta Court of Appeal found an employment relationship even though drivers were paid by their fares and not by the taxi company. The taxi drivers even paid a commission to the company. In reaching this conclusion, the court of appeal distinguished the case of *Yellow Cab Ltd v Board of Industrial Relations*, where the Supreme Court of Canada held on similar facts that the relationship between the company and its drivers was lessor/lessee and not employer/employee.[118] The *Yellow Cab* case was decided under the *Alberta Labour Act* where the determination of a relationship of employment was made through a rigid definition of employment; in the *Prestige Cab Ltd* case, the court of appeal applied a broad, liberal, and purposive interpretation to employment under human rights legislation and reached the opposite result. Similarly, in *Skelly v Assist Realty Ltd*, the British Columbia Council of Human Rights found that a real estate agent and the real estate company of which she was an associate

---

116 *Ibid.*

117 Above note 108 at para 10.

118 *Prestige Cab Ltd*, above note 19 at para 11; *Yellow Cab Ltd v Board of Industrial Relations*, [1980] 2 SCR 761.

were in an employment relationship for the purposes of the *Code*, despite the fact that the company did not pay the realtor; in fact, the realtor paid the company certain monthly and annual fees.[119]

In determining the degree of control exercised by the employer, courts and tribunals often consider whether the employer has the authority to hire and discharge the employee. These factors are considered much more expansively than under the employment law perspective. For example, police officers were traditionally viewed as holders of public office and not as employees, but courts and tribunals have consistently held them to be employees under human rights legislation because of the power of police boards to both hire and dismiss them.[120]

Hiring and discharging were considered as factors in an employment relationship under the common law of master and servant.[121] In the human rights context they are viewed more expansively to include the exercise of authority by a third party that has the consequence of hiring and discharging. This has been applied to government bodies that do not employ someone directly but are deemed to be able to discharge through the exercise of their authority to provide or withhold funding. For example, in *Tulk*, one of the factors considered by the Newfoundland and Labrador Supreme Court in determining that the Ministry of Health and Community Services was the employer was the fact that the ministry could "withhold the funds for the complainant's remuneration if they did not believe she was properly providing home care services, which would effectively result in her termination."[122] This conclusion was reached despite the fact that the complainant was working directly for the personal care recipient.

This reasoning extends to the use of any authority by a third party that may have the effect or consequence of someone being hired or discharged and not just the ability to provide or withhold funding. In *Johnston v St James Community Service Society*, the Human Rights Tribunal of British

---

119 *Skelly v Assist Realty Ltd*, [1991] BCCHRD No 18.

120 The Ontario Divisional Court in *Re Metropolitan Toronto Board of Commissioners of Police* (1974), 27 OR (2d) 48 (Div Ct), reasoned at 51–52 that "the relationship between the police board and the respondent Ahluwalia was not that of an employer/employee in the traditional sense of the words. However, it must be remembered that the Ontario *Human Rights Code* is remedial legislation which must be given a liberal interpretation." See also *Re Prue*, above note 13; *Hartling v Board of Police Commissioners* (1981), 2 CHRR 111 (Ont Bd Inq).

121 *Re Prue*, above note 13 at para 17.

122 *Tulk*, above note 108 at para 17.

Columbia found an employment relationship between the complainant and St James Community Service Society, even though it was a resident of the society that wanted to hire the complainant to care for her children. The female resident who tried to hire the complainant was residing in an emergency women's shelter operated by the society. The society denied the woman permission to hire the complainant because of a policy that prohibited men in the shelter. The tribunal acknowledged that the direct employment relationship would have been with the female resident, not with the society; however, a broad, liberal, and purposive interpretation led it to conclude that the relationship between the complainant and the society was one of employment for the purposes of the *Code* because the society "exercised a high degree of control" over whom their residents could hire.[123]

Courts and tribunals have viewed the question of benefit expansively to mean whether the employer sought to "utilize" the services of the complainant. In *Cormier v Human Rights Commission*, the Alberta Court of the Queen's Bench developed the broad test of "utilization" of services, which is contrasted to the more restrictive approaches in determining whether there was sufficient control to be deemed an employment relationship under the common law of master and servant, labour relations acts, employment standards legislation, and tax law.[124] On that basis the court ruled that there was an employment relationship between a trucking company and an independent trucker who owned his own truck.[125] The "utilization" test was applied to determine whether an employment relationship exists in a number of cases after *Cormier*. For instance, in *Canadian Pacific Ltd v Canada (Human Rights Commission)*, the Federal Court of Appeal found an employment relationship with Canadian Pacific even though the complainant was directly employed as a cook by a company that contracted with CP to provide food services.[126]

123 *Johnston v St James Community Service Society*, 2004 BCHRT 51 at para 12. This decision was set aside by the British Columbia Supreme Court, but not on the basis of the finding that there was a relationship of employment between the complainant and the society. In fact, the court's ruling implicitly supported this finding because it set aside the decision on the basis that the tribunal failed to consider a possible defence available to the employer under s 41 of the *Code*, which permits certain organizations to give preference to members of a particular group: *St James Community Service Society v Johnston*, 2004 BCSC 1807 at para 15.

124 *Cormier*, above note 13 at para 55.

125 *Ibid.*

126 *Canadian Pacific Ltd v Canada (Human Rights Commission)*, [1991] 1 FC 571 (CA) [*Canadian Pacific Ltd*].

One of the most notable differences in the interpretation of employment in human rights legislation is that it can capture relationships that would be categorized as independent contractor in the employment and labour law contexts.[127] The Supreme Court of British Columbia reviewed this type of situation in *HMTQ et al v Emergency Health Services Commission et al*:

> Where there is a relationship between a respondent and complainant that contains some elements of the traditional common law employment relationship or a contract of services, and even where the relationship is unusual or more akin to a contract for services (independent contractor relationship) or to a volunteer-like relationship, courts and tribunals have stretched the meaning of "employment" to ensure that the purposes of human rights legislation are not thwarted in the sense that the targets of discrimination are not left without any remedy.[128]

As previously observed, the Federal Court of Appeal in *Canadian Pacific Ltd v Canada (Human Rights Commission)* interpreted the word "employ" broadly and concluded that it encompassed the relationship between Canadian Pacific Ltd and an employee of a firm with whom Canada Pacific Ltd contracted for services.[129] Likewise, the Alberta Court of Appeal in *Prestige Cab Ltd* found an employment relationship between a taxi company and taxi drivers where the common law would view the drivers as independent contractors.[130]

Justice Clackson, of the Alberta Court of the Queen's Bench, in the 2009 case of *Lockerbie & Hole Industrial Inc v Alberta (Human Rights and Citizenship Commission, Director)*, set out two broad approaches in his effort to "develop a workable test for determining employment in the human rights context."[131] The first approach is to determine the presence of "any of the traditional criteria relied upon to define employment in other legal contexts."[132] If none of these factors are present, the second approach is to consider whether there is an "implied agreement made

---

127 *Ibid.* See also *Sinha v Eastern Shore Memorial Hospital*, [1996] NSHRBID No 3 at para 33. In this case, a doctor with admitting privileges to a hospital was found to be an employee of the hospital for human rights purposes.

128 *HMTQ*, above note 104 at para 152.

129 *Canadian Pacific Ltd*, above note 126.

130 *Prestige Cab Ltd*, above note 19.

131 *Lockerbie*, above note 100 at para 38.

132 *Ibid.*

between the putative employer and the complainant."[133] Justice Clackson described this as a way to "cut through legal fiction to discover agreement." He held that "[a]bsent agreement there can be no employment."[134] In looking for an "implied agreement," it is important to avoid relying entirely on the written agreement as employers can impose agreements on employees that categorize the relationship as something other than one of employment. As the British Columbia Human Rights Tribunal explained in *Yu v Shell Canada Ltd*, "[t]he legal contractual language used by the parties in creating and describing their relationship is also not necessarily determinative."[135] Despite what the written agreement states, the courts have been unequivocal that parties cannot contract out of human rights.[136]

5) Interpreting the Social Areas in Human Rights Legislation: Services

Although courts have commented most frequently about discrimination in the employment context, some of the most interesting results are observed in the application of the broad, liberal, and purposive interpretation to "services" as a social area where discrimination is prohibited.

Services appeared to have been interpreted narrowly by the Supreme Court of Canada in the 1979 case of *Gay Alliance Toward Equality v Vancouver Sun*, where Martland J described services as referring to "such matters as restaurants, bars, taverns, service stations, public transportation and public utilities."[137] After this decision, there was a debate on whether the Court had created an exhaustive list of services to be captured by human rights legislation or whether Martland J's examples were merely illustrative.[138] This decision was first viewed as establishing a defined list of services.[139] The opposite conclusion is observed, for example, in *Rogers*

133 *Ibid.*

134 *Ibid* at para 36.

135 *Yu v Shell Canada Ltd*, 2004 BCHRT 28 at para 9.

136 *Ontario (Human Rights Commission) v Etobicoke (Borough)*, [1982] 1 SCR 202 at 213–14 [*Etobicoke*]; *Cadillac Fairview Corp v Saskatchewan (Human Rights Commission)*, [1999] SJ No 217 at para 16 (CA); *University of Alberta Non-Academic Staff Assn*, above note 30 at para 74; *Parry Sound (District) Social Services Administration Board v OPSEU, Local 324*, 2003 SCC 42 at para 28.

137 [1979] 2 SCR 435 at 455.

138 *Berg*, above note 2 at paras 36–38.

139 Claire Mummé, "At the Crossroads in Discrimination Law: How the Human Rights Codes Overtook the *Charter* in Canadian Government Services Cases" (2012) 9 *Journal*

v Newfoundland, where the Newfoundland Board of Inquiry declared that "[t]he services outlined by Mr. Justice Martland in *Gay Alliance* are not exhaustive of services to which the general public are customarily admitted."[140]

Much of Marland J's reasoning in *Gay Alliance* was subsequently rejected by the Court in *Berg*, although Lamer CJ, writing for the majority, was mostly focused on the artificial distinction created by Martland J between discrimination in the admission process and discrimination in the provision of a service. Arguably, that had already been rejected through the Court's adoption of Lamer J's approach to human rights legislation in *Heerspink*.[141]

Berg remains the leading authority on the interpretation of "services" in the human rights context,[142] although it has been noted that the Supreme Court of Canada in this case did not offer clear direction on how to determine what constitutes a service. Instead, the Court focused on the words limiting the protection in services to those that are customarily available to the public.[143] Despite this confusion, the caselaw is clear: a broad, liberal, and purposive analysis has to be applied to the question of what constitutes a service. In *Ivancicevic v Ontario (Minister of Consumer Services)*, the Human Rights Tribunal of Ontario explained:

> While "services" is not defined in the *Code*, it is to be interpreted in a broad and liberal manner, consistent with the purposes of the *Code*, which includes concern for the effect, or impact, of legislation. It is also clear that the *Code* has primacy over other provincial legislation, and binds the legislature and its agents (*Code*, s. 47).[144]

Courts and tribunals often consider whether a benefit is being provided when determining whether there is a service. The Federal Court of Appeal in *Canada (Attorney General) v Watkin* said that services "contemplate

of Law & Equality 103 at para 16; *Nova Scotia (Human Rights Commission) v Canada Life Assurance Co*, [1992] NSJ No 5 (CA).

140 *Rogers v Newfoundland (Department of Culture, Recreation and Youth – Wildlife Division)*, [1988] NHRBID No 1 at para 12 [*Rogers*]. See also *Kelly v British Columbia (Ministry of Solicitor General, Motor Vehicle Branch)*, [1990] BCCHRD No 9 at para 12; *Hobson v British Columbia Institute of Technology*, [1988] BCCHRD No 2 at para 17; *Sonnenberg v Lang*, [1989] NBJ No 825 (QB).

141 *Berg*, above note 2 at para 50.

142 *HMTQ v McGrath*, 2009 BCSC 180 at para 90.

143 Mummé, above note 139 at para 46.

144 *Ivancicevic v Ontario (Minister of Consumer Services)*, 2011 HRTO 1714 at para 148 [*Ivancicevic*].

something of benefit being 'held out' as services and 'offered' to the public."[145] Similarly, the Ontario Divisional Court in *Braithwaite v Ontario (Attorney General)* adopted the definition of a service formulated by the Human Rights Tribunal as "something which is of benefit that is provided by one person to another or to the public."[146] Both of these definitions appear to be in line with earlier decisions that defined a service as the "doing of something for someone" and as a "benefit conferred on or exertion made on behalf of someone."[147] In *Dreaver v Pankiw*, the Canadian Human Rights Tribunal found that the mailing of newsletters by a member of Parliament to his constituents is not a service under the *Canadian Human Rights Act* because the sender receives the greatest benefit for his political communication needs.[148]

Oddly, some decisions since 2008 appear to suggest a return to a categories-based determination of services.[149] Vice-Chair Judith Keene, of the Human Rights Tribunal of Ontario, rejected this return to a categories-based analysis of services in the 2010 case of *Dopelhamer v Workplace Safety and Insurance Board*, where she reasoned:

> I have read with care the recent decision of my colleague in *Ballieram v Workplace Safety and Insurance Board*, 2010 HRTO 712. That decision, like several decisions of this Tribunal since 2008, reads certain category-based restrictions into the scope of the term "services." While I recognise the value of consistency in Tribunal jurisprudence, I prefer to draw upon the consistency which was well established, from the 1980s until 2008, in the decisions of the Courts which bind this Tribunal, as well as in most of the Tribunal's own jurisprudence on this question. That body of law, consistent with a clear legislative record, interprets the term "services" in a way which does not import category-based limitations which are not found in the *Code* itself.[150]

The lack of a uniform analysis on what constitutes a service has led some tribunals to adopt a common-sense approach to the issue, coupled with the broad, liberal, and purpose analysis of quasi-constitutional legislation. In *Chipperfield v British Columbia (Ministry of Social*

145 2008 FCA 170 at para 31 [*Watkin*].

146 (2007), 88 OR (3d) 455 at para 39 (Div Ct).

147 *Rogers*, above note 140 at para 12.

148 *Dreaver v Pankiw*, 2009 CHRT 8 at para 56, judicial review refused (*sub nom Canada (Canadian Human Rights Commission) v Pankiw*), [2010] FCJ No 657 (FC).

149 *Ballieram v Workplace Safety and Insurance Board*, 2010 HRTO 712.

150 2010 HRTO 765 at para 35 [*Dopelhamer*].

Services), the British Columbia Human Rights Tribunal observed that "[f]requently . . . the proper description of the service is self-evident. Rather, any disagreement is about whether the service is 'customarily available' or whether there is a 'public' relationship between the complainant and the service-provider that engages review under the section."[151] The case involved a claim that the costs of operating a personal vehicle should be covered under legislation that provided funding for transportation services to people with disabilities. The scheme did not cover personal vehicles, although it was clear from the case that the respondent's disabilities were only adequately accommodated through the use of her own vehicle. The respondent argued that the service was the applicant's desire for reimbursement of car repair costs and that since there is no authority for this under the legislation, it was not a "service customarily available to the public."[152] The tribunal adopted a broader view of service that considered more holistically the scheme of transportation assistance provided to people with disabilities.[153]

As courts and tribunals continue to grapple with the question of how to determine whether a government activity constitutes a service for the purposes of human rights legislation, they have held a multitude of government provisions to constitute services through a broad, liberal, and purposive interpretation, including social assistance benefits,[154] disability benefits,[155] workers' compensation benefits,[156] employment insurance,[157]

151 *Chipperfield v British Columbia (Ministry of Social Services)*, [1997] BCHRTD No 20 at para 22 (BCHRT).

152 *Ibid* at para 20.

153 *Ibid* at para 30.

154 *Hendershott v Ontario (Ministry of Community and Social Services)*, 2011 HRTO 482.

155 *Ontario (Director, Disability Support Program) v Tranchemontagne*, 2010 ONCA 593 [*Tranchemontagne*].

156 *Decision No 1529/04I2*, above note 54 at para 62. In this decision, the Ontario Workplace Safety and Insurance Appeals Tribunal stated that "WSIA benefits are analogous to ODSP benefits and there is no apparent justification for excluding benefits under the WSIA from protection under the *Human Rights Code*, while ODSP benefits are included." The tribunal rejected a line of earlier decisions that held workers' compensation benefits were excluded from the protection of human rights legislation. See *Decision No 13/90*, [1990] OWCATD No 33; *Decision No 553/93*, [1995] OWCATD No 27; *Decision No 468/94*, [1995] OWCATD No 664; *Decision No 2452/05I*, [2006] OWSIATD No 669. See also *O'Quinn v Nova Scotia (Workers' Compensation Board)*, [1995] NSJ No 537 at para 63 (CA) [*O'Quinn*]; *Saskatchewan (Workers' Compensation Board) v Saskatchewan (Human Rights Commission)*, [1999] SJ No 457 at paras 3–4 (CA) [*Saskatchewan (Workers' Compensation Board)*].

157 *Canada (Attorney General) v Druken* (1988), [1989] 2 FC 24 at para 3 (CA), leave to appeal to SCC refused, [1988] SCCA No 433.

insured healthcare benefits,[158] public education,[159] the regulation of liquor-licensed premises,[160] the issuance of a driver's licence,[161] birth certificates,[162] the exercise of statutory powers by decision makers,[163] education,[164] and mayoral proclamations.[165] Similar results have been achieved in private sector activities, where a broad, liberal, and purposive interpretation has resulted in "services" encompassing, for example, union organization[166] and a training program for counsellors at a women's shelter.[167]

Since benefits under a government scheme such as workers' compensation are considered a service under human rights legislation, the application of the broad, liberal, and purposive interpretation also means that the bodies that administer these benefit schemes, aside from their adjudicative function, fall within the scope of human rights legislation. The Saskatchewan Court of Appeal in *Saskatchewan (Workers' Compensation Board) v Saskatchewan (Human Rights Commission)* distinguished boards and tribunals from courts on the basis that while they serve an adjudicative function similar to that of courts, this quasi-judicial function does not fully insulate them from scrutiny under human rights legislation: that is because they provide a service through the administration of the scheme under their enabling legislation. The court therefore held that "[s]imply because the Board engages in some functions that are 'quasi-judicial' does not mean that its adjudicative role insulates it from complaint under the *Code*."[168] Thus, for example, in *Dopelhamer* a service

158 *Hogan*, above note 59 at para 12; *DM v Ontario (Minister of Health and Long-Term Care)*, 2013 HRTO 1034 at para 41.

159 *Attis*, above note 19.

160 *Ivancicevic*, above note 144 at para 151.

161 *British Columbia (Superintendent of Motor Vehicles) v British Columbia (Council of Human Rights)*, [1999] 3 SCR 868 at para 23.

162 *XY v Ontario (Minister of Government and Consumer Services)*, 2012 HRTO 726 at para 85.

163 *Dopelhamer*, above note 150 at para 36.

164 *Moore v British Columbia (Education)*, 2012 SCC 61 at paras 28–29 [*Moore*].

165 *Okanagan Rainbow Coalition*, above note 50 at paras 76–79; *Oliver v Hamilton (City)*, [1995] OHRBID No 56 at para 34; *Hudler v London (City)*, [1997] OHRBID No 23 at para 75; *Hill v Fredericton (City) Mayor*, [1998] NBHRBID No 1 at para 34. This is despite the fact that a mayoral declaration is not made under any legal authority and cannot carry any "legal value because it confers no rights and imposes no responsibilities." *Okanagan Rainbow Coalition*, above note 50 at para 53.

166 *Smith v Telecommunications Workers Union*, 2003 BCHRT 33 at para 28.

167 *Vancouver Rape Relief Society*, above note 107 at paras 12–16.

168 *Saskatchewan (Workers' Compensation Board)*, above note 156 at para 13. See also *B v British Columbia (Ministry of Housing and Social Development)*, 2009 BCHRT 299 at para 47.

was found to include the functions performed by a claims adjudicator and a case nurse of the Workplace Safety and Insurance Board.[169]

Human rights tribunals, however, lack jurisdiction to hear complaints against judges and tribunal members because of the principle of judicial and quasi-judicial immunity. In *Gonzalez v British Columbia (Attorney General)*, the Supreme Court of British Columbia explained:

> There is no question that human rights legislation is quasi-constitutional and should be given a broad and liberal application. However, judicial immunity is also a constitutional principle and, as the Supreme Court of Canada held in *Morier*, the immunity of judges must be preserved even when it is alleged they have violated human rights. Judicial immunity is a necessary adjunct to the independence of the judiciary.[170]

This principle has been extended to the quasi-judicial decision-making powers of adjudicators at boards and tribunals.[171] Thus, despite the broad, liberal, and purposive interpretation of human rights legislation, constitutional principles such as judicial and quasi-judicial immunity still prevail. The British Columbia Human Rights Tribunal held that "it is indisputable that where quasi-constitutional human rights protections cannot be reconciled with constitutionally protected rights and privileges, the latter must prevail."[172]

By far the most important result of a broad, liberal, and purposive interpretation of a service has been the conclusion by the courts that a service in the government context includes both administrative decisions and the content of legislation that creates government programs.

---

169 *Dopelhamer*, above note 150 at paras 36–37.

170 *Gonzalez v British Columbia (Attorney General)*, 2009 BCSC 639 at para 49. See also *Chafchak v Taylor (Ontario Superior Court of Justice)*, 2011 HRTO 1425; *Riad v Ontario (Attorney General)*, 2014 HRTO 48; *Tao v Small Claims Court of Toronto*, 2013 HRTO 25.

171 Quasi-judicial immunity has been extended to members of various quasi-judicial tribunals. For example: the Immigration and Refugee Board, in *Ermina v Canada (Minister of Citizenship and Immigration)*, [1998] FCJ No 1785 (TD); the Law Society of Upper Canada, in respect of its decision-making disciplinary processes, in *Edwards v Law Society of Upper Canada*, 2001 SCC 80; members of provincial commissions of public inquiry, in *Morier v Rivard*, [1985] 2 SCR 716; the Ontario Association of Architects, in regard to a determination they made pursuant to their statutory decision-making power, in *Agnew v Ontario Association of Architects* (1987), 64 OR (2d) 8 (Div Ct); members of the Landlord and Tenant Board, in *Babineau v Ontario (Municipal Affairs and Housing)*, 2010 HRTO 2519; and a labour arbitrator, in *Cartier v Nairn*, 2009 HRTO 2208.

172 *Joseph-Tiwary v British Columbia (Ministry of Attorney General)*, 2007 BCHRT 331 at para 18.

Claire Mummé points out that "this is not an intuitive reading of what constitutes a service, particularly given the availability of the *Charter* to regulate this exact type of behaviour."[173] Rather than it being an intuitive reading, it is a consequence of the broad, liberal, and purposive interpretation of quasi-constitutional legislation. As a result of this broad interpretation of a service in the government context, courts and tribunals have been utilizing the primacy of quasi-constitutional human rights statutes to declare provisions in statutes that create government programs inoperable when they are in irreconcilable conflict with human rights legislation. It is important to note that the ability of courts and tribunals to rely on the primacy of human rights legislation to declare conflicting provisions in other statutes inoperable depends, in the first stage of the analysis, on a broad, liberal, and purposive interpretation of "services" to encompass the governmental benefit and the enabling legislation being challenged.

Despite this ability to challenge the legislation creating the service scheme through a broad, liberal, and purposive interpretation of a service under human rights legislation, this does not allow for a bare challenge to a statute, as legislation on its own is not a service. In *Andrews v Canada (Indian and Northern Affairs)*, the Canadian Human Rights Tribunal explained that "[l]aw-making is one of Parliament's most fundamental and significant functions and *sui generis* in its nature," and as such it "is immune from review."[174] The same tribunal, in *Matson v Indian and Northern Affairs Canada*, had earlier established that registration as an Indian under the *Indian Act* constituted a bare challenge to the legislation rather than to a service established under the Act.[175]

Although it is recognized that a statute cannot be directly challenged without a finding of discrimination in the provision of a government service, the tribunal's reasoning in *Matson* and *Andrews* that there was not a service is difficult to reconcile with the caselaw, such as the 2010 decision of the Ontario Court of Appeal in *Tranchemontagne* finding that a disability benefit scheme established by legislation constitutes a service under the *Human Rights Code*.[176] The Supreme Court of Canada heard an appeal of the *Matson* and *Andrews* decisions in *Canada (Canadian*

173 Mummé, above note 139 at para 11.

174 2013 CHRT 21 at para 57 [*Andrews*], judicial review refused (*sub nom Canada (Canadian Human Rights Commission v Canada (Indian and Northern Affairs)*), 2015 FC 398.

175 *Matson v Indian and Northern Affairs Canada*, 2013 CHRT 13, judicial review refused (*sub nom Canada (Canadian Human Rights Commission) v Canada (Indian and Northern Affairs)*), 2015 FC 398 [*Matson*].

176 *Tranchemontagne*, above note 155.

Human Rights Commission) v Canada (Attorney General), but did not provide clarity to the issue as it determined that the task of distinguishing between administrative services and a bare challenge to legislation was a question of mixed fact and law, and that "human rights tribunals are best situated to develop an approach to making such distinction."[177]

The opposite conclusion was reached by the Canadian Human Rights Tribunal in *Beattie v Canada (Aboriginal Affairs and Northern Development)*, in a complaint regarding the refusal to remove the complainant's name from the band list of the Fort Good Hope Band and add it to the band list for the Arctic Red River Band, the band of her adoptive parents.[178] The tribunal reasoned that there was a service in this case because the respondent was exercising discretion in the course of processing the application rather than applying mandatory legislative wording, as in *Matson*.[179]

There are other areas that a service under human rights legislation has been held not to capture. The Federal Court of Appeal in *Canada (Attorney General) v McKenna* and the Canadian Human Rights Tribunal in *Forward and Forward v Citizenship and Immigration Canada* have suggested that the granting of citizenship is not a service, even though it confers a benefit upon an individual. Characterizing citizenship as merely a service overlooks the "fundamental role in defining the relationship between individuals and the state."[180]

It is questionable whether enforcement actions under legislative schemes are considered services. For instance, in *Watkin* the enforcement action of Health Canada in regulating herbal products was found not to be a service because "enforcement actions are not 'held out' or 'offered' to the public in any sense and are not the result of a process which takes place in the context of a public relationship."[181] The Federal Court of Appeal in *Watkin* even explicitly "disavowed" the early groundbreaking decision of the Canadian Human Rights Tribunal in *Bailey et al v Minister of National Revenue*, which held that "all government actions in the performance of a statutory function constitute 'services' within the meaning of section 5 because they are undertaken by the 'public service' for the

177 *Canada (Canadian Human Rights Commission) v Canada (Attorney General)*, 2018 SCC 31 at para 57.

178 *Beattie v Canada (Aboriginal Affairs and Northern Development)*, 2014 CHRT 1.

179 *Ibid* at para 49.

180 *Forward and Forward v Citizenship and Immigration Canada*, 2008 CHRT 5 at para 41; *Canada (Attorney General) v McKenna*, [1999] 1 FC 401 (CA).

181 *Watkin*, above note 145 at para 31. See also *Gould*, above note 30 at para 55.

public good."[182] Older decisions tended to go in the other direction. In the 1986 case of *LeDeuff v Canada (Employment and Immigration Commission)*, for instance, the Canadian Human Rights Tribunal found that the Canadian Employment and Immigration Commission was providing a service to the public when investigating the citizenship of persons charged with criminal offences.[183] Likewise, in that same year the Canadian Human Rights Tribunal found that the activities of a police force in investigating an offence were a service.[184]

6) The Duty to Accommodate and Remedies

When human rights are invoked, an employer, service provider, or landlord is required to accommodate a rights claimant up to the point of undue hardship, and this duty to accommodate is afforded a broad, liberal, and purposive interpretation. The interpretive approach to the duty to accommodate was succinctly described in the case of *Thunder Bay Catholic District School Board v Ontario English Catholic Teachers' Assn (Thunder Bay Secondary Unit)*:

> In satisfying the duty to accommodate an employee with a disability, it seems accepted that a liberal or expansive as opposed to restrictive or fixed perspective is to be adopted by the parties seeking appropriate accommodative measures in the unique factual circumstances of each case, consistent with the underlying expectation that short of the demonstration of undue hardship by the employer, a purposive approach to achieve the broad objectives of human rights legislation is required.[185]

The approach of devising accommodation measures has been described as "broad and flexible,"[186] "innovative yet practical,"[187] and to be "applied

182 *Watkin*, above note 145 at para 32; *Bailey et al v Minister of National Revenue* (1980), 1 CHRR D/193 (CHRT).

183 [1986] CHRD No 6, aff'd [1987] CHRD No 11.

184 *Hum v Canada (Royal Canadian Mounted Police)*, [1986] CHRD No 10. The Canadian Human Rights Tribunal cited two decisions for this proposition: *Gomez v City of Edmonton* (1982), 3 CHRR D/882 (Alta Bd Inq); *Akena v City of Edmonton* (1982), 3 CHRR D/1096 (Alta Bd Inq).

185 [2011] OLAA No 300 at para 73.

186 *Ibid* at para 75.

187 *Meiorin Grievance*, above note 30 at para 64.

with common sense and flexibility in the context of the factual situation presented in each case."[188]

The broad, liberal, and purposive interpretation of the duty to accommodate has resulted in a range of interesting results based on the individual needs of the claimant, such as paid time off work for religious observance,[189] backdating of seniority,[190] and purchase of personal assistive devices such as hearing aids.[191] It has been held that the duty to accommodate "extends beyond investigating whether an employee with a disability is capable of performing an existing job, and requires the employer to investigate whether, short of undue hardship, existing jobs can be adjusted, modified, or adapted to enable the individual to return to (or remain at) work."[192]

The duty to accommodate can also require consideration of options that involve a degree of safety risk to the employee in question. In *Brant (County) v Ontario Public Service Employees Union*, a labour arbitrator held that because of the quasi-constitutional nature of Ontario's *Human Rights Code*, "there needs to be substantial or significant evidence of safety risks to override his quasi-constitutional rights."[193]

Courts and tribunals have also interpreted the remedies available under human rights legislation in a broad, liberal, and purposive fashion. This was recognized in *Hogan*, where the Human Rights Tribunal of Ontario stated that remedy provisions "should be given a broad and liberal interpretation to achieve the legislative philosophy and objective of the *Code*."[194] In *de Montigny v Brossard (Succession)*, the Supreme Court of Canada held that exemplary damages could be awarded under the Quebec *Charter* even in situations where the defendant was deceased through an interpretation that acknowledged the *Charter*'s quasi-constitutional character. It held this despite the fact that punitive or exemplary damages aim at punishing the defendant for egregious misconduct.[195]

188 *Commission scolaire régionale de Chambly v Bergevin Syndicat de l'enseignement de Champlain, Joseph Kadoch*, [1994] 2 SCR 525 at para 32.

189 *Ibid.*

190 *Bellefleur v District of Campbell River Fire Department (No 4)*, 2005 BCHRT 541.

191 Above note 185.

192 *Ontario Nurses' Assn v Community Lifecare Inc (Port Perry) (Clark Grievance)*, [2001] OLAA No 614 at para 42.

193 *Brant (County) v Ontario Public Service Employees Union, Local 256 (Cunnane Grievance)*, [2012] OLAA No 117 at para 37.

194 *Hogan*, above note 59 at para 144. See also *Hill v Misener*, [1997] NSHRBID No 2 at para 46.

195 *de Montigny v Brossard (Succession)*, 2010 SCC 51 at para 45.

7) Interpreting General Terms and Concepts in Human Rights Legislation

In addition to the group of social areas and grounds of discrimination, the broad, liberal, and purposive approach has been applied to the interpretation of general terms and concepts in human rights legislation. As Professor Sullivan points out:

> In responding to general terms and concepts, the approach is organic and flexible. The key provisions of the legislation are adapted not only to changing social circumstances but also to evolving conceptions of human rights.[196]

This is observable in *Citron v Zundel*, where the Canadian Human Rights Tribunal concluded that postings on a website constituted "telephonic communications" under the *Canadian Human Rights Act* through a broad, liberal, and purposive interpretation of that term.[197] The provision in the *Canadian Human Rights Act* made it a discriminatory practice "to communicate telephonically . . . any matter that is likely to expose a person or persons to hatred."[198] The tribunal rejected arguments by the respondent that the provision captured only oral communication by telephone as an "unduly restrictive approach that is inconsistent with a purposive approach to statutory interpretation, and fails to allow for advances in technology."[199] The tribunal had little difficulty finding that the postings were telephonic communications because the internet uses the telephone network and a "static interpretation of s. 13(1), where telephonic communication is restricted to voice transmissions using a conventional telephone device, would dramatically reduce the effectiveness of the Act as an aid to the promotion of equality."[200] Instead, the tribunal interpreted telephonic communication "in a manner that is most likely to promote the underlying objectives of the Act."[201] In so doing, the tribunal explained that it was "especially concerned about an unduly narrow interpretation of *telephonic* at a time of dramatic shifts in the use of different modes of communication."[202]

---

196 Sullivan, above note 2 at 497.
197 *Citron v Zundel*, [2002] CHRD No 1 [*Citron*].
198 *Canadian Human Rights Act*, RSC 1985, c H-6, s 13(1).
199 *Citron*, above note 197 at para 93.
200 *Ibid* at para 86.
201 *Ibid* at para 82.
202 *Ibid* at para 95.

C. A BROAD, LIBERAL, AND PURPOSIVE INTERPRETATION OF ACCESS-TO-INFORMATION AND PRIVACY LEGISLATION

The broad, liberal, and purposive interpretation is now as firmly established for access-to-information and privacy acts as it is for human rights legislation, and the application of this approach similarly results in an expansive understanding of the rights provided under these statutes.[203] As the Federal Court described: "it is well established that the provisions of the *Access Act* and of the *Privacy Act* must be afforded a broad and purposive interpretation."[204] This occurs primarily through a broad, liberal, and purposive interpretation of what constitutes a record under access-to-information legislation, whether a government institution has custody and control over the record, and what constitutes personal information.

1) Determining What Constitutes a Record

The effect of a broad, liberal, and purposive interpretation of access-to-information legislation is observed at the very start of a request for government information. When a government institution receives a request for information, the request itself is to be interpreted broadly. Only records that reasonably relate to the request are deemed responsive,[205] but access-to-information commissions require institutions to "adopt a liberal interpretation of a request, in order to best serve the purpose and spirit of the Act. Generally, ambiguity in the request should be resolved in the requester's favour."[206] Overly narrow interpretations of an access request can result in the decision of a government institution being overturned by the information commissioner on appeal.[207]

The courts and access-to-information commissioners apply a broad, liberal, and purposive interpretation to the issue of whether the requested

---

203 Professor Vincent Kazmierski notes that "[b]y ensuring a purposeful interpretation of access legislation, courts can ensure that existing legislative frameworks provide the best possible protection of access." Vincent Kazmierski, "Accessing with Dinosaurs: Protecting Access to Government Information in the Cretaceous Period of Canadian Democracy" (2001) 25 (3d) *Constitutional Forum* 57 at 62.

204 *Canada (Privacy Commissioner)*, above note 4 at para 46.

205 *Order PO-2694; University of Western Ontario*, [2008] OIPC No 134 at para 18 [*Order PO-2694*], citing *Ontario (Attorney General) v Fineberg* (1994), 19 OR (3d) 197 (Div Ct).

206 *Order PO-2694*, above note 205 at para 18.

207 See, for example, *Order PO-2435; Ontario (Ministry of Health and Long-Term Care)*, [2005] OIPC No 207 at para 19.

information constitutes a record. All access-to-information acts grant access to "records," which are typically broadly defined. The federal *Access to Information Act*, for example, defines a record as "any documentary material, regardless of medium or form."[208] As the British Columbia Supreme Court recognizes, "[c]ourts have consistently found that the definition of 'records' should be liberally interpreted."[209]

The application of this interpretive approach to the question of what constitutes a record has had important consequences in a digital age when records are increasingly being held in electronic format. For instance, the access-to-information request in *Toronto Police Services Board v Ontario (Information and Privacy Commissioner)* required the Toronto Police to create an algorithm to extract and manipulate information contained in a database. The Ontario Court of Appeal, through use of the broad, liberal, and purposive interpretation, determined that the requested information was a "record" under the Act despite the police having to reformat the information for the benefit of the requester. In so doing, Moldaver J, writing for a unanimous Court of Appeal, reasoned:

> A contextual and purposive analysis of s. 2(1)(b) must also take into account the prevalence of computers in our society and their use by government institutions as the primary means by which records are kept and information is stored. This technological reality tells against an interpretation of s. 2(1)(b) that would minimize rather than maximize the public's right of access to electronically recorded information.[210]

The Court of Appeal reversed the decision of the Divisional Court on the basis that it failed to properly apply the broad, liberal, and purposive interpretation:

> The Divisional Court made no mention of these principles of interpretation in constructing s. 2(l)(b) of the Act and in concluding that the Adjudicator's interpretation was unreasonable. This omission led the court to give s. 2(l)(b) a narrow construction — one which, in my

208 *Access to Information Act*, above note 20, s 3. The British Columbia Supreme Court in *Neilson v British Columbia (Information and Privacy Commissioner)*, [1998] BCJ No 1640 (SC) [*Neilson*], considered the federal *Access to Information Act* in comparison to British Columbia's *Freedom of Information and Protection of Privacy Act*, RSBC 1996, c 165. It notes at para 34 that "[b]oth enactments have similar definitions of records."

209 *Neilson*, above note 208 at para 24.

210 *Toronto Police Services Board v Ontario (Information and Privacy Commissioner)*, 2009 ONCA 20 at para 48.

respectful view, fails to reflect the purpose and spirit of the Act and the generous approach to access contemplated by it.[211]

2) Determining Custody and Control

The more common starting point is the question of whether the government institution has custody or control of the requested records. This issue is central to the right of access since the legislation provides the right to access information that is contained in records in the custody or control of a government institution.[212] As the Ontario Court of Appeal explained, "[r]ecords in the custody or under the control of an institution are subject to the access provisions in the Act. Records that are not fall outside the scope of the Act."[213]

In *Canada (Information Commissioner) v Canada (Minister of National Defence)*, the Supreme Court of Canada affirmed the application of the broad, liberal, and purposive interpretation to the question of control, in order to give "a meaningful right of access to government information."[214] The Court in that case rejected the idea that control is limited to the "power to dispose or to get rid of the documents in question."[215] Likewise, in *Canada Post Corp v Canada (Minister of Public Works)*, the Federal Court of Appeal held that "[i]t is not in the power of this Court to cut down the broad meaning of the word 'control' as there is nothing in the Act which indicates that the word should not be given its broad meaning."[216] What this statement means in practical terms is that the question of control is "to be given its broadest possible meaning," up to the limited

211 *Ibid* at para 49. Cited in *Order PO-2761; Carleton University*, [2009] OIPC No 29 at para 24, which concerned a request for access to the "screen shot" of the academic results of a former student of Carleton University rather than a reproduced document.

212 *Access to Information Act*, above note 20, s 4(1); *Canada (Attorney General) v Canada (Information Commissioner)*, 2005 FCA 199 at para 6, leave to appeal to SCC refused, [2005] SCCA No 356.

213 *Ontario (Criminal Code Review Board) v Doe*, [1999] OJ No 4072 at para 19 (CA) [*Doe*].

214 *Canada (Information Commissioner)*, above note 3 at para 48.

215 *Ibid*. Despite this analysis, the Court ultimately found that neither the PMO nor a minister's office is a government institution under the *Access to Information Act*, above note 20. For criticism of this decision and its outcome, see, especially, Kazmierski, above note 203 at 62.

216 [1995] 2 FC 110 at para 3 (CA) [*Canada Post Corp*]. In *Doe*, above note 213 at para 34, the Ontario Court of Appeal approved and reiterated this interpretive approach. See also *Order 02-29, British Columbia (Workers' Compensation Board)*, [2002] BCIPCD No 29 at para 13 [*Order 02-29*]; *Order PO-2286-I; Ontario (Ministry of Community Safety and Correctional Services)*, [2004] OIPC No 131 at para 23.

point that it is being "stretched beyond reason."[217] This broad interpretation means that "control is not limited to *de jure* (legal) control,"[218] and the court approved findings that information was under the control of a government institution in situations where the control is full, ultimate, lasting, *de jure*, *de facto*, immediate, partial, or transient.[219]

The Information and Privacy Commission of Ontario has developed a list of questions to determine the question of control.[220] The exact questions vary somewhat from case to case, although they have been described as reflecting "a purposive approach to the 'control' question."[221]

---

217 *Canada (Information Commissioner)*, above note 3 at para 48.

218 *Canada Post Corp*, above note 216 at paras 32–33; *Order 04-19; Saanich School District No 63*, [2004] BCIPCD No 19 at para 44 [*Order 04-19*].

219 *Canada (Information Commissioner)*, above note 3 at para 48.

220 The questions were developed largely in the following orders: *Order 120*, [1989] OIPC No 84 [*Order 120*]; *Order MO-1251*, [1999] OIPC No 156 [*Order MO-1251*]; *PO-2306; Ontario (Ministry of Education)*, [2004] OIPC No 178; and *PO-2683; University of Toronto*, [2008] OIPC No 121 [*PO-2683*]. The questions were phrased as follows in *Order PO-2739; Ontario (Ministry of the Attorney General)*, [2008] OIPC No 223 at para 23 [*Order PO-2739*]; *Order PO-2968; Ontario (Ministry of Government Services)*, [2011] OIPC No 64 at para 12 [*Order PO-2968*]:

1. Were the records created by an officer or employee of the institution?
2. What use did the creator intend to make of the records?
3. Does the institution have a statutory power or duty to carry out the activity that resulted in the creation of the records?
4. Is the activity in question a "core," "central" or "basic" function of the institution?
5. Does the content of the records relate to the institution's mandate and functions?
6. Does the institution have physical possession of the records, either because it has been voluntarily provided by the creator or pursuant to a mandatory statutory or employment requirement?
7. If the institution does not have possession of the records, are they being held by an officer or employee of the institution for the purposes of his or her duties as an officer or employee?
8. Does the institution have a right to possession of the records?
9. Does the institution have the authority to regulate the records' use and disposal?
10. Are there any limits on the use to which the institution may put the records, what are those limits, and why do they apply to the record?
11. To what extent has the institution relied upon the records?
12. How closely are the records integrated with other records held by the institution?
13. What is the customary practice of the institution and institutions similar to the institution in relation to possession or control of records of this nature, in similar circumstances?

221 *Order MO-1251*, above note 220, cited in *Order PO-1873*, [2001] OIPC No 39 at para 33 [*Order PO-1873*]; *Final Order PO-3009-F; University of Ottawa*, [2011] OIPC No 152 at

These questions serve as a useful starting point, although they are non-exhaustive and cannot be mechanically applied. The result is to determine whether "control has been established in the circumstances of a particular fact situation," which requires consideration of "all aspects of the creation, maintenance and use of particular records."[222] For example, whether the government institution has the power to dispose of the records is far from being determinative of the issue of control. In *Canada Post Corp v Canada (Minister of Public Works)*, Létourneau J stated:

> Had Parliament intended to qualify and restrict the notion of control to the power to dispose of the information, as suggested by the appellant, it could certainly have done so by limiting the citizen's right of access only to those documents that the Government can dispose of or which are under the lasting or ultimate control of the Government.[223]

This statement was applied by the British Columbia Supreme Court in *Neilson v British Columbia (Information and Privacy Commissioner)*, in addressing an argument by a school counsellor that her "raw notes" taken during counselling sessions with a student are not within the control of the school board because the discretion to retain or destroy them is within her exclusive control.[224] The court rejected this argument, and through the application of the broad, liberal, and purposive interpretation found that the notes were within the control of the school board.[225]

The broad, liberal, and purposive interpretation of the question of control is also applied to privacy complaints under privacy acts. An individual claimed in a privacy complaint against the City of Toronto that a city councillor obtained his email address while in his official duties and then subsequently used it for his own personal purposes. The city argued that its bare possession of the emails did not amount to custody or control because the email accounts of councillors were set up by the city for the exclusive purpose of allowing council members to address constituency matters. The Information and Privacy Commission applied

---

para 92 [*Final Order PO-3009-F*]. See also *Order MO-1237*, [1999] OIPC No 131 at para 13 [*Order MO-1237*].

222 *Order 02-29*, above note 216 at para 17, citing *Order 120*, above note 220 at 7. Cited in *Order 04-19*, above note 218 at para 43.

223 *Canada Post Corp*, above note 216 at para 32.

224 *Neilson*, above note 208 at paras 17–18.

225 *Ibid* at para 26. Likewise, in *Order 04-19*, above note 218, the notes prepared by a contractor hired to investigate a harassment complaint were found to be in the control of the school board.

the same broad, liberal, and purposive interpretation it applies to the determination of the custody and control question in access-to-information requests and determined that the email address was in the custody of the city:

> The purposive approach is consistent with the approach that has been applied to access to information decisions. In that context, the courts and this office have applied a broad and liberal approach to the custody or control question . . . . A broad and liberal consideration of the custody or control issue is equally applicable in the context of a privacy complaint investigation, and I will adopt it here.[226]

Courts are particularly diligent in preventing government institutions from circumventing access-to-information legislation through contracting or outsourcing arrangements that include the third party retaining physical control of documents. The mere fact that the records are held by the third party that conducts the work is not determinative of the issue; the broad, liberal, and purposive interpretation requires deeper consideration of whether the record is in the control of the government institution.[227]

---

226 *Privacy Complaint Nos MC10-75 and MC11-18; Toronto (City)*, [2011] OIPC No 116 at para 16.

227 The questions were developed largely in *Greater Vancouver Mental Health Service Society v British Columbia (Information and Privacy Commissioner)*, [1999] BCJ No 198 (SC); *Walmsley v Ontario (Attorney General)* (1997), 34 OR (3d) 611 (CA) [*Walmsley*]; *David v Ontario (Information and Privacy Commissioner)* (2006), 217 OAC 112 (Div Ct); *Order PO-2683*, above note 220; *Order M-165*, [1993] OIPC No 195; *Order MO-1251*, above note 220. In *Order PO-2739*, above note 220 at para 24, and *Order PO-2968*, above note 220 at para 13, the questions were phrased as follows:

1. If the records are not in the physical possession of the institution, who has possession of the records, and why?
2. Is the individual, agency or group who or which has physical possession of the records an "institution" for the purposes of the Act?
3. Who owns the records?
4. Who paid for the creation of the records?
5. What are the circumstances surrounding the creation, use and retention of the records?
6. Are there any provisions in any contracts between the institution and the individual who created the records in relation to the activity that resulted in the creation of the records, which expressly or by implication give the institution the right to possess or otherwise control the records?
7. Was there an understanding or agreement between the institution, the individual who created the record or any other party that the records were not to be disclosed to the Institution? If so, what were the precise undertakings of

Courts and privacy commissioners have held that government institutions "cannot contract out of the Act directly" or "by outsourcing its functions."[228] For example, in *Ontario (Criminal Code Review Board) v Doe*, a case involving a request for backup tapes created and held by a court reporter who was working under contract with the Ontario Criminal Code Review Board, the Ontario Court of Appeal held that

> [t]he Board has argued . . . it will be unable to comply because it is not able to compel the court reporter to deliver the backup tapes to it. I must say I find this a rather surprising proposition. We were told that at some time in the past the Board had used employees to do what independent court reporters now do. If the Board had continued to use employees there would be no issue; the backup tapes would be in the Board's custody and under its control. However, the Board chose to enter into arrangements with independent court reporters to meet its court reporting requirements. Assuming the court reporter now refuses to deliver the backup tapes to the Board, the Board's failure to enter into a contractual arrangement with the reporter that would enable it to fulfil its statutory duty to provide access to documents under its control cannot be a reason for finding that the duty does not exist. Put another way, the Board cannot avoid the access provisions of the Act by entering into arrangements under which third parties hold custody of

---

confidentiality given by the individual who created the records, to whom were they given, when, why and in what form?

8. Is there any other contract, practice, procedure or circumstance that affects the control, retention or disposal of the records by the institution?
9. Was the individual who created the records an agent of the institution for the purposes of the activity in question? If so, what was the scope of that agency, and did it carry with it a right of the institution to possess or otherwise control the records?
10. What is the customary practice of the individual who created the records and others in a similar trade, calling or profession in relation to possession or control of records of this nature, in similar circumstances?
11. To what extent, if any, should the fact that the individual or organization that created the records has refused to provide the institution with a copy of the records to determine the control issue?

228 *Order 04-19*, above note 218 at para 49. The information and privacy commissioner of British Columbia cited the following cases: *Order 00-47; Malaspina University-College*, [2000] BCIPCD No 51 at paras 10–45; *Canada (Information Commissioner) v Canada (Minister of Citizenship and Immigration)*, [2003] 1 FC 219 at para 11 (CA); *Canada (Information Commissioner) v Canada (Immigration and Refugee Board)* (1997), 4 Admin LR (3d) 96 at para 26 (FCTD); *Doe*, above note 213 at para 35, cited in *Order PO-1873*, above note 221.

> the Board's records that would otherwise be subject to the provisions of the Act.[229]

In these scenarios access-to-information commissioners typically ask whether there is a relationship of agency that empowers the agent to act on behalf of the government institution, and whether the government institution has the right to possess or control the records in question.[230] Generally, when there is an agency, the agent has the duty to produce to the government institution all documents in the agent's hands relating to the principal's affairs.[231] However, identifying elements of agency is not sufficient for a finding that an institution has control over records, particularly in situations where there is an independent arm's length relationship.[232]

Even if a government institution does not have control of the record, the broad, liberal, and purposive interpretation results in a deeper consideration on whether the record has been "integrated into the operations of the institution."[233] Although political parties are not institutions for the purposes of the Act, their records can become subject to the Act if they are within the control of a government institution. For instance, in *Order P-267*, the information and privacy commissioner found that records held in the office of the premier of Ontario fall under the purview of the *Access to Information and Protection of Privacy Act* even though they related to the political responsibilities of the premier, not to the institution's mandate and function.[234] In this case, a government institution was found to have control over the political party records because they were intermingled with the institution's other records, and because of the

229 *Doe*, above note 213 at para 35, cited in *Order PO-1873*, above note 221 at para 73. See also *Order MO-1237*, above note 221; *Order MO-1251*, above note 220; *Order MO-1242*, [1999] OIPC No 140 [*Order MO-1242*].

230 Although the question of agency can assist in determining the control issue, a finding one way or another is not necessarily determinative. See *Walmsley*, above note 227; *Order MO-1251*, above note 220. Agency can be created from express or implied consent of the principal and the agent: *Royal Securities Corp v Montreal Trust Co*, [1967] 1 OR 137 (HCJ), aff'd [1967] 2 OR 200 (CA). *Order MO-1251*, above note 220 at para 50; *Order MO-1242*, above note 229 at para 24.

231 *Ibid* at para 29.

232 *Walmsley*, above note 227. For a discussion of records held by a corporation owned solely by a government institution and the piercing of the corporate veil, see, especially, *Simon Fraser University v British Columbia (Information and Privacy Commissioner)*, 2009 BCSC 1481, aff'd 2011 BCCA 334, on the basis that the appeal became moot.

233 *Order PO-2739*, above note 220 at para 74.

234 *Order P-267*, [1992] OIPC No 8.

authority exercised over them by an employee of the government institution. Assistant Commissioner Tom Mitchinson stated:

> [T]hese records have been integrated into the operations of the institution in a manner which constitutes custody under the Act. [It is acknowledged] that no special steps were taken to separate the storage and maintenance of these records from other documents relating to his employment with the institution, and it would appear that these records were integrated with other files held by the institution. In my view, [the employee of the institution] assumed responsibility for the care of these records, and had control over their use. [235]

Similar reasoning has been applied to requests for court records. The courts are not considered government institutions under Ontario's *Freedom of Information and Protection of Privacy Act*, and records held by the courts or even the Ministry of the Attorney General that relate to specific court proceedings are not considered in the custody or under the control of the ministry.[236] However, while records relating to a court action in a court file are not considered under the control of the Ministry of the Attorney General, the situation is different if copies of these records from the court file are held independently from the court file.[237] Likewise, although municipal councillors have been found not to fall within the purview of access-to-information legislation, their records may be determined to be within the control of the municipality.[238]

Information and privacy commissioners have been clear that academic freedom does not automatically exempt records held by university professors. In a case involving a request for information in the possession of professors at the University of Ottawa, the information and privacy commissioner of Ontario determined that the Ontario *Freedom of Information and Privacy Act* does not create a type of "carve-out from academic freedom in a manner that excludes the latter from consideration in the custody and control analysis."[239] The commissioner found that while administrative records are *prima facie* in the university's custody

235 *Ibid.*

236 *Order PO-2446; Ontario (Ministry of the Attorney General,* [2006] OIPC No 13; *Order P-995*, [1995] OIPC No 343; *Order P-1397*, [1997] OIPC No 137.

237 *Order P-994*, [1995] OIPC No 342; *Order PO-2739*, above note 220 at para 56, judicial review denied, *Ontario (Ministry of the Attorney General) v Ontario (Information and Privacy Commissioner)*, 2011 ONSC 172 (Div Ct).

238 *Order MO-1403*, [2001] OIPC No 36 at para 18.

239 *Final Order PO-3009-F*, above note 221 at para 128.

and control, and records in the possession of professors related to personal matters unrelated to the university's mandate are not in its custody or control, records related to teaching or research may be held to be "in the university's custody and/or control if they would be accessible to it by custom or practice, taking academic freedom into account."[240]

A somewhat modified broad, liberal, and purposive interpretive approach is applied to access-to-information legislation in situations involving documents that are subject to solicitor–client privilege. In *Canada (Privacy Commissioner) v Blood Tribe Department of Health*, the leading decision on this point, the Supreme Court of Canada stated that "legislative language that may (if broadly construed) allow incursions on solicitor–client privilege must be interpreted restrictively."[241] This decision has resulted in some confusion on whether the courts have adopted a restrictive interpretive approach rather than a broad one in situations involving documents subject to solicitor–client privilege. The British Columbia Supreme Court clarified in *Central Coast School District No 49 v British Columbia*, that a restrictive interpretation only occurs when a broad, liberal, and purposive analysis results in an encroachment of solicitor–client confidentiality.[242] In this analysis, "a strict or restrictive interpretation will only be resorted to where there are multiple interpretations following a contextual, purposive analysis."[243]

3) Determining What Constitutes Personal Information

Courts and privacy commissioners have likewise interpreted "personal information" in privacy acts broadly. Legislation protecting personal privacy is designed first, to "protect personal information held by government institutions, and second, to provide individuals with a right of access to personal information about themselves."[244] Justice Nöel, of the Federal Court, stated: "[a]n illustration of the broad, purposive approach to statutory interpretation in the context of the *Privacy Act* is the rejection by this Court of an unduly restrictive interpretation of the term 'personal information.'"[245] In *Canada (Information Commissioner) v Canada*

240 *Ibid* at para 181.

241 2008 SCC 44 at para 11.

242 In *Central Coast School District No 49 v British Columbia*, 2012 BCSC 427 at para 48.

243 *Ibid* at para 49.

244 *Lavigne*, above note 4 at para 24.

245 *Canada (Privacy Commissioner) v Canada (Labour Relations Board)*, [1996] 3 FC 609 at para 46 (TD).

(Solicitor General), Jerome J, of the Federal Court, found a correlation between the intent of the *Privacy Act*, which is "clearly to protect the privacy or identity of individuals," and the fact that "the definition of personal information is deliberately broad," which he viewed as "entirely consistent with the great pains that have been taken to safeguard individual identity."[246]

In *Sutherland v Canada (Minister of Indian and Northern Affairs)*, Rothstein J, of the Federal Court, stressed that personal information is protected unless it is established that an exception applies:

> Because the purpose of the *Privacy Act* is to protect the privacy of "personal information," the general rule is that information about identifiable individuals is "personal information" and only if a specific exception applies, would such information not be "personal information." It follows that a party wishing to demonstrate that information about an identifiable individual is not "personal information" must show that an exception applies.[247]

The broad, liberal, and purposive interpretation of privacy, therefore, results in putting the onus for demonstrating that something does not constitute personal information on the person claiming an exception.

The Alberta Court of Queen's Bench in *University of Alberta v Alberta (Information and Privacy Commissioner)* held that an individual does not have to be specifically named in a record for it to be considered personal information if the individual is identifiable through the larger context. That case involved an access request under Alberta's *Freedom of Information and Protection of Privacy Act* for a statistical summary of teaching effectiveness and the number of published papers of faculty members in a department. This was found to contain personal information because some of the complainant's colleagues had identified him from the summary.[248]

In *Ontario (Attorney General) v Ontario (Information and Privacy Commissioner)*, the Ontario Divisional Court established a test that considers whether it is reasonable to expect that the requested information,

---

246 *Canada (Solicitor General)*, above note 32 at para 11.

247 *Sutherland v Canada (Minister of Indian and Northern Affairs)*, [1994] 3 FC 527 at para 22 (TD).

248 *University of Alberta v Alberta (Information and Privacy Commissioner)*, 2009 ABQB 112; *Freedom of Information and Protection of Privacy Act*, RSA 2000, c F-25.

when combined with information available from other sources, could result in an individual being identified.[249]

There is little caselaw at present on the broad, liberal, and purposive interpretation of the second category of privacy legislation dealing with privacy rights in the private sector. Given the Supreme Court of Canada's determination in the 2013 case of *Alberta (Information and Privacy Commissioner) v United Food and Commercial Workers* that this kind of privacy statute is quasi-constitutional, the appropriate interpretive approach is arguably the same as other quasi-constitutional statutes.[250] A similar expansive interpretation has been applied to the definition of personal information under the federal *Personal Information Protection and Electronic Documents Act* as under the *Privacy Act*. In *Girao v Zarek Taylor Grossman, Hanrahan LLP*, the Federal Court held that, as under the *Privacy Act*, information is personal under *PIPEDA* if it is about an identifiable individual, and that a person is identifiable if the information disclosed can result in identification when combined with publicly available information.[251]

D. A BROAD, LIBERAL, AND PURPOSIVE INTERPRETATION OF LANGUAGE RIGHTS

As with human rights, access-to-information, and privacy legislation, the broad, liberal, and purposive interpretation of language rights legislation has also resulted in notable outcomes. Restricting the study of this interpretive approach to its use in quasi-constitutional language statutes is more of a challenge, however, because, as previously mentioned, the

---

249 *Ontario (Attorney General) v Ontario (Information and Privacy Commissioner)*, [2001] OJ No 4987 at para 15 (Div Ct), aff'd (*sub nom Ontario (Attorney General) v Pascoe*), [2002] OJ No 4300 (CA). This was applied by an adjudicator of the information and privacy commissioner of Ontario in *Order PO-2811; Ontario (Ministry of Community Safety and Correctional Services)*, [2009] OIPC No 127.

250 *Alberta (Information and Privacy Commissioner) v United Food and Commercial Workers, Local 401*, 2013 SCC 62 at paras 19 and 22. See also *Mountain Province Diamonds Inc v De Beers Canada Inc*, 2014 ONSC 2026 at para 37; *Personal Information Protection Act*, SA 2003, c P-6.5.

251 *Girao v Zarek Taylor Grossman, Hanrahan LLP*, 2011 FC 1070 at para 32; *Personal Information Protection and Electronic Documents Act*, SC 2000, c 5. In reaching this conclusion, the Federal Court relied on one of its own decisions under the federal *Privacy Act*, *Canada (Information Commissioner) v Canada (Transportation Accident Investigation and Safety Board)*, 2005 FC 384 at para 43, rev'd 2006 FCA 157, leave to appeal to SCC refused, [2006] SCCA No 259.

broad, liberal, and purposive interpretation is applied not only to language rights legislation, but also to the language rights found in section 133 of the *Constitution Act, 1867*, the *Charter*, and the *Criminal Code*. As the Supreme Court of Canada explained in *Beaulac*, "[l]anguage rights must in all cases be interpreted purposively, in a manner consistent with the preservation and development of official language communities in Canada."[252] Moreover, the caselaw often involves an interplay between constitutional and statutory forms of language rights. The intention is to focus on the interpretation of quasi-constitutional statutes to the extent possible, and the discussion of the other forms of language rights will be limited to the formation of general principles that apply to quasi-constitutional legislation.

1) Language Rights as Substantive Rights

The broad, liberal, and purposive interpretation has resulted in the determination by the Supreme Court of Canada that language rights are substantive rights and not "exceptional, or as something in the nature of a request for an accommodation."[253] Justice Louise Charron summarized these principles as follows in *DesRochers v Canada (Industry)*:

> Before considering the provisions at issue in the case at bar, it will be helpful to review the principles that govern the interpretation of language rights provisions. Courts are required to give language rights a liberal and purposive interpretation. This means that the relevant provisions must be construed in a manner that is consistent with the preservation and development of official language communities in Canada . . . Indeed, on several occasions this Court has reaffirmed that the concept of equality in language rights matters must be given true meaning . . . Substantive equality, as opposed to formal equality, is to be the norm, and the exercise of language rights is not to be considered a request for accommodation.[254]

In *Beaulac*, the decision heralded as the Court's return to a broad, liberal, and purposive interpretation of language rights, Bastarache J held

252 *Beaulac*, above note 36 at para 25. For the application of this approach to language rights more generally see especially Marc Cousineau, "Survol des droits linguistiques: enfin de vrais droits linguistiques au Canada" (2000–2001) 32 *Ottawa Law Review* 117.

253 *Ibid* at para 24.

254 2009 SCC 8 at para 31.

that "[l]anguage rights are not negative rights, or passive rights; they can only be enjoyed if the means are provided."[255] Justice Bastarache conducted a thorough review of the broad, liberal, and purposive interpretive approach, and when he applied it to the language rights in the *Criminal Code*, he found that it "creates an absolute right of the accused to equal access to designated courts in the official language that he or she considers to be his or her own," which consequently led to the conclusion that the courts "are therefore required to be institutionally bilingual."[256]

Not surprisingly, the conclusion that language rights are substantive and not merely procedural has its most profound effect in cases involving litigants asserting their right to use French in court proceedings. The right to an interpreter for languages other than English and French is protected by the *Charter* to ensure a fair trial, and courts have been clear that linguistic rights are not merely an extension of the right to a fair trial.[257]

Cases involving the assertion of language rights in a court proceeding occur most frequently under the *Criminal Code* as in *Beaulac*, although several decisions in this area have involved the quasi-constitutional provincial language rights statutes. In *R v Pooran*, a broad, liberal, and purposive interpretation of the right in Alberta's *Languages Act* to use French in court resulted in the conclusion that this is a right to a French-speaking prosecutor and a French-speaking judge, not merely to an interpreter, in a prosecution under the *Traffic Safety Act*.[258] In this decision Brown J, of the Provincial Court of Alberta, stated:

> If litigants are entitled to use either English or French in oral representations before the courts yet are not entitled to be understood except through an interpreter, their language rights are hollow indeed. Such a narrow interpretation of the right to use either English or French is illogical, akin to the sound of one hand clapping, and has been emphatically overruled by *Beaulac*.[259]

The same result was achieved in the Manitoba case of *R v Rémillard*, a case which involved notices for traffic offences issued only partly in

255 *Beaulac*, above note 36 at para 20.

256 *Ibid* at para 28.

257 *Ibid* at para 41.

258 *R v Pooran*, 2011 ABPC 77 [*Pooran*]. *Languages Act*, RSA 2000, c L-6, s 4(1), states that "[a]ny person may use English or French in oral communication in proceedings before the following courts . . . ."; *Traffic Safety Act*, RSA 2000, c T-6.

259 *Pooran*, above note 258 at para 21.

French.[260] In quashing the offence notices, the trial judge in this case was mindful of the substantive nature of language rights as required by the Supreme Court of Canada in *DesRochers* and *Beaulac* when applying the broad, liberal, and purposive interpretation:

> When a court is interpreting the scope of a language right where some efforts have already been made by a government to provide a linguistic service, care must be taken to not unconsciously diminish the scope of the government's obligation by minimizing the practical effect of an allegedly insufficient service or inadequately translated document. This sort of minimization could occur where (like in the case at bar) a government's identifiable but inadequate efforts are used as a reference point by the Crown to emphasize how little of the document was not translated. Implicit in such an argument, is the suggestion that that which has not yet been translated, will not cause any practical harm or inconvenience to the citizen seeking the service. For such an argument to have any relevance in a case involving language rights, a court would have to accept that it is appropriate to determine the scope of a government's linguistic obligation with reference to whether members of a linguistic minority (Anglophone or Francophone) already have the capacity to cope using the official language of the majority. In my view, such a utilitarian argument (and its subtle but insidious implications) represents a threat to the required broad and liberal interpretation of language rights. Such an argument has no place in my legal determination as to scope (what is the City's linguistic obligation?) nor my factual determination concerning compliance (has the City provided the service required by its obligation?).[261]

Similar applications of official languages acts have been made in the civil context. In *Kilrich Industries Ltd v Halotier*, the Yukon Court of Appeal held that the lack of a French version of the rules of court denied a francophone litigant his fundamental language rights as required by Yukon's *Languages Act*.[262] While the *Languages Act* does not explicitly require the rules of court to be published in both French and English, the court concluded that a broad, liberal, and purposive interpretation of the right to use French or English in the court process necessitates a French

260 *R v Rémillard*, [2005] MJ No 467 (Prov Ct), aff'd 2009 MBCA 112.

261 *Ibid* at para 69 (Prov Ct).

262 *Kilrich Industries Ltd v Halotier*, 2007 YKCA 12 [*Kilrich Industries*]; *Languages Act*, RSY 2002, c 133.

version of the rules.[263] The court ordered a new trial and declared the rules of court of no force and effect; however, it suspended the application of the order for one year to allow the Legislative Assembly to enact the rules in a manner compliant with the Act.[264]

A broad, liberal, and purposive interpretation of New Brunswick's quasi-constitutional *Official Languages Act* has resulted in the determination that peace officers must make an "active offer" of services available in both English and French, even though this is not explicitly required by the Act; furthermore, a failure to provide such an active offer can result in the dismissal of criminal charges. In *R v Losier*, the New Brunswick Provincial Court held that "a peace officer in New Brunswick must inform every member of the public with whom he communicates of their right to be served in the official language of their choice."[265] Since this had not occurred, the court concluded that "[t]he violation of Mr. Losier's language rights by a police officer who was totally aware of his duty is serious, and any evidence obtained as a result must be excluded . . ."[266] The same court stated the following in *R v McGraw*:

> Following the decision by our Court of Appeal in *R v Losier*, 2011 NBCA 102, it is well established that police officers have an obligation to make an active offer to the driver of any intercepted vehicle. Failure by a peace officer to make an active offer to any member of the public constitutes a violation of subsection 31(1) of the *Official Languages Act* and of subsection 20(2) of the *Charter of Rights*.[267]

The Federal Court relied on the broad, liberal, and purposive interpretation of the federal *Official Languages Act* in *Thibodeau v Air Canada* to assert that Air Canada had to achieve substantive results with respect to language rights.[268] This case began as a complaint to the commissioner of official languages that Air Canada had failed to provide French language services on one of its subsidiary carriers on a flight from Montreal to Ottawa. Air Canada acknowledged the statutory French language requirements but argued that the statutory regime did not require full bilingualism overnight and that it could be found liable only if it had not exercised due

263 *Kilrich Industries*, above note 262 at paras 62–63.
264 *Ibid* at paras 106 and 108.
265 2010 NBPC 24 at para 15; *Official Languages Act*, SNB 2002, c O-05.
266 *R v Losier*, above note 265 at para 27.
267 *R v McGraw*, 2012 NBQB 358 at para 21. See also *R v Gaudet*, 2010 NBQB 27 at para 41.
268 *Thibodeau*, above note 6.

diligence and care with respect to its obligation. Air Canada claimed to have met the statutory standard because it began conducting surveys on the demand for French language service once the obligation to provide bilingual services was imposed; furthermore, it had sent a message to its regional carriers informing them of their official languages obligations.[269] The Federal Court explicitly rejected this argument because Air Canada was proposing an interpretation of the *Official Languages Regulations*, which imposed the bilingual standard, that compared it to wording found in the *Canadian Aviation Regulations* and the *Aeronautics Act*, rather than to the *Official Languages Act*.[270] The court reasoned that

> the respondents ought instead to conduct a comparative study of the words used in the OLA [*Official Languages Act*] if they wish to find out how to interpret their duties under the ACPPA. The *Canadian Aviation Regulations* are not regulations based on a quasi-constitutional enactment. Subsection 10(2) of the ACPPA refers to a quasi-constitutional enactment, the OLA. Consequently, the words in subsection 10(2) of the ACPPA must be construed in light of the language used in the OLA.[271]

The court proceeded with a broad, liberal, and purposive interpretation and concluded that "obligation is one of result" because of the similarities to constitutional language rights guarantees.[272] It then ordered Air Canada to "make the necessary arrangements with its unions to ensure compliance with the OLA, bearing in mind that this statute is quasi-constitutional in nature."[273]

2) Expanding the Scope of Language Rights

In a somewhat similar fashion to the results achieved with the broad, liberal, and purposive interpretation of human right statutes, this interpretive approach has expanded the scope of quasi-constitutional language rights to areas that a more restrictive interpretation would not have achieved.

269 *Ibid* at paras 30 and 63.

270 *Ibid* at paras 39–40; *Aeronautics Act*, RSC 1985, c A-2; *Canadian Aviation Regulations*, SOR/96-443; *Official Languages (Communications with and Services to the Public) Regulations*, SOR/1992-48; *Official Languages Act*, RSC 1985, c 31 (4th Supp). Air Canada is made subject to the *Official Languages Act* through the *Official Languages (Communications with and Services to the Public) Regulations*, s 10.

271 *Thibodeau*, above note 6 at para 40.

272 *Ibid* at para 48.

273 *Ibid* at para 101.

For example, in *Ndem v General Accident Assurance Co of Canada*, the Ontario Financial Services Commission held that the regime under the *Insurance Act* concerning accident benefits and the evaluation process is both a government agency and a service under Ontario's *French Language Services Act* through a broad, liberal, and purposive interpretation of language rights.[274] This conclusion was reached even though the provisions of the *French Language Services Act* were silent on whether the Act applies in these circumstances because the arbitrator reasoned that "a purposive analysis is most useful where the legislation is unclear or permits alternative interpretations."[275]

The Supreme Court of Canada grappled with a similar issue in *Charlebois v Saint John (City)*, in trying to determine whether the application of New Brunswick's *Official Languages Act* extends to municipalities even though municipalities are not listed in the definition of "institution" under the Act.[276] In this case the plaintiff of a civil action objected that the pleadings from the defendant City of Saint John were in English only and argued that the *Official Languages Act* required the city to adopt the language of the plaintiff's choice in the proceedings. The Supreme Court of Canada was split 5:4 on this issue. The majority decision, written by Charron J, held that the word "institution" in the *Official Languages Act* does not include municipalities.[277] The dissenting opinion, written by Bastarache J, concluded that municipalities fall under the term "institution." Justice Bastarache reasoned that the broad, liberal, and purposive interpretation of the *Official Languages Act* requires one to ask "whether it was necessary to limit the scope of the newly defined term . . ."[278]

In *Lalonde* the Ontario Court of Appeal upheld a decision of the Divisional Court quashing the directions of the Health Services Restructuring Commission, which ordered the Montfort Hospital in Ottawa to reduce its health services based, in part, on a large, liberal, and purposive interpretation of Ontario's *French Language Services Act*.[279] The Montfort Hospital is the only hospital in Ontario where French is the primary working language, and it is meant to serve the francophone community of eastern Ontario and educate and train French-speaking healthcare professionals.

---

274 *Ndem*, above note 17 at para 73.

275 *Ibid* at para 38.

276 *Charlebois v Saint John (City)*, 2005 SCC 74.

277 *Ibid*.

278 *Ibid* at para 15.

279 *Lalonde*, above note 6 at para 188.

The *French Language Services Act* provides the right to "communicate in French with, and to receive available services in French from, any head or central office of a government agency" located in an area of Ontario that is designated to receive French language services under the Act. There was no question that the Montfort was designated as a government agency under the Act and that it was within an area of Ontario designated to receive French language services.[280] The real issue was what "available services" signifies. The provincial government argued that "available services" provides a limited right to receive services in French to the extent of the services being currently offered by the government agency. According to this argument, the *French Language Services Act* does not provide a standard on the types or extent of services to be offered, but rather requires the services to be offered in French only once they are established. Thus, if the Montfort offered ten services one year and then reduced its services to two the following year, the only requirement would be to provide French language rights to those two remaining services.[281] The court rejected this argument and instead interpreted "available services" as requiring services to be maintained to at least the same levels as when the agency was designated under the Act.[282]

Courts apply the broad, liberal, and purposive interpretation when devising a remedy for a breach of quasi-constitutional language rights legislation. This is seen in *Lavigne v Canada (Human Resources Development)*, which involves a complaint to the commissioner of official languages by an anglophone employee of a federal government department in Montreal who claimed he obtained poor results in his job performance review because he was denied training and the opportunity to work in English.[283] The government department admitted to violating the plaintiff's rights under the *Official Languages Act*, but argued that the court could not impose damages under the Act. The Federal Court disagreed, and through a broad, liberal, and purposive interpretation of the *Official Languages Act* found that the department's interpretation "is restrictive and incompatible with the interpretation of the nature and purposes of the Act that was given by the Federal Court of Appeal in *Canada (Attorney General) v Viola*."[284] The court observed that

---

280 *Ibid*; *French Language Services Act*, RSO 1990, c F.32, s 5(1).

281 *Lalonde*, above note 6 at para 159.

282 *Ibid* at para 160.

283 *Lavigne v Canada (Human Resources Development)*, [1997] 1 FC 305 (TD).

284 *Ibid* at para 19.

> the 1988 *Official Languages Act* is a statute designed to create practical and effective legal rights and obligations. To accomplish this objective, and to ensure that the Act is indeed an effective instrument for the protection of the language rights of Canadians, damages must be included among the realm of remedies available to the Court under subsection 77(4). The ability of the Court to award damages is, in my view, essential to the enforcement of guaranteed quasi-constitutional rights.[285]

The broad, liberal, and purposive interpretation allowed the court in this case to make an inference that "[h]ad the legislator intended to limit the Court's powers under that specific provision to grant a remedy so as to exclude damages, it would have stated so explicitly."[286]

E. A NARROW INTERPRETATION OF DEFENCES AND EXEMPTIONS IN QUASI-CONSTITUTIONAL LEGISLATION

In addition to interpreting the rights contained in quasi-constitutional statutes broadly and liberally, the Supreme Court of Canada has endorsed a narrow interpretation of the defences, exceptions, exemptions, exclusions, and other limitations to the rights contained in these statutes. This section will consider the application of this narrow interpretation and how it helps promote the purpose of quasi-constitutional legislation. The application of this approach is observed most frequently in human rights and access-to-information legislation. That is because these statutes explicitly contain defences to discriminatory practice and exemptions to the general rule of access to government information, although it applies equally to privacy acts and statutes upholding language rights.

1) A Purposive Approach and a Narrow Interpretation of Limitations to Rights

Just as a broad and liberal interpretation of the rights contained in quasi-constitutional legislation is a consequence of the purposive approach, so is a narrow interpretation of the limitations to these rights. In the human rights context, Dickson CJ, writing for a unanimous Supreme Court of Canada in *CNR v Canada (Human Rights Commission)*, cautiously

285 *Ibid* at para 25.
286 *Ibid* at para 20.

warned that "[w]e should not search for ways and means to minimize those rights and to enfeeble their proper impact."[287] Since the purpose of human rights legislation is, as declared by the Supreme Court of Canada in *O'Malley*, "the removal of discrimination," defences to discrimination are considered to be the exception. Justice McIntyre, for a unanimous Court, observed in the 1982 decision of *Ontario (Human Rights Commission) v Etobicoke (Borough)* "that under the *Code* non-discrimination is the rule of general application and discrimination, where permitted, is the exception."[288] In *Dickason v University of Alberta*, Cory J stated for the majority that "while rights should receive a broad interpretation, defences to the exercise of those rights should be interpreted narrowly."[289] This principle was described most succinctly by the Canadian Human Rights Tribunal in *Citron*: "[t]he Act is thus to be given a large and liberal interpretation: protected rights must be interpreted broadly, while defences and exceptions are read narrowly."[290]

The narrow interpretation of exceptions and exemptions in access-to-information and privacy legislation is likewise a result of a purposive interpretation of those statutes. The Supreme Court of Canada found that in the context of the federal *Access to Information Act*, "Parliament intended the Act to apply liberally and broadly with the citizen's right of access to such information being denied only in limited and specific exceptions."[291] The Federal Court further explained in *Canadian Broadcasting Corp v Canada (Information Commissioner)* that "[t]he spirit of the Act is based on the principle of disclosure. Under the Act, non-disclosure of information under the control of government institutions is the exception."[292] This is referenced in the legislation's purpose statements. The purpose statement in the federal *Access to Information Act* reads as follows:

> The purpose of this Act is to extend the present laws of Canada to provide a right of access to information in records under the control of a government institution in accordance with the principles that

287 *CNR*, above note 30 at para 24.

288 *Etobicoke*, above note 136 at 208.

289 *Dickason v University of Alberta*, [1992] SCJ No 76 at para 17 [*Dickason*]. See also *Boisbriand*, above note 1 at para 29.

290 *Citron*, above note 197 at para 74.

291 *Canada Post Corp*, above note 216 at para 34. Cited in *Bronskill*, above note 16 at para 5 (FC). See also *Canada (Information Commissioner) v Canada (Commissioner of the Royal Canadian Mounted Police)*, 2003 SCC 8; *Rubin*, above note 21.

292 2010 FC 954 at para 14 [*Canadian Broadcasting Corp*], aff'd 2011 FCA 326. See also *Canada Post Corp*, above note 216 at para 34.

> government information should be available to the public, that necessary exceptions to the right of access should be limited and specific . . . .[293]

The restrictive interpretation of the defences contained in human rights legislation was first observed in the dissenting opinion of Dickson CJ in *Bhinder*, where he stated that "the *bona fide* exception must be interpreted narrowly so as not to conflict with the remedial aims of the Act."[294] This is in reference to a type of defence commonly found in human rights legislation where such things as a job requirement or a mandatory age of retirement — *prima facie* contraventions of the human rights legislation — are permitted to continue under the circumstances because they are *bona fide* occupational requirements. Justice Abella described the *bona fide* defences in *New Brunswick (Human Rights Commission) v Potash Corporation of Saskatchewan Inc*:

> There is no doubt that the words "*bona fide*" have a unique pedigree in human rights jurisprudence. When the words are used together with "occupational qualification," "occupational requirement" or "reasonable justification," they have a well-understood meaning and represent an accepted term of art in the human rights world.[295]

As previously mentioned, *Bhinder* involved a Sikh who was found to have been discriminated against by his employer's policy requiring the use of hard hats as it interfered with his religious headdress. Yet, while this decision helped establish the restrictive interpretation of the *bona fide* occupational requirement, the effects of this approach were not immediately obvious in this case: the Court ultimately determined that CN's hard hat policy met the *bona fide* requirement defence. In fact, the Court found the *bona fide* occupational requirement defence to have been met in several decisions following *Bhinder*.[296]

An important consideration in the restrictive interpretation of the *bona fide* occupational requirement is the Supreme Court of Canada's point in *Etobicoke* that the complainant only needs to establish a *prima facie* case of discrimination and then the more onerous burden of proving

293 *Access to Information Act*, above note 20, s 2.

294 *Bhinder*, above note 48 at para 6. See also Sullivan, above note 2 at 497.

295 *Potash*, above note 1 at para 18.

296 See, for example, *Caldwell v St Thomas Aquinas High School*, [1984] 2 SCR 603; *Zurich Insurance Co v Ontario (Human Rights Commission)*, [1992] 2 SCR 321 [*Zurich Insurance*]; *Saskatchewan (Human Rights Commission) v Saskatoon (City)*, [1989] 2 SCR 1297; *Dickason*, above note 289.

the *bona fide* occupational requirement defence falls on the respondent.[297] This point was emphasized by the Court in *O'Malley*, where it overturned the decision of the Board of Inquiry, which had dismissed the human rights complaint.[298] Justice McIntyre, who wrote the unanimous decision, was extremely critical of the Board of Inquiry's "[reluctance] . . . to impose a strict burden of proof upon the employer."[299] This viewpoint was reiterated by the Court in the 2012 decision of *Moore v British Columbia (Education)*.[300]

The narrow interpretation and strict burden of proof in making out a *bona fide* requirement has made it an onerous defence. This is displayed in decisions at the tribunal level. In *Stanley v Canada (Royal Canadian Mounted Police)*, the Canadian Human Rights Tribunal stated that

> [g]iven the admonition by McIntyre J. in *Bhinder* to give narrow scope to provisions like section 14(a) of the CHRA [*Canadian Human Rights Act*], it is to be expected that, in the great majority of cases in which the BFOR question is addressed, the balance of interests will be struck in favour of the complainant.[301]

A review tribunal under the *Canadian Human Rights Act* in *Bader v Canada (National Health and Welfare)* overturned the original decision of the Canadian Human Rights Tribunal on the basis that the evidence relied upon by the respondent was not of sufficient quality and weight to meet the *bona fide* requirement defence. The review tribunal found that, in attempting to make out the *bona fide* requirement defence, the respondent relied on information that was "unscientific," "inherently unreliable," and based "exclusively on perceptions and opinions." As a result it held that the original tribunal "made manifest and palpable errors in respect to the facts and the law."[302]

The terms "defences" and "exceptions" are used somewhat interchangeably in human rights legislation. For instance, the Supreme Court of Canada has referred to the *bona fide* occupational requirement as

297 *Etobicoke*, above note 136.
298 *O'Malley*, above note 18.
299 *Ibid* at para 24.
300 *Moore*, above note 164 at para 33.
301 *Stanley v Canada (Royal Canadian Mounted Police)*, [1987] CHRD No 3.
302 *Bader v Canada (National Health and Welfare)*, [1998] CHRD No 1 at paras 150, 167, and 315.

both an exception and as a defence.[303] When an exception or defence is advanced, there is no question that the human rights legislation applies to the situation: the applicant must make out a *prima facie* case of discrimination while the respondent can avail herself to the defences or exceptions contained in the statute itself. Justice Cory explained for the majority in *Dickason v University of Alberta* that

> [t]he right against discrimination provided in human rights statutes will be subject to any defence provided by those same statutes to those who discriminate. However, as McIntyre J. recognized in *Ontario Human Rights Commission v Borough of Etobicoke* " . . . a defence which allows discrimination to continue stands as an exception to the rule of non-discrimination.[304]

Justice Sopinka provided the Court's rationale for the narrow construction of defences and exceptions to discrimination in *Zurich Insurance Co v Ontario (Human Rights Commission)*: "[a]s the last protection of the most vulnerable members of society, exceptions to such legislation should be narrowly construed."[305]

2) The Interpretation of Exclusions and Exemptions

There is no question that human rights legislation is invoked when defences and exceptions are relied upon; exclusions and exemptions, on the other hand, are circumstances where human rights legislation does not apply.

The jurisprudence appears to consider an exclusion as a limited circumstance, provided by the legislation itself, where the protection against discrimination does not apply. Section 10 of Ontario's *Human Rights Code*, for example, provides a specific exclusion to what constitutes a service: "'services' does not include a levy, fee, tax, or periodic payment imposed by law."[306] This exclusion has been interpreted narrowly. In one case the Ontario Workplace Safety and Insurance Appeals Tribunal interpreted the words "periodic payment" in the immediate context of the

---

303 In *Bhinder*, above note 48 at para 6, Dickson CJ said: "the *bona fide* exception must be interpreted narrowly." In contrast, in *Dickason*, above note 289 at para 60, L'Heureux-Dubé J referred to it as "a defence of *bona fide* occupational qualification."

304 *Dickason*, *ibid* at para 17.

305 *Zurich Insurance*, above note 296 at para 18.

306 *Human Rights Code*, above note 49, s 10.

words "levy, fee, tax" and rejected the argument that this excludes workers' compensation benefits.[307]

Some human rights statutes explicitly limit their application to "services" that are "customarily available to the public." For instance, section 5 of the *Canadian Human Rights Act* provides: "[i]t is a discriminatory practice in the provision of goods, services, facilities or accommodation customarily available to the general public . . ."[308] Similar to exclusions, the Supreme Court of Canada refers to this language as "limiting provisions."[309]

The Court has outright rejected the argument that this requires a service to be offered to all members of the public for the application of human rights legislation to be invoked; it has, instead, adopted a much more restrictive interpretation. In *Berg*, Lamer CJ said that "[s]uch an absolute position, requiring the 'public' to include every member of a 'community' cannot be maintained if human rights legislation is to have any impact."[310] In *Saskatchewan (Human Rights Commission) v Saskatchewan (Department of Social Services)*, the Saskatchewan Court of Appeal stated:

> . . . The fact that a service is offered to the public does not mean that it must be offered to all members of the public. The government can impose eligibility requirements to ensure that the program or services reaches the intended client group. The only restriction is that the government cannot discriminate among the client group, that is, the elderly, the poor or others, on the basis of the enumerated characteristics set out in the *Code*.[311]

The results of this narrow interpretation of these limiting words are significant. In *O'Quinn v Nova Scotia (Workers' Compensation Board)*, the Nova Scotia Court of Appeal found that workers' compensation benefits are services despite the fact that they are "available only to the worker or

---

307 *Decision No 1529/04I2*, above note 54 at paras 44–52.

308 *Canadian Human Rights Act*, above note 198, s 5.

309 Chief Justice Lamer, writing for the majority in *Berg*, above note 2 at para 28, stated that "[m]ost, but not all, human rights Acts contain similar limiting provisions." See also the comments of the Nova Scotia Court of Appeal in *O'Quinn*, above note 156 at para 29.

310 *Berg*, above note 2 at para 54. See also *O'Quinn*, above note 156 at para 22, where the Nova Scotia Court of Appeal referred to how the Court in *Berg* rejected the approach in *Jenkins v Workers' Compensation Board of Prince Edward Island* (1986), 31 DLR (4th) 536 (PEISCAD).

311 *Saskatchewan (Human Rights Commission) v Saskatchewan (Department of Social Services)* (1988), 9 CHRR 5181 at 25 (Sask CA).

his dependants."[312] In *Re Singh* the Federal Court of Appeal concluded that the Department of External Affairs and the Canada Employment and Immigration Commission were engaged in the provision of services customarily available to the general public when they determined who should be granted visitor visas to allow close relatives to sponsor family members.[313] Finally, in *Chiang v Natural Sciences and Engineering Research Council*, the Canadian Human Rights Tribunal found that the activities of the Natural Sciences and Engineering Research Council of Canada (NSERC) are services customarily available to members of the public even though they are aimed at scientists.[314]

Exemptions to human rights legislation are similar to exclusions, although the caselaw suggests that they are wider sweeping circumstances that go to the core of human rights legislation rather than the narrower exclusions that are provided in the legislation itself. An example of an exemption to human rights legislation is the argument that human rights legislation does not apply to the actions of Parliament or the provincial legislatures because of parliamentary privilege. In *Ontario (Speaker of the Legislative Assembly) v Ontario (Human Rights Commission)*, the Ontario Court of Appeal found that the *Human Rights Code* of Ontario could not be used to challenge the daily recital of the Lord's Prayer by the Speaker of the Ontario legislature because it was a matter inherently related to the conduct of proceedings within the legislature, and the *Code* did not apply because of parliamentary immunity.[315]

Although parliamentary privilege or immunity may insulate legislatures from human rights legislation on matters of their own procedure, it does not do so in other contexts such as employment. In *Canada (House of Commons) v Vaid* the Speaker of the House of Commons unsuccessfully challenged the jurisdiction of the Canadian Human Rights Tribunal on the basis that parliamentary privilege insulates the Speaker's power to hire, manage, and dismiss employees. This case involved a complaint to the Canadian Human Rights Commission by the chauffeur of the Speaker of the House of Commons. The chauffeur said he had been discriminated against by his employer on the basis of race, colour, nation, or

---

312 *O'Quinn*, above note 156 at para 20; Nova Scotia *Human Rights Act*, RSNS 1989, c 214.

313 *Re Singh*, [1989] 1 FC 430 (CA).

314 [1992] CHRD No 3.

315 *Ontario (Speaker of the Legislative Assembly) v Ontario (Human Rights Commission)*, [2001] OJ No 2180 (CA).

ethnic origin. In rejecting the Speaker's argument, Binnie J, writing for a unanimous Supreme Court of Canada, explained that

> the language used by Parliament in the *Canadian Human Rights Act* is wide enough to cover its own employees and that the sweeping exemption now asserted by the appellants has not been shown to be intended by Parliament nor, on general principles, is it necessary or justifiable as parliamentary privilege.[316]

Justice Binnie's underlying rationale for this conclusion was that the "*Canadian Human Rights Act* is a quasi-constitutional document and we should affirm that any exemption from its provisions must be clearly stated."[317]

Justice Binnie's comments were relied upon by the Federal Court in *Pankiw v Canada (Human Rights Commission)*, a case involving a complaint to the Canadian Human Rights Commission that a member of Parliament had violated the *Canadian Human Rights Act* through discriminatory comments contained in printed mail-outs sent to his constituents. The Federal Court conducted an in-depth review of the law surrounding parliamentary privilege and considered the quasi-constitutional status of human rights legislation to be an important factor to consider:

> Another contextual factor is the status which the CHRA [*Canadian Human Rights Act*] has attained. As stated at paragraph 81 of *Vaid*, above, the CHRA is a quasi-constitutional document and "we should affirm that any exemption from its provisions must be clearly stated," and in terms of the application of the CHRA to employees of Parliament, examining the language of section 2 . . . of that Act, there is no indication that it was not intended to extend to employees of Parliament, and in the words of Justice Binnie "[t]here is no reason to think that Parliament 'intended' to impose human rights obligations on every federal employer except itself."[318]

The Supreme Court of Canada has endorsed a similar narrow interpretation of the limitations in access-to-information legislation and the right to access personal information under privacy acts. As previously mentioned, courts have held that access-to-information regimes are "based on

316 *Canada (House of Commons) v Vaid*, 2005 SCC 30 at para 5.

317 *Ibid* at para 81.

318 *Pankiw v Canada (Human Rights Commission)*, 2006 FC 1544 at para 109, aff'd 2007 FCA 386, leave to appeal to SCC refused, [2008] SCCA No 95.

the principle of disclosure," while "non-disclosure of information under the control of government institutions is the exception."[319] What this means, first, is that the general right to access government information is only restricted to the extent of the exemptions explicitly provided for in the statute. The terms "exception" and "exemption" are used somewhat interchangeably in the caselaw and the legislation. The term "exemption" is used in the federal *Access to Information Act* and the *Privacy Act*,[320] while the provincial schemes, which combine access-to-information and privacy rights in one statute, generally use the term "exception."[321]

Whether a record falls within a specific exemption provided by the Act is a separate inquiry from the question of custody or control, and the analysis is conducted through a narrow interpretation of exemptions. Moreover, even when an exemption to access is found to apply, access-to-information regimes contain severance provisions that require disclosure of any parts of a record that do not contain exempt material.[322]

The Federal Court of Appeal explained in *Rubin v Canada (Minister of Transport)* that where there is ambiguity on the interpretation of an exemption, the court is to "choose the interpretation that infringes on the public's stated right to access to information contained in section 4 of the Act the least."[323] This has affected the scope of the exemptions under the access-to-information regimes. In *Moseley v Spray Lakes Sawmills*, the Alberta Court of Appeal held that the exception for litigation privilege "will not automatically apply to statements taken or reports made

---

319 *Canadian Broadcasting Corp*, above note 292 at para 14. See also *Canada Post Corp*, above note 216 at para 34.

320 *Access to Information Act*, above note 20, s 13; *Privacy Act*, RSC 1985, c P-21, s 18.8.

321 *Freedom of Information and Protection of Privacy Act*, above note 208, Division 2, s 12; *Freedom of Information and Protection of Privacy Act*, above note 248, Division 2, s 16; *The Freedom of Information and Protection of Privacy Act*, CCSM c F175, Division 3, s 17; *Access to Information and Protection of Privacy Act*, SNL 2002, c A-1.1, Part III; *Right to Information and Protection of Privacy Act*, SNB 2009, c R-10.6, Division B, s 17; *Freedom of Information and Protection of Privacy Act*, SNS 1993, c 5, s 2 and Division 2, s 14; *Freedom of Information and Protection of Privacy Act*, RSPEI 1988, c F-15.01, Division 2, s 14; *Access to Information and Protection of Privacy Act*, SNWT (Nu) 1994, c 20, Division B, s 13; *Access to Information and Protection of Privacy Act*, RSY 2002, c 1, s 1. The Ontario and Nova Scotia acts refer to both exemptions and exceptions: *Freedom of Information and Protection of Privacy Act*, RSO 1990, c F31, s 12.

322 *Access to Information Act*, above note 20, s 2(1); *Merck Frosst Canada Ltd v Canada (Health)*, 2012 SCC 3 at para 25 [*Merck Frosst*].

323 *Rubin*, above note 21 at para 24, cited in *3430901 Canada Inc v Canada (Minister of Industry)*, 2001 FCA 254 at para 27.

by insurance adjusters investigating serious personal injury accidents."[324] The court further stressed the fact that "litigation privilege has been carefully confined to narrow limits in order to preserve the public interest in full disclosure."[325] This principle was applied by the information and privacy commissioner of Alberta to a request for a report arising from a fire, which was created for the purpose of pursuing at fault parties, resulting in the conclusion that the report was not subject to the litigation privilege exemption.[326]

In *Canada (Information Commissioner) v Canada (Minister of National Defence)*, Charron J, noted earlier for her endorsement of the broad, liberal, and purposive interpretation to the question of control on behalf of a majority Supreme Court of Canada, was criticized for her interpretation of exceptions to disclosure, which she emphasized as "necessary exceptions."[327] Professor Vincent Kazmierski questioned this approach since section 2 of the Act states that "necessary exceptions to the right of access should be limited and specific.[328] As such, Professor Kazmierski expresses concern "that Justice Charron's emphasis on the necessity of the exceptions may lead to an expansive interpretation of the exceptions to the right to access in future cases."[329]

In addition to interpreting the exemptions to disclosure in access-to-information regimes narrowly, the courts have also applied a narrow interpretation to the procedural protections provided to third parties related to the disclosure of their confidential commercial information held by government. Access-to-information regimes contain provisions that give third parties an opportunity to make representations as to why the requested records should not be disclosed.[330] The Supreme Court of Canada has recognized the fact that "the important goal of disclosure must be balanced with the legitimate private interests of third parties and the public interest in promoting innovation and development."[331] In *Merck Frosst*, the Supreme Court of Canada held that there is "a fairly low threshold to trigger the obligation to give notice," although the Court outright rejected Merck Frosst's argument that the right is automatic

324 *Moseley v Spray Lakes Sawmills (1980) Ltd*, [1996] AJ No 380 at para 24 (CA).

325 *Ibid* at para 26.

326 *Order F2009-015; St Albert (City) (Re)*, [2009] AIPCD No 43 at para 90.

327 *Canada (Information Commissioner)*, above note 3 at para 89.

328 Kazmierski, above note 203 at 62.

329 *Ibid* at 63.

330 *Access to Information Act*, above note 20, ss 27 & 28.

331 *Merck Frosst*, above note 322 at para 23.

with certain categories of records.[332] In that case Cromwell J also endorsed a much narrower understanding of the term "trade secrets" than the one advanced by Merck Frosst. In contrast to Charron J's interpretation of exceptions in *Canada (Information Commissioner)*, Cromwell J's approach has been described as more in keeping with the broad, liberal, and purposive interpretation of the right to access and the corresponding narrow interpretation of exceptions.[333] Even though this case involved a private party, not a government institution, Professor Kazmierski emphasizes the importance of ensuring a restrictive interpretation of the limitations to the right to access.[334]

Access-to-information regimes provide a process of independent review by a commission when access is denied by the government institutions to ensure that the application of an exemption is justified. Privacy legislation likewise allows for complaints to a privacy commissioner to ensure compliance with the legislation. The commissioners have statutory authority to compel the production of documents to investigate a privacy complaint or to determine whether an exception to access has been properly applied. The courts have applied a broad, liberal, and purposive interpretation to the powers granted to commissioners under access-to-information and privacy legislation to ensure that there is proper recourse for independent review of decisions by government institutions.[335]

Although exceptions and exemptions to quasi-constitutional language rights are not as common as those contained in human rights, access-to-information, and privacy legislation, those that exist are similarly narrowly interpreted. The Ontario Court of Appeal in *Lalonde* had to address an exemption from the *French Language Services Act* that allowed services in French to be limited "as circumstances make reasonable and necessary, if all reasonable measures and plans for compliance with this Act have been taken or made."[336] The court interpreted this exception narrowly by first, focusing on the word "necessary," which was interpreted to mean "that existing services can only be limited when this is the only course of action that can be taken."[337] In acknowledging that

332 *Ibid* at para 63.

333 Kazmierski, above note 203 at 63.

334 *Ibid.*

335 *Canadian Broadcasting Corp*, above note 292 at para 37. See also *Canada (Information Commissioner) v Canada (Minister of National Defence)*, [1999] FCJ No 522 at para 27 (CA).

336 *Lalonde*, above note 6 at para 164.

337 *Ibid.*

the provincial government has the discretion to change and to limit the services offered by Montfort Hospital, the court held that "it cannot simply invoke administrative convenience and vague funding concerns as the reasons for doing so."[338]

In considering the application of the broad, liberal, and purposive interpretation to quasi-constitutional legislation, this chapter demonstrated that this interpretive approach considerably expands the rights provided in quasi-constitutional law. This expansion occurs both through a broad, liberal, and purposive interpretation of the rights themselves and through a narrow and restrictive interpretation of any provisions that seek to limit the scope of these rights. Although this interpretive approach displays one of the defining features of quasi-constitutional legislation and its concrete differences with regular legislation, what remains to be explored is its theoretical basis and relationship to constitutional law, which will be considered in Chapter 4. The next chapter, Chapter 3, will consider the influence of quasi-constitutional legislation in the interpretation of regular statutes because of its primacy. As will be seen, the broad, liberal, and purposive interpretation of quasi-constitutional legislation has a bearing on the full effect of primacy.

FURTHER READINGS

COUSINEAU, MARC. "Survol des droits linguistiques: enfin de vrais droits linguistiques au Canada" (2000–2001) 32 *Ottawa Law Review* 117.

D'SILVA, ALAN LW. "Giving Effect to Human Rights Legislation: A Purposive Approach" (1991) 3 *Windsor Review of Legal and Social Issues* 45.

KAZMIERSKI, VINCENT. "Accessing with Dinosaurs: Protecting Access to Government Information in the Cretaceous Period of Canadian Democracy" (2016) 25:3 *Constitutional Forum* 57.

SAMSON, MÉLANIE. "Interprétation large et libérale et interprétation contextuelle : convergence ou divergence?" (2008) 49:2 *Cahiers de droit* 297.

SULLIVAN, RUTH. *Sullivan on the Construction of Statutes*, 5th ed (Markham, ON: LexisNexis, 2008) ch 17.

338 *Ibid* at para 168.

CHAPTER 3

The Primacy of Quasi-constitutional Legislation

The primacy of quasi-constitutional legislation involves giving it priority and an elevated legal status vis-à-vis other statutes to advance fundamental rights. Primacy has thus been described as providing quasi-constitutional legislation with a form of "precedence over other incompatible legislative enactments."[1] Many quasi-constitutional statutes contain a primacy provision, although this function is recognized by the courts passed on the fundamental character of quasi-constitutional legislation; the same results have therefore been achieved even in the absence of an express provision.

Primacy is most often observed when there is a perceived conflict between a quasi-constitutional statute and a regular one, but a quasi-constitutional statute can also guide the interpretation of a regular statute even in the absence of conflict. The courts have adopted a two-stage approach to primacy whereby they first try to interpret a regular statute in accordance with the quasi-constitutional one to avoid conflict. Quasi-constitutional statutes significantly affect the interpretation of other statutes, and courts and tribunals use this interpretive function to effectively review other legislation and ensure compliance with fundamental rights. This aspect of primacy is notably similar to the weak-form model of constitutionalism and judicial review in several Commonwealth jurisdictions, where

1 Claire Mummé, "At the Crossroads in Discrimination Law: How the Human Rights Codes Overtook the *Charter* in Canadian Government Services Cases" (2012) 9 *Journal of Law & Equality* 103 at para 5.

the role of the judiciary in scrutinizing legislation for compliance with fundamental rights is based on interpretation rather than invalidation.

When conflict cannot be avoided through interpretation, courts and tribunals, in some instances, can proceed to the second stage and either declare the conflicting provision in the regular statute inoperable or formulate a comparable remedy. This is one of the most significant attributes of quasi-constitutional legislation, which was first developed under the *Canadian Bill of Rights* and is now being increasingly used under human rights legislation, primarily when discrimination is found in a service created by a statute. Since these cases can typically be pursued either under human rights legislation or section 15(1) of the *Charter*, the courts have been influenced by the analytical framework developed under the *Charter*. Unlike the use of the *Charter*, however, human rights legislation cannot be used to directly challenge legislation; rather, it requires discrimination in one of the social areas covered by human rights legislation. The literature has focused largely on the cases involving discrimination in the provision of government services and the analytical framework adopted by the courts, but even in this context it has been observed that the primacy of quasi-constitutional legislation has been "relatively unexplored."[2] Although this remedy is issued most frequently in the services context, there is no theoretical reason to restrict it to this social area, and this chapter will examine declarations of inoperability in cases involving discrimination in employment as well as in services.

Even though declarations of inoperability have only been explicitly endorsed by the courts as a remedy under the *Canadian Bill of Rights* and human rights legislation, this chapter will consider some of the emerging trends under access-to-information, privacy, and language rights legislation. These cases are often determined on the first stage of the analysis, yet an interpretation that applies the quasi-constitutional statute and declines to apply the conflicting one can be practically indistinguishable from a declaration of inoperability.

Section A of this chapter discusses the two-stage approach to primacy under the *Canadian Bill of Rights*, and how the interpretive function is being applied under the five categories of quasi-constitutional legislation. It then considers the similarities between this aspect of primacy and developments in other Commonwealth jurisdictions that have adopted

2 *Ibid. Canadian Charter of Rights and Freedoms*, Part I of the *Constitution Act, 1982*, being Schedule B to the *Canada Act 1982* (UK), 1982, c 11 [*Charter*].

a weak-form model of constitutionalism and judicial review. Section B focuses on declarations of inoperability and comparable remedies when a regular statute is in irreconcilable conflict with a quasi-constitutional one, including the analytical framework developed by the courts. The focus of this chapter is on the practical application of primacy, whereas theoretical questions and the broader history of the cross-fertilization between human rights and section 15(1) of the *Charter* will be largely reserved for chapters 4 and 5.

A. THE PRIMACY OF QUASI-CONSTITUTIONAL LEGISLATION AND STATUTORY INTERPRETATION

In applying the two-stage approach to primacy, a court or tribunal first tries to interpret a statute in accordance with the quasi-constitutional one in order to avoid conflict. This approach was developed under the *Canadian Bill of Rights* and has since been extended to the other categories of quasi-constitutional legislation. It has a substantial impact on the interpretation of regular statutes, and even beyond the question of conflict, it is recognized that all legislation is to be interpreted consistent with human rights when it is capable of more than one interpretation. The primacy of access-to-information and privacy acts means that they prevail over confidentiality provisions or other methods of accessing records unless the regular statute indicates otherwise. Language rights statutes influence the interpretation of other legislation to ensure the broadest degree of French language services.

Primacy also means that quasi-constitutional legislation prevails over private law instruments, such as contracts and collective agreements, which cannot be used to diminish quasi-constitutional rights. Relatedly, courts will scrutinize whether the enforcement of a foreign judgment, a forum selection, or a choice of law clause is contrary to quasi-constitutional principles. Finally, the primacy of Canadian quasi-constitutional legislation displays some notable similarities to the weak-form model of judicial review in the Commonwealth, which primarily mandates courts to interpret statutes consistently with rights instruments.

1) The *Canadian Bill of Rights* and the Two-Stage Approach to Primacy

The primacy of quasi-constitutional legislation can be traced back to the *Canadian Bill of Rights*, section 2:

> Every law of Canada shall, unless it is expressly declared by an Act of the Parliament of Canada that it shall operate notwithstanding the *Canadian Bill of Rights*, be so construed and applied as not to abrogate, abridge or infringe or to authorize the abrogation, abridgment or infringement of any of the rights or freedoms herein recognized and declared . . .

Professor Ruth Sullivan refers to section 2 as establishing a rule of interpretation but notes that it has had "little impact on the interpretative practice of Canadian courts."[3] This was largely due to the interpretive approach adopted by the Supreme Court of Canada whereby the enumerated rights were interpreted as "frozen," or as they existed in the common law when the *Canadian Bill of Rights* was enacted in 1960.[4] This narrow interpretation was adopted by the Court because of the declaratory nature of section 1, which merely recognizes rights that "have existed and shall continue to exist." As a result, the Court reasoned that the purpose of the *Canadian Bill of Rights* was not to protect rights "in an abstract sense," or to define new rights and freedoms, but rather to codify rights found in the common law "as they existed in Canada immediately before the statute was enacted."[5] The Court's restrictive interpretation of the *Canadian Bill of Rights*, considered briefly in Chapter 2, will be considered in more detail in Chapter 5 in the context of how it affected the development of a special approach to the interpretation of other quasi-constitutional statutes. The immediate concern is how the primacy of quasi-constitutional legislation affects the interpretation of other statutes; it is thus sufficient

---

3 Ruth Sullivan, *Sullivan on the Construction of Statutes*, 5th ed (Markham, ON: LexisNexis, 2008) at 505. *Canadian Bill of Rights*, SC 1960, c 44.

4 The term "frozen concept" of rights was formulated by Walter Tarnopolsky. See Walter Tarnopolsky, "A New Bill of Rights in the Light of the Interpretation of the Present One by the Supreme Court of Canada" in Law Society of Upper Canada, ed, *The Constitution and the Future of Canada* (Toronto: R De Boo, 1978) 161 at 181–91. See also Joel Bakan et al, eds, *Canadian Constitutional Law*, 4th ed (Toronto: Emond Montgomery, 2010) at 715.

5 *Robertson and Rosetanni v The Queen*, [1963] SCR 651 at 654; *R v Burnshine*, [1975] 1 SCR 693 at 702 [*Burnshine*]. See also *Smythe v The Queen*, [1971] SCR 680, and the dissent of Pigeon J in *R v Drybones*, [1970] SCR 282 at 305 [*Drybones*].

to say that the restrictive interpretation of the *Canadian Bill of Rights* means that it is rare, although not impossible, for other statutes to be found to conflict with it.

A statute was first found to conflict with the *Canadian Bill of Rights* in the 1970 case of *R v Drybones*. That case concerned an Indigenous person in the Northwest Territories who was convicted under the *Indian Act* for being intoxicated off reserve. The *Indian Act* imposed a much harsher penalty against an Indigenous person for this offence, including a minimum fine and a term of imprisonment of up to three months, compared to the penalty imposed against a non-Indigenous person under the territorial liquor ordinance, which imposed a maximum term of improvement of only thirty days and no minimum fine. The provision in the *Indian Act* clearly conflicted with the *Canadian Bill of Rights*, and the Supreme Court of Canada accordingly found that Drybones was denied equality before the law because he was treated more harshly solely because he was an Indigenous person.[6]

The *Drybones* decision resolved a decade-long debate of "conflicting judicial opinions" on the question of the impact of the *Canadian Bill of Rights* on other legislation, which was occurring in parallel to the debate about its interpretation.[7] *Drybones* is well known for the confirmation from the Supreme Court of Canada that a provision in another statute found in conflict with the *Canadian Bill of Rights* can be declared inoperable. At this stage it is important to note that the Court declared the impugned provision of the *Indian Act* inoperable only because it could not interpret it consistently with the *Canadian Bill of Rights*. Justice Ritchie, writing for the majority in *Drybones*, recognized that "[t]he difficulty with sec. 94(a) of the *Indian Act* is that it admits of no construction or application that would avoid conflict with sec. 1(b) of the *Canadian Bill of Rights* as appellant's counsel interprets it."[8]

The Supreme Court of Canada has therefore adopted a two-stage approach to the primacy of the *Canadian Bill of Rights*, which first requires courts to try to construe conflicting statutes in accordance with its enumerated rights, and only if conflict cannot be avoided through interpretation will the conflicting provision in the regular statute be declared

---

6 *Drybones*, *ibid.*

7 Peter W Hogg, *Constitutional Law of Canada*, 5th ed (Toronto: Carswell, 2007) at 35-5; Bakan et al, eds, above note 4 at 714. For the early judicial debate of the question, see, especially, DM Gordon, "The *Canadian Bill of Rights*" (1961) 4 *Canadian Bar Journal* 431.

8 *Drybones*, above note 5 at 293.

inoperable.[9] This approach was described by Bora Laskin CJ in the 1975 case of *R v Burnshire*:

> It is important to appreciate that the *Canadian Bill of Rights* does not invariably command a declaration of inoperability of any federal legislation affected by its terms. That may be the result, under the principle enunciated in the *Drybones* case, *supra*, if a construction and application compatible with the *Canadian Bill of Rights* cannot reasonably be found. The primary injunction of the *Bill*, however, is to determine whether a challenged measure is open to a compatible construction that would enable it to remain an effective enactment. If the process of construction in the light of the Bill yields this result, it is unnecessary and, indeed, it would be an abuse of judicial power to sterilize the federal measure.[10]

The same analysis was extended to the *Alberta Bill of Rights* due to its similarities to the *Canadian Bill of Rights*.[11]

The primacy of the *Canadian Bill of Rights* and the requirement to interpret other legislation in accordance with it was a significant development because it departed from the established rules of statutory interpretation. These rules begin with an underlying presumption that the entire body of legislation is meant to work together and operate without conflict among statutes.[12] Courts thus only find conflict to exist "when provisions are so inconsistent that they are incapable of standing together."[13] The presumption in favour of a coherent statute book is succinctly explained by the Newfoundland Court of Appeal in *Newfoundland (Human Rights Commission) v Newfoundland (Workplace Health, Safety and Compensation Commission)*: "where possible, potentially conflicting legislation is interpreted so that inconsistency or conflict is avoided."[14]

The courts therefore strive to reconcile statutes that are seemingly in conflict through the adoption of maxims meant to resolve the conflict

9 Hogg, above note 7 at 35-4.

10 *Burnshine*, above note 5 at 714.

11 *R v JD*, 1977 ALTASCAD 89 at paras 95–99.

12 *Friends of The Oldman River Society v Canada (Minister of Transport)*, [1992] 1 SCR 3 at para 42; *Pointe-Claire (City) v Quebec (Labour Court)*, [1997] 1 SCR 1015 at para 61; *Human Rights Commission v Workplace Health, Safety and Compensation Commission*, 2005 NLCA 61 at para 13 [*Human Rights Commission*]; *Diamond v Robbins*, 2006 NLCA 1 at para 49; Sullivan, above note 3 at 325.

13 *Thibodeau v Air Canada*, 2014 SCC 67 at para 89 [*Thibodeau* SCC].

14 *Human Rights Commission*, above note 12 at para 13.

in a fashion that respects the legislature's intentions. The two most important maxims for our purposes are *generalia specialibus non derogant*, which ensures that the provisions of specific legislation apply in priority sequence over general legislation, and *leges posteriores priores contrarias abrogant*, which results in implied repeal of an earlier statute by a latter one when two statutes are in conflict. These maxims aim at an interpretation that respects the intent of the legislature and are therefore based on the underlying theory of legislative supremacy, which involves the notion that a legislature cannot bind a subsequent legislature on the substance of legislation.

The interpretive strategies traditionally developed to avoid conflict have little to no application when a potential conflict involves a quasi-constitutional statute; in this instance, the court must adopt an interpretation that brings a regular statute in line with the quasi-constitutional one. How this remains consistent with legislative supremacy will be examined in Chapter 4. At this stage, it is enough to say that a quasi-constitutional statute always prevails over ordinary legislation to avoid conflict, and that "[t]he maxims *leges posteriors priores contrarias abrogant* and *generalia specialibus non derogant* have no application when resolving conflicts."[15] The two-stage approach to primacy, first developed under the *Canadian Bill of Rights*, has been adopted for the other categories of quasi-constitutional legislation, which have had a more significant impact on the interpretation of other legislation.

2) The Primacy of Human Rights and the Interpretation of Regular Statutes

How the primacy of quasi-constitutional legislation is used to interpret regular statutes in a fashion that upholds fundamental rights is most clearly demonstrated under human rights legislation. Many human rights statutes include a primacy provision. The following is an example from the Ontario *Human Rights Code*:

> Where a provision in an Act or regulation purports to require or authorize conduct that is a contravention of Part I, this Act applies and

15 *Ibid* at para 34.

> prevails unless the Act or regulation specifically provides that it is to apply despite this Act.[16]

Some of the earliest human rights statutes contained provisions essentially declaring the opposite: that they will not enlarge, restrict, or otherwise alter the provisions of any other statute.[17] Legislatures gradually repealed such limiting clauses, which no longer exist.

The Ontario *Human Rights Code* uses the term "prevails," while the heading to the provision refers to "primacy." Other provincial human rights statutes contain provisions that seek to achieve the same result with different terminology such as "paramountcy,"[18] "precedence,"[19] "supersedes,"[20] and "[n]o provision of any Act . . . may derogate."[21] The jurisprudence has not placed much weight on these differences, which suggests that these terms are largely interchangeable. In *Newfoundland (Human Rights Commission) v Newfoundland (Workplace Health, Safety and Compensation Commission)*, both the majority and dissenting justices of the Court of Appeal agreed that there was no legal significance to the distinctions between "takes precedence over," as found in Newfoundland's

---

16 *Human Rights Code*, RSO 1990, c H.19, s 47(2) [Ontario *Human Rights Code*]. A similar provision is found in British Columbia's *Human Rights Code*, RSBC 1996, c 210, s 4: "If there is a conflict between this Code and any other enactment, this Code prevails." See also British Columbia's repealed *Human Rights Act*, SBC 1984, c 22, s 22(2): "Where there is a conflict between a provision of this Act and a provision of another enactment, this Act prevails."

17 See, for example, *Alberta Human Rights Act*, SA 1966, c 39, s 2: "Nothing in this Act shall be construed as enlarging or restricting or otherwise altering the force and effect of any provision in any other Act."

18 In Manitoba, *The Human Rights Code*, CCSM c H175, s 58, provides: "Unless expressly provided otherwise herein or in another Act of the Legislature, the substantive rights and obligations in this Code are paramount over the substantive rights and obligations in every other Act of the Legislature, whether enacted before or after this Code."

19 The Newfoundland *Human Rights Act, 2010*, SNL 2010, c H-13.1, s 5, provides: "This Act shall take precedence over other Acts where they conflict with this Act whether those Acts were enacted before or after this Act comes into force." The identical provision was found in the now repealed *Human Rights Code*, RSNL 1990, c H-14, s 5.

20 See Yukon's *Human Rights Act*, RSY 2002, c 116, s 39: "This Act supersedes every other Act, whether enacted before or after this Act, unless it is expressly declared by the other Act that it shall supersede this Act." See also Nunavut's *Human Rights Act*, SNu 2003, c 12, s 5(1): "This Act supersedes every other Act or regulation, whether enacted or made before or after this Act, unless it is expressly declared by the other Act that it shall supersede this Act." The term "paramountcy" is used in the headings of both statutes.

21 *Charter of Human Rights and Freedoms*, CQLR c C-12, s 52 [Quebec *Charter*].

legislation, and "are paramount over," which is contained in Manitoba's *Human Rights Code*.[22]

The most profound difference at face value is found in the *Alberta Human Rights Act* and *The Saskatchewan Human Rights Code*: they contain provisions that expressly state that other statutes are inoperative when they purport to authorize something prohibited under these human rights statutes.[23] The Nova Scotia *Human Rights Act*, in contrast, does not include a general primacy provision, but instead contains a provision that deems discriminatory regulations "void and of no legal effect."[24]

Since the Supreme Court of Canada's decision in *Insurance Corporation of British Columbia v Heerspink*, all human rights statutes arguably have primacy even without an express primacy provision.[25] Justice Lamer (later chief justice) concurred with the majority decision of Ritchie J, but made the following *obiter* comments about the importance of human rights legislation:

> When the subject matter of a law is said to be the comprehensive statement of the "human rights" of the people living in that jurisdiction, then there is no doubt in my mind that the people of that jurisdiction have through their legislature clearly indicated that they consider that law, and the values it endeavours to buttress and protect, are, save their constitutional laws, more important than all others. Therefore, short of that legislature speaking to the contrary in express and unequivocal language in the *Code* or in some other enactment, it is intended that the *Code* supersede all other laws when conflict arises.
>
> As a result, the legal proposition *generalia specialibus non derogant* cannot be applied to such a code. Indeed the *Human Rights Code*, when in conflict with "particular and specific legislation", is not to be treated as another ordinary law of general application. It should be recognized for what it is, a fundamental law.
>
> Furthermore, as it is a public and fundamental law, no one, unless clearly authorized by law to do so, may contractually agree to suspend its operation and thereby put oneself beyond the reach of its protection.[26]

---

22 *Human Rights Commission*, above note 12 at para 18.

23 *Alberta Human Rights Act*, RSA 2000, c A-25.5, s 1(1); *The Saskatchewan Human Rights Code*, SS 1979, c S-24.1, s 44.

24 *Human Rights Act*, RSNS 1989, c 214, s 10(1).

25 [1982] 2 SCR 145 [*Heerspink*].

26 *Ibid* at 157–58.

The Court did not employ the term "quasi-constitutional" in *Heerspink*, but the decision has since been recognized as the first judicial statement on the quasi-constitutional character of human rights legislation. Professor Sullivan, for example, states that "[s]ince the Supreme Court of Canada's decision in *Insurance Corporation of British Columbia v Heerspink*, legislation enacted to protect human rights has been recognized as having a quasi-constitutional status."[27]

Justice Lamer's comments on the primacy of human rights statutes were not based on the presence of a primacy provision, but rather on their overall importance and fundamental character. This reasoning was applied by a unanimous Supreme Court of Canada three years later in *Winnipeg School Division No 1 v Craton*. Justice McIntyre, who wrote the unanimous judgment, cited Monnin CJ's judgment of the Manitoba Court of Appeal with approval:

> Human rights legislation is public and fundamental law of general application. If there is a conflict between fundamental law and other specific legislation, unless an exception is created, the human rights legislation must govern.[28]

Accordingly, although a number of human rights statutes do not contain a primacy provision, including those at the federal level, New Brunswick, Nova Scotia, Prince Edward Island, and the Northwest Territories, they nonetheless hold primacy and therefore prevail when in conflict with other statutes unless the conflicting statute provides a clear exception.[29] Even though there were earlier suggestions about the primacy of all human rights legislation, the Supreme Court of Canada's decisions in *Heerspink* and *Craton* confirmed this conclusion.[30] The Federal Court of

---

27 Sullivan, above note 3 at 497.

28 *Winnipeg School Division No 1 v Craton*, [1985] 2 SCR 150 at para 8 [*Craton* SCC]; *Craton v Winnipeg School Division No 1*, [1983] MJ No 141 at para 7 (CA) [*Craton* CA].

29 *Canadian Human Rights Act*, RSC 1985, c H-6; *Human Rights Act*, RSNB 2011, c 171; *Human Rights Act*, RSPEI 1988, c H-12; *Human Rights Act*, SNWT 2002, c 18. Claire Mummé states that "[s]ome [human rights] codes declare their supremacy and quasi-constitutionality explicitly, such that the review of other incompatible enactments can be considered mandated by legislative intent. However, some codes are silent on the issue of supremacy and have been held to be supreme and quasi-constitutional by judicial pronouncement." Mummé, above note 1 at para 5. See also Maxime St-Hilaire, "The Codification of Human Rights in Canada" (2012) 42 *Revue de droit de l'Université de Sherbrooke* 505 at para 83.

30 In *Bailey et al v Minister of National Revenue* (1980), 1 CHRR D/193 at 71 (CHRT), the Canadian Human Rights Tribunal found that the *Canadian Human Rights Act* had

Appeal explicitly recognized the primacy of the *Canadian Human Rights Act* over other statutes in *Canada (Attorney General) v Druken*, which the Supreme Court of Canada endorsed by denying leave to appeal.[31] The primacy of the *Canadian Human Rights Act* over regular legislation is now recognized and regularly invoked by the Federal Court and the Canadian Human Rights Tribunal.[32] The theoretical basis of how a statute can hold primacy in the absence of a primacy provision will be explored in Chapter 4.

The two-stage approach to primacy developed under the *Canadian Bill of Rights* is equally applicable to human rights legislation. *Heerspink* was ultimately decided by the Supreme Court of Canada at the first stage of the analysis by interpreting the *Insurance Act* in a manner consistent with the *Human Rights Code* of British Columbia to avoid conflict. The insurance company in that case cancelled Robert Heerspink's fire insurance policy at his properties because it considered him to be a "moral hazard" after he was charged with the offence of trafficking marijuana. The *Insurance Act* provided that a policy can be terminated by an insurance company with fifteen days' notice:

> 5(1) This contract may be terminated
> (a) by the insurer giving to the insured fifteen days' notice of termination by registered mail, or five days' written notice of termination personally delivered; or
> (b) by the insured at any time on request.[33]

This provision was undoubtedly more specific on the question of the termination of an insurance policy than the general right not to be discriminated against in the provision of services under the *Human Rights*

---

primacy without an explicit provision two years before the Supreme Court of Canada's decision in *Heerspink*, above note 25.

31 *Canada (Attorney General) v Druken*, [1989] 2 FC 24 at para 7 (CA) [*Druken*], aff'g (*sub nom Druken v Canada (Employment and Immigration Commission)*) (1987), 8 CHRR D/4379 (CHRT), leave to appeal to SCC refused, [1988] SCCA No 433. See also the dissenting reasons of Dickson CJ and Lamer J in *Bhinder v Canadian National Railway Co*, [1985] 2 SCR 561 at paras 18–19 [*Bhinder*]; and the dissenting reasons of McLachlin J and L'Heureux-Dubé J in *Cooper v Canada (Human Rights Commission)*, [1996] 3 SCR 854 at para 100 [*Cooper*].

32 See, for example, *Canada (Attorney General) v Uzoaba*, [1995] 2 FC 569 (TD) [*Uzoaba*]; *Franke v Canada (Canadian Armed Forces)*, [1998] CHRD No 3 at paras 753–66, aff'd (*sub nom Canada (Canadian Human Rights Commission) v Canada (Canadian Armed Forces) (re Franke)*), [1999] 3 FC 653 (TD).

33 *Insurance Act*, RSBC 1960, c 197, s 5(1).

Code. On that basis Munroe J, of the Supreme Court of British Columbia, applied the maxim *generalia specialibus non derogant* and held that "the *Insurance Act*, stat. con. 5, takes precedence over the *Human Rights Code*, s. 3, because the former is particular and specific legislation while the latter is of a more general nature and does not purport specifically to alter the provisions of said statutory condition."[34]

Justice Lamer, on the other hand, made it clear that *generalia specialibus non derogant* cannot be applied to the *Human Rights Code*, which holds primacy even with respect to more specific legislation. These comments were made in *obiter*, and the Court ultimately interpreted the *Insurance Act* in a manner that avoided conflict with the *Code*. Justice Ritchie, who wrote for the majority, agreed with Hinkson J, of the Court of Appeal, that a conflict between the *Insurance Act* and the *Code* could be avoided when the provision of the *Insurance Act* was interpreted to include the requirement that "reasonable cause exists" for the termination of the policy.[35] The term "reasonable cause" was not found in the *Insurance Act*, although the *Code* prohibited discrimination "unless reasonable cause exists for such denial or discrimination." The language of the *Code* was therefore used to guide the interpretation of the *Insurance Act* and avoid conflict.

This reasoning is now employed by lower courts and tribunals to interpret regular statutes in a manner that avoids conflicts with human rights legislation. A labour arbitrator in *Canadian Pipe Co v United Steelworkers of America*, for example, interpreted a regulation under Ontario's *Employment Standards Act*, which requires severance pay to be calculated based on the thirteen-week period prior to the layoff, as not applying to employees on sick leave during this period.[36] The case involved a plant closure and the resulting layoff of employees. The employer's position was that five employees were not entitled to termination or severance pay since they had earned nothing during the thirteen-week period before the layoff. The employees grieved this decision as inconsistent with the *Human Rights Code* because they were on sick leave during the period in question. The arbitrator interpreted the provision in the *Employment*

34 *Insurance Corporation of British Columbia v Heerspink*, 1979 CanLII 600 at para 21 (BCSC).

35 *Heerspink*, above note 25 at 153, aff'g (*sub nom Heerspink v Insurance Corp of British Columbia*) (1981), 121 DLR (3d) 464 (BCCA).

36 *Canadian Pipe Co v United Steelworkers of America, Local 8233 (Lowery Grievance)*, [1998] OLAA No 569 [*Lowery Grievance*].

Standards Act in accordance with the *Human Rights Code* by finding that the calculation based on the thirteen weeks before their layoff simply was not meant to apply to employees who did not work during this period, and only if the regulation could not be interpreted in this fashion did he find that it was inoperable, or, in his words, "ineffective."[37] The arbitrator phrased it as follows:

> So far as possible, the regulation should be interpreted in a manner consistent with the principles of the *Code*. There will be no conflict if it is interpreted as inapplicable to employees who are absent from work during the entire 13 week period to which it refers. I believe it can and should be so interpreted. If it cannot be so interpreted, however, if it must be read as providing that long term employees who are absent from work during those particular 13 weeks are to receive nothing for severance pay, then the regulation will simply be ineffective in its application to those whose absences were due to handicap. Section 47 of the *Code* makes it clear that its provisions prevail over an Act or regulation that purports to require or authorize conduct that contravenes Part I of the *Code*. If doing to the grievors what the employer says the regulation permits or requires results in discrimination on the basis of handicap, as I have found it does, then the regulation is no defence to the charge that the employer has violated the *Code* by failing to pay severance pay to the grievors.[38]

This case most clearly demonstrates the two-stage approach and the need to first try to interpret seemingly conflicting legislation consistently with human rights legislation.

In some instances a court or tribunal will depart from the requirements of a legislative scheme to ensure compliance with human rights. In *Canada (Attorney General) v Uzoaba*, the Federal Court upheld an order requiring the Correctional Service of Canada to reinstate the complainant in a position at a higher classification than the one he held at the time of the hearing. In rejecting the attorney general's argument that the human rights tribunal could not overrule the statutory scheme set out in the *Public Service Employment Act* for promotions on the basis of merit, the court held that "if the power of a Human Rights Tribunal to order a promotion in the Public Service conflicts with the *Public Service Employment Act*, I

37 *Ibid* at paras 19–24.

38 *Ibid* at para 27.

am satisfied that the provisions of the [*Canadian Human Rights*] *Act* must prevail."[39] Likewise, in *Saskatchewan (Human Rights Commission) v Ripplinger*, the Court of Appeal of Saskatchewan rejected the argument that the respondent in a human rights complaint did not discriminate against the complainant by not installing a wheelchair ramp because he followed the requirements set out in *The Uniform Building and Accessibility Standards Act*, which the respondent unsuccessfully argued, "overrules the *Code* because *UBAS* [*Uniform Building and Accessibility Standards Act*] is specific legislation while the *Code* is vague and is of a more general nature."[40]

The primacy of human rights legislation can be triggered by the duty to accommodate, which prevails over the requirements of other statutes.[41] In *Buttar v Halton Regional Police Services Board*, the Human Rights Tribunal of Ontario concluded that the duty to accommodate under the *Human Rights Code* can result in the extension of a twelve-month probationary period for a rookie police constable as established under the *Police Services Act*.[42] The plain meaning of section 44(1) of the *Police Services Act* imposed a single twelve-month probationary period:

> 44(1) A municipal police officer's probationary period begins on the day he or she is appointed and ends on the later of,
> (a) the first anniversary of the day of appointment;
> (b) the first anniversary of the day the police officer completes an initial period of training at the Ontario Police College.[43]

39 *Uzoaba*, above note 32 at para 18.

40 *Saskatchewan (Human Rights Commission) v Ripplinger* (1996), 141 Sask R 34 at paras 17 and 27 (CA). While the court found that there was no operational conflict, at para 27 it held that, "if there was, unless expressly declared by the Legislature that *UBAS* is to operate notwithstanding the *Code*, the *Code* would prevail by operation of s. 44. I note as well in s. 15 of the *UBAS* a permit issued in accordance with Part IV does not authorize any person to construct a building that does not comply with the provisions of any other Act or law."

41 Ian McKenna, "Legal Rights for Persons with Disabilities in Canada: Can the Impasse Be Resolved?" (1997–1998) 29 *Ottawa Law Review* 153 at para 33; *Abetkoff v Saskatchewan Indian Gaming Authority* (2002), 47 CHRR 322 at para 41 (Sask HRT).

42 *Buttar v Halton Regional Police Services Board*, 2013 HRTO 1578 [*Buttar*].

43 *Police Services Act*, RSO 1990, c P.15, s 44(1).

The tribunal concluded that the primacy of the *Human Rights Code* over the *Police Services Act* and the duty to accommodate a disability under the *Code* can result in an extension of the twelve-month probationary period.[44]

The primacy of human rights legislation is most apparent when there is a perceived conflict with another statute, although regular statutes are also to be interpreted consistently with human rights legislation when they are capable of more than one interpretation. In *Bell ExpressVu Limited Partnership v Rex*, the Supreme Court of Canada held that "*Charter* values" may be applied "where a statutory provision is subject to differing, but equally plausible interpretations."[45] This reasoning has been extended to include quasi-constitutional human rights legislation in addition to *Charter* values. The Ontario Divisional Court explained in *Pavon v Ontario (Director, Ontario Disability Support Program)* that the *Ontario Disability Support Program Act*, a statute providing income support and benefits to people with disabilities, is to be interpreted consistently with the *Charter* and human rights:

> given that by definition the very persons the statute is designed to support are persons with disabilities, I consider it axiomatic that the Act must be interpreted in a manner that does not discriminate on the basis of disability and in a manner that recognizes the right of persons with disabilities to reasonable accommodation. Where more than one interpretation of a provision is possible, the court should adopt the interpretation that accords with human rights and *Charter* values, rather than one that would undermine them.[46]

The Divisional Court had to choose between two plausible interpretations of a limitation period, and it chose the interpretation that was more consistent with *Charter* values and human rights.

---

44 *Buttar*, above note 42 at para 151. The tribunal ultimately found that the strict imposition of the twelve-month probationary period did not contravene the *Code* because the medical information available to the police suggested that the applicant's disability, which was preventing him from performing his duties, would not improve over time and that the applicant's disabilities could therefore not be accommodated. For the obligation to accommodate under human rights legislation in the provision of service, see, for example, *McLoughlin v British Columbia (Ministry of Environment, Lands and Parks)*, [1999] BCHRTD No 47.

45 *Bell ExpressVu Limited Partnership v Rex*, 2002 SCC 42 at para 62.

46 *Pavon v Ontario (Director, Ontario Disability Support Program)*, 2013 ONSC 4309 at para 45.

3) The Primacy of Access to Information and Privacy and the Interpretation of Regular Statutes

All provincial access-to-information and privacy statutes contain a primacy provision that holds that they prevail over any other acts. The primacy provision in Ontario's *Freedom of Information and Protection of Privacy Act* provides:

> 67(1) This Act prevails over a confidentiality provision in any other Act unless subsection (2) or the other Act specifically provides otherwise.[47]

The provision then lists specific confidentiality provisions found in other statutes that prevail.[48] Similar provisions are found in other provincial access-to-information and privacy statutes,[49] and an identical provision is found in Ontario's *Municipal Freedom of Information and Protection of Privacy Act*.[50]

The federal *Access to Information Act* does not contain an explicit primacy provision, although it has this effect because the presumption in favour of access is restricted only through a schedule to the Act referencing provisions in other statutes.[51] The *Access to Information Act* therefore has primacy over all statutes other than the specific provisions from other statutes listed in the schedule. The federal *Privacy Act* does not contain a primacy provision, but it has been recognized to have this effect by the

---

47 *Freedom of Information and Protection of Privacy Act*, RSO 1990, c F.31, s 67(1).

48 *Ibid*, s 67(2).

49 *Freedom of Information and Protection of Privacy Act*, RSA 2000, c F-25, s 5 [Alberta *Freedom of Information and Protection of Privacy Act*]; *Freedom of Information and Protection of Privacy Act*, RSBC 1996, c 165, s 79; *The Freedom of Information and Protection of Privacy Act*, SS 1990–91, c F-22.01, s 23(1); *The Freedom of Information and Protection of Privacy Act*, CCSM c F175, s 5(2); *An Act Respecting Access to Documents Held by Public Bodies and the Protection of Personal Information*, CQLR c A-2.1, s 168; *Right to Information and Protection of Privacy Act*, SNB 2009, c R-10.6, s 5(2); *Freedom of Information and Protection of Privacy Act*, SNS 1993, c 5, s 4A(1); *Freedom of Information and Protection of Privacy Act*, RSPEI 1988, c F-15.01, s 5(2); *Access to Information and Protection of Privacy Act*, SNL 2015, c A-1.2, s 7(1); *Access to Information and Protection of Privacy Act*, RSY 2002, c 1, s 4; *Access to Information and Protection of Privacy Act*, SNWT 1994, c 20, s 4; *Access to Information and Protection of Privacy Act*, SNWT (Nu) 1994, c 20, s 4(2).

50 *Municipal Freedom of Information and Protection of Privacy Act*, RSO 1990, c M.56, s 53.

51 *Access to Information Act*, RSC 1985, c A-1, s 24 and Schedule II.

Supreme Court of Canada.[52] Alberta's statute providing for the protection of personal privacy in the private sector contains a primacy provision.[53]

The primacy of access-to-information legislation has affected the interpretation of regular statutes providing for confidentiality or other forms of access to records. In *Ontario (Community Safety and Correctional Services) v Ontario (Information and Privacy Commissioner)*, the Supreme Court of Canada described the primacy of Ontario's *Freedom of Information and Protection of Privacy Act* to mean that "an institution cannot refuse to disclose a record requested under *FIPPA* [*Freedom of Information and Protection of Privacy Act*] on the basis that its governing legislation mandates that the information contained in the record be kept confidential."[54] The case involved an access request for information held in a sex offender registry established under what is known as *Christopher's Law*. The ministry refused to disclose the records under the access request on the basis that *Christopher's Law* requires the ministry and the police to keep the information contained in the registry confidential. The confidentiality provision in *Christopher's Law* read as follows:

> no person shall disclose to another person information obtained from the sex offender registry in the course of his or her duties under this Act or received in the course of his or her duties under this Act except as provided by this Act.[55]

The Supreme Court of Canada endorsed the interpretation adopted by the information and privacy commissioner of Ontario, who considered the provision a restriction on disclosure by the police in the course of their duties under that Act, and not as limiting any right to access under the *Freedom of Information and Protection of Privacy Act*.[56] The practical effect of this decision is that *Christopher's Law* prohibits officials from disclosing information from the sex offender registry in the course of their duties, and it is an offence if they do so; however, some information may be

---

52 *Dagg v Canada (Minister of Finance)*, [1997] 2 SCR 403 at para 48 [*Dagg*]; *HJ Heinz Co of Canada Ltd v Canada (Attorney General)*, [2006] 1 SCR 441 at para 26 [*HJ Heinz Co*]. Both La Forest J in *Dagg* and Deschamps J in *HJ Heinz Co* used the term "paramount."

53 *Personal Information Protection Act*, SA 2003, c P-6.5, s 4(6).

54 *Ontario (Community Safety and Correctional Services) v Ontario (Information and Privacy Commissioner)*, 2014 SCC 31 at para 11 [*Ontario (Community Safety and Correctional Services)*].

55 *Christopher's Law (Sex Offender Registry), 2000*, SO 2000, c 1, s 10(1).

56 *Ontario (Community Safety and Correctional Services)*, above note 54 at para 16.

obtained under an access-to-information request because of the primacy of access-to-information legislation.

4) The Primacy of Language Rights and the Interpretation of Regular Statutes

Several Canadian language rights statutes contain a primacy provision. The federal *Official Languages Act* contains a primacy provision that allows it to prevail over all other federal statutes and regulations in the event of an inconsistency, except the *Human Rights Act*.[57] Oddly, as previously noted, the federal *Human Rights Act* does not have a primacy provision. The primacy provision in the *Official Languages Act* of New Brunswick holds that it prevails in the event of a conflict with another act, with the exception of the *Education Act* and any measures to promote the equality of the two official linguistic communities.[58] The primacy provision in Nunavut's *Official Languages Act* similarly provides that it prevails when there is a conflict with any act other than the *Human Rights Act*.[59] The language rights statutes in the three territories contain a clause that deems any statutes or regulations not published in both English and French to be of no force and effect.[60]

The remaining provincial language rights statutes do not have an explicit primacy provision, although they arguably have this status given their fundamental quasi-constitutional character. In *Thibodeau v Air Canada*, the Federal Court suggested that the *Official Languages Act* holds primacy over regular statutes not only because of its primacy provision, but because it is quasi-constitutional:

> Section 82 of the OLA [federal *Official Languages Act*] provides that in the event of any inconsistency between Parts I to V and any other Act of Parliament or regulation thereunder, those Parts prevail to the extent of the inconsistency . . . . But the OLA is a quasi-constitutional statute and by its very nature prevails over other legislation.[61]

---

57 *Official Languages Act*, RSC, 1985, c 31 (4th Supp), s 82(1).

58 *Official Languages Act*, SNB 2002, c O-0.5, ss 3(1) & 3(2).

59 *Official Languages Act*, SNu 2008, c 10, s 2(2) [Nunavut *Official Languages Act*].

60 *Languages Act*, RSY 2002, c 133, s 13; *Official Languages Act*, RSNWT 1988, c O-1, s 15(2); Nunavut *Official Languages Act*, above note 59, s 7(1).

61 *Thibodeau v Air Canada*, 2005 FC 1156 at para 81 [*Thibodeau* FC], aff'd *(sub nom Air Canada v Thibodeau)*, 2007 FCA 115.

This conclusion was also reached by the information and privacy commissioner of Ontario in *Re: Workplace Safety and Insurance Board* while considering Ontario's *French Language Services Act*, which does not contain a primacy provision:

> Unlike the *Code*, the FLSA [*French Language Services Act*] does not contain a clause that gives it primacy over other legislation. However, given that the Court of Appeal has clearly stated that 'language rights are to be treated as fundamental human rights,' it logically follows . . .[62]

The same reasoning applies to other language rights statutes.

The primacy of language rights legislation has affected the interpretation of other legislation. In *Re: Workplace Safety and Insurance Board*, for example, the information and privacy commissioner of Ontario found that an institution that is covered by the *French Language Services Act* has to provide requesters with their personal information in French in response to their access requests, even if the information was not held in French.[63] Under the *Freedom of Information and Protection of Privacy Act*, an institution is required to provide a copy of the requester's personal information only in its existing form or in a comprehensible form.[64] In considering a request for access to personal information in French, the commissioner extended the reasoning from the Supreme Court of Canada's 2006 decision in *Tranchemontagne v Ontario (Director, Disability Support Program)*, that an administrative tribunal cannot decline to apply the *Human Rights Code* unless its enabling statute grants it the authority. In so doing it substituted human rights legislation with the *French Language Services Act* and thereby interpreted the words "comprehensible format" to mean "in the French language."[65]

5) The Primacy of Quasi-constitutional Legislation and Private Law

One advantage of human rights statutes over the *Canadian Bill of Rights* is that they provide protection in both the private and public spheres,

62 *Order PO-2696; Workplace Safety and Insurance Board*, [2008] OIPC No 144 at para 71 [*Order PO-2696*].

63 *Ibid.*

64 *Freedom of Information and Protection of Privacy Act*, above note 47, ss 48(3) & (4).

65 *Order PO-2696*, above note 62 at paras 66–70; *Tranchemontagne v Ontario (Director, Disability Support Program)*, 2006 SCC 14 at paras 24–25 [*Tranchemontagne* SCC].

albeit in a defined group of social areas where discrimination is prohibited, for example, employment, services, accommodations, vocational associations, and the formation of contracts. Beginning in *Heerspink*, the Supreme Court of Canada has held that parties cannot contract out of human rights legislation to put a person "beyond the reach of its protection."[66] Human rights legislation has this effect despite not containing an "explicit restriction on such contracting out."[67]

In *Ontario Human Rights Commission v Etobicoke*, the Supreme Court of Canada rejected the argument that a mandatory retirement condition in a collective agreement should be considered a *bona fide* occupational qualification and requirement simply because it was agreed upon in good faith during statutorily required collective bargaining; it did so because this approach would permit parties to contract out of human rights.[68] Instead, the Court found that the consequence of attempting to contract out of human rights legislation is that "contracts having such effect are void, as contrary to public policy."[69] Thus, for example, provisions in collective agreements that authorize the termination of employment because of a specified period of continuous absence from work will not be enforced when absence is due to a disability.[70] Similar reasoning applies to discrimination policies of employers that are not *bona fide* occupational requirements, regardless of whether such policies result in direct or adverse effect discrimination.[71] At the same time, parties to a contract can "raise and further protect the human rights of the people affected," since human rights legislation is viewed as "a floor beneath which the parties cannot contract out."[72] A provision in a contract or collective agreement

66 *Heerspink*, above note 25 at 158.

67 *Ontario (Human Rights Commission) v Etobicoke (Borough)*, [1982] 1 SCR 202 at 213 [*Etobicoke*].

68 *Ibid*. See also *Whitehouse v Yukon*, [2000] YHRBAD No 2 at para 29.

69 *Etobicoke*, above note 67.

70 *Glengarry Industries/Chromalox Components v United Steelworkers of America, Local 6976 (Kincaid Grievance)*, [1989] OLAA No 2; *Ontario Nurses' Assn v Etobicoke General Hospital* (1993), 14 OR (3d) 40 (Div Ct); *Alcan Rolled Products Co v United Steelworkers of America, Local 343 (Discharge Grievance)*, [1996] OLAA No 44 at paras 86–98; *Lowery Grievance*, above note 36 at para 24.

71 *Bhinder*, above note 31; *Ontario Human Rights Commission and O'Malley v Simpsons-Sears Ltd*, [1985] 2 SCR 536 [*O'Malley*].

72 *Newfoundland Association of Public Employees v Newfoundland (Green Bay Health Care Centre)*, [1996] 2 SCR 3 at para 26 [*Green Bay Health Care Centre*]. See also *University of Alberta Non-Academic Staff Assn v University of Alberta*, [1997] AJ No 803 at paras 75–76 (QB).

that covenants not to discriminate does not, however, transform a dispute from a human rights issue to a contractual dispute or a breach of the collective agreement; it therefore does not oust the jurisdiction of a human rights tribunal.[73]

The Supreme Court of Canada has attributed the inability to contract out of human rights to its quasi-constitutional status. In *Newfoundland Association of Public Employees v Newfoundland (Green Bay Health Care Centre)*, Major J explained that "[t]he rationale for the rule against contracting out of human rights legislation is in part because of its quasi-constitutional status." He further reasoned that it is to prevent "the exploitation of inequality of bargaining power," because "those without bargaining power might be coerced or forced to give up their rights under human rights legislation."[74]

Just as the courts have held that parties cannot contract out of human rights legislation and cannot enforce policies that discriminate directly or indirectly, they have reached the same conclusion about language rights statutes because of their quasi-constitutional status. Since the *Official Languages Act* applies to Air Canada, the Federal Court, in *Thibodeau v Air Canada*, found the airline could not bargain out of language rights in the collective agreement. Justice Beaudry quoted with approval the following statement from the commissioner of official languages of Canada:

> The OLA is quasi-constitutional legislation and as such the public's rights are not negotiable. The respondents should not be required to negotiate the public's language rights with the union. They must persuade the union representatives that the seniority provisions cannot contravene the duty to provide services in both official languages on designated flights. They must clearly state that the assignment of bilingual flight attendants to designated bilingual flights is not negotiable.[75]

Courts have accordingly found that the right to communicate with and receive services in the official language of one's choice prevails over a work rule or a collective agreement.[76]

---

73 *Cadillac Fairview Corp v Saskatchewan (Human Rights Commission)*, [1999] SJ No 217 at para 15 (CA), leave to appeal to SCC refused, [1999] SCCA No 492.

74 *Green Bay Health Care Centre*, above note 72 at para 21. See also *Dickason v University of Alberta*, [1992] SCJ No 76 at para 36.

75 *Thibodeau* FC, above note 61 at para 16.

76 *Ibid* at para 101; *Collins v VIA Rail Canada Inc*, 2009 FC 860 at para 80; *Bonner v VIA Rail Canada Inc*, 2009 FC 857 at para 78; *Seesahai v VIA Rail Canada Inc*, 2009 FC 859

The primacy of quasi-constitutional legislation also has an impact in the realm of private international law. When the Supreme Court of Canada expanded the common law rule to allow for the recognition and enforcement of foreign orders other than final money judgments in *Pro Swing Inc v Elta Golf Inc*, it recognized that it had to move away from the traditional common law rule that restricted courts from considering the substantive or procedural law of the foreign jurisdiction that issued the final judgment, to ensure that non-money judgments "do not disturb the structure and integrity of the Canadian legal system."[77] This requires, at the very least, consideration of public policy, which is comprised of constitutional and quasi-constitutional values. The Court found that a consent decree from an Ohio court was problematic "in light of the quasi-constitutional status attributed to privacy," because it required the disclosure of "all credit card receipts, accounts receivable, contracts, etc.," and it therefore did not accede to the request to enforce the consent decree.[78] Although privacy rights were specifically implicated in *Pro Swing Inc v Elta Golf Inc*, the case speaks more broadly about the need to take into account quasi-constitutional laws in efforts to enforce foreign judgments in Canadian courts, which clearly prevail over the application of foreign judgments and the foreign law.

More recently, in *Douez v Facebook, Inc*, the Supreme Court of Canada dealt with quasi-constitutional rights in the context of a forum selection and choice of law clause.[79] A resident of British Columbia brought an action against Facebook in that province for infringement of her privacy rights under the provincial *Privacy Act* because it used her name and profile picture in advertisements without her consent. Facebook sought to have the action stayed because its terms of use include a forum selection and choice of law clause requiring that disputes be resolved in California according to California law.

---

at para 81; *Norton v VIA Rail Canada Inc*, 2009 FC 704 at para 77; *Temple v VIA Rail Canada Inc*, 2009 FC 858 at para 79.

77 *Pro Swing Inc v Elta Golf Inc*, 2006 SCC 52 at para 15.

78 *Ibid* at paras 59–64. In a comparative analysis of privacy laws in Canada, the United States, and Europe, Avner Levin and Mary Jo Nicholson conclude that "Canada and the US have vastly different attitudes and motivations when it comes to protecting privacy." Avner Levin & Mary Jo Nicholson, "Privacy Law in the United States, the EU and Canada: The Allure of the Middle Ground" (2005) 2 *University of Ottawa Law & Technology Journal* 357 at para 49.

79 *Douez v Facebook, Inc*, 2017 SCC 33.

The Court was divided on the issue. Three justices, including Karakatsanis J, Wagner J, and Gascon J, found that the forum selection clause was enforceable because the *Privacy Act* did not override it, but held that it should not be enforced at the second stage of the analysis, which requires consideration of "all the circumstances," including public policy considerations such as the quasi-constitutional nature of privacy rights. In making this determination, they explicitly referred to Canadian courts having a greater interest in adjudicating cases involving "constitutional and quasi-constitutional rights because these rights play an essential role in a free and democratic society and embody key Canadian values," and the "inherent public good in Canadian courts deciding these types of claims."[80] Justice Abella concurred with the outcome but instead found that the foreign selection clause was not enforceable; she similarly invoked the quasi-constitutional status of privacy rights in support of her conclusion.[81] The dissent, which included McLachlin CJ and Côté J, believed that the principles of private international law justified the enforcement of forum selection clauses and that "strong cause" for not enforcing the forum selection clause in the circumstances was not shown. The dissent did not mention the quasi-constitutional status of privacy rights.

6) The Primacy of Quasi-constitutional Legislation and the Interpretive Mandate in the Commonwealth

The primacy of Canadian quasi-constitutional legislation can be considered alongside developments in other Commonwealth jurisdictions where courts are increasingly using statutory rights instruments to review other legislation. The *Human Rights Act* in the United Kingdom, the *New Zealand Bill of Rights Act*, the *Human Rights Act* of the Australian Capital Territory, and the *Charter of Human Rights and Responsibilities Act* of the state of Victoria are often collectively referred to as the new Commonwealth, parliamentary, or weak-form model of constitutionalism and judicial review.[82] These statutes do not provide a strong-form model of rights protection and judicial review as under the American

80 *Ibid* at para 58.

81 *Ibid* at paras 80 and 104.

82 *Human Rights Act, 1998* (UK), c 42 [UK *Human Rights Act*]; *New Zealand Bill of Rights Act 1990* (NZ), 1990/109 [New Zealand *Bill of Rights*]; *Human Rights Act 2004* (ACT), A2004-5 [ACT *Human Rights Act*]; *Charter of Human Rights and Responsibilities Act 2006* (Vic), Act No 43 of 2006 [Victoria *Charter*].

Bill of Rights; however, they influence other legislation far beyond that found in the common law approach to rights protections traditionally followed in the Commonwealth. They do so in a manner that displays some similarities to the interpretive approach to the primacy of Canadian quasi-constitutional legislation. Several terms that are generally used synonymously have been employed to capture the developments in the Commonwealth: these include "new Commonwealth model,"[83] "parliamentary bill of rights model,"[84] "the model of democratic dialogue,"[85] and the "weak-form" model of judicial review.[86]

Although the United Kingdom does not have a written constitution in the American sense, the courts have begun to recognize certain statutes and common law principles as constitutional. A shortlist of statutes includes the *Petition of Right 1628*, the *Bill of Rights 1689*, the *Act of Settlement 1701*, the *Act of Union 1707*, the *Treaty of Union with Ireland Act 1800*, the *Representation of the People Acts 1832–84*, the *European Communities Act 1972*, the *Human Rights Act 1998*, the *Scotland Act 1998*, the *Northern Ireland Act 1998*, the *Constitutional Reform Act 2005*, and the *Government of Wales Act 2006*. By some accounts the *Human Rights Act* is the "cornerstone" of the UK's constitution.[87] The weak-form model of judicial review in the Commonwealth, which includes constitutional statutes of the United Kingdom, provides an interesting comparison for quasi-constitutional legislation in Canada as these statutes display a graduated type of legal system involving statutes that were enacted through the regular legislative process.

Some people consider the *Charter* as the Canadian example of the weak-form model in the Commonwealth because the notwithstanding

---

83 Stephen Gardbaum, "The New Commonwealth Model of Constitutionalism" (2001) 49 *American Journal of Comparative Law* 707.

84 Janet Hiebert, "Parliamentary Bill of Rights: An Alternative Model?" (2006) 69 *Modern Law Review* 7.

85 Alison Young, *Parliamentary Sovereignty and the Human Rights Act* (Oxford: Hart, 2009) ch 5. Kent Roach also refers to "dialogic judicial review." Kent Roach, "Dialogic Judicial Review and Its Critics" (2004) 23 *Supreme Court Law Review* (2d) 49.

86 Mark Tushnet, "Alternative Forms of Judicial Review" (2003) 101 *Michigan Law Review* 2781. Jeremy Waldron refers to "weak judicial review." Jeremy Waldron, "The Core of the Case Against Judicial Review" (2006) 115 *Yale Law Journal* 1346.

87 Vernon Bogdanor, *The New British Constitution* (Oxford: Hart, 2009) at xiii. The UK *Human Rights Act*, above note 82, was described by Lord Irvine of Lairg as occupying "a special place in our programme of reform." Lord Irvine of Lairg, *Human Rights, Constitutional Law and the Development of the English Legal System: Selective Essays* (Oxford: Hart, 2003) at 97.

clause in section 33 allows Parliament to override the judicial authority to review legislation.[88] However, since the *Charter* is constitutionally entrenched — in contrast to the statutory form of the rights regimes that constitute the weak-form model in the Commonwealth — there has been some disagreement over whether the *Charter* properly fits within the weak or strong-form model of judicial review. Jeremy Waldron views the *Charter* as falling within the strong-form model because of the infrequent use of the notwithstanding clause.[89] The frequency that the notwithstanding clause is invoked, however, is a practical consideration related to political culture. It does not speak to the theoretical question of whether the *Charter* can be properly classified as an example of the weak-form model.

More important than the frequency that the notwithstanding clause is used is the fact that the *Charter* embodies a form of judicial supremacy that is balanced with what Janet Hiebert refers to as "temporary but renewable" political dissent.[90] Others view it as balancing judicial supremacy with legislative supremacy.[91] As such, the *Charter* can be more appropriately described as being based on the doctrine of judicial supremacy with a mechanism that allows for incursions of legislative supremacy. This represents a compromise of sorts between the two purer forms of parliamentary and judicial supremacy, but still differs from the weak-form model, which seeks a form of judicial review in statutory form that does not outright adopt judicial and constitutional supremacy. For this reason, quasi-constitutional statutes in Canada, because of their statutory form, are more appropriately characterized as the Canadian example of the weak-form model.

---

88 See, for example, Mark Tushnet, *Weak Courts, Strong Rights: Judicial Review and Social Welfare Rights in Comparative Constitutional Law* (Princeton, NJ: Princeton University Press, 2008) at 31 [Tushnet, *Weak Courts, Strong Rights*]; Jeffrey Goldsworthy, "Homogenizing Constitutions" (2003) 23 *Oxford Journal of Legal Studies* 483 at 483; Jeffrey Goldsworthy, "Judicial Review, Legislative Override, and Democracy" (2003) 38 *Wake Forest Law Review* 451 at 454–59; Stephen Gardbaum, *The New Commonwealth Model of Constitutionalism: Theory and Practice* (Cambridge: Cambridge University Press, 2013) at 27 [Gardbaum, *The New Commonwealth Model of Constitutionalism*].

89 Jeremy Waldron, "The Core of the Case Against Judicial Review" (2006) 115 *Yale Law Journal* 1346 at 1356–57.

90 Janet Hiebert, "Rights-Vetting in New Zealand and Canada" (2005) 3 *New Zealand Journal of Public and International Law* 63 at 64.

91 Barbara Billingsley, "Section 33: The *Charter*'s Sleeping Giant" (2002) 21 *Windsor Yearbook of Access to Justice* 331; Richard Albert, "Advisory Review: The Reincarnation of the Notwithstanding Clause" (2008) 45 *Alberta Law Review* 1037 at paras 1 and 6.

The primary characteristic of the weak-form model of judicial review is what Mark Tushnet calls the "interpretative mandate," whereby statutes are interpreted in accordance with rights-protecting statutes.[92] Rather than containing primacy provisions, the Commonwealth statutes refer to "interpreting" or "reading" other legislation to make it compatible with human rights.[93] For example, the UK's *Human Rights Act*, section 3, provides that "[s]o far as it is possible to do so, primary legislation and subordinate legislation must be read and given effect in a way which is compatible with the Convention rights."

The interpretive mandate was devised as a form of judicial review that is not conflated to judicial supremacy.[94] Tushnet observes that the interpretive mandate as a form of judicial review is most clearly revealed in situations where the interpretation of a statute in accordance with rights appears to be a radical departure from the face-value wording of the statute.[95] In other words, the interpretation of a regular statute that departs radically from a conventional interpretation may be as contentious as striking down the statute.[96] The 2004 case of *Ghaidan v Mendoza* from the House of Lords is an example. Lord Nicholls described the extent of the interpretive mandate under the UK *Human Rights Act* in quite expansive terms:

> Section 3 enables language to be interpreted restrictively or expansively. But section 3 goes further than this. It is also apt to require a court to read in words which change the meaning of the enacted legislation, so as to make it Convention-compliant. In other words, the intention of Parliament in enacting section 3 was that, to an extent bounded only

---

92 Tushnet, *Weak Courts, Strong Rights*, above note 88 at 25–26.

93 UK *Human Rights Act*, above note 82, s 3; New Zealand *Bill of Rights*, above note 82, s 6; ACT *Human Rights Act*, above note 82, s 30; Victoria *Charter*, above note 82, s 6. The preliminary provision of the *Civil Code of Québec*, CQLR c C-1991, may be comparable: "The *Civil Code of Québec*, in harmony with the *Charter of human rights and freedoms* (chapter C-12) and the general principles of law, governs persons, relations between persons, and property." In *Quebec (Commission des droits de la personne et des droits de la jeunesse) v Communauté urbaine de Montréal*, 2004 SCC 30 [*Larocque*], LeBel J, for a unanimous Supreme Court of Canada, stated at para 20 that "the *Code*, as jus commune of Quebec, must be interpreted in harmony with the *Quebec Charter*."

94 Janet Hiebert, "New Constitutional Ideas: But Can New Parliamentary Models Resist Judicial Dominance When Interpreting Rights?" (2004) 82 *Texas Law Review* 1963 at 1965.

95 Tushnet, *Weak Courts, Strong Rights*, above note 88 at 25.

96 TRS Allan, *The Sovereignty of Law: Freedom, Constitution and Common Law* (Oxford: Oxford University Press, 2013) at 41.

> by what is "possible", a court can modify the meaning, and hence the effect, of primary and secondary legislation.[97]

Lord Steyn went as far as referring to the interpretive mandate as allowing a court to "read in and read down . . . supply missing words, so long as they are consistent with the fundamental features of the legislative scheme," even if it involves stretching the interpretation to "almost (but not quite) to breaking point."[98] This approach contains some notable similarities to the methods used to interpret regular statutes consistently with quasi-constitutional statutes in Canada.

The rights statutes in the United Kingdom, Australia, and New Zealand, and the courts that interpret and apply them, differ in their application of the interpretive mandate, and while there are broad similarities across the Commonwealth, one cannot refer to a completely unified approach. In contrast to the expansive effect of the interpretive mandate in the United Kingdom, the courts in New Zealand are generally viewed as having taken a more restrained approach.[99] Likewise, despite some obvious similarities, it has been suggested that constitutional statutes in the United Kingdom and quasi-constitutional legislation in Canada constitute distinct categories.[100] An apparent difference is that while the courts in Canada have adopted both a broad, liberal, and purposive interpretation of quasi-constitutional legislation, and have confirmed their influence over regular statutes because of their primacy, courts in the United Kingdom are developing the latter in the form of the interpretive mandate but they have rejected the former function. Despite some early suggestions from the courts that constitutional statutes in the United Kingdom should be interpreted "generously and purposively,"[101] this approach was rejected by the Supreme Court in *Imperial Tobacco Ltd v The Lord Advocate (Scotland)* and *Attorney General v National Assembly for Wales Commission*.[102] Second, quasi-constitutional status in Canada is

---

97 *Ghaidan v Mendoza*, [2004] UKHL 30 at para 32.

98 *Ibid* at para 67.

99 Gardbaum, *The New Commonwealth Model of Constitutionalism*, above note 88 at 145. See, especially, *Quilter v Attorney-General*, [1997] NZCA 207. The Court of Appeal subsequently applied the *New Zealand Bill of Rights Act* with more vigour in the 2000 case of *R v Poumako*, [2000] NZCA 69.

100 Vanessa MacDonnell, "A Theory of Quasi-constitutionality" (2016) 53 *Osgoode Hall Law Journal* 508 at 512.

101 *Robinson v Secretary of State for Northern Ireland*, [2002] UKHL 32 at para 11.

102 *Imperial Tobacco Ltd v The Lord Advocate (Scotland)*, [2012] UKSC 61 at para 14; *Attorney General v National Assembly for Wales Commission*, [2012] UKSC 53 at para 80;

currently limited generally to statutes that uphold fundamental rights, whereas the category of constitutional statutes in the United Kingdom also captures statutes that establish "the legal relationship between citizen and State in some general, overarching manner."[103]

B. THE PRIMACY OF QUASI-CONSTITUTIONAL LEGISLATION AND DECLARATIONS OF INOPERABILITY

Despite the influence of quasi-constitutional legislation in the interpretive exercise, there are instances when even a strained interpretation of a statute cannot bring its interpretation in line with a quasi-constitutional one. Under some circumstances courts and tribunals can proceed to declare a conflicting provision in a regular statute inoperable or devise a comparable remedy. This remedy was first developed under the *Canadian Bill of Rights*, although the Supreme Court of Canada's adoption of a restrictive interpretation of that statute resulted in few instances of conflict. The influence of the *Canadian Bill of Rights* diminished further with the patriation of the Constitution. Its relevance today is primarily with two rights not replicated in the *Charter*. Declarations of inoperability have had a more widespread impact under human rights legislation, particularly since the Court endorsed a broad, liberal, and purposive interpretation and held that all administrative tribunals can presumptively interpret and apply human rights. The Court's emphasis on the need for flexibility when devising remedies for quasi-constitutional legislation has resulted in remedies similar to declarations of inoperability, which can be seen under access-to-information, privacy, and language rights legislation. The significance of declarations of inoperability under quasi-constitutional legislation is most apparent when compared to developments in other Commonwealth jurisdictions, where the range of remedies to address a statute conflicting with a fundamental right is more limited.

1) Declarations of Inoperability Under the *Canadian Bill of Rights*

As previously observed, the first use of a quasi-constitutional statute to render a conflicting statute inoperable was in the 1970 *Drybones* decision,

---

Farrah Ahmed & Adam Perry, "Constitutional Statutes" (2017) 37 *Oxford Journal of Legal Studies* 461 at 465.

103 *Thoburn v Sunderland City Council*, [2002] EWHC 195 at para 62 (Admin) [*Thoburn*].

where a unanimous Supreme Court of Canada held that the *Canadian Bill of Rights* rendered a section of the *Indian Act* inoperable. Given that an Indigenous person convicted under the *Indian Act* for being intoxicated off reserve was subject to a harsher penalty than a non-Indigenous person was under the territorial liquor ordinance, the Supreme Court of Canada found that Drybones was denied equality before the law under the *Canadian Bill of Rights*. Since the conflict between these two statutes was irreconcilable through interpretation, paragraph 94(b) of the *Indian Act* was declared inoperative and Drybones's conviction was overturned.[104]

The infrequent use of this remedy was not a repudiation of the principles established in *Drybones*, but rather a result of a narrow and frozen interpretation that reduces the likelihood of conflict with other legislation.[105] The courts, therefore, through a restrictive interpretive approach, consistently managed to bypass this important function of the *Canadian Bill of Rights*.

The continued relevance of the *Canadian Bill of Rights* following the constitutional entrenchment of the *Charter* is with respect to the two rights not replicated in the *Charter*. These include the right to property with "the right not to be deprived thereof except by due process of law," and the guarantee to a fair hearing whenever a person's rights are to be determined. Similar quasi-constitutional protections to property and a fair hearing outside the criminal context are also found in the *Alberta Bill of Rights* and the Quebec *Charter*.[106]

These quasi-constitutional protections of procedural fairness in the administrative law context are significant. *Charter* protections of procedural fairness are limited to cases involving liberty or security of the person under section 7,[107] or where one is charged with an offence and section 11(d) is triggered, which rarely applies in the administrative context.[108]

In a partial revitalization of the *Canadian Bill of Rights*, the courts began to declare provisions in other statutes that violated these procedural

---

104 *Drybones*, above note 5; *Indian Act*, RSC 1970, c I-6, s 94(b).

105 For examples of cases where a provision was held inoperable due to conflict with the *Canadian Bill of Rights*, see, especially, *Singh v Canada (Minister of Employment and Immigration)*, [1985] 1 SCR 177 [*Singh*]; *MacBain v Lederman*, [1985] 1 FC 856 (CA) [*MacBain*]; *R v Hayden*, [1983] MJ No 27 (CA), leave to appeal to SCC refused, [1983] SCCA No 210; *R v Benson*, [1984] 3 CNLR 134 (Sask Prov Ct).

106 *Alberta Bill of Rights*, RSA 2000, c A-14, s 1(a); Quebec *Charter*, above note 21, ss 6, 7, and 23.

107 See, for example, *Charkaoui v Canada (Citizenship and Immigration)*, 2007 SCC 9.

108 See, for example, *Guindon v Canada*, 2015 SCC 41.

safeguards inoperable.[109] In *Singh v Canada (Minister of Employment and Immigration)*, Beetz J, who wrote on behalf of two other justices, found that the refugee determination process in the *Immigration Act* violated the right to a fair hearing under the *Canadian Bill of Rights* because refugee status could be denied without a hearing. He therefore held that the offending provisions were inoperable because of their conflict with the *Canadian Bill of Rights*.[110] In comparison, Wilson J, who also wrote for two other justices, found that the provisions were invalid under section 7 of the *Charter* and thus of no force and effect.[111] Justice Beetz cautioned that the *Canadian Bill of Rights* should not be allowed to "fall into neglect" because of the additional rights it protects over the *Charter*, which are preserved under section 26 of the *Charter* as "any other rights or freedoms that exist in Canada."[112]

Even more significant than *Singh* is *MacBain v Lederman*, where provisions of the *Human Rights Act*, which allowed the Human Rights Commission to select the members of the tribunal, were successfully challenged under the *Canadian Bill of Rights* as giving rise to a reasonable apprehension of bias.[113] Unlike in *Singh*, the provisions in this case could not be challenged under section 7 of the *Charter* because the right to "life, liberty and security of the person" was not implicated. Most notably, as will be discussed in detail below, this appears to be the only case where a court relied on one quasi-constitutional statute to declare provisions in another quasi-constitutional statute inoperable. Since the challenge was to the *Human Rights Act*, this case leaves little doubt that the *Canadian Bill of Rights* remains relevant and able to render conflicting provisions in other statutes inoperable, despite both the restrictive interpretation it has received and the entrenchment of the *Charter*. As a result of *Singh* and *MacBain*, the Quebec Court of Appeal in *Air Canada c Canada (Procureure générale)* observed that "[s]ince *Drybones*, and even more so since the adoption of the *Canadian Charter of Rights and Freedoms* in 1982, the courts have not

109 *MacBain*, above note 105. See also *Northwest Territories v Public Service Alliance of Canada*, 2001 FCA 162 at para 60. Lorne Sossin similarly observed that "[a]fter the enactment of the *Charter*, the *Bill of Rights* seemed to be granted a new lease on life by the Supreme Court of Canada." Lorne Sossin, "The Quasi-revival of the *Canadian Bill of Rights* and Its Implications for Administrative Law" (2004) 25 *Supreme Court Law Review* (2d) 191 at 196.

110 *Singh*, above note 105 at paras 116–17 and 125.

111 *Ibid* at 74–75.

112 *Ibid* at paras 84–85.

113 *MacBain*, above note 105.

hesitated to invoke the *Canadian Bill of Rights* to declare inoperative any contrary legislative provisions enacted by the Canadian Parliament."[114]

The procedural protections for property rights in the *Canadian Bill of Rights* relate to an adjudicative process that may affect personal property. In *Kazemi Estate v Islamic Republic of Iran*, LeBel J explained that the process "guarantees fairness in the context of a hearing before a Canadian court or a tribunal," but "does not create a self-standing right to a fair hearing where the law does not [otherwise] allow for an adjudicative process."[115]

In terms of the specifics of the procedural guarantees, Major J held in *Authorson v Canada (Attorney General)* that "the *Bill of Rights* guarantees notice and some opportunity to contest a governmental deprivation of property rights only in the context of an adjudication of that person's rights and obligations before a court or tribunal."[116] The right to property and due process under the *Canadian Bill of Rights*, however, cannot be used to challenge the passage of legislation, since "due process does not require . . . notice and a hearing before Parliament prior to the passage of expropriative legislation."[117] The only procedural guarantee in the passage of legislation that may affect the right to property is the regular parliamentary process of three readings and royal assent, and the *Canadian Bill of Rights* cannot be used to impose additional procedural safeguards.[118]

Ocean Port Hotel Ltd v British Columbia (General Manager, Liquor Control and Licensing Branch) further highlights the importance of quasi-constitutional procedural rights.[119] This case is not about the *Canadian Bill of Rights*, although it displays the difference between common law procedural protections and quasi-constitutional ones; the former can be easily displaced by statute whereas the latter require the legislature to invoke a clear override to their primacy.[120] The Supreme Court of Canada therefore distinguished common law procedural principles in this case to the situation it addressed in *2747-3174 Québec Inc v Quebec (Régie des permis d'alcool)*, where it was dealing with the Quebec *Charter of Human Rights and Freedoms*, recognized as quasi-constitutional and containing a

114 *Air Canada c Canada (Procureure générale)*, [2003] RJQ 322 at para 43 (CA). [English translation in Sossin, above note 109 at 207–8].

115 *Kazemi Estate v Islamic Republic of Iran*, 2014 SCC 62 at para 116.

116 *Authorson v Canada (Attorney General)*, [2003] 2 SCR 40 at para 42.

117 *Ibid* at para 12.

118 *Ibid* at para 37.

119 [2001] 2 SCR 781 [*Ocean Port Hotel*].

120 Sossin, above note 109 at 197.

provision that provides a "full and equal, public and fair hearing by an independent and impartial tribunal."[121]

Aside from these two rights, the Federal Court, in *Bear v Canada*, also suggested that other rights contained in the *Canadian Bill of Rights* may be relied upon in circumstances that precede the patriation of the Constitution, since the *Charter* does not have retroactive effect.[122] The alleged discrimination in the *Bear* case crystallized in 1966, when the applicant could have been allowed to participate in the Canada Pension Plan at its inception, long prior to the entrenchment of the *Charter* and the coming into force of section 15(1) in 1985. Although this decision was reversed by the Federal Court of Appeal on the basis that the jurisprudence following *Drybones* established that the *Canadian Bill of Rights* did not guarantee equal benefit of the law, it did not reject the finding that the *Canadian Bill of Rights* can be used for situations that predate the *Charter*.[123] Finally, the other rights protected by the *Canadian Bill of Rights* could also be relied upon in the unlikely scenario that Parliament invokes the section 33 notwithstanding clause of the *Charter* but does not interfere with the primacy of the *Canadian Bill of Rights*.

The same reasoning has been applied to the *Alberta Bill of Rights*, which is almost identical to the *Canadian Bill of Rights*.[124] The continued relevance of this statute is accordingly practically confined to the same two categories of rights. This in itself is significant because it extends these rights to the provincial level in Alberta while the *Canadian Bill of Rights* is limited to the federal government. The courts declare provisions inoperable when they conflict with the *Alberta Bill of Rights*. In *Lavallee v Alberta (Securities Commission)*, the Alberta Court of Queen's Bench found that a provision in the *Alberta Securities Act* that made it mandatory for the Alberta Securities Commission to admit all relevant evidence at a hearing without regard to whether it should be excluded in some cases, could in some limited instances deprives individuals of the right to enjoyment of property without due process of law. The court therefore declared the provision inoperable "only where the admission of relevant evidence would violate due process of law."[125]

121 *Ocean Port Hotel*, above note 119 at para 28; *2747-3174 Québec Inc v Quebec (Régie des permis d'alcool)*, [1996] 3 SCR 919; Quebec *Charter*, above note 21, s 23.

122 *Bear v Canada (Attorney General)*, 2001 FCT 1192.

123 *Bear v Canada (Attorney General)*, 2003 FCA 40 at paras 39–40.

124 See, for example, *Alberta (Attorney General) v Gares*, [1976] AJ No 360 at para 156 (SCTD).

125 *Lavallee v Alberta (Securities Commission)*, 2009 ABQB 17 at para 207.

2) Declarations of Inoperability Under the Human Rights Legislation

The ability to use human rights legislation to declare conflicting provisions in other statutes inoperable is most often observed in cases involving government services, although it can also occur under the other social areas. In the government services context, claims are brought challenge programs established by legislation in a manner similar to a constitutional challenge under section 15(1) of the *Charter*, but in a more accessible and cost-effective manner before an administrative tribunal.[126] The effectiveness of this remedy depends on a broad interpretation of a government service to include the statutory provisions that establish a service, since unlike section 15(1) of the *Charter*, human rights legislation cannot be used to directly challenge legislation. However, the similarity in outcomes between inoperability and invalidity — which involves the impugned provision not being applied — has affected the analysis adopted by the courts under human rights legislation, which has been influenced by the framework under the *Charter*.

a) Accessibility of Human Rights Before Administrative Tribunals

The effect of the primacy of quasi-constitutional legislation has increased considerably since the Supreme Court of Canada confirmed in *Nova Scotia (Workers' Compensation Board) v Martin* that administrative tribunals can presumptively consider the whole law, including human rights legislation, when deciding cases properly before them, provided that their enabling legislation does not limit this jurisdiction.[127]

Tribunals therefore must interpret and apply the law, including their enabling statute, in light of the primacy of human rights legislation. In *Walmer Developments v Wolch*, for example, the Ontario Divisional Court found that the Ontario Rental Housing Tribunal erred in evicting a

---

126 Mummé, above note 1 at para 2.

127 *Nova Scotia (Workers' Compensation Board) v Martin*, 2003 SCC 54 at para 45 [*Martin*]. See also *Tranchemontagne* SCC, above note 65 at paras 24–25; *Council of Canadians with Disabilities v VIA Rail Canada Inc*, 2007 SCC 15 at para 14; *British Columbia (Workers' Compensation Board) v Figliola*, 2011 SCC 52 at para 53. In *Martin*, the Court held that statutory tribunals can interpret and apply the *Charter*, which was a reversal of the majority's decision in *Cooper*, and the adoption of McLachlin CJ's dissenting view in *Cooper*, above note 31 at para 100. See also Wayne A MacKay, "Evolving Fundamental Principles and Merging Public Law Silos: The Reshaping of Canada's Constitutional Landscape" (2013) 61 *Supreme Court Law Review* (2d) 83 at paras 72–75.

tenant for his conduct, even though a case for eviction had been made out, because it failed to consider whether his conduct was due to a disability that should be accommodated under the *Human Rights Code*.[128] In addition to administrative tribunals, labour arbitrators are also to interpret and apply human rights legislation.[129] The Ontario Court of Appeal has held correctness or reasonableness as the standard of review when quasi-constitutional rights or values are concerned.[130]

There are numerous administrative tribunals that adjudicate cases where the substantive issues in dispute are often intertwined with human rights claims. A few examples from Ontario include the Health Services Appeal and Review Board, which decides an individual's eligibility for publicly funded healthcare services; the Special Education Tribunal, which hears appeals from parents who are not satisfied with a school board's identification or placement of a child with exceptional learning needs; the Workplace Safety and Insurance Appeals Tribunal, which addresses workers' compensation matters; the Social Benefits Tribunal, which deals with disputes over social assistance, such as eligibility for income support and benefits for people with disabilities; the Ontario Labour Relations Board, which handles various employment and labour relations matters; and the Grievance Settlement Board, which provides dispute resolution services to Crown employers and unions.

---

128 *Walmer Developments v Wolch* (2003), 67 OR (3d) 246 (Div Ct). *Human Rights Code* considerations in eviction proceedings were procedurally considered under s 84(1) of the *Tenant Protection Act, 1997*, SO 1997, c 24, which provided:

> Upon an application for an order evicting a tenant or subtenant, the Tribunal may, despite any other provision of this Act or the tenancy agreement, (a) refuse to grant the application unless satisfied, having regard to all the circumstances, that it would be unfair to refuse; or (b) order that the enforcement of the order of eviction be postponed for a period of time.

This provision is now found in s 83 of the *Residential Tenancies Act, 2006*, SO 2006, c 17. The *Residential Tenancies Act* also provides at s 3(4): "If a provision of this Act conflicts with a provision of another Act, other than the *Human Rights Code*, the provision of this Act applies." The same provision was found in the *Tenant Protection Act*, s 2(4). The Divisional Court further held that these same considerations are to be applied by co-ops in their eviction proceedings, and by the courts when hearing an application for a writ of possession under the *Co-Operative Corporations Act*, before evicting a co-op member with a disability for reasons related to the disability. See, for example, *Eagleson Co-Operative Homes, Inc v Théberge*, [2006] OJ No 4585 at para 21 (Div Ct).

129 *Parry Sound (District) Social Services Administration Board v OPSEU, Local 324*, 2003 SCC 42; *Brown v Westfair Foods Ltd*, 2002 SKQB 154.

130 *Lalonde v Ontario (Commission de restructuration des services de santé)* (2001), 56 OR (3d) 505 at para 186 (CA) [*Lalonde*].

This development is a result of both the interplay of human rights with the substantive issues addressed by many administrative tribunals, and the ability of these forums to provide the timely and efficient adjudication that human rights claims require.[131] This is particularly important when a tribunal has exclusive jurisdiction to interpret and apply a comprehensive administrative scheme, as that body will not lose its exclusive jurisdiction when a case involves a human rights issue, in contrast to some human rights tribunals that have been found not to have exclusive jurisdiction over human rights legislation.[132] The Supreme Court of Canada, in the 2006 *Tranchemontagne* decision, explained that "[i]n its present form, the *Code* can be interpreted and applied by a myriad of administrative actors. Nothing in the current legislative scheme suggests that the OHRC [Ontario Human Rights Commission] is the guardian or the gatekeeper for human rights law in Ontario."[133] The Court confirmed that the legislation did not permit the Social Benefits Tribunal to decline to exercise jurisdiction in favour of the Human Rights Tribunal of Ontario, and that ultimately the question is not which forum is preferable but rather "which of two forums has jurisdiction in the first place."[134] In reaching this conclusion the Court recognized the practical importance of having an efficient and accessible method of adjudicating human rights issues.[135] Such accessibility of human rights legislation is consistent with the Court's description of human rights legislation as "the law of the people."[136]

Since the Court set out the rule in *Mackin v New Brunswick (Minister of Finance)* and *Wynberg v Ontario* "that damages will not be awarded for the harm suffered as a result of a mere enactment or application of a law that is subsequently declared to be unconstitutional" without evidence of "conduct that is clearly wrong, in bad faith or an abuse of power," complainants will not be disadvantaged by bringing their challenge of a government program created by legislation to administrative tribunals that

---

131 Lesli Bisgould, "Twists and Turns and Seventeen Volumes of Evidence, or How Procedural Developments Might Have Influenced Substantive Human Rights Law" (2012) 9 *Journal of Law and Equality* 5 at para 12.

132 *Tranchemontagne* SCC, above note 65 at para 39; *Larocque*, above note 93 at para 13.

133 *Tranchemontagne* SCC, above note 65 at para 39.

134 *Ibid* at para 44.

135 *Ibid* at para 47.

136 *Ibid* at para 33; *Martin*, above note 127 at para 29; *Quebec (Attorney General) v Quebec (Human Rights Tribunal)*, 2004 SCC 40 at paras 28 & 29.

do not have the statutory remedial authority of human rights tribunals, as they will likely not be foregoing a damage claim.[137]

b) Declarations of Inoperability in the Government Services Context

The courts adopted a broad, liberal, and purposive approach to the interpretation of human rights legislation at a rather early stage after their enactment but took well over a decade after the *Drybones* decision to begin declaring statutes in conflict with human rights inoperable. This remedy under human rights legislation finds support in Lamer J's *obiter* comments in *Heerspink*, although he never explicitly used the term "inoperable." Justice Lamer stated more generally that "the *Code* supersedes all other laws when conflict arises."[138] Although there were early suggestions at the tribunal level that statutes conflicting with human rights legislation could be declared inoperable, the explicit recognition by a unanimous Supreme Court of Canada came three years after *Heerspink* in *Craton*. That case involved a challenge to the authorization of mandatory retirement policies under Manitoba's *Public Schools Act* as constituting discrimination on the basis of age contrary to the *Human Rights Act*. Justice McIntyre dismissed the appeal from the majority judgment of Monnin CJ, of the Court of Appeal, who found that a clear conflict with the *Human Rights Act* rendered a provision of the *Public Schools Act* inoperable.[139] In so doing, McIntyre J quoted extensively from the opinion of Lamer J in *Heerspink*.

The Ontario Court of Appeal's 2010 decision in *Ontario (Director, Disability Support Program) v Tranchemontagne* provides one of the clearest examples of a statutory provision establishing a government program being declared inoperable for its conflict with human rights legislation.[140] The case first arose in 2001 when the Social Benefits Tribunal found that it did not have jurisdiction to hear a *Code* challenge to section 5(2) of the *Ontario Disability Support Program Act, 1997*, which explicitly denies income support to people who suffer from addictions:

---

137 *Mackin v New Brunswick (Minister of Finance)*, 2002 SCC 13 at paras 78–81; *Wynberg v Ontario* (2006), 82 OR (3d) 561 at para 192 (CA). See also *Abbey v Ontario (Minister of Community and Social Services)*, 2018 ONSC 1899.

138 *Heerspink*, above note 25 at 158.

139 *Craton* SCC, above note 28 at para 4; *Craton* CA, above note 28 at paras 7–9.

140 *Ontario (Director, Disability Support Program) v Tranchemontagne*, 2010 ONCA 593 [*Tranchemontagne* CA].

> 5(2) A person is not eligible for income support if,
> (a) the person is dependent on or addicted to alcohol, a drug or some other chemically active substance;
> (b) the alcohol, drug or other substance has not been authorized by prescription as provided for in the regulations; and
> (c) the only substantial restriction in activities of daily living is attributable to the use or cessation of use of the alcohol, drug or other substance at the time of determining or reviewing eligibility.[141]

As previously observed, the case eventually reached the Supreme Court of Canada in 2006. The Court held that the tribunal has jurisdiction to apply the *Human Rights Code*. Justice Bastarache, who wrote for the majority, addressed the differences between inoperability under human rights legislation and invalidity under the Constitution. This theoretical difference will be reviewed in Chapter 4; suffice to say at this point that with this distinction in mind, the Court remitted the case back to the tribunal so it could rule on the applicability of section 5(2) of the Act. With its jurisdiction to apply the *Code* confirmed, the tribunal found that section 5(2) contravened the *Code* by denying a service on the basis of disability, and it ordered that the provision not be applied. The issue that made its way to the Ontario Court of Appeal from this decision was the analytical framework to be applied, which will be considered in detail below. The legislation being challenged, however, does not have to display such a direct form of discrimination for it to be declared inoperable, and the question is whether there is an adverse discriminatory effect due to a statutory rule which on its face appears to be neutral.[142]

Administrative tribunals are now issuing declarations of inoperability or comparable remedies when a government program that is established by legislation is found to be discriminatory. In *Hendershott v Ontario (Ministry of Community and Social Services)*, the Human Rights Tribunal of Ontario found that providing a social assistance recipient fewer benefits for the support of her children because she lives and is dependent on her parents constitutes a breach of the *Human Rights Code*. It ordered the respondent to "cease to consider the fact that a minor parent is living with her or his own parents in the calculation of benefits for the minor

141 *Ontario Disability Support Program Act, 1997*, SO 1997, c 25, Schedule B, s 5(2).

142 *Ross v Brunswick Hotel (1977) Ltd* (1994), 26 CHRR 141 at paras 48–50 (Sask Bd Inq).

parent's children."[143] Likewise, the same tribunal, in *Ivancicevic v Ontario (Minister of Consumer Services)*, ordered that a provision in the *Licences to Sell Liquor* regulation that prevents prescribed users of medical marijuana from holding marijuana while attending liquor-licensed establishments in Ontario should not be applied.[144] The applicant in *Ivancicevic*, who was a prescribed user of medical marijuana to alleviate chronic pain, challenged the regulation and sought an order permitting him to smoke marijuana on uncovered patios where it is legally permissible to smoke tobacco. The tribunal found that the restriction on smoking marijuana at licensed establishments rose to the level of undue hardship because of the serious risk associated with second-hand smoke. However, it also found that restricting the mere possession of medical marijuana while attending licensed establishments is contrary to the *Code*. It accordingly ordered that the provision should not be enforced.[145] In *Dhillon v British Columbia (Ministry of Transportation and Highways)*, the British Columbia Human Rights Tribunal held that a provision of the *Motor Vehicle Act* making it an offence to ride a motorcycle without a safety helmet discriminates against Sikhs who cannot wear helmets because of their turbans, and it ordered the respondent ministry to "cease the contravention or any similar contravention and refrain from committing the same or a similar contravention."[146]

c) The Broad Range of Remedies Under Human Rights Legislation

One interesting aspect of some tribunal decisions is that declarations of inoperability have a wider impact beyond the immediate case. In *Druken*,

143 *Hendershott v Ontario (Ministry of Community and Social Services)*, 2011 HRTO 482 at para 134 [*Hendershott*].

144 *Ivancicevic v Ontario (Minister of Consumer Services)*, 2011 HRTO 1714 at para 224 [*Ivancicevic*]. The applicant had an authorization to possess marijuana pursuant to the federal government's *Marihuana Medical Access Regulations*, SOR/2001-227. The challenge was to s 45(2) of the *Licences to Sell Liquor*, RRO 1990, Reg 719, under the *Liquor Licence Act*, RSO 1990, c L.19, which prohibits the possession or use of marijuana in licensed establishments. Section 45(2) of the *Licences to Sell Liquor* reads as follows: "The licence holder shall not permit a person to hold, offer for sale, sell, distribute or consume a controlled substance as defined in the *Controlled Drugs and Substances Act* (Canada) on the premises or in the adjacent washrooms, liquor and food preparation areas and storage areas under the exclusive control of the licence holder."

145 *Ivancicevic*, above note 144 at para 218.

146 *Dhillon v British Columbia (Ministry of Transportation and Highways, Motor Vehicle Branch)*, [1999] BCHRTD No 25 at para 56 [*Dhillon*].

the Federal Court of Appeal justified a tribunal's jurisdiction to make a general declaration of inoperability based on a provision in the *Human Rights Act* that allows remedies "in order to prevent the same or a similar practice from occurring in the future."[147] The Canadian Human Rights Tribunal, in *McAllister-Windsor v Canada (Human Resources Development)*, found that a provision of the *Unemployment Insurance Act* resulted in discrimination on the basis of sex and disability, and it ordered the respondent to cease applying that section of the Act. It suspended the order for a twelve-month period to allow the respondent time to consult with the Canadian Human Rights Commission and remedy the problem.[148]

Provincial human rights statutes contain similarly broad remedial provisions. In Ontario, for example, the Human Rights Tribunal is given the authority to make "[a]n order directing any party to the application to do anything that, in the opinion of the Tribunal, the party ought to do to promote compliance with this Act."[149] The tribunals in *Hendershott*, *Ivancicevic*, and *Dhillon* relied on the broad remedial authority in the legislation when they suggested that the inoperability of the provisions in question was wider than the immediate case.[150]

It is to be determined whether a declaration of inoperability issued by another administrative tribunal in a case properly before it can affect the future application of the impugned provision since the remedial authority in human rights legislation is to be exercised by human rights tribunals.[151] Since the Ontario Court of Appeal confirmed the inoperability of the provision in the *Ontario Disability Support Program Act* denying people with alcoholism and addictions income support and benefits in the 2010 *Tranchemontagne* decision, the Social Benefits Tribunal has been considering alcoholism and substance addictions when determining whether an individual qualifies as a person with a disability, and increasingly without

147 *Druken*, above note 31 at para 9; *Canadian Human Rights Act*, above note 29, s 53(2).

148 *McAllister-Windsor v Canada (Human Resources Development)*, [2001] CHRD No 4 at para 84.

149 Ontario *Human Rights Code*, above note 16, s 45.2(1). The tribunal can make such an order even if it is not requested by the parties according to s 45.2(2)(b) of the *Human Rights Code*.

150 *Hendershott*, above note 143 at paras 105 and 128; *Ivancicevic*, above note 144 at paras 215–18 and 224; *Dhillon*, above note 146 at paras 55–56.

151 See, for example, the remedy provision in the Ontario *Human Rights Code*, above note 16, s 45.2(1), which speaks to the remedies that can be issued by the Human Rights Tribunal: "On an application under section 34, the Tribunal may make one or more of the following orders if the Tribunal determines that a party to the application has infringed a right under Part I of another party to the application."

any mention of the impugned provision and the fact that it was even declared inoperable.[152] This, however, is likely attributed to the tribunal following the precedent set by the Court of Appeal compared to the remedial provisions in the *Code* available to the Human Rights Tribunal of Ontario.

Moreover, with these broad remedial provisions, courts and tribunals have moved beyond simple declarations of inoperability and are requiring service providers to take positive measures to address the discriminatory effect that results from the operation of legislation. The Court of Appeal of Saskatchewan, in *Saskatchewan (Human Rights Commission) v Saskatchewan (Department of Social Services)*, found that a section of *The Saskatchewan Assistance Act* was discriminatory because it provided for a lower basic allowance to a single person compared to the basic allowance provided to each person in a childless marriage.[153] Holding the provision inoperable would not advance the rights claim, although the Court of Appeal notes that the parties had agreed that the complainant had suffered damages in the amount of $55 per month as a result of the discriminatory legislation. Similarly, a declaration of inoperability would not have been an appropriate remedy in *Chipperfield v British Columbia (Ministry of Social Services)*, which involved a challenge to a scheme that provided funding for transportation services to people with disabilities, because it did not cover the costs of operating a personal vehicle, the mode of transportation that best accommodated the applicant's disabilities. The tribunal ordered that the respondent "cease its contravention

---

152 See, for example, *1312-12993 (Re)*, 2014 ONSBT 3304 at para 12 where member Hummelen, of the SBT, stated:

> In determining whether or not the Tribunal is able to consider the Appellant's impairments relating to Alcohol/Substance Abuse for the purposes of him qualifying as a person with a disability under the *Ontario Disability Support Program Act*, the Tribunal notes that on September 16, 2010, the Court of Appeal of Ontario dismissed the Ministry of Community and Social Services (MCSS) appeal in *Ontario (Director, Disability Support Program) v. Tranchemontagne* and held that the addiction exclusion provision set out under subsection 5(2) of the *Ontario Disability Support Program Act* (*ODSPA*) is discriminatory and inconsistent with the Ontario *Human Rights Code*. The Tribunal is therefore free to consider this Appellant's substance abuse . . . .

For cases that do not refer to *Tranchemontagne* or to the impugned provision, see, for example, *1404-03880R (Re)*, 2016 ONSBT 1117 at paras 12–21; *1508-08220 (Re)*, 2016 ONSBT 3596 at paras 22 and 32; *1607-05178 (Re)*, 2017 ONSBT 4222 at paras 15 and 17.

153 *Saskatchewan (Human Rights Commission) v Saskatchewan (Department of Social Services)*, [1988] SJ No 464 (CA).

of the *Code*," and required it to pay 50 percent of the applicant's vehicle costs to bring it in line with the 50 percent of taxi costs covered by the scheme.[154]

Courts and tribunals are therefore using these broad remedial provisions to devise remedies that are increasingly comparable to those available under the *Charter*. This is revealed in a comparison of two similar cases involving the issuance of birth certificates to transgendered persons that resulted in substantively similar outcomes, despite one case being decided under Ontario's *Human Rights Code* and the other being decided under section 15 of the *Charter*. In *XY v Ontario (Minister of Government and Consumer Services)*, the Ontario Human Rights Tribunal found that the requirement under the *Vital Statistics Act* that transgendered persons must undergo transsexual surgery before their sex designation can be changed on their birth certificate constitutes discrimination under the *Code*, and that as a remedy the surgical requirement ought not to be applied.[155] The tribunal declined to specify the manner by which the needs of transgendered persons are to be met; it opted instead to direct the respondent to take steps to eliminate the discriminatory effect of the birth certificate scheme and accommodate transgendered people up to the point of undue hardship.[156]

Two years after the *XY v Ontario* decision, the Alberta Court of Queen's Bench, in *CF v Alberta (Vital Statistics)*, found that a similar requirement in Alberta's *Vital Statistics Act* was inconsistent with section 15 of the *Charter* and, therefore, of no force or effect. It consequently ordered the respondent to issue a birth certificate to the applicant listing her as a female.[157] Although a more direct result was achieved under the *Charter*, the result under the *Code* was substantively similar, and, indeed, the Alberta Court of Queen's Bench in *CF v Alberta* cited *XY v Ontario*. The tribunal in *XY v Ontario* appears to have heeded LeBel J's advice in *Quebec (Commission des droits de la personne et des droits de la jeunesse) v Communauté urbaine de Montréal* on "the need for flexibility and imagination in the crafting of remedies for infringements of fundamental human rights."[158]

---

154 *Chipperfield v British Columbia (Ministry of Social Services)*, [1997] BCHRTD No 20 at para 64.

155 *XY v Ontario (Minister of Government and Consumer Services)*, 2012 HRTO 726 at para 294 [*XY v Ontario*].

156 *Ibid* at paras 295–97.

157 *CF v Alberta (Vital Statistics)*, 2014 ABQB 237 at paras 63–65.

158 *Larocque*, above note 93 at para 26.

d) Declarations of Inoperability Under the Other Social Areas in Human Rights Legislation

Most attention has been placed on declarations of inoperability in cases involving discrimination in the provision of a government service, yet there is no theoretical reason to restrict this remedy to service cases. Primacy provisions in human rights legislation do not limit this effect to services, nor does the explicit recognition in the *Alberta Human Rights Act* and *The Saskatchewan Human Rights Code* that provisions of other statutes are inoperative if they conflict with them. Indeed, declarations of inoperability have been issued by courts and tribunals in cases involving discrimination in employment.

In *Quebec (Commission des droits de la personne et des droits de la jeunesse) v Communauté urbaine de Montréal*, a case concerning discrimination in employment, the Supreme Court of Canada found that a bylaw establishing minimum hearing standards for a position as a municipal police officer was inoperable because it conflicted with the Quebec *Charter*. The municipality was thus required to consider the candidate's job application without taking into account his hearing loss.[159] This case involved a bylaw, although Dickson CJ in *Bhinder v Canadian National Railway Co* stated the following about a statute in the employment context:

> The Tribunal determined that federal legislation and regulations were to be construed and applied in such a way as to be consistent with the *Canadian Human Rights Act*. Thus, if the policy of an employer is discriminatory under the Act, it will not be rendered non-discriminatory simply by reason of there being a statutory requirement mandating that policy. In effect, the Tribunal held that federal legislation is inoperative to the extent it conflicts with the *Canadian Human Rights Act*.[160]

The chief justice wrote for the minority in *Bhinder*, and the majority did not need to address this point; nonetheless, similar reasoning has been adopted by tribunals when declaring statutory provisions inoperable in the employment context.

In *Friesen v Regina (City) Commissioners of Police*, the Saskatchewan Board of Inquiry held a provision of the *Police Act* inoperable because of a conflict with *The Saskatchewan Human Rights Code*.[161] The complainant in that case alleged that the respondents — a staff sergeant, the Regina Board

159 *Ibid* at paras 28–29.

160 *Bhinder*, above note 31 at para 18.

161 *Friesen v Regina (City) Commissioners of Police* (1990), 13 CHRR 11 (Sask Bd Inq) [*Friesen*].

of Police Commissioners, and the City of Regina — discriminated against him during their hiring practices on the basis of a physical disability. The respondents appeared to be immune from the human rights complaint on the basis of Saskatchewan's *Police Act*, section 19, which provided:

> Neither the commission nor any member thereof nor any person acting under its instructions or under the authority of this Act . . . shall be personally liable for any loss or damage suffered by any person by reason of anything in good faith done, or omitted to be done, pursuant to or in the exercise or supposed exercise of the powers conferred by this Act.[162]

The Board of Inquiry held this provision inoperable because granting immunity to the respondents could have the effect of authorizing the type of discrimination prohibited under the *Code*. In reaching this conclusion, the Board of Inquiry noted that section 44 of the *Code* renders other statutory provisions inoperable only when they "authorize or require the doing of anything prohibited by this Act," but reasoned that it captures the immunity granted by the *Police Act* when the *Code* is given a broad, liberal, and purposive interpretation.[163]

e) Declarations of Inoperability Under Human Rights Legislation and the Analytical Framework

Given the practical similarities between declarations of inoperability with orders of invalidity, the courts have incorporated aspects of the analysis from section 15 of the *Charter* in cases brought under human rights legislation. The theoretical differences between inoperability and invalidity will be explored in Chapter 4 in the context of the theory of quasi-constitutionality, but for immediate purposes it is important to recognize that since the impugned provision is not applied in both instances, there has been pressure to merge the applicant-friendly test for establishing discrimination under human rights legislation with the analysis under section 15(1) of the *Charter*.[164] The evolution of the analytical framework and the history of cross-fertilization between human rights legislation and the *Charter* more generally will be reviewed in Chapter 5 in the context of the development of quasi-constitutionality, and the focus here is on the framework itself and its application.

162 *The Police Act*, RSS 1978, c P-15, s 19.

163 *Friesen*, above note 161 at para 47.

164 Mummé, above note 1 at para 3.

The Supreme Court of Canada initially turned to its established jurisprudence under human rights legislation in its first decision under section 15(1) of the *Charter* in *Andrews v Law Society of British Columbia*.[165] In the 1999 decision of *Law v Canada (Minister of Employment and Immigration)*, however, the Court established a more onerous framework for section 15(1) of the *Charter*: one that required claimants to demonstrate that differential treatment on the basis of an enumerated or analogous ground impugned their human dignity.[166] Consequently, government lawyers began arguing that the framework under *Law* should supplant the *prima facie* case analysis from *Ontario Human Rights Commission v Simpsons-Sears Ltd* (*O'Malley*) in the crossover cases because of their similarity.[167]

The Ontario Court of Appeal established the analytical framework when a government service created by legislation is being challenged under human rights legislation in the 2010 *Tranchemontagne* decision. The Court of Appeal relied heavily on the Supreme Court of Canada's decision of *R v Kapp*, a case decided under section 15(1) of the *Charter*, and set out the following framework in the human rights context:

1. Does the law create a distinction based on an enumerated or analogous ground?
2. Does the distinction create a disadvantage by perpetuating prejudice or stereotyping?[168]

After establishing this two-part test, however, the court highlighted the differences between human rights legislation and the *Charter*, as first observed in *Andrews*, and suggested that

> [i]n the human rights context, in most instances, it will be evident that a *prima facie* case of discrimination has been established based solely on the claimant's evidence showing a distinction based on a prohibited ground that creates a disadvantage (in the sense of withholding a benefit available to others or imposing a burden not imposed on others). An inference of stereotyping or of perpetuating disadvantage or prejudice will generally arise based on that evidence alone.[169]

---

165 *Andrews v Law Society of British Columbia*, [1989] 1 SCR 143 at para 37.
166 *Law v Canada (Minister of Employment and Immigration)*, [1999] 1 SCR 497.
167 Mummé, above note 1 at paras 2 and 59; *O'Malley*, above note 71.
168 *Tranchemontagne* CA, above note 140 at para 86.
169 *Ibid* at para 90.

This statement was relied upon by the Human Rights Tribunal of Ontario in *Hendershott*, in which Vice-Chair Leslie Reaume set out the clearest articulation of the test to be applied in most cases under the *Code*.[170]

In many instances prejudice or stereotyping can be inferred where the prohibited ground of discrimination stems from a historical disadvantage, as in *Tranchemontagne* where the Court of Appeal recognized that it is well known that addicts and social assistance recipients are subject to stigma and prejudice. In *Hendershott*, Vice-Chair Reaume referred to the example of a woman whose employment is terminated due to her pregnancy, which is obviously a form of disadvantage that perpetuates prejudice or stereotyping, and "falls within the range of human experiences which were intended to be captured by the *Code*."[171]

On the other hand, cases may arise where a complainant is able to demonstrate a distinction that creates a disadvantage that does not concern substantive equality, and an inquiry about prejudice and stereotyping can distinguish between a mere distinction and a valid human rights issue. Vice-Chair Reaume expresses the view that the Court of Appeal employed the terms "historical disadvantage," "prejudice," and "stereotyping" "to distinguish between those allegations which raise implications for substantive equality and those which may not." In these circumstances, she explains that, "[a]t the risk of over-simplification, the Court of Appeal appears to be suggesting that some cases will beg the question 'is this really a human rights issue?'"[172]

There may ultimately be little difference from establishing the conventional *prima facie* case when the analytical framework from section 15(1) of the *Charter* is applied in this fashion under human rights legislation by focusing, in most cases, solely on the question of whether the law creates a distinction based on an enumerated or analogous ground. In the 2015 decision of *Moore v British Columbia (Education)*, a unanimous Supreme Court of Canada affirmed that a *prima facie* case of discrimination requires the complainant to establish the following:

170 *Hendershott*, above note 143 at para 40. See also *Ivancicevic*, above note 144 at paras 176–79.

171 *Hendershott*, above note 143 at para 45.

172 *Ibid* at para 51. For a case where it was found that a distinction does not have the effect of creating a disadvantage by perpetuating prejudice or stereotyping, see *1312-13573 (Re)*, 2016 ONSBT 5636 at paras 41–49.

1) a characteristic protected from discrimination under the *Code*;
2) an adverse impact experienced with respect to the service; and
3) the protected characteristic being a factor in the adverse impact.

Once a *prima facie* case is established, the burden then shifts to the respondent to provide a justification based on the exemptions available under the specific human rights statute.[173]

The *Moore* decision did not directly involve a challenge to a government program established by legislation, but rather concerned funding and services available for special education. The case, therefore, did not directly invoke the principle of primacy and the ability of human rights legislation to render conflicting statutes inoperable. Questions related to the relationship between human rights legislation and the *Charter*, however, were still raised both in the lower court and in oral arguments before the Supreme Court of Canada. Justice Abella, who wrote for a unanimous Court, did not directly address these issues.

The literature suggests that the *Moore* decision now establishes the framework and supplants the Ontario Court of Appeal's ruling in *Tranchemontagne*.[174] Given the extent of the controversy and debate on the question of the appropriate framework to be adopted under human rights legislation, it remains to be seen whether lower courts and tribunals will accept this decision as marking a departure from *Tranchemontagne*. That is particularly so since *Moore* did not directly involve a challenge to a program established by legislation and the Court was silent on the issue. Nonetheless, the approach in *Tranchemontagne*, as applied by the Human Rights Tribunal of Ontario in *Hendershott*, may ultimately differ little in practice from the *prima facie* case test as set out in *Moore*.

f) Declarations of Inoperability and Bare Challenges to Legislation

The ability to declare a provision of a statute inoperable when it is in irreconcilable conflict with human rights legislation does not allow a statute to be challenged in a vacuum without a discriminatory effect in one of the social areas.[175] This is one of the most significant differences between a challenge under human rights legislation compared to one

173 *Moore v British Columbia (Education)*, 2012 SCC 61 at para 33.

174 Bruce Ryder, "The Strange Double Life of Canadian Equality Rights" (2013) 63 *Supreme Court Law Review* (2d) 261 at para 51.

175 *Public Service Alliance of Canada v Canada Revenue Agency*, 2012 FCA 7 at para 6 [*Public Service Alliance*], leave to appeal to SCC refused, [2012] SCCA No 102.

under the *Charter*. In *Gale Estate v Hominick*, the Manitoba Court of Appeal described this principle:

> Human rights legislation does not create and does not pretend to create a mechanism to determine the validity of or to strike down allegedly discriminatory provincial legislation. In other words, it is not a provincial *Charter of Rights and Freedoms* with the potential to limit the ability of the legislature to enact laws of general application.[176]

Similarly, the Human Rights Tribunal of Ontario, in *Freitag v Penetanguishene (Municipality)*, stated that "I see nothing in the *Code* that would give the Tribunal the power to rule on the bare question of whether legislation, in whole or in part, breaches the *Code*."[177]

In *Matson v Indian and Northern Affairs Canada*, the Canadian Human Rights Tribunal found that registration of Indian status according to the *Indian Act* is not a service under the *Canadian Human Rights Act* and that the case involved a bare challenge to legislation. The tribunal contrasted the registration process to the situation in other cases where a service was found:

> The basis of the conflict between legislation in *Heerspink*, *Craton* and *Larocque* was couched in the terms of a "discrimination" complaint under the applicable human rights legislation in those cases. The complaints themselves were not challenges to the wording of other laws.[178]

As first observed in Chapter 2, this case, along with a similar decision by the Canadian Human Rights Tribunal in *Andrews v Canada (Indian and Northern Affairs)*, appear to depart from the established jurisprudence on what constitutes a service and the two decisions are difficult to reconcile with cases such as *Tranchemontagne* where a legislative provision establishing a service was successfully challenged.[179] The Supreme Court of Canada did not provide clarity to the issue in the appeal of these

176 *Gale Estate v Hominick*, [1997] MJ No 154 at para 15 (CA), leave to appeal to SCC refused, [1997] SCCA No 275.

177 2009 HRTO 1712 at para 17 [*Freitag*].

178 *Matson v Canada (Indian and Northern Affairs)*, 2013 CHRT 13 at para 93, judicial review refused, (*sub nom Canada (Canadian Human Rights Commission) v Canada (Indian and Northern Affairs)*), 2015 FC 398.

179 *Andrews v Canada (Indian and Northern Affairs)*, 2013 CHRT 21, judicial review refused, (*sub nom Canada (Human Rights Commission) v Canada (Attorney General)*), 2015 FC 398. In contrast to *Matson* and *Andrews*, discrimination was found when Indian and Northern Affairs Canada had discretion in the course of processing an application in *Beattie v Canada (Aboriginal Affairs and Northern Development)*, 2014 CHRT 1 at para 49.

two decisions in *Canada (Canadian Human Rights Commission) v Canada (Attorney General)*, and it dismissed the appeal on the basis that determining whether the complaint concerned discrimination in the provision of a service or a direct attack on legislation was a question of mixed law and fact to be determined by the tribunal, and that the tribunal's decision on this point "fell within the range of possible, acceptable outcomes."[180] Consequently, the determination of this vital issue is left to individual tribunals with no additional guidance on how this is to be performed. Undoubtedly, this leaves open the possibility of divergent approaches to the issue by various tribunals with limited possibility of interference by a reviewing court.

Relatedly, the remedies under human rights legislation, while overall broad, do not allow for the reading-in of statutory language to bring it into compliance with human rights, or to require the legislature to adopt new provisions.[181] The Ontario Divisional Court reached this conclusion in *Malkowski v Ontario (Human Rights Commission)*, in which the applicant was challenging the under-inclusiveness of the Ontario *Building Code* that did not require movie theatres to install rear window caption boards for the hearing impaired. In dismissing the judicial review application, the Divisional Court reasoned that "the *Code* does not authorize the addition to legislation of words that are not there in order to bring the *Building Code* into compliance with the *Code*."[182] Similarly, the applicant in *Freitag* alleged that the *Accessibility for Ontarians with Disabilities Act* infringes the *Human Rights Code* because it makes accessibility advisory committees mandatory only for municipalities with a population of 10,000 or more, and requested that the Act be amended. The Human Rights Tribunal of Ontario held that there is "nothing in the *Code* that would give the Tribunal the power to rule on the bare question of whether legislation, in whole or in part, breaches the *Code*."[183] Cases such as *Freitang* and *Malkowski* are now cited for the principle that the development and passage of legislation and regulations is not a service under the *Code*.[184]

180 *Canada (Canadian Human Rights Commission) v Canada (Attorney General)*, 2018 SCC 31 at paras 57 and 66.

181 The Newfoundland Court of Appeal in *Human Rights Commission*, above note 12 at para 38, stated: "A board of inquiry has no power to read down or read in legislative changes to ensure compliance with the *Human Rights Code*."

182 *Malkowski v Ontario (Human Rights Commission)*, [2006] OJ No 5140 at para 31 (Div Ct) [*Malkowski*].

183 *Freitag*, above note 177 at paras 10 and 17; *Accessibility for Ontarians with Disabilities Act, 2005*, SO 2005, c 11.

184 *Ball v Ontario (Community and Social Services)*, 2010 HRTO 360 at para 154; *Sprague v Elections Ontario*, 2017 HRTO 410 at para 17; *Lee v Toronto (City)*, 2012 HRTO 412 at

Tribunals, therefore, routinely dismiss applications at summary hearings when they constitute a bare question of whether another statute is contrary to human rights legislation, although they refuse to do so if the applicant alleges a discriminatory effect. This is observed in *Wheaton v Ottawa*, where the Ontario Human Rights Tribunal denied the respondent's motion to dismiss the application at a summary hearing.[185] The applicant in that case alleged that a City of Ottawa bylaw prohibiting the use of voice amplifiers by street performers discriminated against her as a woman because female street performers are less able than males to project their voices without use of a microphone. The respondent City of Ottawa brought a motion to dismiss the application as having no reasonable prospect of success because it constitutes a bare challenge to a bylaw. In denying the respondent's motion, the tribunal noted that the discriminatory effect was the alleged impact that the bylaw had on the applicant in preventing her from performing because she is a woman.[186]

The same tribunal denied a similar motion in *Dream Team v Toronto (City)*, which involved a challenge to a municipal zoning bylaw that established minimum separation distance standards for the development and location of supportive housing for people with mental health disabilities.[187] The tribunal noted that the alleged discrimination concerned the effect of the bylaw's restriction on where the applicants could live because of their mental health needs.[188] The Ontario Divisional Court dismissed an application for judicial review and confirmed that the tribunal's decision did not involve a determination of jurisdiction, but rather a question of interpreting and applying the *Code*.[189]

3) Remedies Comparable to Declarations of Inoperability Under Access-to-Information and Privacy Legislation

Holding a statutory provision inoperable when it is in irreconcilable conflict with a quasi-constitutional statute is a remedy that has been developed under the *Canadian Bill of Rights* and human rights legislation, and it has not been explicitly endorsed or applied by the courts

para 7. See also *Public Service Alliance*, above note 175.

185 *Wheaton v Ottawa (City)*, 2013 HRTO 1597 [*Wheaton*]. See also *Hodgson v Fort Erie (Town)*, 2014 HRTO 1073.

186 *Wheaton*, above note 185 at para 8.

187 *Dream Team v Toronto (City)*, 2012 HRTO 25.

188 *Ibid* at para 25.

189 *Toronto (City) v The Dream Team*, 2012 ONSC 3904 at paras 15 and 19.

with respect to the other categories of quasi-constitutional legislation. Comparable results, however, can occur without a court issuing an explicit declaration of inoperability, and this remains the preferred approach to primacy under access-to-information and privacy legislation. Due to the way access-to-information and privacy statutes operate and interact with other statutes, declarations of inoperability are not required to apply them in priority sequence over other legislation.

When the courts interpret a statute to avoid a conflict and make it compatible with a quasi-constitutional right, the outcome, in some instances, can be similar to a declaration of inoperability. The difference between interpreting an ordinary statute in order to avoid a conflict with a quasi-constitutional one and declaring it to be inoperable as a result of the conflict is one of degree, not of kind. As Trevor Allan explains, "[t]he distinction between an interpretation of statute that avoids the infliction of serious harm on individuals, out of all proportion to any advancement of the public good, on the one hand, and the non-application (or invalidation) of a wicked statute, on the other, is only a distinction of degree."[190]

Such an approach is particularly suitable for the primacy of access-to-information legislation, where the right to access is applied over a conflicting statute that contains a confidentiality provision, unless the conflicting statute contains a clear override provision. As previously observed, the broad right to access government information under the federal *Access to Information Act* is limited only by other statutes listed in the Act itself. Primacy, therefore, means that the right to access is applied while any other statute providing for confidentiality is not applied in the circumstances of an access-to-information request, unless the statute is specifically listed in the access-to-information legislation as an exemption.

This principle applies equally to provincial access-to-information statutes. As previously observed, in *Ontario (Community Safety and Correctional Services) v Ontario (Information and Privacy Commissioner)*, the Supreme Court of Canada found that the primacy provision in the *Freedom of Information and Protection of Privacy Act* meant that the confidentiality clause in *Christopher's Law* had no application in that case.[191] The Court did not declare the confidentiality clause in *Christopher's Law* inoperable, although clearly the method of resolving conflict between the two statutes means that it was not applied and there remained no

190 Allan, above note 96 at 41.

191 *Ontario (Community Safety and Correctional Services)*, above note 54 at para 32.

reason to declare it inoperable. Thus, given the operation of the right to access information, courts do not outright declare a conflicting statute inoperable, although the outcome is similar when they apply the quasi-constitutional statute and refrain from applying the conflicting one.

Labour arbitrators and labour relations boards have been found to have jurisdiction to determine questions about privacy and access to information if those questions flow from the employment relationship.[192] In *Economic Development Edmonton (Re)*, the Alberta Labour Relations Board rejected the employer's argument that the board has no jurisdiction to order the disclosure of personal information that the union sought from the employer, comprising the names, addresses, and telephone numbers of the employees for whom the union had bargaining rights, and that it must, instead, wait for a decision of the information and privacy commissioner.[193] In concluding that it had jurisdiction to hear this matter, the board held that it had to consider whether production of the information is prohibited by the *Freedom of Information and Protection of Privacy Act*.[194] A similar outcome was reached by the Ontario Labour Relations Board in *Ottawa-Carleton District School Board (Re)*, which rejected the employer's argument that it lacks jurisdiction to direct the disclosure of this type of personal information that the union sought from the employer because the union is to obtain the information through a request under the *Municipal Freedom of Information and Protection of Privacy Act*.[195] The board explained that it

> is not deprived of jurisdiction to deal with the matters which fall under the Act because the union has another means of obtaining the information through the access procedures of the *MFIPPA* [*Municipal Freedom of Information and Protection of Privacy Act*]. The union is entitled to come to the Board to seek relief if a provision of the Act has been violated. There is nothing in the Act or the *MFIPPA* to suggest otherwise.[196]

Although these decisions involved a public sector employer whose records fall under the *Freedom of Information and Protection of Privacy Act*,

---

192 Sandra M Anderson, "Alberta's Statutory Privacy Regime and Its Impact on the Workplace" (2006) 43 *Alberta Law Review* 647 at para 61.

193 *Economic Development Edmonton (Re)*, [2002] Alta LRBR 161 at para 20. See also *Economic Development Edmonton (Re)*, [2002] Alta LRBR 186.

194 *Ibid.*

195 *Ottawa-Carleton District School Board (Re)*, [2001] OLRD No 4575; *Municipal Freedom of Information and Protection of Privacy Act*, RSO 1990, c M.56.

196 *Ottawa-Carleton District School Board (Re)*, above note 195 at para 10.

the same reasoning has been applied to private sector employers under the province's *Personal Information Protection Act*.[197] Given this jurisdiction to consider quasi-constitutional access-to-information and privacy rights, labour arbitrators and labour relations boards must accordingly prioritize them in the interpretive exercise whenever they conflict with other statutes.

4) Remedies Comparable to Declarations of Inoperability Under Language Rights Legislation

Aside from the *Canadian Bill of Rights* and human rights legislation, courts have come closest to holding conflicting statutes inoperable under language rights statutes. The courts have not directly declared other statutes inoperable when in conflict with language rights legislation, although there have been some interesting developments in that direction.

In *Canada (Commissioner of Official Languages) v Canada (Department of Justice)*, the Federal Court ordered the Department of Justice to ensure that the quasi-constitutional language rights contained in the *Official Languages Act* and the *Criminal Code* were respected by provincial and municipal governments that were delegated authority for administering the prosecution of federal contraventions.[198] Defendants prosecuted under the federal *Contraventions Act* had the benefit of constitutional and quasi-constitutional rights related to the judicial aspects of prosecution under sections 530 and 530.1 of the *Criminal Code* and section 16 of the *Charter*; they also had rights related to the administrative aspects of prosecutions under the *Official Languages Act* and section 20 of the *Charter*. When the Department of Justice delegated its powers under the *Contraventions Act* to the Ontario government, which subsequently transferred certain powers to municipalities, not all municipalities were subject to the French language service provisions in Ontario's *Courts of Justice Act* or the *French Language Services Act*. Moreover, even when applicable these statutes did not provide the same level of language rights as the federal *Official Languages Act* and the *Criminal Code*. The court found that there was a duty to uphold constitutional and quasi-constitutional language

197 *Aysa Pharm Inc (Re)*, [2012] Alta LRBR 36 at paras 94–98; Alberta *Freedom of Information and Protection of Privacy Act*, above note 49; *Personal Information Protection Act*, above note 53.

198 *Canada (Commissioner of Official Languages) v Canada (Department of Justice)*, [2001] FCJ No 431 at para 194 (TD).

rights, and that it would be wrong to say that the delegation "could make Part IV of the OLA, or section 20 of the *Charter*, inoperative."[199] The court went a step further and held that "Part IV of the OLA and section 20 of the *Charter* still apply, and if any conflict arises with the *French Language Services Act* of Ontario, the OLA and section 20 of the *Charter* must prevail."[200]

Another interesting case is *Lalonde v Ontario (Commission de restructuration des services de santé)*, in which the Ontario Court of Appeal upheld the judgment of the Divisional Court quashing the directions of the Health Services Restructuring Commission to substantially reduce the French language health services of the Montfort Hospital, in part, because this direction violated the *French Language Services Act*. The court found that Ontario was bound by the *French Language Services Act* to continue providing the same level of health services offered at Montfort as when it was first designated bilingual under the Act and the province failed to demonstrate that the reduction was "reasonable and necessary."[201]

Although the Supreme Court of Canada has not directly commented on the possibility of language rights legislation being used to render provisions in other statutes inoperable, it did not close off the possibility in the 2014 case of *Thibodeau v Air Canada*, even though the majority found no conflict with the *Official Languages Act* in that case.[202] The case began with the Federal Court awarding damages against Air Canada under the *Official Languages Act* for failing to provide bilingual services on certain flights, despite the fact that liability on flights is strictly limited under an international convention, the *Montreal Convention*, incorporated into Canadian law under the *Carriage by Air Act*.[203] The Federal Court found that the *Montreal Convention* conflicted with the remedy provision in the *Official Languages Act* because it excludes a damage award and that the *Official Languages Act* prevails because its primacy results "in the displacement of the *Montreal Convention*."[204]

This decision was overturned by the Federal Court of Appeal, which found that the statutes did not conflict but rather could be applied

199 *Ibid* at paras 143 and 148.

200 *Ibid* at para 149.

201 *Lalonde*, above note 130 at para 188.

202 *Thibodeau* SCC, above note 13.

203 *Thibodeau v Air Canada*, 2011 FC 876 [*Thibodeau* FC]; *Convention for the Unification of Certain Rules for International Carriage by Air*, 28 May 1999, 2242 UNTS 350 [*Montreal Convention*]; *Carriage by Air Act*, RSC 1985, c C-26.

204 *Thibodeau* FC, above note 203 at paras 76 and 82–83.

concurrently.[205] A majority of the Supreme Court of Canada agreed with the Federal Court of Appeal and found that there was no conflict because the *Official Languages Act* simply authorizes courts to grant "appropriate and just" remedies and does not provide for damages to be granted in every case. According to the Court, this displays that the exclusion of a remedy for damages under the *Montreal Convention* is not a direct contradiction of the *Official Languages Act*.[206] Given the harmonious interpretation of the *Montreal Convention* with the *Official Languages Act*, there was no need for the Court to directly address the Federal Court's finding on the displacement of the *Montreal Convention*. Instead, the Court simply stated that "there is no conflict between the general remedial powers under the OLA and the exclusion of damages under the *Montreal Convention* and there is no need to consider which would prevail if there were."[207]

Administrative tribunals also have the duty to interpret and apply language rights legislation and consider its primacy over their governing statutes if it arises in an issue properly before them. As previously discussed, in *Re: Workplace Safety and Insurance Board*, the Information and Privacy Commission of Ontario found that an institution covered by the *French Language Services Act* is required to translate a francophone requester's personal information into French when responding to an access request.[208]

5) Declarations of Inoperability Under Quasi-constitutional Legislation and Comparable Remedies in the Commonwealth

Declarations of inoperability go well beyond the scope of remedies available under the weak-form model of judicial review in the Commonwealth, where the duty of the courts to interpret other statutes consistently with human rights cannot affect the validity or continuing operation of legislation.[209] Instead, provisions in the UK *Human Rights Act*, the *Human Rights Act* of the Australian Capital Territory, and the State of Victoria *Charter* authorize courts to declare provisions in other statutes incompatible when they cannot be interpreted in a manner consistent with the

205 *Air Canada v Thibodeau*, 2012 FCA 246 at para 24.
206 *Thibodeau* SCC, above note 13 at paras 97–98.
207 *Ibid at* para 5.
208 *Order PO-2696*, above note 62 at para 81.
209 UK *Human Rights Act*, above note 82, s 3(2); New Zealand *Bill of Rights*, above note 82, s 4; Victoria *Charter*, above note 82, s 32(3).

rights statute.[210] Such authority is not found in the *New Zealand Bill of Rights Act*, but the Court of Appeal in the 2017 decision of *Attorney General v Taylor* upheld a declaration issued by the High Court that a statute prohibiting prisoners from voting is inconsistent with the right to vote in the *New Zealand Bill of Rights Act*.[211] Declarations of incompatibility provide a modest and uncontroversial role for the courts in protecting rights compared to declarations of inoperability. When a conflict with a rights-protecting statute cannot be resolved through interpretation, the court is required to apply the provision in question; it can simply point out the discord in a declaratory statement and leave it to the legislature to take any corrective action.

Declarations of incompatibility are consistent with legislative supremacy, but they also fail to provide the individual rights claimant with a remedy. They therefore defy the legal maxim *ubi jus ibi remedium* — where there is a right, there must be a remedy. In the 2006 case of *Burden v The United Kingdom*, the European Court of Human Rights, therefore, held that a declaration was not an effective remedy under the *Human Rights Act* because it is not binding on the parties; instead, it depended on the executive and Parliament to amend the law.[212] The court, however, suggested that the future development of a constitutional convention viewing such a declaration as a binding obligation may make this an effective remedy.[213] In contrast, a declaration of inoperability under quasi-constitutional legislation in Canada provides a full remedy to the litigant whose rights have been infringed.

A remedy that more closely resembles declarations of inoperability was developed in the United Kingdom for irreconcilable conflicts with the *European Communities Act 1972*. The long-standing principle of the European Court of Justice that Community law holds primacy over national law is supported in the United Kingdom by section 2 of the *European Communities Act*.[214] To ensure consistency with the doctrine of

210 UK *Human Rights Act*, above note 82, s 4; ACT *Human Rights Act*, above note 82, s 32(2); Victoria *Charter*, above note 82, s 36. In the Victoria *Charter*, it is referred to as a "declaration of inconsistent interpretation."

211 *Taylor v Attorney-General of New Zealand*, [2015] NZHC 1706 at para 109.

212 *Burden v The United Kingdom*, [2008] ECHR 357 at para 40.

213 *Ibid* at para 43.

214 See, especially, *Van Gend en Loos v Nederlandse Administratie der Belastingen*, [1963] ECR 1 (ECJ); *Flaminio Costa v ENEL*, [1964] ECR 585 (ECJ); *Amministrazione della Finanze dello Stato v Simenthal SpA*, [1978] ECR 628 (ECJ). *European Communities Act 1972* (UK), c 68.

parliamentary sovereignty, UK courts have applied the priority of Community law as a rule of statutory construction, whereby national legislation is to be interpreted in accordance with Community law.[215] The courts first contended with the issue of a UK statute being in irreconcilable conflict with Community law in the *Factortame* litigation, where nationality requirements for registration of fishing vessels under UK law conflicted with Community law. To deal with the conflict, the House of Lords "disapplied" the UK law to uphold the priority of Community law.[216] The case provided limited reasoning for the special status of the *European Communities Act 1972*, but Laws LJ in the 2002 decision of *Thoburn v Sunderland City Council* attributed it to its constitutional status.[217]

It has since been suggested that this remedy should be extended to other constitutional statutes in the UK.[218] This could only occur under the *Human Rights Act* only with legislative change since the statute provides that the interpretation of other legislation compatible with rights "does not affect the validity, continuing operation or enforcement of any incompatible primary legislation."[219]

While the temporary disapplication of legislation in the United Kingdom is a remedy only available under *European Communities Act 1972*, the courts have begun to modify the traditional interpretive approaches in cases involving other constitutional statutes. Lord Justice Laws, in *Thoburn*, held that constitutional statutes are not subject to implied repeal but rather require express words.[220] In *BH & Anor v Lord Advocate*, the Supreme Court of the United Kingdom appears to have agreed as it held that the *Scotland Act 1998* is "incapable of being altered otherwise than by an express enactment."[221] The 2011 decision of *R (Governors of Brynmawr Foundational School) v The Welsh Ministers (Brynmawr)* also established the principle that constitutional statutes are not subject to the maxim of *generalia specialibus non derogant*.[222] Farrah Ahmed and Adam Perry point

215 *Garland v British Rail Engineering Ltd (No 2)*, [1982] UKHL 2 at para 178. See also Jay Arangonés, "*Regina v Secretary of State for Transport ex Parte Factortame Ltd.*: The Limits of Parliamentary Sovereignty and the Rule of Community Law" (1990) 14 *Fordham International Law Journal* 778.

216 *R v Secretary of State for Transport, Ex p Factortame Ltd (No 2)*, [1991] 1 AC 603 (HL).

217 *Thoburn*, above note 103.

218 Bogdanor, above note 87 at 80.

219 *Human Rights Act, 1998* (UK), above note 82, s 4.

220 *Thoburn*, above note 103 at para 63.

221 *BH & Anor v Lord Advocate*, [2012] UKSC 24 at para 30.

222 *R (Governors of Brynmawr Foundational School) v The Welsh Ministers*, [2011] EWHC 519.

to this line of decisions as effectively challenging "the Diceyan orthodoxy that a statute's constitutionality is irrelevant in law."[223]

6) Primacy and Resolving Conflict Among Quasi-constitutional Statutes

When two quasi-constitutional statutes appear to conflict, both must be interpreted broadly, liberally, and purposively, and one is not to be interpreted as being subordinate to the other. To the extent possible, quasi-constitutional statutes are to be interpreted harmoniously. This approach was first confirmed by the Supreme Court of Canada in *Dagg v Canada (Minister of Finance)*, a case which La Forest J categorized as involving "a clash between two competing legislative policies — access to information and privacy."[224] Justice La Forest adopted the following statement of Isaac CJ, of the Federal Court of Appeal, on the intersection of the federal *Access to Information Act* and the *Privacy Act*:

> [T]here is nothing in the language of either statute which suggests, let alone compels, the conclusion that the one is subordinate to the other. They are each on the same footing. Neither is pre-eminent. There is no doubt that they are complementary and must be construed harmoniously with each other according to well-known principles of statutory interpretation in order to give effect to the stated parliamentary intention and in order to ensure the attainment of the stated parliamentary objectives.[225]

In the context of that case, La Forest J determined that while access to information is the general rule, the exception for personal information should not be interpreted restrictively because "to do so would effectively read the *Privacy Act* as subordinate to the *Access to Information Act*."[226] While La Forest J wrote in dissent, the majority agreed with his approach to the interpretation of the two statutes, "particularly that they must be . . . read together."[227]

The same reasoning has been adopted and applied by the Supreme Court of Canada with respect to the intersection of other

---

223 Ahmed & Perry, above note 102 at 464.

224 *Dagg*, above note 52 at para 45.

225 *Ibid* at para 51; *Dagg v Canada (Minister of Finance)*, [1995] 3 FC 199 at 217 (CA).

226 *Dagg*, above note 52 at para 51.

227 *Ibid* at para 1.

quasi-constitutional statutes. Justice Gonthier, for a unanimous Court in *Lavigne v Canada (Office of the Commissioner of Official Languages)*, considered "the application of the *Official Languages Act* and the *Privacy Act* in relation to each other," and held that "[t]he two Acts must be interpreted and applied harmoniously."[228] The Court accordingly rejected an argument by the commissioner of official languages that the personal information the office collects is to remain private unless it could be disclosed under the *Official Languages Act*, on the basis that the effect of this interpretation would "exempt the *Official Languages Act* from the application of the *Privacy Act*," and would thus consequently defeat "the complainant's right to obtain access to personal information about him under the *Privacy Act*."[229]

Situations may still arise where quasi-constitutional statutes conflict and cannot be interpreted harmoniously. Some primacy provisions account for the prevalence of quasi-constitutional statutes over all other legislation except human rights legislation, which always take precedence. The primacy provision in the *Official Languages Act*, for example, holds that it prevails over other enactments except for the *Human Rights Act*.[230] Such provisions provide a clear order for resolving conflicts between quasi-constitutional statutes in favour of human rights legislation.

It is rare to have such a clear legislative indication of which quasi-constitutional statute is to prevail when two are in conflict, and the courts have devised a method by which they look at the two quasi-constitutional legislative schemes in their entirety to determine the values that should be paramount in a given case. In *HJ Heinz Co of Canada Ltd v Canada (Attorney General)*, for instance, the Supreme Court of Canada held that while the *Privacy Act* and the *Access to Information Act* strike a careful balance between privacy rights and the right to access information, within the two schemes, the acts provide the greatest protection to personal privacy.[231] Justice Deschamps wrote for the majority Court that, "[b]y including a mandatory privacy exemption in the *Access to Information Act* itself, Parliament ensured that

228 *Lavigne v Canada (Office of the Commissioner of Official Languages)*, 2002 SCC 53 at para 46.

229 *Ibid.*

230 *Official Languages Act*, RSC 1985, c 31, s 82(2).

231 *HJ Heinz Co*, above note 52 at para 31.

both statutes recognize that the protection of the privacy of individuals is paramount over the right of access."[232]

Justice Deschamps found that HJ Heinz Co had a broad right to seek a review of the decision by a federal agency to release responsive records that contained personal information, and she explicitly rejected the arguments by the appellant and intervener that the review mechanism was limited to confidential business information and that a person wishing to complain about the disclosure of personal information was required to seek a remedy under the *Privacy Act*. She reached this conclusion on the basis that such an interpretation "forces an individual to wait until the personal information is disclosed and the damage is done," and that it "fails to give actual content to the right to privacy and also fails to satisfy the clear legislative goals underlying the *Access Act* and the *Privacy Act*."[233] This case likewise accounts for the primacy of the *Privacy Act* in the absence of an express provision.

It is also possible for a conflict between two quasi-constitutional statutes to result in the provision of one statute being declared inoperable. As mentioned above, this occurred in *MacBain*, where the Federal Court of Appeal declared provisions in the federal *Human Rights Act* inoperable due to irreconcilable conflict with the right to a fair hearing under the *Canadian Bill of Rights*.[234] In that case the Federal Court of Appeal found that the adjudicative structure of the *Canadian Human Rights Act* contained an inherent bias because there was a direct connection between the commissioner as the prosecutor of the complaint and the tribunal as decision maker, which contravened the right to a fair hearing in section 2(e) of the *Canadian Bill of Rights*. This case is significant because it demonstrates the continued relevance of the *Canadian Bill of Rights*, particularly since the conflicting statute was the *Human Rights Act*. However, while the case involved two quasi-constitutional statutes, it can also be argued that it only truly involved one quasi-constitutional principle — the right to a fair hearing under the *Canadian Bill of Rights* — as the conflicting provisions in the *Human Rights Act* pertained to the appointment process of adjudicators rather than to a quasi-constitutional right.

These principles have been applied by administrative tribunals. As previously observed, in *Re: Workplace Safety and Insurance Board* the information and privacy commissioner of Ontario considered the *French*

232 *Ibid* at para 2.

233 *Ibid.*

234 *MacBain*, above note 105.

Language Services Act while interpreting the *Freedom of Information and Protection of Privacy Act*. The issue in that case was whether a requester had the right to his personal information translated into French. The information and privacy commissioner considered both the Supreme Court of Canada's 2006 decision in *Tranchemontagne*, which requires tribunals to consider and apply the *Human Rights Code*, and the Ontario Court of Appeal's decision in *Lalonde*, which suggests that the *French Language Services Act* is akin to human rights legislation.[235] Although the *Freedom of Information and Protection of Privacy Act* does not require an institution to create a record in response to an access request, the Information and Privacy Commission interpreted it in a manner that is consistent with the *French Language Services Act* and found that an institution has an obligation to translate a francophone requester's personal information into French in response to an access request, unless section 7 of that Act applies. Section 7 allows for limits, "as circumstances make reasonable and necessary, if all reasonable measures and plans for compliance with this Act have been taken or made."[236]

The courts in the United Kingdom have also begun to consider the implications of a possible conflict between two constitutional statutes. In *HS2 Action Alliance Ltd v Secretary of State for Transport*, the Supreme Court of the United Kingdom referred to the possibility of conflict between constitutional statutes, in that case, the *European Communities Act 1972* and the *Bill of Rights 1689*, as requiring "further considerations," which raises the possibility that the *European Communities Act 1972* does not automatically trump other constitutional statutes.[237] The Court held "that there may be fundamental principles, whether contained in other constitutional instruments or recognised at common law, of which Parliament when it enacted the *European Communities Act 1972* did not either contemplate or authorise the abrogation."[238] In resolving the issue the Supreme Court ultimately did not find a conflict, nor did it articulate what considerations would have to be taken into account in the event of a conflict.[239]

---

235 *Order PO-2696*, above note 62 at paras 63 and 70.

236 *Ibid* at para 82.

237 *HS2 Action Alliance Ltd v Secretary of State for Transport*, [2014] UKSC 3 at para 208 [*HS2*]. See Mark Elliott, "Constitutional Legislation, European Union Law and the Nature of the United Kingdom's Contemporary Constitution" (2014) 10 *European Constitutional Law Review* 379.

238 *HS2*, above note 237 at para 207.

239 Ahmed & Perry, above note 102 at 464.

Primacy is a legal principle that distinguishes quasi-constitutional legislation from regular statutes and characterizes the relationship between the two when they interact. Whereas Chapter 2 considered the special interpretive approach applied to quasi-constitutional legislation, primacy reveals the influence of quasi-constitutional legislation in the interpretation of regular statutes. The focus of this chapter was on the practical aspects of primacy under the five groups of quasi-constitutional statutes, and the application of the two-stage approach whereby a court or tribunal first strives to interpret a statute consistently with the quasi-constitutional one, and only if a conflict cannot be avoided through interpretation will the conflicting provision in the regular statute be declared inoperable.

The significance of this remedy was viewed alongside similar developments in other Commonwealth countries, as well as orders of invalidity under the *Charter*. Declarations of inoperability go beyond the range of remedies in other Commonwealth countries, and they represent the most advanced form of judicial review in the weak-form model. Given the notable similarities in outcomes when a statute is challenged under section 15(1) of the *Charter*, as the impugned provision is not applied, the courts have grappled with establishing the analytical framework to be applied when a government service established by legislation is challenged under human rights legislation. This chapter sets out the elements of the analytical framework and its practical application, while its development will be considered in Chapter 5. The theoretical basis of primacy, including the differences with invalidity under the Constitution, will be considered in Chapter 4.

FURTHER READINGS

AHMED, FARRAH, & ADAM PERRY. "Constitutional Statutes" (2017) 37 *Oxford Journal of Legal Studies* 461.

GARDBAUM, STEPHEN. *New Commonwealth Model of Constitutionalism: Theory and Practice* (Cambridge: Cambridge University Press, 2013).

———. "The New Commonwealth Model of Constitutionalism" (2001) 49 *American Journal of Comparative Law* 707.

HIEBERT, JANET. "New Constitutional Ideas. But Can New Parliamentary Models Resist Judicial Dominance when Interpreting Rights?" (2004) 82 *Texas Law Review* 1963.

———. "Parliamentary Bill of Rights: An Alternative Model?" (2006) 69 *Modern Law Review* 7.

HOGG, PETER W. *Constitutional Law of Canada*, 5th ed (Toronto: Carswell, 2007) ch 35.

MUMMÉ, CLAIRE. "At the Crossroads in Discrimination Law: How the Human Rights Codes Overtook the Charter in Canadian Government Services Cases" (2012) 9 *Journal of Law and Equality* 103.

SOSSIN, LORNE. "The Quasi-Revival of the Canadian Bill of Rights and Its Implications for Administrative Law" (2004) 25 *Supreme Court Law Review* (2d) 191.

TUSHNET, MARK. "Alternative Forms of Judicial Review" (2003) 101 *Michigan Law Review* 2781.

CHAPTER 4

The Theory of Quasi-constitutionality

Quasi-constitutional law is fundamental law by virtue of its association to the provisions and normative elements of the Constitution, and this accounts for both its primacy over regular legislation and the broad, liberal, and purposive approach to its interpretation. The primacy of quasi-constitutional legislation, with resulting declarations of inoperability, provides courts and tribunals with a method of judicial review over regular legislation, although it is a form of judicial review which differs from constitutional supremacy and the legislation is not invalidated.

Primacy is best understood as an interpretive approach adopted by the courts, in recognition of the fundamental nature of the rights upheld by quasi-constitutional legislation, which prioritizes a quasi-constitutional statute over a regular statute when the two statutes conflict. Primacy is recognized by the courts even in the absence of an express primacy provision, although the courts account for the legislature's intention through its role in enacting legislation protecting fundamental rights. Legislative supremacy is also maintained through the legislature's ability to override, amend, or repeal quasi-constitutional legislation. Such derogation, however, will only be recognized by courts and tribunals only with use of clear legislative language that rebuts the presumption that the legislature intends to uphold fundamental rights.

A declaration of inoperability therefore differs theoretically from the invalidation of a statute that violates a constitutional right or was enacted contrary to a constitutional or statutory manner and form provision, which connotes that the impugned provision was never legally enacted in the first place. Despite the theoretical differences, on a more practical level the outcomes are remarkably similar as the impugned provision is not applied. The similarities are most apparent when a human rights tribunal issues a declaration of inoperability that purports to have a broader impact beyond the immediate case. In this instance, inoperability is no longer a case-specific example of statutory interpretation that is guided by the fundamental nature of rights; courts and tribunals must, instead, rely on legislative intent through provisions in human rights legislation meant to prevent future violation of rights.

The fundamental nature of rights also forms the basis of the broad, liberal, and purposive interpretation of quasi-constitutional legislation, which is similarly balanced with legislative intent. There is a long tradition of interpreting remedial legislation broadly, liberally, and purposively, which has been extended by legislatures to all legislation through interpretation acts. Yet, as was displayed in Chapter 2, unique results are achieved through the broad, liberal, and purposive interpretation of quasi-constitutional legislation over other legislation, and comparisons can be made to constitutional law. For this reason, courts often emphasize the special nature of quasi-constitutional statutes for their interpretive approach, and the conventional theories of statutory interpretation fail to provide a proper account of their function. The interpretation of quasi-constitutional legislation finds its basis in constitutional principles and is promoted through legislative intent in the substantive legislative provisions. The courts achieve this through a purposive analysis that identifies the fundamental nature of quasi-constitutional legislation by way of the doctrine of presumed legislative intent, and through more direct measures such as preambles, purposive statements, and interpretation acts. At the same time, while the interpretive exercise is based on the presumption that the legislature intends to honour and advance fundamental rights, courts remain diligent not to encroach upon the substantive provisions of the statute. They will, therefore, depart from the broad, liberal, and purposive interpretation when there is clear statutory language to the contrary.

This chapter has four sections. Section A presents the theoretical differences and practical similarities between inoperability under quasi-constitutional legislation and the invalidity of a statute when it conflicts with either the Constitution or a legislative manner and form provision. Section B situates the theoretical basis of quasi-constitutionality in the concept of fundamental law, which will be shown to be rooted in both the provisions and normative elements of the Constitution. Section C then reviews the balance that courts achieve between the fundamental nature of rights and legislative intent when applying the principle of primacy. Finally, Section D explores these same principles of the fundamental nature of rights and legislative intent in the adoption of the broad, liberal, and purposive interpretation of quasi-constitutional legislation.

A. THE PRIMACY OF QUASI-CONSTITUTIONAL LEGISLATION COMPARED TO INVALIDITY

The starting point in uncovering the basis of primacy is to consider the theoretical differences and practical similarities between inoperability and invalidity. The most direct account from the Supreme Court of Canada was outlined by Bastarache J, who wrote for the majority in the 2006 decision of *Tranchemontagne v Ontario (Director, Disability Support Program)*:

> This primacy provision has both similarities and differences with s. 52 of the *Constitution Act, 1982*, which announces the supremacy of the Constitution. In terms of similarities, both provisions function to eliminate the effects of inconsistent legislation. At the end of the day, whether there is a conflict with the Code or the Constitution, the ultimate effect is that the other provision is not followed and, for the purposes of that particular application, it is as if the legislation was never enacted. But in my view, the differences between the two provisions are far more important. A provision declared invalid pursuant to s. 52 of the *Constitution Act, 1982* was never validly enacted to begin with. It never existed as valid law because the legislature enacting it never had the authority to pass it. But when a provision is inapplicable pursuant to s. 47 of the Code, there is no statement being made as to its validity. The legislature had the power to enact the conflicting provision; it just so happens that the legislature also enacted another law that takes precedence.[1]

Unlike a declaration of invalidity, a declaration of inoperability does not question the legal validity of a provision, but rather prioritizes one statute over another one in the interpretive exercise. This bears some resemblance to the paramountcy rule, which holds a provincial law inoperable to the

1 *Tranchemontagne v Ontario (Director, Disability Support Program)*, 2006 SCC 14 at para 35 [*Tranchemontagne* SCC]. *Constitution Act, 1982*, being Schedule B to the *Canada Act 1982* (UK), 1982, c 11.

extent of an inconsistency if it conflicts with a federal law or frustrates the purpose of a federal law.[2]

This relationship establishes the basic differences between invalidity and inoperability, although further elaboration is necessary to understand the roles of constitutional supremacy, legislative supremacy, and the fundamental nature of rights in declarations of invalidity and inoperability.

First, a statutory provision can be held invalid if it is found to violate a fundamental constitutional right, or if it was enacted contrary to a constitutional manner and form requirement. In both instances, invalidity is based on constitutional supremacy, even though in the former the courts are almost always addressing a fundamental right. A provision in a statute found to contravene the right to equality in section 15(1) of the *Charter*, for example, is of no force or effect because it conflicts with a fundamental right that has been constitutionally entrenched. Similarly, a statute enacted solely in English is of no force and effect if a constitutional manner and form requires it to be enacted both in English and in French.

Second, a statutory provision can also be held invalid if it was enacted contrary to a statutory manner and form requirement. Invalidity, in this instance, is based on legislative supremacy.

In contrast, primacy and the inoperability of a provision is a result of an interpretive approach that prioritizes a quasi-constitutional statute over a regular statute because of the fundamental nature of the rights it upholds, and when a conflict between the two cannot be reconciled through interpretation, the conflicting provision in the regular statute is not applied or declared inoperable. Since primacy is a function of statutory interpretation, a declaration of inoperability that applies beyond the immediate case is based on the broad remedial provisions in human rights legislation meant to prevent the future violation of rights.

1) Manner and Form

The primacy of quasi-constitutional legislation is distinct from the principles of manner and form.[3] Both self-imposed manner and form

2 *Saskatchewan (Attorney General) v Lemare Lake Logging Ltd*, 2015 SCC 53 at paras 15–22; *Rothmans, Benson & Hedges Inc v Saskatchewan*, 2005 SCC 13 at para 11; Luanne A Walton, "Paramountcy: A Distinctly Canadian Solution" (2003–2004) 15 *National Journal of Constitutional Law* 335.

3 Luc Tremblay observes that the new view of parliamentary sovereignty "does not fit the body of judicial decisions dealing with quasi-constitutional legislation in Canada." See Luc B Tremblay, *The Rule of Law, Justice and Interpretation* (Montreal: McGill-Queen's

provisions and primacy challenge the conventional conception of legislative supremacy, the former by recognizing that one legislature can bind a subsequent one procedurally and the latter by ousting the doctrine of implied repeal in the interpretive exercise. However, self-imposed manner and form requirements are still entirely based on legislative supremacy, albeit in modified form as articulated by the new view, while the primacy of quasi-constitutional legislation is not dependent on an express provision and is an interpretive approach rooted in the fundamental nature of rights.

Manner and form provisions outline specific procedural requirements that must be followed for legislation to be validly enacted; they can be in both statutory and constitutional forms.[4] The 1952 South African case of *Harris v Minister of the Interior* is commonly cited as an example of a constitutional manner and form requirement that binds a sovereign legislature. In that decision the Appeal Division of the Supreme Court of South Africa held that a 1951 Act of the Nationalist South African government meant to further its racist ideology by removing the voting rights of coloured voters was "invalid and not a law," because it was not enacted in accordance with certain provisions in the *South Africa Act* that required a two-thirds majority vote of both Houses of Parliament sitting together.[5] What distinguishes this case from decisions before the enactment of the *Statute of Westminster* in 1931 is that the Parliament in South Africa was sovereign —not a colonial parliament — when it tried to restrict the franchise in 1951, yet the Court held that it was required to follow the process, or "manner and form," contained in its constitution.

Earlier decisions, such as the 1932 case of *New South Wales v Trethowan*, resulted in a similar outcome when a law was enacted in a method other than that in the prescribed manner and form, although many of these early cases concerned non-sovereign legislatures and were thus decided under the *Colonial Laws Validity Act, 1865*. [6] It is in the *Colonial Laws Validity Act* that the term "manner and form" originates, in the context

University Press, 1997) at 93. In contrast, Professor Hogg asserts that "theory under which primacy clauses are effective has never been articulated by the Court, but it must rest on the principle that a legislative body may bind itself as to manner and form." Peter W Hogg, *Constitutional Law of Canada*, 5th ed (Toronto: Carswell, 2007) at 12-18.

4 Katherine Swinton, "Challenging the Validity of an Act of Parliament: The Effect of Enrolment and Parliamentary Privilege" (1976) 14 *Osgoode Hall Law Journal* 345 at 383–84.

5 *Harris v Minister of the Interior*, [1952] 2 S Afr LR 428 (App Div).

6 *New South Wales v Trethowan*, [1932] AC 526 (JCPC); *Colonial Laws Validity Act 1865* (UK), 28 & 29 Vict, c 63; *Statute of Westminster, 1931* (UK), 22 & 23 Geo V, c 4, s 2.

of authorizing colonial legislatures to amend their constitutions in a procedure that is in accordance with existing legislation.[7] It is also worth noting that the *Colonial Laws Validity Act* merely affirmed a general principle already well established by 1865: that the Imperial Parliament was sovereign, and if a colonial legislature enacted a law inconsistent with an imperial statute, that law was *ultra vires* and thus void.

Parliament and provincial legislatures are bound by manner and form provisions in the Canadian Constitution. In *Re Initiative and Referendum Act*, for example, a proposed bill of the Manitoba Legislative Assembly that would permit an initiative to become law once voted upon by a majority of voters in a referendum without passage by the legislature and without royal assent was found invalid because it was contrary to the legislative process — the constitutional manner and form requirement of enacting legislation — as set out in the *British North America Act, 1867*, now the *Constitution Act, 1867*.[8] Viscount Haldane, who delivered the judgment of the Judicial Committee of the Privy Council, phrased the principle in the following way: "Sect. 92 of the Act of 1867 entrusts the legislative power in a Province to its Legislature, and to that Legislature only . . . . it does not follow that it can create and endow with its own capacity a new legislative power not created by the Act to which it owes its own existence."[9]

One can now point to section 52(1) of the *Constitution Act, 1982* for the Constitution's supremacy, and the corresponding requirement of Parliament and the provincial legislatures to follow its procedural requirements:

> The Constitution of Canada is the supreme law of Canada, and any law that is inconsistent with the provisions of the Constitution is, to the extent of the inconsistency, of no force or effect.

In the *Manitoba Language Rights Reference*, however, the Supreme Court of Canada explained that this section only enshrines an older principle:

> Section 52 of the *Constitution Act, 1982* does not alter the principles which have provided the foundation for judicial review over the years. In a case where constitutional manner and form requirements have not

7 Robin Elliot, "Rethinking Manner and Form: From Parliamentary Supremacy to Constitutional Values" (1991) 29 *Osgoode Hall Law Journal* 215, n 1.

8 *Constitution Act, 1867* (UK), 30 & 31 Vict, c 3, reprinted in RSC 1985, App II, No 5. *Re the Initiative and Referendum Act*, [1919] AC 935 (JCPC).

9 *Ibid* at para 14. See also *Gallant v The King*, [1948] PEIJ No 1 (SC).

been complied with, the consequence of such non-compliance continues to be invalidity.[10]

The principle of manner and form has not been controversial in Canada as it has been in the United Kingdom, where Parliament is unconstrained by a written constitution, and where there has been a lively debate on the validity of rules of procedure self-imposed by Parliament in legislative form. Such rules of procedure are at odds with the classical conception of legislative supremacy as expressed by AV Dicey, who is perceived as leaving no room for one parliament to bind a subsequent parliament, even with regard to matters of procedure.[11] Dicey proceeded to demonstrate that all attempts by Parliament to pass acts that would tie the enactment of future legislation were unsuccessful.[12]

Some constitutional scholars maintain the classical view of legislative supremacy, though many have moved towards what is referred to as the "new view" of legislative supremacy, first developed by Sir Ivor Jennings.[13] Central to Jennings's understanding of manner and form is the distinction between legal and political sovereignty, whereby Parliament holds the former and the electorate holds the latter.[14] Legal sovereignty involves the power of Parliament to enact laws that the courts must recognize, and it necessarily includes "the power to change the law affecting itself."[15] Further building on this idea, RFV Heuston displays the distinction between the areas of power that a sovereign legislature has authority to legislate over and the composition and procedural rules for enacting legislation.[16] As Jeffrey Goldsworthy notes, the Westminster Parliament is sovereign "if it has unlimited power as to the substance of legislation, even if it is governed by judicially enforceable norms that determine its composition, and the procedure and form by which it must legislate."[17]

10 *Reference re Manitoba Language Rights*, [1985] 1 SCR 721 at para 52 [*Manitoba Language Rights Reference*].

11 AV Dicey, *Introduction to the Study of the Law of the Constitution*, 10th ed (London: Palgrave Macmillan, 1959) at 39–40.

12 This is supported by Professor ECS Wade in the Introduction to the 10th edition of Dicey's book, *ibid* at xii–xiii.

13 For the classical view, see, especially, HWR Wade, "The Basis of Legal Sovereignty" (1955) 13:2 *Cambridge Law Journal* 172.

14 W Ivor Jennings, *The Law and the Constitution*, 4th ed (London: University of London Press, 1952) at 139.

15 *Ibid* at 143.

16 RFV Heuston, *Essays in Constitutional Law* (London: Stevens & Sons, 1961) at 6.

17 Jeffrey Goldsworthy, *The Sovereignty of Parliament: History and Philosophy* (Oxford: Clarendon Press, 1999) at 16. For elaboration on Goldsworthy's point, see Pavlos

According to the new view, therefore, the courts lack the authority to question the validity of the legislation based on its substance, but they maintain the authority to question the validity of legislation on the basis of whether it was enacted in accordance with the procedural manner and form requirements established by the legislature.[18]

The judicial basis to this approach can be found in the 1965 case of *Bribery Commission v Ranasinghe*, an appeal to the Privy Council from Ceylon, where Lord Pearce held that both a sovereign and non-sovereign legislature can be bound by procedural rules that effectively entrench a law from a simple majority in Parliament.[19] The widespread acceptance of the new view in Canadian constitutional thought has led one commentator to label it the "new orthodoxy."[20]

Professor Peter Hogg rejects the traditional view of parliamentary sovereignty that continues to oppose the validity of manner and form provisions on the basis that "[i]t seems implausible that a legislative body should be disabled from making changes to its present structure and procedures."[21] He explains that an effective self-imposed manner and form provision must apply to itself in addition to the protected category of law, and in those circumstances can operate in a fashion similar to a constitutional one.[22] He cites the Supreme Court of Canada decision in *R*

Eleftheriadis, "Parliamentary Sovereignty and the Constitution" (2009) 22 *Canadian Journal of Law and Jurisprudence* 267 at paras 44–45.

18 Hogg, above note 3 at 12.12. See also Elliot, above note 7 at 225–26; François Chevrette & Hebert Marx, *Droit constitutionnel : Notes et jurisprudence* (Montréal: Presses de l'Université de Montréal, 1982) at 93.

19 *The Bribery Commissioner v Pederick Ranasinghe (Ceylon)*, [1964] UKPC 20.

20 Tremblay, above note 3 at 91. See also Hogg, above note 3 at 12-11; Walter Surma Tarnopolsky, *The Canadian Bill of Rights*, 2d rev ed (Toronto: Carswell, 1978) at 87–112; Elliot, above note 7 at 225–26; Chevrette & Marx, above note 18 at 93.

21 Hogg, above note 3 at 12-14.

22 *Ibid* at 12–13 and n 54e. The Ontario Superior Court, for example, found that the *Taxpayer's Protection Act*, SO 1999, c 7, Schedule A, did not impose "an effective manner and form requirement," in *Canadian Taxpayers Federation v Ontario* (2004), 73 OR (3d) 621 at para 50 (SCJ). This statute prohibited the introduction of legislation in Ontario that would create a new tax without first holding a referendum. This law was effectively bypassed by the government by first passing legislation to amend the *Taxpayer's Protection Act* to provide an exception for a new healthcare tax. The government then passed a second bill in the legislature that levied a new tax. This was not an effective manner and form requirement because the court found that the referendum requirement did not apply to the manner and form provision. See also *Greater Vancouver (Regional District) v British Columbia*, 2011 BCCA 345 at paras 32–42, where the British Columbia Court of Appeal undertook a comprehensive study of statutory manner and form provisions.

v Mercure as the leading case on self-imposed manner and form requirements.[23] The Court in that decision held that Saskatchewan legislation was invalid because of the failure of the legislature to enact it in both English and French, contrary to a statutory requirement that resembled section 133 of the *Constitution Act, 1867*. The case was factually similar but conceptually different from the situation in the *Manitoba Language Rights Reference* case, since the requirement in Saskatchewan was in statutory form compared to the same requirement in the *Manitoba Act, 1870*, which is part of the Constitution.[24] In both cases there existed a procedural requirement that legislation was to be enacted in both English and French. The manner and form requirement in this case was not self-imposed in the strict sense since it precedes the founding of the province of Saskatchewan, but Professor Hogg justified it on the basis that it was imposed by the legislature's predecessor. The legislature was bound by the requirement until it repealed or amended it, and a statute enacted in English only was accordingly invalid.[25]

Mercure may more appropriately be viewed as a manner and form requirement in a provincial constitution. A constitutional manner and form provision of this nature, which can be amended or repealed by a majority vote in the provincial legislature, was at issue in *Eurig Estate (Re)*.[26] In that case, the Supreme Court of Canada held that an attempt to impose a tax through an order in council under a power delegated by statute was constitutionally invalid because, by combination of sections 53 and 90 of the *Constitution Act, 1867*, laws of this nature must originate in the Legislative Assembly. This rule can be changed unilaterally by the province, but until this occurs it is constitutionally binding. Justice Major explained:

> By virtue of s. 45 of the *Constitution Act, 1982*, the legislature of each province retains the discretion to exclusively make laws amending the constitution of the province. That power must be read in association with s. 52(1) of the *Constitution Act*, which stipulates that any law that is inconsistent with the provisions of the Constitution is, to the extent of the inconsistency, of no force or effect. Subsection 52(1) effectively requires any provincial legislation that seeks to amend the constitution of the province to do so expressly . . . . Otherwise, the legislation is

---

23 Hogg, above note 3 at 12-11; *R v Mercure*, [1988] 1 SCR 234 [*Mercure*].

24 *Manitoba Language Rights Reference*, above note 10.

25 *Mercure*, above note 23 at paras 65–66.

26 *Eurig Estate (Re)*, [1998] 2 SCR 565.

> liable to being struck down on the basis that it is inconsistent with the Constitution.[27]

In *Mercure* La Forest J seems to have blurred the distinction between statutory manner and form requirements and constitutional ones that can be amended by provincial legislatures. In the final analysis, however, when discussing the rule that statutes in Saskatchewan must be enacted in both English and French, he emphasized that it comes from the province's "constituent" statute; he concludes, in effect, that it is constitutionally binding until changed.[28] Justice La Forest therefore appears to treat the rule as being part of the constitution of the province, and consequently constitutionally binding until it is amended.

Kilrich Industries Ltd v Halotier may provide a clearer if not a perfect example. Yukon's *Languages Act* contains a manner and form provision that explicitly states that other statutes enacted contrary to its requirements are invalid: "No Act or regulation made after December 31, 1990, will be of any force or effect if it has not been published in English and French at the time of its coming into force."[29] The Yukon Court of Appeal found that the failure to publish the Rules of Court in French as well as in English, as required by the *Languages Act*, rendered them invalid. In reaching this conclusion, the court stated that "the Legislature is bound by its own 'manner and form' requirements, even where they are not constitutionally entrenched."[30] While the Yukon Court of Appeal referred to a self-imposed manner and form requirement in this case, the Yukon Legislative Assembly is not a sovereign legislature but rather a creature of the federal *Yukon Act*. Additionally, the ordinance cannot be unilaterally amended by the Legislative Assembly without the concurrence of

27 *Ibid* at para 35. See also Warren J Newman, "Defining the 'Constitution of Canada' Since 1982: The Scope of the Legislative Powers of Constitutional Amendment Under Sections 44 and 45 of the *Constitution Act, 1982*" (2003) 22 *Supreme Court Law Review* (2d) 423 at paras 146–47.

28 *Mercure*, above note 23 at para 62.

29 *Languages Act*, RSY 2002, c 133, s 13(1) [Yukon *Languages Act*].

30 *Kilrich Industries Ltd v Halotier*, 2007 YKCA 12 at para 101.

Parliament by way of amendment to the *Yukon Act*.[31] The enabling statutes of the two other territories contain the same requirement.[32]

The theoretical basis of manner and form rests on constitutional supremacy in the case of entrenched manner and form requirements, and on legislative supremacy in the case of the self-imposed variety. The debate on whether one parliament can bind a subsequent parliament therefore ensues entirely within the doctrine of legislative supremacy; it does not involve a competing theory. This means that the courts will uphold manner and form provisions contained in legislation, but they will not read-in their own procedural requirements. In *Authorson v Canada*, for example, a unanimous Supreme Court of Canada rejected an argument that the right not to be deprived of property except by due process of law under the *Canadian Bill of Rights* entitles parties affected by expropriation legislation to notice and a hearing before Parliament because the "long-standing parliamentary tradition has never required that procedure."[33]

Trevor Allan has been critical of limiting the debate on self-imposed manner and form requirements within the doctrine of parliamentary sovereignty. He has boldly claimed that "relevant questions of manner and form cannot be severed from questions of moral and political substance."[34] As will be shown below, this is at the core of the theoretical difference between manner and form and the primacy of quasi-constitutional legislation.

2) The Primacy of Quasi-constitutional Legislation: Beyond Manner and Form

In contrast to constitutional or statutory manner and form provisions that establish procedures for enacting legislation, primacy involves prioritizing

31 *Yukon Act*, SC 2002, c 7, s 27(1): "The ordinance entitled the *Languages Act* made on May 18, 1988 under the former Act and any successor to it may not be repealed, amended or otherwise rendered inoperable by the Legislature without the concurrence of Parliament by way of an amendment to this Act."

32 *Northwest Territories Act*, RSC 1985, c N-27, s 43; *Nunavut Act*, SC 1993, c 28, s 38. The official languages acts of the territories are the Northwest Territories *Official Languages Act*, RSNWT 1988, c O-1; and Nunavut *Official Languages Act*, SNu 2008, c 10.

33 *Authorson v Canada (Attorney General)*, [2003] 2 SCR 40 at para 12 [*Authorson*]; Hogg, above note 3 at 12-11 and n 46. *Canadian Bill of Rights*, SC 1960, c 44.

34 TRS Allan, *The Sovereignty of Law: Freedom, Constitution and Common Law* (Oxford: Oxford University Press, 2013) at 147 [Allan, *The Sovereignty of Law*].

quasi-constitutional legislation in the interpretive exercise. Although the two are based on distinct theoretical grounds, there are substantially similar outcomes in practice as the impugned provision is not applied. Since primacy is achieved in the context of statutory interpretation, a declaration of inoperability has traditionally been viewed as a case-specific remedy. As such, when human rights tribunals issue declarations of inoperability that have a broader impact than the immediate case, they rely on remedial provisions meant to prevent the future violation of rights.

The primacy of quasi-constitutional legislation is a departure from the interpretive strategies traditionally used to avoid conflict between statutes, and the court or tribunal must instead adopt an interpretation consistent with the quasi-constitutional one. The Supreme Court of Canada first established that the doctrine of *generalia specialibus non derogant*, which ensures that specific legislation is prioritized over general legislation, does not apply to quasi-constitutional human rights legislation in the 1982 decision of *Insurance Corporation of British Columbia v Heerspink*.[35] Rather, quasi-constitutional legislation applies in priority sequence even over more specific statutes. In *Winnipeg School Division No 1 v Craton*, decided three years after *Heerspink*, the Supreme Court of Canada also declared that the doctrine *leges posteriores priores contrarias abrogant*, which results in the implied repeal of an earlier statute by a latter one when two statutes are in conflict, similarly does not apply to quasi-constitutional human rights legislation.[36] The implied repeal of an earlier statute by a later one has been called a "logical consequence" of legislative supremacy because it prevents one Parliament from binding a subsequent one[37] and has been recognized by British courts as an important constitutional principle since at least the 1930s.[38] Instead, the Court in *Craton* held that human rights legislation "may not be altered, amended or repealed, nor may exceptions be created to its provisions, save by clear legislative pronouncement."[39]

In *Canada (Attorney General) v Druken*, the Federal Court of Appeal described the operation of the doctrine of implied repeal as it relates to human rights legislation in the following terms:

35 [1982] 2 SCR 145 at 152 [*Heerspink*].

36 *Winnipeg School Division No 1 v Craton*, [1985] 2 SCR 150 at para 8 [*Craton*].

37 Vernon Bogdanor, *The New British Constitution* (Oxford: Hart, 2009) at 60.

38 *Vauxhall Estates v Liverpool Corporation*, [1932] 1 KB 723; *Ellen Street Estates Ltd v Minister of Health*, [1934] 1 KB 590.

39 *Craton*, above note 36 at para 8.

> The rule appears to be that when human rights legislation and other legislation cannot stand together, a subsequent inconsistent enactment, unless clearly stated to create an exception to it, is not to be construed as repealing the subsisting human rights legislation. On the other hand, when the human rights legislation is the subsequent enactment, it does repeal by implication the other inconsistent legislation.[40]

The application of these principles in *Druken* resulted in a section of the *Unemployment Insurance Act* being held to have been impliedly repealed by the *Human Rights Act* when it came into force in 1977.

At the same time, it was acknowledged that a quasi-constitutional statute cannot be impliedly repealed in this fashion because of its primacy. This principle was most succinctly explained by Greckol J, of the Alberta Court of Queen's Bench, in *Gwinner v Alberta (Human Resources and Employment)* with respect to human rights legislation as "supremacy legislation prevails regardless of temporal sequence."[41] The courts have not been as explicit about the categories of quasi-constitutional legislation other than the *Canadian Bill of Rights* and human rights statutes, although the same reasoning logically applies given the recognition by the courts that these statutes hold primacy even in the absence of a primacy provision.[42]

The Supreme Court of Canada has also made it clear that the *Canadian Bill of Rights* applies to statutes enacted after it. Justice Laskin in *Curr v The Queen* clarified that "federal law enacted after the date of the *Canadian Bill of Rights* as well as pre-existing federal law may be found to run foul of the prescriptions of the *Canadian Bill of Rights*."[43] In *Singh v Canada (Minister of Employment and Immigration)*, Beetz J said, "I do not see any reason not to apply the principle in the *Drybones* case to a provision enacted after the *Canadian Bill of Rights*."[44] Interestingly, Professor Walter Tarnopolsky observed that the majority decision in *R v Drybones* could have been made on the basis of the doctrine of implied repeal because the *Indian Act* was a prior act of Parliament and the *Canadian*

40 *Canada (Attorney General) v Druken* (1988), [1989] 2 FC 24 at para 6 (CA) [*Druken*].

41 *Gwinner v Alberta (Human Resources and Employment)*, 2002 ABQB 685 at para 70.

42 See, especially, *Thibodeau v Air Canada*, 2005 FC 1156 at para 81, aff'd (*sub nom Air Canada v Thibodeau*) 2007 FCA 115 [*Thibodeau*]; *Order PO-2696; Workplace Safety and Insurance Board*, [2008] OIPC No 144 at para 71 [*Order PO-2696*].

43 *R v Curr*, [1972] SCR 889 at 893.

44 *Singh v Canada (Minister of Employment and Immigration)*, [1985] 1 SCR 177 at para 121.

Bill of Rights a subsequent one.[45] Nonetheless, it has been pointed out that while the Court has declared that the *Canadian Bill of Rights* prevails over later statutes, "their reasoning was not extensive."[46]

The Supreme Court of Canada has relied on section 2 of the *Canadian Bill of Rights* for its primacy over all other enactments, although the human rights statutes at issue in *Heerspink*, *Craton*, and *Druken* did not have a primacy provision. Justice Estey, writing for a majority Supreme Court of Canada in *Scowby v Glendinning*, looked back at the Court's decisions in *Heerspink* and *Craton* and explained that "[h]uman rights codes are fundamental laws intended to apply to all other legislation of the enacting body in the absence of express words in that legislation denying it that power."[47] These cases therefore reveal that the ability to render inoperable a statute in conflict with quasi-constitutional legislation has much less to do with parliamentary intent than the nature of the rights that it upholds.

The notion that quasi-constitutional legislation holds primacy and an elevated legal status vis-à-vis other legislation, even without a primacy provision, has not been particularly controversial, although it has not been extensively studied in the literature.[48] As observed in Chapter 3, much of the literature on declarations of inoperability has largely focused on the appropriate analytical framework when human rights legislation is used to challenge a government program established by legislation. In contrast, in the United Kingdom questions surrounding the importance of constitutional statutes and their relationship with other statutes have generated more interest. For this reason, the literature on constitutional

45 *R v Drybones*, [1970] SCR 282 [*Drybones*]; Tarnopolsky, above note 20 at 141–42.

46 Joel Bakan et al, eds, *Canadian Constitutional Law*, 4th ed (Toronto: Emond Montgomery, 2010) at 715.

47 *Scowby v Glendinning*, [1986] 2 SCR 226 at para 9.

48 A notable critic is Professor Hogg who, after acknowledging that human rights legislation takes precedence over inconsistent statutes in the complete absence of a primacy clause suggests that "[t]his reasoning is dubious," and that "in the absence of a primacy clause, the Court is in no position to create priorities between public policies." Above note 3 at 12-17 and n 67. For the literature that considers this function, see, especially, Claire Mummé, "At the Crossroads in Discrimination Law: How the Human Rights Codes Overtook the *Charter* in Canadian Government Services Cases" (2012) 9 *Journal of Law & Equality* 103; Tremblay, above note 3 at 104–8; Vanessa MacDonnell, "A Theory of Quasi-constitutionality" (2016) 53 *Osgoode Hall Law Journal* 508; Ruth Sullivan, *Sullivan on the Construction of Statutes*, 5th ed (Markham, ON: LexisNexis, 2008) at 340; Maxime St-Hilaire, "The Codification of Human Rights in Canada" (2012) 42 *Revue de droit de l'Université de Sherbrooke* 505; Shirish Pundit Chotalia, *The 2000 Annotated Canadian Human Rights Act* (Scarborough, ON: Carswell, 1999) at 4.

statutes in the United Kingdom has recently been recognized as a source of potential guidance on the theoretical basis of quasi-constitutionality in Canada despite the differences between the two concepts.[49]

Luc Tremblay refers to the view that quasi-constitutionality is based entirely upon the presence of a primacy provision as "orthodox," and he engages the rule of law to explain the courts' consideration of the content and underlying values of statutes when determining whether they have primacy.[50] Doing this necessarily entails more than a mere formalistic view of the rule of law. It moves towards a substantive understanding whereby the rule of law does not detail specific rights, but rather serves as a safeguard against the violation of rights overall.[51] In the United Kingdom, David Jenkins has similarly argued that the normative significance of some statutes means "that they themselves embody or generate higher-order principles that weave into a common law constitutional fabric," and that the core principles of constitutional statutes transcend their text even if some of their provisions are amended over time.[52]

When the term "inoperative" was first used in the context of quasi-constitutional legislation under the *Canadian Bill of Rights* in *R v Drybones*, it was described by the Supreme Court of Canada as a distinct remedy from invalidity in that it only applied to the immediate case. Justice Ritchie, who wrote the majority judgment, justified the remedy on that basis:

> I think a declaration by the courts that a section or portion of a section of a statute is inoperative is to be distinguished from the repeal of such a section and is to be confined to the particular circumstances of the case in which the declaration is made. The situation appears to me to be somewhat analogous to a case where valid provincial legislation in an otherwise unoccupied field ceases to be operative by reason of conflicting federal legislation.[53]

---

49 MacDonnell, above note 48 at 512.

50 Tremblay, above note 3 at 88, n 189 and 104. Tremblay distinguishes between the enactments that contain primacy provisions and those that do not by referring to the latter as "special nature enactments." This distinction may no longer be necessary given the caselaw from the Supreme Court of Canada attributing primacy to quasi-constitutional statutes that do not contain a primacy provision. See also St-Hilaire, above note 48 at para 83.

51 See, especially, Allan, *The Sovereignty of Law*, above note 34, ch 3.

52 David Jenkins, "Common Law Declarations of Unconstitutionality" (2009) 7 *International Journal of Constitutional Law* 183 at 201.

53 *Drybones*, above note 45 at 294–95.

The early literature also supported this distinction between inoperability and invalidity. Professor Tarnopolsky concluded that "[t]he specific choice of the term 'inoperative' as an alternative, to 'void,' or 'invalid,' must have been intended to restrict the effect of these decisions to the particular fact circumstances."[54] The courts appear to continue to support limiting declarations of inoperability under the *Canadian Bill of Rights* to the immediate case. In *Northwest Territories v Public Service Alliance of Canada*, the Federal Court of Appeal looked back at Ritchie J's comment in *Drybones* and held that "[t]his means that a finding of inoperability is restricted to the case at bar and its particular fact circumstances."[55]

As observed in Chapter 3, courts and tribunals have acknowledged the wider impact of inoperability under human rights legislation in more systemic type cases, and it can no longer be said that this remedy is limited to the circumstances of the immediate case. Tribunal decisions do not form a legal precedent under the doctrine of *stare decisis*, yet human rights tribunals are suggesting that their declarations of inoperability have a wider impact beyond the immediate case before them. Unlike the general operation of primacy, however, which is not necessarily dependent on a primacy provision, the wider impact of an order of inoperability on future cases appears to be contingent on legislative intent, as courts and tribunals justify the result based on the broad remedial authority in human rights legislation. This is likely because tribunals can account for the fundamental nature of quasi-constitutional legislation in the interpretive exercise, while questions about the operation of a provision beyond the immediate are no longer within the context of statutory interpretation.

Druken represents the first time an appellate-level court considered the issue of whether a declaration of inoperability from a human rights tribunal affects the future application of the impugned provision.[56] The Federal Court of Appeal in *Druken*, of course, did not find that statutory human rights tribunals possess the inherent jurisdiction of the superior courts, although it reached a conclusion that allows tribunals to achieve substantively similar results by relying on the broad remedial provisions of the *Human Rights Act* that expressly authorize measures "to prevent the same or a similar practice from occurring in the future."[57] The court provided the following reasons:

---

54 Tarnopolsky, above note 20 at 140.

55 *Northwest Territories v Public Service Alliance of Canada*, [2001] 3 FC 566 at para 60 (CA).

56 Mummé, above note 48 at para 30.

57 *Canadian Human Rights Act*, RSC 1985, c H-6, s 53(2).

> The Attorney General proceeded from the position that a tribunal has no power to make a general declaration of invalidity to the proposition that a tribunal has no right to order that legislation, which it has found unjustifiably discriminatory in its necessary application, is not to be further applied. The argument would be no different had the offending legislation been found implicitly repealed. In my view, such a limitation on a tribunal's power to make an order is inconsistent with paragraph 41(2)(a) of the *Human Rights Act* which expressly authorizes the tribunal to order that measures be taken "in order to prevent the same or a similar practice from occurring in the future." That is not intended only to prevent repetition of the discriminatory practice vis-à-vis the particular complainant; it is intended to prevent its repetition at all by the person found to have engaged in it.[58]

Interestingly, the court accepted the primacy of the *Human Rights Act*, and the corresponding principle that a conflicting provision in another statute is inoperable, even in the absence of an express primacy provision, but it justified the broader impact of such a decision beyond the immediate case on the express remedial language in the Act. The Supreme Court of Canada seemingly accepted the Federal Court of Appeal's reasoning as it denied leave to appeal. Human rights tribunals that issue declarations of inoperability that affect the future application of the impugned provision similarly rely on the broadly worded remedial provisions.[59]

Professor Tarnopolsky considered the new view perspective of parliamentary sovereignty in light of the early debate on the constitutional entrenchment of the *Canadian Bill of Rights*. He has suggested as an alternative that Parliament could have included a self-imposed manner and form provision that would provide a more onerous amending process.[60] This interesting proposal of combining primacy with a manner and

58 *Druken*, above note 40 at para 13, leave to appeal to SCC refused, [1988] SCCA No 433. See also *Québec (Commission des droits de la personne et des droits de la jeunesse) v Montréal (City)*; *Québec (Commission des droits de la personne et des droits de la jeunesse) v Boisbriand (City)*, 2000 SCC 27 at para 27, where a unanimous Supreme Court of Canada made a broad statement that "given its fundamental and quasi-constitutional status, human rights legislation prevails over other legislation," without any mention of a primacy provision [*Boisbriand*].

59 See, especially, *Hendershott v Ontario (Ministry of Community and Social Services)*, 2011 HRTO 482 at para 128; *Ivancicevic v Ontario (Minister of Consumer Services)*, 2011 HRTO 1714 at para 224; *Dhillon v British Columbia (Ministry of Transportation and Highways, Motor Vehicle Branch)*, [1999] BCHRTD No 25 at para 56.

60 Tarnopolsky, above note 20 at 112.

form provision in quasi-constitutional legislation has never been formally adopted by a legislature, although, as previously noted, Yukon's *Languages Act* contains a manner and form provision that explicitly states that statutes that are not enacted in both English and French are of no force or effect.[61] This statute does not contain an express primacy provision, although it would be interpreted to have primacy by the courts given its quasi-constitutional status. The Nova Scotia *Human Rights Act*, which does not include a primacy provision, instead contains a provision that deems discriminatory regulations "void and of no legal effect."[62] This is a partial manner and form provision as it applies only to subordinate legislation. Since primacy is based on the underlying nature and purpose of quasi-constitutional legislation, the courts have relied upon the concept of fundamental law, which will be considered in detail below.

B. QUASI-CONSTITUTIONAL LAW AS FUNDAMENTAL LAW

Chief among the similarities between quasi-constitutional legislation in Canada and constitutional statutes in the United Kingdom is that the courts have turned to the concept of fundamental law in the absence of an express primacy provision. In *Heerspink* Lamer J held that human rights legislation "is not to be treated as another ordinary law of general application," but rather "should be recognized for what it is, a fundamental law."[63] The Supreme Court of Canada has consistently referred to human rights legislation as fundamental law since *Heerspink* and, indeed, has gone as far as calling it its "most important characteristic."[64]

The fundamental nature of human rights legislation has received the most attention by the courts, although the other categories of quasi-constitutional law have also been declared as fundamental. The Supreme Court of Canada described the *Canadian Bill of Rights* as having been "designed and adopted to perform a more fundamental role than ordinary

---

61 Yukon *Languages Act*, above note 29, s 13.

62 *Human Rights Act*, RSNS 1989, c 214, s 10(1) [Nova Scotia *Human Rights Act*].

63 *Heerspink*, above note 35 at 158.

64 *Tranchemontagne* SCC, above note 1 at para 33. See also *Craton*, above note 36 at para 8; *Battlefords and District Co-operative Ltd v Gibbs*, [1996] 3 SCR 566 at para 18; *Quebec (Commission des droits de la personne et des droits de la jeunesse) v Communauté urbaine de Montréal*, 2004 SCC 30 at para 20. The Human Rights Tribunal of Ontario said that it was "trite" that human rights legislation is fundamental law in *Arzem v Ontario (Minister of Community and Social Services)*, 2006 HRTO 17 at para 12. See also *Canadian National Railway v Seeley*, 2013 FC 117 at para 65, aff'd 2014 FCA 111.

statutes in this country."[65] Access-to-information legislation was held to embody "values that are fundamental,"[66] and reflect the "fundamental principle that access may be had to government information."[67] The protection of privacy was likewise called a "fundamental value in our society"[68] and "fundamental in the Canadian legal system."[69] In spite of its previous reluctance, the Court now firmly asserts that language rights are fundamental.[70] Finally, the common law protection of the good reputation of an individual is also described as being of "fundamental importance."[71]

The courts in the United Kingdom have similarly relied on the concept of fundamental law to support the distinction between constitutional statutes and regular ones. Lord Justice Laws in *Thoburn v Sunderland City Council* found that constitutional legislation "enlarges or diminishes what we would now regard as fundamental constitutional rights,"[72] and Lord Hope in *BH & Anor v Lord Advocate* referred to the *Scotland Act 1998* as a "fundamental constitutional" statute in support of the conclusion that it can be altered only through express language.[73]

Relying on the concept of fundamental law in support of the primacy of quasi-constitutional legislation is significant because it invokes an ancient maxim that predates parliamentary sovereignty. In England the concept is most commonly associated with Sir Edward Coke and the idea of English customary, or immemorial, law, although its origin has been attributed to the sixteenth-century Continental theologian Théodore de Bèze, who

65 *Law Society of Upper Canada v Skapinker*, [1984] 1 SCR 357 at para 10 [*Skapinker*].

66 *Canada (Information Commissioner) v Canada (Minister of National Defence)*, 2011 SCC 25 at para 79 [*Canada (Information Commissioner)*].

67 *Macdonell v Quebec (Commission d'accès à l'information)*, [2002] 3 SCR 661 at para 62 [*Macdonell*].

68 *R v Osolin*, [1993] 4 SCR 595 at 614.

69 *Lavigne v Canada (Office of the Commissioner of Official Languages)*, 2002 SCC 53 at para 24 [*Lavigne*]. This applies equally to legislation protecting personal privacy in the private sector such as the federal *Personal Information Protection and Electronic Documents Act*, SC 2000, c 5 [*PIPEDA*]. Justice Lemieux, of the Federal Court, held that "I have no hesitation in classifying *PIPEDA* as a fundamental law of Canada just as the Supreme Court of Canada ruled the federal *Privacy Act* enjoyed quasi-constitutional status." *Eastmond v Canadian Pacific Railway*, 2004 FC 852 at para 100.

70 *Solski (Tutor of) v Quebec (Attorney General)*, 2005 SCC 14 at para 2 [*Solski*]. See also *Lalonde v Ontario (Commission de restructuration des services de santé)*, [2001] OJ No 4767 at para 132 (CA) [*Lalonde*].

71 *Hill v Church of Scientology of Toronto*, [1995] 2 SCR 1130 at paras 116 and 120 [*Hill*].

72 *Thoburn v Sunderland City Council*, [2003] QB 151 at para 62 (Admin) [*Thoburn*].

73 *BH & Anor v Lord Advocate*, [2012] UKSC 24 at para 30 [*BH & Anor*].

referred to "*les loix fondamentales d'un Royaume.*"[74] Fundamental law as a concept reached its height in the seventeenth century, although understanding of it varied considerably. JW Gough tells us that it was "vague and ill-defined,"[75] and JGA Pocock has referred to it as the "most important and elusive of seventeenth-century concepts."[76] Fundamental law was variously associated with natural law, ancient immemorial law, customary law, an original contract, and even the whole common law.[77] Yet despite the variety of perspectives, Gough identified a "normal usage" denoting "the essential presuppositions of the historic constitution," which has since been associated with constitutional theory, particularly judicial review, and the inability to amend or repeal a constitution through the regular process.[78] These factors display the outcomes of the fundamental nature of quasi-constitutional legislation, but its roots are based in the provisions and normative elements of the Constitution.

1) Fundamental Law and Constitutional Theory

The trend in modern accounts of fundamental law is to associate the concept with constitutional theory, particularly the inability to amend or repeal fundamental law through the regular legislative process and the use of fundamental law to judicially review other laws. This comes primarily from American rather than English authors, who were unmoved by Dicey and the doctrine of parliamentary sovereignty. The emphasis on parliamentary sovereignty is generally considered to have precipitated the decline of fundamental law as a legal concept, which gradually lost its force over the course of the late eighteenth and early nineteenth centuries. Gough explains the divergent paths taken by English and American authors:

74 Martyn P Thompson, "The History of Fundamental Law in Political Thought from the French Wars of Religion to the American Revolution" (1986) 91 *American Historical Review* 1103 at 1106.

75 JW Gough, *Fundamental Law in English Constitutional History* (Oxford: Clarendon Press, 1955) at 2.

76 JGA Pocock, *The Ancient Constitution and the Feudal Law: A Study of English Historical Thought in the Seventeenth Century*, 2d ed (Cambridge: Cambridge University Press, 1987) at 48.

77 Thompson, above note 74 at 1118.

78 Gough, above note 75 at 159.

> English constitutional and legal historians nowadays are generally inclined to belittle the idea of fundamentals, and to suggest that it arose in the past from a misunderstanding of the true character of English law and the true omnipresence of the legislature. They emphasize the impossibility of attaching any precise meaning to the fundamental laws or fundamental rights which used to be invoked in England, and are therefore inclined to dismiss them as errors and confusions which we have outgrown. American writers, on the other hand, treat the notion of fundamental law with more respect, and some have thought that in its appearance in seventeenth-century England they could discern anticipations of the principles of the American constitution.[79]

American writers looked to the English authors of the seventeenth century as the precursors to their constitutional principles, chiefly Sir Edward Coke's *obiter dicta* in *Dr. Thomas Bonham's Case*, where he stated: "when an Act of Parliament is against Common right and reason, or repugnant, or impossible to be performed, the Common Law will control it, and adjudge such Act to be void."[80] In Federalist Papers No 78, Alexander Hamilton wrote in support of judicial review by describing a constitution as fundamental law:

> The interpretation of the laws is the proper and peculiar province of the courts. A constitution is, in fact, and must be regarded by the judges, as a fundamental law. It therefore belongs to them to ascertain its meaning, as well as the meaning of any particular act proceeding from the legislative body. If there should happen to be an irreconcilable variance between the two, that which has the superior obligation and validity ought, of course, to be preferred; or, in other words, the Constitution ought to be preferred to the statute, the intention of the people to the intention of their agents.[81]

Coke was not cited by Hamilton or by Marshall CJ when he established the basis of judicial review in *Marbuy v Madison*, although it has been asserted that "there is little doubt" that they drew upon his "now-ancient maxim."[82]

---

79 Gough, above note 75 at v.

80 *Dr Bonham's Case* (1610), 8 Co Rep 114 (CP).

81 Alexander Hamilton, "The Federalist Papers: No 78," online: http://avalon.law.yale.edu/18th_century/fed78.asp.

82 James R Stoner Jr, "Common Law, Natural Law and the Constitution" in Douglas E Edlin, ed, *Common Law Theory* (Cambridge: Cambridge University Press, 2007) 171 at 171.

This association of fundamental law with a constitutional order, judicial review, and an amending process that departs from the regular method is now commonly accepted as the principal understanding of the concept.[83] As Gough explains:

> What were these fundamental laws, which were invoked so freely in the seventeenth century? Nowadays fundamental law has a precise meaning as a technical term in political science. It is applied to some framework of government, such as the Constitution of the United States . . .
>
> In this sense a law is fundamental when it cannot be altered or repealed by ordinary legislative procedure. It is generally associated with the principle of judicial review, by which a supreme court has the last word in cases where the validity of legislative enactments is challenged, and can pronounce whether they are or are not in conformity with the fundamental provisions of the constitution.[84]

Despite the stark distinction between American and English authors when Gough wrote in 1955, fundamental law is now being invoked by judges and academics alike in the United Kingdom. Dicey asserted that "[t]here is under the English constitution no marked or clear distinction between laws which are not fundamental or constitutional and laws which are fundamental or constitutional,"[85] yet in *BH & Anor* the Supreme Court of the United Kingdom held that the *Scotland Act 1998* cannot be impliedly repealed because of its constitutional status, which has accordingly led to the suggestion that constitutional statutes in the United Kingdom are "quasi-entrenched."[86] Quasi-constitutional statutes in Canada have also been described as quasi-entrenched because they are exempt from the doctrine of implied repeal.[87]

Relying on fundamental law as the theoretical basis of quasi-constitutionality may appear odd at first glance, but the concept became appealing with the emergence of the rights movement in Canada after the Second World War, as it provided a theoretical foundation for rights while avoiding the historical baggage of natural law theory and the enduring debate with legal positivism. Fundamental law was first mentioned

83 Martyn P Thompson acknowledges that is how fundamental law is typically viewed, but he finds it to be a distortion of history. See Thompson, above note 74 at 1103.

84 Gough, above note 75 at 2.

85 Dicey, above note 11 at 85.

86 Farrah Ahmed & Adam Perry, "The Quasi-entrenchment of Constitutional Statutes" (2014) 73 *Oxford Journal of Legal Studies* 514 at 515.

87 Sullivan, above note 48 at 497; MacDonnell, above note 48 at 527.

in the context of a quasi-constitutional statute in 1960 before the Special Committee on Human Rights on the proposed *Canadian Bill of Rights*. Professor Maxwell Cohen described the dilemma between the renewed interest in natural law as the foundation of rights and the unease with the concept in the common law tradition in his testimony before the Special Committee. He pointed to fundamental law as the alternative:

> English law was both comfortable and uncomfortable with ideas of natural law, which makes some of the language in this bill difficult, it seems to me, to handle.
>
> It was comfortable, it seems to me where — as Professor Lower said yesterday — it recognized something called fundamental law, something that went a long way back, to *Magna Carta*, which no one, in the opinion of some constitutionalists, could ever change. So the British common law ideals of fundamental law were not far removed in their method from natural law ideas, and to that extent British law has always had a little bit of the naturalist in it, even though it tended to reject it for a very long time.
>
> But it was uncomfortable with natural law to the point where it did not believe that a specific statute could be overruled by natural law; and there was this great fight that I mentioned a while ago, in which it was perfectly clear that parliament could, if it wished to do so, offend whatever might be the natural law.
>
> So far as civil liberties are concerned in English law, the debate on civil liberties tended to be very much concerned with these ideas of fundamental law.[88]

In addition to fundamental law being more consistent with the common law tradition, Professor AR Lower pointed out that the situation in Canada did not directly parallel the decline of fundamental law and corresponding rise of parliamentary sovereignty that occurred in the United Kingdom, as a form of a fundamental law was retained in Canada through the written Constitution.[89] The concept of fundamental law therefore provided the necessary transcendent principle underlying rights as it was part of the common law tradition, and it actively existed in Canada at the time of the enactment of the *Canadian Bill of Rights*. All

88 Canada, Special Committee on Human Rights and Fundamental Freedoms, *Minutes of Proceedings and Evidence*, 24th Parl, 3rd Sess, No 5 (21 July 1960) at 367 (Maxwell Cohen, professor of law and acting dean of the law faculty at McGill University).

89 *Ibid*, (20 July 1960) at 313 (AR Lower, professor of history at Queen's University).

quasi-constitutional laws have since been recognized by the courts as fundamental law because they uphold fundamental rights.

Consistent with the modern understanding of fundamental law, the courts have associated the concept with constitutionalism, including the inability to amend or repeal through the regular legislative process and judicial review. With respect to constitutional law, Brossard JA, of the Quebec Court of Appeal, cited Jennings for this principle:

> With a written constitution, this is an end which in principle is fairly easy to accomplish. Certain "fundamental rights" are inserted in the constitution, and every institution of government is forbidden to change them. A fundamental right can then be limited or taken away only by constitutional amendment, and if the process is in any[ ]way difficult or formal, such a limitation becomes plain for all to see. Nearly all written constitutions contain such provisions, though with varying definiteness of expression.[90]

Quasi-constitutional statutes are statutory instruments, and the onerous amendment process in part V of the *Constitution Act, 1982* does not apply to them; however, as noted above, the courts reject that they can be impliedly repealed and instead require clear legislative language for amendment or repeal. This idea was initially framed by Lamer J in *Heerspink* as "express and unequivocal language,"[91] and by McIntyre J in *Craton* as follows:

> Human rights legislation is of a special nature and declares public policy regarding matters of general concern. It is not constitutional in nature in the sense that it may not be altered, amended, or repealed by the Legislature. It is, however, of such nature that it may not be altered, amended, or repealed, nor may exceptions be created to its provisions, save by clear legislative pronouncement. To adopt and apply any theory of implied repeal by later statutory enactment to legislation of this kind would be to rob it of its special nature and give scant protection to the rights it proclaims.[92]

---

90 *Libman c Québec (Procureur général)*, [1995] RJQ 2015 at para 75 (CA). Justice Brossard was dissenting in part, although the majority opinion was reversed by the SCC in *Libman v Quebec (Attorney General)*, [1997] 3 SCR 569.

91 *Heerspink*, above note 35 at 158.

92 *Craton*, above note 36 at para 8.

A comparable approach is now applied to constitutional statutes in the United Kingdom; these statutes cannot be impliedly repealed because of their fundamental character.

Courts also refer to the judicial review that occurs as a result of primacy as an indicator of the fundamental nature of quasi-constitutional legislation. This stems back to the comments by Lamer J in *Heerspink*, which is arguably the most commonly cited statement on the fundamental character of quasi-constitutional laws:

> [T]he *Human Rights Code*, when in conflict with "particular and specific legislation," is not to be treated as another ordinary law of general application. It should be recognized for what it is, a fundamental law.[93]

The Saskatchewan Court of Appeal similarly explained:

> The Supreme Court of Canada has stated that when human rights legislation comes into conflict with other, more specific legislation, the provisions of the *Code* prevail. Next to constitutional law, human rights provisions are more important than all other laws. They have been defined as quasi constitutional rights and statutes. They are not treated as laws of general application but rather as fundamental laws. Unless the legislature has expressly provided otherwise, the *Code* takes precedence over all other laws when there is a conflict.[94]

Although the courts most commonly address these principles with respect to human rights legislation, a similar approach is adopted under other categories of quasi-constitutional legislation, even in the absence of a primacy provision.[95]

2) Fundamental Law as Association with the Constitution

Judicial review and the methods of amendment or repeal display the consequences or effects of the fundamental nature of quasi-constitutional legislation, but not the reasons why the rights upheld by these statutes are considered fundamental. Instead, the courts associate the fundamental rights in quasi-constitutional laws with those found in the Constitution.

93 *Heerspink*, above note 35 at 158.

94 *Cadillac Fairview Corp v Saskatchewan (Human Rights Commission)*, [1999] SJ No 217 at para 29 (CA), leave to appeal to SCC refused, [1999] SCCA No 492.

95 See, especially, *Thibodeau*, above note 42; and *Order PO-2696*, above note 42.

The Supreme Court of Canada has referred to human rights legislation as being "almost constitutional,"[96] the *Canadian Bill of Rights* as falling "somewhere between a statute and a constitutional instrument," in recognition of the fact that it was "designed and adopted to perform a more fundamental role than ordinary statutes in this country,"[97] to access to information as a "derivative right" to the freedom of expression under section 2(b) of the *Charter*,[98] and to the *Official Languages Act* and the *Privacy Act* as being "closely linked to the values and rights set out in the Constitution, and that this explains the quasi-constitutional status, that this Court has recognized them as having."[99]

Given these links to the Constitution, the recent scholarship has focused on the role of quasi-constitutional legislation in the implementation of constitutional obligations, or "constitutional imperatives."[100] This principle was most succinctly described by LeBel J in his dissenting opinion in *Canada (Information Commissioner) v Canada (Minister of National Defence)*: "[s]tatutes that protect *Charter* rights have often been found to have quasi-constitutional status."[101] The clearest example is found in the Federal Court decision in *Canada (Attorney General) v Viola*, which was adopted by a unanimous Supreme Court of Canada in *Lavigne v Canada (Office of the Commissioner of Official Languages)*:

> The 1988 *Official Languages Act* is not an ordinary statute. It reflects both the Constitution of the country and the social and political compromise out of which it arose. To the extent that it is the exact reflection of the recognition of the official languages contained in subsections 16(1) and (3) of the *Canadian Charter of Rights and Freedoms*, it follows the rules of interpretation of that *Charter* as they have been defined by the Supreme Court of Canada. To the extent also that it is an extension of the rights and guarantees recognized in the *Charter* . . . and its taking precedence over other statutes in accordance with subsection 82(1), it belongs to that privileged category of quasi-constitutional legislation which reflects "certain basic goals of our society" and

96 *Robichaud v Canada (Treasury Board)*, [1987] 2 SCR 84 at para 13 [*Robichaud*].

97 *Skapinker*, above note 65 at para 10.

98 *Ontario (Public Safety and Security) v Criminal Lawyers' Association*, 2010 SCC 23 at para 30 [*Criminal Lawyers' Association*]. *Canadian Charter of Rights and Freedoms*, Part I of the *Constitution Act, 1982*, being Schedule B to the *Canada Act 1982* (UK), 1982, c 11.

99 *Lavigne*, above note 69 at para 25.

100 MacDonnell, above note 48 at 511.

101 *Canada (Information Commissioner)*, above note 66 at para 79.

must be so interpreted "as to advance the broad policy considerations underlying it."[102]

The Federal Court, in the 2013 decision of *Chopra v Canada (Attorney General)*, found that these pronouncements "demonstrate the kind of characteristics required to grant a piece a law quasi-constitutional status," and the Supreme Court of Canada was therefore able to conclude in *Lavigne* that "[t]he fact that the *Official Languages Act* is a legislative measure taken in order to fulfil the constitutional duty in respect of bilingualism is not in doubt."[103]

The links to the Constitution are also observed in the right to access government information; as noted above, the Supreme Court of Canada has referred to access as a "derivative right" to the freedom of expression in section 2(b) of the *Charter*.[104] Lower courts have similarly suggested that "freedom of expression cannot be exercised properly or fully without access to information," and that "there is little importance to the constitutional guarantee of freedom of expression if this freedom does not include a meaningful right of access to information."[105]

This degree of correlation between a constitutional obligation and the quasi-constitutional statute implementing it may not be necessary, as not all quasi-constitutional statutes stem from constitutional provisions that impose positive obligations.[106] The Federal Court in *Chopra* has also pointed out that the mere fact that "a right guaranteed under the *Charter* is at stake will not elevate that statute to a quasi-constitutional status," and it rejected the claim that the *Public Servants Disclosure Protection Act* is quasi-constitutional.[107]

In addition to the furtherance of constitutional obligations, more important are the theoretical links between quasi-constitutionality and the normative elements of the Constitution. In *Reference re Secession of Quebec*, the Supreme Court of Canada set out a non-exhaustive list of "four fundamental and organizing principles of the Constitution," which include democracy, the protection of minorities, federalism,

102 *Canada (Attorney General) v Viola*, [1991] 1 FC 373 at para 16 (CA); *Lavigne*, above note 69 at para 23.

103 *Chopra v Canada (Attorney General)*, 2013 FC 644 at para 74 [*Chopra*], aff'd 2014 FCA 179; *Lavigne*, above note 69 at para 21.

104 *Canada (Information Commissioner)*, above note 66 at para 79.

105 *R v CHNS*, [1983] YJ No 16 at para 16 (Terr Ct).

106 MacDonnell, above note 48 at 514–18.

107 *Chopra*, above note 103 at para 74; *Public Servants Disclosure Protection Act*, SC 2005, c 46.

constitutionalism, and the rule of law.[108] Since the Court referred to these principles as informing and sustaining the constitutional text, it is the specific provisions of the Constitution that implement or actualize them.[109] It can likewise be argued that quasi-constitutional laws embody these constitutional principles and similarly help to implement and actualize them.

Of the four foundational constitutional principles the courts have said the most about the relationship between the principle of democracy and quasi-constitutional law. Most recently, in the 2017 decision of *Douez v Facebook*, three justices of the Supreme Court of Canada held that quasi-constitutional rights "play an essential role in a free and democratic society and embody key Canadian values."[110]

With human rights legislation this relationship is due primarily to the importance of equality and inclusion to the principle of democracy. As Michael Ignatieff explains, "the rights revolution is a story of inclusion, of how previously excluded groups obtained rights of equality. In this sense, the tension of rights has widened and deepened our democracy."[111] The Court views democracy as embodying certain values such as "respect for the inherent dignity of the human person, commitment to social justice and equality, accommodation of a wide variety of beliefs, respect for cultural and group identity, and faith in social and political institutions which enhance the participation of individuals and groups in society."[112] This was most notably recognized by McIntyre J in *Andrews v Law Society of British Columbia*, who held that "[d]iscrimination is unacceptable in a democratic society because it epitomizes the worst effects of the denial of equality, and discrimination reinforced by law is particularly repugnant."[113] A similar statement was made by L'Heureux-Dubé J in *Canada (Attorney General) v Mossop* in reference to the *Canadian Human Rights Act*: "[t]he *Act*, in prohibiting certain forms of discrimination, has the

108 *Reference re Secession of Quebec*, [1998] 2 SCR 217 at para 32 [*Quebec Secession Reference*].

109 Sujit Choudhry & Robert Howse, "Constitutional Theory and the Quebec Secession Reference" (2000) 13 *Canadian Journal of Law and Jurisprudence* 143 at 155.

110 *Douez v Facebook, Inc*, 2017 SCC 33 at para 58 [*Douez*].

111 Michael Ignatieff, *The Rights Revolution* (Toronto: House of Anansi Press, 2000) at 1.

112 *R v Oakes*, [1986] 1 SCR 103 at 136, cited in *Quebec Secession Reference*, above note 108 at para 64.

113 *Andrews v Law Society of British Columbia*, [1989] 1 SCR 143 at para 35.

express purpose of promoting the value of equality which lies at the centre of a free and democratic society."[114]

Justice Cory's majority judgment in *Hill v Church of Scientology of Toronto* displays the link between the quasi-constitutional common law right to the preservation of a person's good reputation and democracy. He explained that defamatory statements are not related to the "core values" that underline the freedom of expression, but rather "are detrimental to the advancement of these values and harmful to the interests of a free and democratic society."[115] In contrast, the good reputation of an individual helps advance and promote the principle of democracy:

> Democracy has always recognized and cherished the fundamental importance of an individual. That importance must, in turn, be based upon the good repute of a person. It is that good repute which enhances an individual's sense of worth and value. False allegations can so very quickly and completely destroy a good reputation. A reputation tarnished by libel can seldom regain its former lustre. A democratic society, therefore, has an interest in ensuring that its members can enjoy and protect their good reputation so long as it is merited.[116]

On this basis Cory J concluded that "[i]t follows that the protection of the good reputation of an individual is of fundamental importance to our democratic society."[117]

In *Lavigne* Gonthier J held that the federal *Privacy Act* serves as "a reminder of the extent to which the protection of privacy is necessary to the preservation of a free and democratic society."[118] In making this statement he relied largely on *Dagg v Canada*, where La Forest J reasoned that privacy was vital to the individual's autonomy, unique personhood, and ability to engage in "one's own thoughts, actions and decisions," and on that basis concluded that "[t]he protection of privacy is a fundamental value in modern, democratic states."[119]

---

114 *Canada (Attorney General) v Mossop*, [1993] 1 SCR 554 at para 97 [*Mossop*]. Justice L'Heureux-Dubé wrote in dissent, but her comments were adopted by the Federal Court in *Vilven v Air Canada*, 2009 FC 367 at para 76.

115 *Hill*, above note 71 at para 106.

116 *Ibid* at para 108.

117 *Ibid* at para 120.

118 *Lavigne*, above note 69 at para 25. See also *Canada (Information Commissioner) v Canada (Commissioner of the Royal Canadian Mounted Police)*, 2003 SCC 8 at para 25.

119 *Dagg v Canada (Minister of Finance)*, [1997] 2 SCR 403 at para 65 [*Dagg*].

This reasoning was extended to legislation protecting personal privacy in the private sector by the Supreme Court of Canada, such as the federal *Personal Information Protection and Electronic Documents Act* (*PIPEDA*) and equivalent provincial legislation, which have likewise been found to promote democracy. In *Alberta v United Food and Commercial Workers*, a unanimous Court stated: "[i]nsofar as PIPA [Alberta *Personal Information Protection Act*] seeks to safeguard informational privacy, it is 'quasi-constitutional' in nature . . . . The importance of the protection of privacy in a vibrant democracy cannot be overstated."[120]

Access-to-information legislation even more clearly advances the foundational constitutional principle of democracy. This right has been described by the Supreme Court of Canada as effectively being able to "increase transparency in government, contribute to an informed public, and enhance an open and democratic society."[121] In this respect, access-to-information legislation has been deemed "fundamental to our democracy,"[122] because "[i]t helps to ensure first, that citizens have the information required to participate meaningfully in the democratic process, and secondly, that politicians and bureaucrats remain accountable to the citizenry."[123] The Court referred to access to information as "a derivative right" to the freedom of expression in section 2(b) of the *Charter* because "it is a necessary precondition of meaningful expression on the functioning of government."[124] Justice McMahon, of the Alberta Court of Queen's Bench, cited the Supreme Court of Canada's jurisprudence

---

120 *Alberta (Information and Privacy Commissioner) v United Food and Commercial Workers, Local 401*, 2013 SCC 62 at para 22. This has also been applied to the federal *PIPEDA*, above note 69; see *Mountain Province Diamonds Inc v De Beers Canada Inc*, [2014] OJ No 1554 at para 37 (SCJ).

121 *Criminal Lawyers' Association*, above note 98 at para 1, cited in *Canada (Information Commissioner)*, above note 66 at para 15, by Charron J writing for the majority, and in the dissenting opinion of LeBel J at para 78. The Federal Court similarly said that "[t]he purpose of the *Access to Information Act* is to enshrine an essential component of democracy: the public's right to government information (s 2 of the Act). This right to government information is mandatory for both public scrutiny of government activities, as well as the full and meaningful participation in public debate and discussion." *Bronskill v Canada (Canadian Heritage)*, 2011 FC 983 at para 4.

122 Justice LeBel in *Canada (Information Commissioner)*, above note 66 at para 79.

123 *Dagg*, above note 119 at para 61, cited in *Lavigne*, above note 69 at para 25. See also *Macdonell*, above note 67 at para 15; *Toronto Police Services Board v Ontario (Information and Privacy Commissioner)*, 2009 ONCA 20 at paras 46–47; Vincent Kazmierski, "Something to Talk About: Is There a *Charter* Right to Access Government Information?" (2008) 31 *Dalhousie Law Journal* 351.

124 *Criminal Lawyers' Association*, above note 98 at para 30.

on the link between access-to-information regimes and democracy as implying that "[t]he public's right to information is a powerful weapon in the defence of democracy."[125]

The Supreme Court of Canada described the protection of minorities in the *Quebec Succession Reference* both as an independent foundational constitutional principle as well as one that operates in symbiosis with the principle of democracy. The Court began by recounting how the concern for the protection of minorities has grown exponentially since the entrenchment of the *Charter*, but it also acknowledged that its origins are much older and that it was "one of the key considerations motivating the enactment of the *Charter*."[126] The Court did not directly refer to quasi-constitutional statutes, but behind this statement is the long history of provincial anti-discrimination and human rights legislation, as well as the drive for a charter of rights that first resulted in the enactment of the *Canadian Bill of Rights*.[127]

In *Solski (Tutor of) v Quebec (Attorney General)*, the Supreme Court of Canada stated that "[t]he protection of minority language rights by s. 23 of the Canadian *Charter* is an integral part of the broader protection of minority rights, a principle recognized as foundational to Canada's Constitution in *Reference re Secession of Quebec*."[128] This is because language has been recognized to be far more than a means of communication, but rather what the Court calls, "part and parcel of the identity and culture of the people speaking it."[129] This statement applies equally to quasi-constitutional language rights statutes because, as the Ontario Court of Appeal observed in *Lalonde v Ontario (Commission de restructuration des services de santé)*, such statutes "build on the language rights contained in the *Constitution Act, 1867* and the *Charter* to advance the equality of status or use of the French language."[130]

---

125 *Calgary Police Service v Alberta (Information and Privacy Commissioner)*, 2010 ABQB 82 at para 74.

126 *Quebec Secession Reference*, above note 108 at para 81.

127 For a concise summary of the development of anti-discrimination and human rights legislation in Canada, see, especially, Ian A Hunter, "Human Rights Legislation in Canada: Its Origin, Development and Interpretation" (1976) 15 *University of Western Ontario Law Review* 21.

128 *Solski*, above note 70 at para 2.

129 *Mahe v Alberta*, [1990] 1 SCR 342 at para 32, cited by the Ontario Court of Appeal in *Lalonde*, above note 70 at para 134.

130 *Ibid* at para 129.

Language rights advance the principle of federalism since the protection of language rights provided much of the impetus for Canada's federal structure.[131] This is not only a historic relic of Canada's federal origin, but an ongoing reality. As La Forest J explained in *Mercure*, "rights regarding the English and French languages . . . are basic to the continued viability of the nation."[132] Quasi-constitutional language rights ordinances in the three territories also protect Indigenous languages.

The Supreme Court of Canada has referred to the rule of law at its most basic level as protecting a sense of a "stable, predictable and ordered society."[133]Accordingly, when a court is asked to enforce a foreign judgment in Canada, it is to take into account whether it would violate constitutional and quasi-constitutional rights. The Court in *Pro Swing Inc v Elta Golf Inc*, for example, referred to the violation of the rule of law that would occur if a foreign judgment that circumvented quasi-constitutional rights was allowed to be enforced in Canada.[134] As observed in Chapter 3, the Court in that case was concerned about the enforcement of a consent decree from an Ohio court that required the disclosure of information that was protected under the quasi-constitutional *PIPEDA*. More recently in *Douez*, the Court held that the public good of having Canadian courts adjudicate claims involving constitutional or constitutional rights should be taken into account when determining whether to enforce a forum selection and choice of law clause in a contract.[135]

Quasi-constitutional statutes also more directly promote rule of law values. This is most clearly observed under the *Canadian Bill of Rights* and the Quebec *Charter of Human Rights and Freedoms*, which protect the right to a fair hearing.[136] Rule of law values are also more broadly promoted by quasi-constitutional legislation since human rights statutes prevent decision making on discriminatory grounds, freedom of information legislation creates transparency, and language rights legislation makes laws and legal processes accessible. Some quasi-constitutional statutes even directly refer to the rule of law. The *Human Rights Act* of Nova

131 *Lalonde, ibid* at para 86.

132 *Mercure*, above note 23 at para 46, cited in *Lalonde, ibid* at para 112.

133 *Quebec Secession Reference*, above note 108 at para 70. The rule of law was first recognized by the Supreme Court of Canada as constituting "a fundamental postulate of our constitutional structure" in *Roncarelli v Duplessis*, [1959] SCR 121 at 142.

134 *Pro Swing Inc v Elta Golf Inc*, 2006 SCC 52 at paras 59–60.

135 *Douez*, above note 110 at paras 58–59. See also *Demers c Yahoo! Inc*, 2017 QCCS 4154.

136 *Canadian Bill of Rights*, above note 33, s 2(e); *Charter of Human Rights and Freedoms*, CQLR c C-12, s 23.

Scotia, for example, stipulates that one of its purposes is to "recognize that human rights must be protected by the rule of law."[137]

The courts in the United Kingdom have similarly invoked the concept of fundamental law as the basis of constitutional statutes; however, identifying fundamental values has been more challenging as the courts cannot turn to a written constitution for guidance. Jenkins's notion that some statutes in the United Kingdom have normative significance and are woven together with common law principles into a broader "constitutional fabric," as detailed above, has been questioned because it is not obvious which principles are part of the constitution.[138] Despite the challenge, it has been argued that identifying fundamental principles is a role that courts must necessarily fulfill when a legal system recognizes a hierarchy between regular laws and constitutional ones to prevent their "casual or incidental erosion."[139] Nonetheless, devising a definition of what makes a statute constitutional in the United Kingdom has been an elusive undertaking.[140]

The concept of fundamental law is the theoretical basis of quasi-constitutionality and connotes an association with the Constitution and the foundational principles that underpin it. The relationship of certain rights to the foundational principles of the Canadian Constitution is what establishes their fundamental nature and distinguishes them from rights that are merely acquired by law.[141] Fundamental rights in statutory or common law form help advance the foundational constitutional principles and accordingly are recognized as quasi-constitutional. The next section will explore how the courts balance the fundamental nature of rights with legislative intent when considering the primacy of quasi-constitutional legislation.

---

137 Nova Scotia *Human Rights Act*, above note 62, s 2(c).

138 Jenkins, above note 52; Ahmed & Perry, above note 86 at 469.

139 Mark Elliott, "Embracing 'Constitutional' Legislation: Towards Fundamental Law?" (2003) 54 *Northern Ireland Legal Quarterly* 25 at 32.

140 See, especially, Ahmed & Perry, above note 86 at 464; David Feldman, "The Nature and Significance of 'Constitutional' Legislation" (2013) 129 *Law Quarterly Review* 343; Jenkins, above note 52.

141 See, for example, *Globe and Mail v Canada (Attorney General)*, 2010 SCC 41 at para 34, where the Supreme Court of Canada distinguished between a fundamental right which is quasi-constitutional and a right acquired by law, such as a social and economic right.

C. FUNDAMENTAL RIGHTS AND LEGISLATIVE INTENT

By invoking the concept of fundamental law, the courts are necessarily relying on the doctrine of presumed legislative intent, and they resolve conflict between two statutes by prioritizing the quasi-constitutional statute that they believe the legislature enacted to protect fundamental rights. The presence of a primacy provision is not necessarily the only indication of the legislature's intention regarding a statute's relative importance; indeed, the content of the statute is often even more revealing of its overall significance as primacy provisions are sometimes used for more mundane matters.

In balancing the fundamental nature of rights with legislative intent, courts and tribunals recognize that the legislature can override quasi-constitutional rights or amend or repeal the legislation's provisions; however, they are diligent in ensuring that the legislature intended to derogate from a law upholding fundamental rights by accepting only clear and unequivocal statutory language. Hence, quasi-constitutional legislation is not subject to the doctrine of implied repeal; courts and tribunals require explicit language invoking the derogation.

1) Presumed Legislative Intent and Primacy

When courts give effect to the intentions of the legislature through the provisions of a statute, they maintain an underlying presumption that the legislature did not seek to undermine the basic tenets of the legal order, including that it did not intend to subvert fundamental rights. As Neil Craik explains:

> Quite apart from this practice of direct judicial review, the courts often engage in indirect review when they interpret legislation in light of common law constitutional values such as respect for individual autonomy and private property rights. In such cases the courts presume that the legislature, in enacting a particular provision, did not intend to violate long recognized constitutional values or authorize its delegates to do so.[142]

Such an approach was applied by La Forest J, of the New Brunswick Court of Appeal, in *New Brunswick v Estabrooks Pontiac Buick Ltd*:

142 Neil Craik et al, eds, *Public Law: Cases, Materials, and Commentary* (Toronto: Emond Montgomery, 2011) at 361.

> This approach of the courts to legislative action permitted them to exercise an important role in the protection of individual liberties even in the absence of an entrenched *Bill of Rights*. If the legislation is clear, of course, the intent of the Legislature must be respected. But what these presumptions ensure is that a law that appears to transgress our basic political understandings should be clearly expressed so as to invite the debate which is the lifeblood of parliamentary democracy.[143]

Justice La Forest called this presumption a constitutional principle in the British sense, and he asserted that the intention to modify or abolish this principle must be clearly stated by the legislature.[144] He also warned that courts are to apply the principle "with great caution to ensure that its application conforms to changing social values and affords the Legislature the widest possible scope in the performance of its task of adjusting private rights to meet evolving social realities."[145]

Justice La Forest set out the general principles of presumed legislative intent in *Estabrooks*, although he was not specifically addressing quasi-constitutional legislation. The use of presumed legislative intent in the context of a quasi-constitutional statute is first observed in the comments of Lamer J in *Heerspink*:

> When the subject matter of a law is said to be the comprehensive statement of the "human rights" of the people living in that jurisdiction, then there is no doubt in my mind that the people of that jurisdiction have through their legislature clearly indicated that they consider that law, and the values it endeavours to buttress and protect, are, save their constitutional laws, more important than all others. Therefore, short of that legislature speaking to the contrary in express and unequivocal language in the Code or in some other enactment, it is intended that the Code supersede all other laws when conflict arises.
>
> As a result, the legal proposition *generalia specialibus non derogant* cannot be applied to such a code. Indeed the *Human Rights Code*, when in conflict with "particular and specific legislation," is not to be treated as another ordinary law of general application. It should be recognized for what it is, a fundamental law.

143 *New Brunswick v Estabrooks Pontiac Buick Ltd*, [1982] NBJ No 397 at para 25 (CA) [*Estabrooks*].

144 *Ibid* at para 30.

145 *Ibid* at para 32.

> Furthermore, as it is a public and fundamental law, no one, unless clearly authorized by law to do so, may contractually agree to suspend its operation and thereby put oneself beyond the reach of its protection.[146]

Justice La Forest expressed the principle of presumed legislative intent in negative terms to prevent the erosion of rights. Justice Lamer, on the other hand, applied it in positive terms by identifying the *Human Rights Code* as fundamental law that the legislature enacted as a comprehensive scheme for the protection of rights. He accordingly found that it held primacy over all other enactments. The courts use this approach to attribute primacy to quasi-constitutional statutes that do not contain an express primacy provision.

Justice Lamer's approach to presumed legislative intent in the enactment of human rights legislation reflects the development of anti-discrimination law, which evolved in legislative rather than common law form. Unlike the *Canadian Bill of Rights*, which the Supreme Court of Canada interpreted as merely codifying existing common law, Lamer J observed that the legislature intended to establish fundamental law through comprehensive human rights legislation. Professor Denise Réaume refers to such an approach as the "top-down model" of anti-discrimination law, which she describes as a circumstance where the legislature seeks to "bring to life a grand theory about the norms regulating human interaction."[147] Taking guidance from the overall importance and comprehensiveness of human rights legislation and finding that it holds primacy over other enactments due to the fundamental nature of the rights it upholds is consistent with the classic description of presumed legislative intent as an "*a priori* scheme of values which the legislature was deemed to adhere."[148]

An express primacy provision is therefore not the only method of uncovering legislative intent, and it can reasonably be presumed that Parliament is motivated by principles of justice and the common good when enacting legislation. That is particularly so when, as Lamer J points out, the statute "is said to be the comprehensive statement of the 'human rights,' of the people living in that jurisdiction." As Trevor Allan recognizes, "[t]he presumption that elected legislators intend to honour the most fundamental requirements of the rule of law can scarcely be

146 *Heerspink*, above note 35 at 157–58.

147 Denise G Réaume, "Of Pigeonholes and Principles: A Reconsideration of Discrimination Law" (2002) 40 *Osgoode Hall Law Journal* 113 at para 2.

148 JA Corry, "Administrative Law and the Interpretation of Statutes" (1936) 1 *University of Toronto Law Journal* 286 at 296.

controversial in a liberal democracy that preserves a basic separation of powers between the principal organs of government."[149]

A closer examination of primacy provisions reveals that they are not limited to quasi-constitutional legislation; indeed, at times they are used to address mundane matters. Primacy provisions are found in a number of statutes other than quasi-constitutional ones to address a range of matters such as public sector salaries, back-to-work legislation, expropriation, and land-use planning.[150] Contrary to primacy provisions in quasi-constitutional statutes, those found in regular statutes are often limited to balancing interest in a specific subject area; thus, they do not establish the primacy of the legislation more broadly.[151] For example, an Ontario statute designed to restrain public sector salaries contains a primacy provision that holds that it prevails over other compensation plans.[152] Back-to-work statutes enacted in response to striking teachers in Ontario contain primacy provisions that make these statutes prevail over the *Education Act* and collective agreements.[153] Ontario's *Fire Protection and Prevention Act, 1997* holds that the more restrictive rule applies in the event of a conflict between the fire code and a municipal bylaw respecting the keeping and manufacturing of explosives.[154] Some statutes also have a reverse primacy provision that holds that other statutes prevail in the event of a conflict.[155] Even when primacy provisions in regular statutes are worded more broadly, they are sometimes qualified so as not to be interpreted to reduce any rights or entitlement in remedial legislation, such as the *Employment*

---

149 TRS Allan, "Constitutional Dialogue and the Justification of Judicial Review" (2003) 23 *Oxford Journal of Legal Studies* 563 at 571–72 [Allan, "Constitutional Dialogue"].

150 See, for example, *Public Sector Compensation Restraint to Protect Public Services Act, 2010*, SO 2010, c 1, Schedule 24, s 12(1); *Broader Public Sector Executive Compensation Act, 2014*, SO 2014, c 13, Schedule 1, s 23; *Back to School Act (Hamilton-Wentworth District School Board), 2000*, SO 2000, c 23, ss 2(2) and 22(3) [repealed]; *Back to School Act (Simcoe Muskoka Catholic District School Board), 2002*, SO 2002, c 20, ss 2(2) and 21(5) [repealed]; *Expropriations Act*, RSO 1990, c E.26, s 2(4); *Ontario Planning and Development Act*, RSO 1990, c O.35, s 10.

151 See, for example, *Greenbelt Act, 2005*, SO 2005, c 1, s 8; *Adjudicative Tribunals Accountability, Governance and Appointments Act, 2009*, SO 2009, c 33, Schedule 5, s 6(4); *Public Service of Ontario Act, 2006*, SO 2006, c 35, Schedule A, s 43(3).

152 *Public Sector Compensation Restraint to Protect Public Services Act, 2010*, SO 2010, c 1, Schedule 24, s 12(1).

153 Above note 150.

154 SO 1997, c 4, s 12(5).

155 See, for example, *Adjudicative Tribunals Accountability, Governance and Appointments Act, 2009*, SO 2009, c 33, Schedule 5, s 14(5); *Statutory Powers Procedure Act*, RSO 1990, c S.22, s 21.2(3).

Standards Act and the *Workplace Safety and Insurance Act*.[156] Most important, primacy provisions in regular statutes sometimes expressly state that they do not prevail over human rights legislation.[157]

The *Canadian Human Rights Act* provides the clearest example of a primacy provision not necessarily being the most indicative of a statute's relative importance. The *Canadian Human Rights Act* does not contain a primacy provision but has been held to prevail when in conflict with other statutes due to the fundamental nature of the rights it upholds and its quasi-constitutional status.[158] If a court or tribunal were to conclude that Parliament's intention was for the *Canadian Human Rights Act* to be treated as a regular statute simply because it lacks a primacy provision, it would reach the wrong outcome based on an insufficient assessment of legislative intent. Indeed, the *Canadian Human Rights Act* prevails even over some quasi-constitutional statutes, as the primacy provision in the *Official Languages Act* holds that it prevails over all other statutes except the *Canadian Human Rights Act*.[159] Accordingly, a broader contextual analysis that considers the purpose of a statute and its content is often more revealing of a legislature's intention regarding statute's relative importance than the presence of a primacy provision.

2) Overriding Primacy

The theoretical basis of all legislation in the doctrine of legislative supremacy also gives Parliament and provincial legislatures the right to retain the final word; and they can legislatively override the primacy of quasi-constitutional legislation. As Maxime St-Hilaire explains with respect to human rights legislation, they "are ordinary statutes on the formal level. Their adoption is not an exercise of the constitution-making power. Consequently, they cannot set out the conditions of validity of statutes."[160] This is readily observed in the wording of some primacy provisions, which

156 *Public Sector Compensation Restraint to Protect Public Services Act, 2010*, above note 150, s 12(1); *Broader Public Sector Accountability Act, 2010*, SO 2010, c 25, s 7.17(1).

157 See, for example, *Broader Public Sector Executive Compensation Act, 2014*, SO 2014, c 13, Schedule 1, s 17(a); *Residential Tenancies Act, 2006*, SO 2006, c 17, s 3(4).

158 See, especially, *Druken*, above note 40; *Canada (Attorney General) v Uzoaba*, [1995] 2 FC 569 (TD); *Franke v Canada (Canadian Armed Forces)*, [1998] CHRD No 3 at paras 753–66, aff'd (*sub nom Canada (Canadian Human Rights Commission) v Canada (Canadian Armed Forces) (re Franke)*), [1999] 3 FC 653 (TD).

159 *Official Languages Act*, RSC 1985, c 31 (4th Supp), s 82.

160 St-Hilaire, above note 48 at para 83.

hold that the quasi-constitutional statute prevails unless a provision in another statute specifically provides otherwise.

Courts and tribunals recognize that the legislature retains the ability to override quasi-constitutional rights, but they diligently seek to ensure that the legislature intended to derogate from a law upholding fundamental rights by accepting only clear statutory language. The doctrine of implied repeal thus does not apply to quasi-constitutional legislation. Courts and tribunals therefore look for explicit language invoking the derogation to ensure that the legislature truly sought to override fundamental quasi-constitutional rights. The method by which the primacy of quasi-constitutional legislation can be overridden was formulated by McIntyre J in *Craton*:

> It is not constitutional in nature in the sense that it may not be altered, amended, or repealed by the Legislature. It is, however, of such a nature that it may not be altered, amended or repealed, nor may exceptions be created to its provisions, save by clear legislative pronouncement.[161]

Justice Major made a similar statement with regard to the *Canadian Bill of Rights* in *Authorson*: "[i]f Parliament wishes to circumvent the protections of the *Bill of Rights*, it must do so explicitly by stating that the legislation in question operates notwithstanding the *Bill of Rights*."[162] As a result of this function, the Ontario Court of Appeal has referred to quasi-constitutional status as occupying "a uniquely protected sphere in the legal orbit."[163]

It has also been recognized that constitutional statutes in the United Kingdom cannot be repealed impliedly but rather require express words. It was clear from the House of Lord's decision in *R v Secretary of State for Transport, ex parte Factortame Ltd (No 2)* that the *European Communities Act 1972* could not be impliedly repealed, but the courts have since suggested that the same is true of all constitutional statutes, beginning with the assertion by Laws LJ in *Thoburn* that "[o]rdinary statutes may be impliedly repealed. Constitutional statutes may not."[164] Accordingly, what is required for the repeal of a constitutional statute or the abrogation of a fundamental right is "express words," or "unambiguous words on the face

161 *Craton*, above note 36 at para 8.

162 *Authorson*, above note 33 at para 10.

163 *Ford Motor Co of Canada v Ontario (Human Rights Commission)*, [2001] OJ No 4937 at para 47 (CA).

164 *Thoburn*, above note 72 at para 63.

of the later statute."[165] In reaching this conclusion, Laws LJ referred to the doctrine of implied repeal as "the common law's own creature."[166] In *BH & Anor*, the Supreme Court of the United Kingdom subsequently held that the *Scotland Act 1998* was "incapable of being altered otherwise than by an express enactment," because of its constitutional status.[167]

Overriding the primacy of a quasi-constitutional statute, therefore, requires the use of specific language that the statute in question will prevail notwithstanding any conflict with the quasi-constitutional one. An example of a clear legislative override is found in section 4(6) of the *Broader Public Sector Executive Compensation Act*, which reads: "Subsections (4) and (5) prevail over the *Freedom of Information and Protection of Privacy Act*."[168] In the case of the federal *Access to Information Act*, which incorporates by reference select provisions from other statutory instruments that override the general right to access government information, the courts are diligent in ensuring that the requested documents fit within the provision of the Act with the overriding effect.[169]

Courts and tribunals accordingly will not accept that a legislature intended to override the primacy of a quasi-constitutional statute short of clear statutory language that explicitly invokes the override. In the 2006 *Tranchemontagne* decision, for example, the Supreme Court of Canada rejected an argument that the Social Benefits Tribunal lacked jurisdiction to apply the *Human Rights Code* on the basis of a provision in the *Ontario Works Act, 1997*, which bars the tribunal from determining "the constitutional validity of a provision of an Act or a regulation."[170] Justice Bastarache provided the following reasons:

> [T]he legislature could not possibly have intended that the *Code* be denied application by analogy to the Constitution. While it clearly prohibited the SBT [Social Benefits Tribunal] from considering the

---

165 *Ibid.*

166 *Ibid* at para 60.

167 *BH & Anor*, above note 73 at para 30.

168 *Broader Public Sector Executive Compensation Act, 2014*, above note 157, s 5(6).

169 See, for example, *Hibernia Management and Development Co v Canada-Newfoundland and Labrador Offshore Petroleum Board*, 2012 FC 417 at para 46; *Husky Oil Operations Ltd v Canada-Newfoundland and Labrador Offshore Petroleum Board*, 2014 FC 1170 at paras 39–41; *Canadian Council of Christian Charities v Canada (Minister of Finance)*, [1999] FCJ No 771 at para 9 (TD); *Summers v Canada (Minister of National Revenue)*, 2014 FC 880 at paras 54–56; *Siemens Canada Ltd v Canada (Minister of Public Works and Government Services)*, 2001 FCT 1202 at paras 12–20, aff'd 2002 FCA 414.

170 *Ontario Works Act, 1997*, SO 1997, c 25, Schedule A, s 67(2).

> constitutional validity of laws and regulations, it equally clearly chose not to invoke the same prohibition with respect to the *Code*.[171]

He further stated that "[c]onsistent with the human rights regime it crafted, the legislature has afforded the *Code* the possibility of broad application even while denying the SBT the authority to determine constitutional issues."[172] *Tranchemontagne* SCC best displays the extent to which quasi-constitutional statutes are immune from implied repeal. The *Ontario Disability Support Program Act, 1997* is much more specific legislation than the *Human Rights Code*, and it was enacted seven years after the *Code*; however, the *Code* still has primacy.

The courts have held that the same degree of clarity is required to override the primacy of the other categories of quasi-constitutional legislation. In *Ontario (Community Safety and Correctional Services) v Ontario (Information and Privacy Commissioner)*, the Supreme Court of Canada was unsatisfied that the establishment of an offence for breaches of confidentiality in *Christopher's Law* ousted the right to access information under the *Freedom of Information and Protection of Privacy Act*.[173] In rejecting the ministry's argument that the confidentiality provision made *Christopher's Law* prevail, the Court stated that "[h]ad the legislature intended the confidentiality provision in *Christopher's Law* to prevail over *FIPPA*, it could easily have included specific language to that effect." It cited several statutes in which the legislature included specific language to make the override clear.[174] Consequently, the information and privacy commissioner of Ontario does not accept that confidentiality clauses override the right to access in the *Freedom of Information and Protection of Privacy Act* unless they explicitly state that they do.[175]

The case of *Saunders v Kentville (Town)* before the Nova Scotia Board of Inquiry under the *Human Rights Act* illustrates how tribunals rely on the reasons of McIntyre J in *Craton* when considering whether the override has been invoked.[176] The respondent police board in that case unsuccessfully argued that the Board of Inquiry lacked jurisdiction to

171 *Tranchemontagne* SCC, above note 1 at para 32.

172 *Ibid.*

173 *Ontario (Community Safety and Correctional Services) v Ontario (Information and Privacy Commissioner)*, 2014 SCC 31 at para 33.

174 *Ibid* at paras 33–35.

175 See, for example, *Order PO-3174; Ontario (Ministry of Health and Long-Term Care) (Re)*, [2013] OIPC No 52 at para 23.

176 *Saunders v Kentville (Town)*, [2004] NSHRBID No 9.

hear the human rights complaint because the exclusive jurisdiction under the *Police Act* to deal with the discipline of police officers had primacy over the *Human Rights Act* by virtue of section 49(1), which states, "[w]hen there is a conflict between this Act and another Act, the provisions of this Act prevail." In rejecting this argument, the presiding chair cited *Craton* and found that the provision "is not a sufficiently clear statement from the legislature that it intends to deprive a police officer of all rights to file a complaint under the *Nova Scotia Human Rights Act*."[177]

A well-known statutory override was previously found in section 67 of the *Canadian Human Rights Act*: "Nothing in this Act affects any provision of the *Indian Act* or any provision made under or pursuant to that Act." The provision was interpreted as not exempting all decisions made by First Nations governments. In *Shubenacadie Indian Band v Canada (Human Rights Commission)*, the Federal Court rejected the argument that the Canadian Human Rights Commission lacked jurisdiction to hear a complaint about a band council's refusal to provide social assistance to non-Indigenous spouses of band members:

> While undoubtedly section 67 recognizes that certain provisions of the *Indian Act* and Regulations may conflict with the *Canadian Human Rights Act* and in such cases the *Indian Act* and Regulations will prevail, I do not think section 67 is to be interpreted as taking out of the scope of the *Canadian Human Rights Act* all decisions of Indian band councils provided they are made under the Indian Band Council Procedure Regulations. If it was Parliament's intention to immunize all decisions of Indian band councils from overview by the Human Rights Commission, Parliament would have expressly so provided rather than enacting section 67. Section 67 immunizes decisions authorized by the *Indian Act* and Regulations, but not all decisions made by Indian band councils.[178]

---

177 *Ibid* at para 18.

178 *Shubenacadie Indian Band v Canada (Canadian Human Rights Commission) (Re MacNutt)*, [1998] 2 FC 198 at para 31 (TD), aff'd [2000] FCJ No 702 (CA), leave to appeal to SCC refused, [2000] SCCA No 398.

This provision was repealed in 2008 with a three-year grace period for First Nations governments.[179]

Legislatures are cautious and exercise restraint when overriding the primacy of quasi-constitutional legislation. It has been noted that there is only one instance of a statutory override to the primacy of the *Canadian Bill of Rights*, which was to deal with the 1970 October Crisis in Quebec.[180] The use of override provisions is more common among some of the other categories of quasi-constitutional legislation. Overrides to the primacy of human rights legislation are typically used for public health and safety purposes. In Ontario, for example, override provisions to the primacy of the *Human Rights Code* include upholding mandatory retirement of firefighters,[181] age distinctions in accident benefits,[182] workers' compensation benefits,[183] medical tests for the possession of a driver's licence,[184] and the prohibition of minors from gambling facilities.[185]

There is also an intrinsic safeguard in that only a sovereign legislature can override primacy through legislation. Bodies such as municipalities and cooperative boards that have delegated authority from the legislature to pass subordinate laws, such as bylaws and directives, are clearly precluded from utilizing the override. The exception to this is that some primacy provisions explicitly authorize the use of the override through regulation.[186] In all circumstances, regardless of whether the quasi-constitutional statute contains a primacy provision, it can be overridden only by "clear legislative pronouncement," as outlined by McIntyre J in *Craton*. The same criteria would logically apply to primacy provisions that do not explicitly account for their override.

---

179 *An Act to amend the Canadian Human Rights Act*, SC 2008, c 30, ss 1 and 3. See David Newman, "A Double Standard: Indians Are Not Protected Against Political Discrimination" (2007) 32 *Manitoba Law Journal* 117; Kirsty Gover, "When Tribalism Meets Liberalism: Human Rights and Indigenous Boundary Problems in Canada" (2014) 64 *University of Toronto Law Journal* 206 at 240.

180 Hogg, above note 3 at 35-4; *Public Order (Temporary Measures) Act*, SC 1970-71-72, c 2, s 12.

181 *Fire Protection and Prevention Act*, above note 154, s 53.1(5).

182 *Statutory Accident Benefits Schedule*, O Reg 34/10, s 10.1, enacted under the *Insurance Act*, RSO 1990, c I.8.

183 *Workplace Safety and Insurance Act, 1997*, SO 1997, c 16, Schedule A, s 2.1(1).

184 *Drivers' Licences*, O Reg 340/94, s 19, enacted under the *Highway Traffic Act*, RSO 1990, c H.8. For the application of this provision, see *Beattie v Ontario (Minister of Transportation)*, 2014 HRTO 1478.

185 *Gaming Control Act, 1992*, SO 1992, c 24, s 2(8).

186 *Human Rights Code*, RSO 1990, c H.19, s 47(2).

There is arguably little disagreement between the legislatures and the courts that all quasi-constitutional statutes hold primacy in the absence of a primacy provision. There are no clear examples of a legislature amending a quasi-constitutional statute or enacting an override after a finding by a court or tribunal that a quasi-constitutional statute has primacy in the absence of a primacy provision. Instead, Parliament appears to acknowledge that the *Canadian Human Rights Act* holds primacy. The "Guide to Making Federal Acts and Regulations" lists four groups of laws that need to be considered during the drafting and enactment of a new bill: (1) the Constitution, (2) quasi-constitutional legislation, (3) statutes of general application, and (4) common law principles.[187] The *Canadian Human Rights Act* is listed as a quasi-constitutional statute with the explanation that "[t]he courts have recognized that Acts dealing with human rights prevail over other legislation. The *Canadian Human Rights Act* therefore prevails over other federal Acts." In contrast, the Guide cites the primacy provisions in the *Canadian Bill of Rights* and the *Official Languages Act* for this same function. Rather than disputing the primacy of the *Canadian Human Rights Act*, the Guide requires that it be accounted for when bills are being drafted as it "can limit policy choices in preparation of Acts and regulations." The Guide further asserts that "[t]he *Canadian Human Rights Act* is an important aspect of our national human rights protection. Human rights legislation sets out many of the fundamental values of our society."

The difference between requiring clear legislative language for the amendment or repeal of quasi-constitutional legislation and the amendment process set out in part V of the *Constitution Act, 1982* is revealed most clearly in *Reference re Supreme Court Act*. The Supreme Court of Canada held that certain sections of the *Supreme Court Act* could be amended only through the constitutional amendment process.[188] The Court found that sections 5 and 6 of the *Supreme Court Act*, a statute which was enacted through the regular legislative process, entered into the constitutional realm; thus, it could be amended only through the rigorous constitutional process because the Court's composition is established in

187 Privy Council Office, "Guide to Making Federal Acts and Regulations: Cabinet Directive on Law-Making," online: www.canada.ca/en/privy-council/services/publications/guide-making-federal-acts-regulations.html.

188 *Reference re Supreme Court Act, ss 5 and 6*, 2014 SCC 21 [*Reference re Supreme Court Act*]; *Supreme Court Act*, RSC 1985, c S-26.

the *Constitution Act, 1982*.[189] The *Supreme Court Act* does not contain a primacy provision, but this case raises the question of the continuing relevance of primacy when a statute without that provision becomes constitutionally protected.

This appears to have occurred with respect to the federal statutes implementing treaties with Indigenous peoples. Some of the modern treaties with Indigenous peoples, consisting of land claims and self-government agreements such as the 1975 *James Bay and Northern Quebec Agreement*, and the statutes implementing these agreements, contain primacy provisions.[190] These treaties and their implementing legislation were never declared to be quasi-constitutional by the courts before becoming constitutionally protected in 1982 with the inclusion of section 35 in the *Constitution Act, 1982*, which recognizes and affirms the existing treaty rights of Indigenous peoples. Given both the presence of a primacy provision and the fundamental nature of Indigenous rights, the argument can be advanced that the principles of quasi-constitutionality apply to these treaties and their implementing legislation. Indeed, there is some similarity between the Supreme Court of Canada's assertion in *Craton* that quasi-constitutional legislation can be amended or repealed only with "clear legislative pronouncement," and a similar statement in *R v Sparrow* that the extinguishment of an Indigenous right prior to 1982 could be accepted with evidence of "a clear and plain intention."[191]

This subject merits comprehensive study, particularly given the dissenting opinion of four justices in the 2010 case of *Quebec (Attorney General) v Moses* that the primacy provisions in the *James Bay and Northern*

189 *Reference re Supreme Court Act*, above note 188 at para 19. See also Ian Peach, "*Reference re Supreme Court Act, ss 5 and 6*: Expanding the Constitution of Canada" (2014) 23 *Constitutional Forum* 1.

190 *James Bay and Northern Quebec Agreement*, 1975, s 2.5, enabled by the *James Bay and Northern Quebec Native Claims Settlement Act*, SC 1976-77, c 32, s 8; *An Act Approving the Agreement Concerning James Bay and Northern Quebec*, CQLR c C-67, s 6. See also *Eeyou Marine Region Land Claims Agreement Act*, SC 2011, c 20, s 6; *Gwich'in Land Claims Settlement Act*, SC 1992, c 53, s 8; *Maanulth First Nations Final Agreement Act*, SC 2009, c 18, s 5; *Nisga'a Final Agreement Act*, SC 2000, c 7, s 6; *Nunavik Inuit Land Claims Agreement Act*, SC 2008, c 2, s 6; *Nunavut Land Claims Agreement Act*, SC 1993, c 29, s 6; *Tla'amin Final Agreement Act*, SC 2014, c 11, s 5; *Tlicho Land Claims and Self-Government Act*, SC 2005, c 1, s 5; *An Act to give effect to the Westbank First Nation Self-Government Agreement*, SC 2004, c 17, s 5; *Western Arctic (Inuvialuit) Claims Settlement Act*, SC 1984, c 24, s 4; *Yale First Nation Final Agreement Act*, SC 2013, c 25, s 5; *Yukon First Nations Land Claims Settlement Act*, SC 1994, c 34, s 13; *Yukon First Nations Self-Government Act*, SC 1994, c 35, s 3.

191 *Craton*, above note 36 at para 8; *R v Sparrow*, [1990] 1 SCR 1075 at para 38.

Quebec Agreement Act "have never been repealed, and they continue to bind both governments."[192] The relevance of this statement to the primacy of quasi-constitutional legislation is that this group of dissenting Supreme Court justices also referred to the primacy provision as "an intention to elevate the Agreement to supra-legislative status."[193] This term has not been widely used by the courts, although the Quebec *Charter* has been called "supra-legislative."[194] Given the effect that the primacy of quasi-constitutional legislation has over other statutes, parallels can be drawn to the suggestion that quasi-constitutional legislation is quasi-entrenched.

Courts and tribunals recognize the primacy of quasi-constitutional legislation even without an express primacy provision because of the fundamental nature of rights they uphold, while also remaining faithful to legislative intent by attributing this function both to the legislature's enactment of the legislation upholding these rights and the presumption that it did not intend to derogate from them without clear legislative language. This balance between fundamental rights and legislative intent in the interpretive exercise is best described as "faithful to the legislative intent, fairly construed, within the constraints of reason that the rule of law provides."[195] Such an approach departs from the conventional reading of Dicey which elevates parliamentary sovereignty and downgrades the rule of law to a mere formality that everyone is bound by law. The two principles are, instead, viewed as equal and codependent; being fundamental, they motivate the legislature and likewise inform the courts in the interpretive exercise.[196] Similarly, exempting constitutional statutes from implied repeal in the United Kingdom has been recognized as a method of accepting a hierarchy between constitutional and non-constitutional statutes that does not undermine legislative supremacy.[197]

---

192 *Quebec (Attorney General) v Moses*, 2010 SCC 17 at para 92.

193 *Ibid.*

194 *Association des procureurs aux poursuites criminelles et pénales et Directeur des poursuites criminelles et pénales*, 2014 QCCFP 26 at para 43; *MT c Québec (Société de l'assurance automobile)*, 2014 QCTAQ 0869 at para 151.

195 Allan, "Constitutional Dialogue," above note 149 at 565.

196 See, for example, Allan, *The Sovereignty of Law*, above note 34 at 168.

197 Elliott, above note 139 at 31.

D. A BROAD, LIBERAL, AND PURPOSIVE INTERPRETATION: FUNDAMENTAL RIGHTS AND LEGISLATIVE INTENT

The broad, liberal, and purposive interpretation applied to quasi-constitutional legislation is similarly based on a balance between the fundamental nature of rights and legislative intent. The courts apply an interpretive approach that advances the fundamental nature of rights protected by quasi-constitutional legislation through some of the principles developed for the interpretation of the Constitution, while also maintaining a more concrete connection to legislative intent by relying on preambles, purpose statements, and interpretation acts. These interpretive aids are assigned a supportive role to the fundamental nature of rights protected by quasi-constitutional legislation that requires a broad, liberal, and purposive interpretation. The courts will depart from the broad, liberal, and purposive interpretation only when this interpretive approach defeats the purpose of legislation.

1) Constitutional Interpretation and the Interpretation of Quasi-constitutional Legislation

The courts apply a broad, liberal, and purposive interpretation to several categories of legislation, including reform and social welfare legislation based on the presumption that the legislature seeks to protect vulnerable persons and disadvantaged groups.[198] Examples of statutes that have been interpreted in this fashion include the *Employment Insurance Act*, Ontario's *Employment Standards Act*, and the *Ontario Disability Support Program Act*.[199]

At the same time, the broad, liberal, and purposive interpretation is applied with more vigour to quasi-constitutional statutes because of the fundamental rights they protect and their links to the Constitution:

---

198 Sullivan, above note 48 at 486–87; William D Popkin, *Statutes in Court: The History and Theory of Statutory Interpretation* (Durham, NC: Duke University Press, 1999) at 118.

199 Pierre-André Côté, Mathieu Devinat, & Stéphane Beaulac, *The Interpretation of Legislation in Canada*, 4th ed (Toronto: Carswell, 2011) at 534; *Canadian Pacific Ltd v Canada (Attorney General)*, [1986] 1 SCR 678 at para 25; *Canada (Attorney General) v Abrahams*, [1983] 1 SCR 2; *Hills v Canada (Attorney General)*, [1988] 1 SCR 513; *Re Rizzo & Rizzo Shoes Ltd*, [1998] 1 SCR 27 at paras 8 and 22; *Helping Hands Agency Ltd v British Columbia (Director of Employment Standards)* (1995), 131 DLR (4th) 336 (BCCA); *Ontario (Ministry of Labour) v Hamilton (City)* (2002), 58 OR (3d) 37 at para 27 (CA); *Gray v Director of the Ontario Disability Support Program* (2002), 59 OR (3d) 364 at paras 9–12 (CA).

the unique results achieved from this approach were outlined in Chapter 2.[200] Justice Binnie wrote for a unanimous Supreme Court of Canada in *Canada (House of Commons) v Vaid* when he held that "such interpretative principles apply with special force in the application of human rights laws."[201] The special force and vigour of the broad, liberal, and purposive interpretation endorsed by the Court in *Vaid* was applied to access-to-information and privacy acts.[202] In *R v Beaulac* the Court confirmed that "[l]anguage rights must in all cases be interpreted purposively, in a manner consistent with the preservation and development of official language communities in Canada," and it rejected the argument that such an interpretation will discourage legislation extending these rights on the basis that it "is inconsistent with the requirement that language rights be interpreted as a fundamental tool for the preservation and protection of official language communities where they do apply."[203]

In devising a special approach to the interpretation of quasi-constitutional legislation, the courts are guided by the approach applied to the interpretation of the Constitution, as the Supreme Court of Canada "has repeatedly stressed that it is inappropriate to rely solely on a strictly grammatical analysis, particularly with respect to the interpretation of legislation which is constitutional or quasi-constitutional in nature."[204] Nonetheless, important differences arise because of the statutory form of quasi-constitutional legislation.

The courts adopted a broad, liberal, and purposive interpretation of the Constitution based on its distinctiveness from legislation. Chief Justice Dickson described the differences between the two forms of law and the corresponding need for a different interpretive approach in *Hunter v Southam Inc*:

> The task of expounding a constitution is crucially different from that of construing a statute. A statute defines present rights and obligations. It is easily enacted and as easily repealed. A constitution, by contrast, is drafted with an eye to the future. Its function is to provide a continuing

200 Mélanie Samson, "Interprétation large et libérale et interprétation contextuelle : Convergence ou divergence?" (2008) 49 *Cahiers de droit* 297 at para 3; Sullivan, above note 48 at 457 and 497; MacDonnell, above note 48 at 510.

201 2005 SCC 30 at para 80.

202 *Canada (Information Commissioner) v Canada (Minister of Industry)*, 2006 FC 132 at para 55, aff'd 2007 FCA 212.

203 [1999] 1 SCR 768 at para 25 [*Beaulac*].

204 *Boisbriand*, above note 58 at para 30.

> framework for the legitimate exercise of governmental power and, when joined by a *Bill* or a *Charter of Rights*, for the unremitting protection of individual rights and liberties. Once enacted, its provisions cannot easily be repealed or amended. It must, therefore, be capable of growth and development over time to meet new social, political and historical realities often unimagined by its framers. The judiciary is the guardian of the constitution and must, in interpreting its provisions, bear these considerations in mind. Professor Paul Freund expressed this idea aptly when he admonished the American courts "not to read the provisions of the Constitution like a last will and testament lest it become one."
>
> The need for a broad perspective in approaching constitutional documents is a familiar theme in Canadian constitutional jurisprudence.[205]

In mandating an interpretation of the Constitution that underscores its enduring character compared to regular legislation, the Court adopted the approach first developed by the Privy Council in *Edwards v Attorney General of Canada*, the *Persons Case*, which established that a woman could be a "fit and qualified person" under section 24 of the *British North America Act, 1867* for the purpose of an appointment to the Senate.[206] The federal government argued that the term "persons" referred only to men. It relied on a static interpretation that focused on the fact that at the time of the Act's enactment in 1867, it was understood that only men were eligible for public service. Lord Sankey rejected this argument on the basis that it was not the role of the courts "to cut down the provisions of the Act by a narrow and technical construction, but rather to give it a large and liberal interpretation," and most memorably, that "the *British North America Act* planted in Canada a living tree capable of growth and expansion within its natural limits."[207] The *Edwards* decision is commonly viewed as the case that displaced originalism with a more progressive interpretation of constitutional law.[208]

The Supreme Court of Canada was quick to extend this living tree metaphor and the resulting broad, liberal, and purposive interpretive

---

205 *Hunter v Southam Inc*, [1984] 2 SCR 145 at 155. See also *Skapinker*, above note 65 at para 10; *R v Big M Drug Mart Ltd*, [1985] 1 SCR 295 at paras 116–17.

206 *Edwards v Attorney General of Canada*, [1930] AC 124 (JCPC).

207 *Ibid* at 136.

208 Bradley W Miller, "Beguiled by Metaphors: The 'Living Tree' and Originalist Constitutional Interpretation in Canada" (2009) 22 *Canadian Journal of Law and Jurisprudence* 331 at para 7.

approach to the *Charter* once the Constitution was patriated in 1982.[209] In the 1985 decision of *Re BC Motor Vehicle Act*, Lamer J said that "the newly planted 'living tree' which is the *Charter* is to have the possibility of growth and adjustment over time."[210] It is now viewed as commonplace for the *Charter* to be interpreted in this fashion.[211]

Lord Sankey's living tree metaphor and the subsequent adoption of the broad, liberal, and purposive approach for the interpretation of the *Charter* is based on a clear difference between statutory interpretation and constitutional interpretation.[212] Much of the literature on statutory and constitutional interpretation similarly focuses on the distinction between the two forms of law.[213] Justifying an interpretive approach based on the distinctions between the various forms of law has provided utility in the interpretation of the Constitution and regular statutes, although it holds less value for the interpretation of quasi-constitutional legislation where the lines between the two are not as distinct and the caselaw reveals interconnectedness.

The Supreme Court of Canada adopted the broad, liberal, and purposive interpretation of quasi-constitutional statutes in order to advance the fundamental rights they protect.[214] Justice (later Chief Justice) McLachlin, writing for a unanimous Court in *Meiorin Grievance*, stated that "because of their status as 'fundamental law,' human rights statutes must be interpreted liberally, so that they may better fulfill their objectives."[215] Similarly, in *Tranchemontagne* SCC Bastarache J stated:

> The most important characteristic of the *Code* for the purposes of this appeal is that it is fundamental, quasi-constitutional law . . . Accordingly, it is to be interpreted in a liberal and purposive manner, with a

209 Wayne A MacKay, "Evolving Fundamental Principles and Merging Public Law Silos: The Reshaping of Canada's Constitutional Landscape" (2013) *Supreme Court Law Review* (2d) 83 at para 38.

210 *Re BC Motor Vehicle Act*, [1985] 2 SCR 486 at para 53.

211 Côté, Devinat, & Beaulac, above note 199 at 532.

212 The Honourable Justice Robert J Sharpe, "The *Persons Case* and the Living Tree Theory of Constitutional Interpretation" (2013) 64 *University of New Brunswick Law Journal* 1 at para 40.

213 William N Eskridge, *Dynamic Statutory Interpretation* (Cambridge, MA: Harvard University Press, 1994) at 5–7; Frank B Cross, *The Theory and Practice of Statutory Interpretation* (Stanford, CA: Stanford University Press, 2009) at 34.

214 MacKay, above note 209 at para 46.

215 *British Columbia (Public Service Employee Relations Commission) v British Columbia Government and Service Employees' Union (BCGSEU) (Meiorin Grievance)*, [1999] 3 SCR 3 at para 44.

> view towards broadly protecting the human rights of those to whom it applies.[216]

This interpretive approach is used most frequently with respect to human rights legislation, although, as displayed in Chapter 2, these rules of construction apply to all legislation recognized as quasi-constitutional.

The Supreme Court of Canada's focus on the fundamental nature of quasi-constitutional law does not make the living tree doctrine, as developed for the interpretation of constitutional law, directly transferable to quasi-constitutional legislation because legislative intent maintains a role in the interpretation of quasi-constitutional legislation. The living tree doctrine is commonly viewed to include a purposive analysis, an organic, or progressive interpretation, and a more limited role for the original intent of the framers.[217] The purposive analysis of quasi-constitutional legislation, considered at length in Chapter 2, involves an effort to uncover the purpose or intent behind the statute and then undertake an interpretation of its provisions that advances this overarching purpose.

A progressive or organic interpretation involves a continuous adaptation of constitutional provisions for new conditions, contexts, and ideas that were not necessarily envisioned by the framers, and thereby not freezing its interpretation at the time of enactment.[218] This occurs, for example, when new social phenomena or technology could not have been anticipated at the time of enactment, and the court engages in what has been described as "gap filling."[219] A progressive interpretation of human rights legislation was advanced by L'Heureux-Dubé J in her dissenting opinion in *Mossop*:

> Human rights codes are documents that embody fundamental principles, but which permit the understanding and application of these principles to change over time. These codes leave ample scope for interpretation by those charged with that task. The "living tree" doctrine, well understood and accepted as a principle of constitutional interpretation, is particularly well suited to human rights legislation. The enumerated grounds of discrimination must be examined in the context of contemporary values, and not in a vacuum. As with other types

216 *Tranchemontagne* SCC, above note 1 at para 33. See also *B v Ontario (Human Rights Commission)*, 2002 SCC 66 at para 44.

217 Miller, above note 208 at para 5; MacKay, above note 209 at para 33.

218 *Reference re Same-Sex Marriage*, 2004 SCC 79 at para 23.

219 Miller, above note 208 at para 14.

> of legislation, the meaning of the enumerated grounds in s. 3 of the Act is not "frozen in time" and the scope of each ground may evolve.[220]

This approach was applied by the Canadian Human Rights Tribunal in *Citron v Zundel*, when it held that postings on a website constituted "telephonic communications," which it justified on the basis of a purposive analysis.[221] The tribunal rejected the respondent's argument that communicating telephonically is limited to voice communications because it is an "unduly restrictive approach that is inconsistent with a purposive approach to statutory interpretation, and fails to allow for advances in technology."[222] Professor Ruth Sullivan explains that "new concepts may be loosely tied to particular provisions in the Act, the main justification for introducing them is that they accord with and tend to promote the general policies and goals of the Act."[223]

It is in the two interrelated aspects of the living tree doctrine of a purposive analysis and a progressive interpretation where the living tree doctrine is most applicable to the interpretation of quasi-constitutional legislation. The third aspect of the living tree doctrine as applied to constitutional law is not as straightforwardly transferable to quasi-constitutional legislation. Bradley Miller demonstrates that the intention of the framers can play a role in the interpretation of the Constitution, although such intention is often attributed little to no weight, or is merely used as a "gratuitous reference" and does not play a significant part in the court's reasoning.[224] Miller also maintains that courts often fail to even assess the intentions of the framers, and in more extreme situations they adopt an interpretation that is clearly contrary to the intentions of the framers.[225] The case of *Egan v Canada* is arguably the clearest example of the latter, as the Supreme Court of Canada read-in sexual orientation as an analogous

---

220 *Mossop*, above note 114 at para 109. This was cited by the Nova Scotia Board of Inquiry under the *Human Rights Act* in *Reid v Truro (Town)*, [2009] NSHRBID No 2 at para 97. Wayne MacKay states that "[i]n this passage, L'Heureux-Dubé J. clearly links constitutional and statutory interpretation and applies the 'living tree' doctrine, thus merging the constitutional and human rights silos." See MacKay, above note 209 at para 48. See also *Giant Grosmont Petroleums Ltd v Gulf Canada Resources Ltd*, 2001 ABCA 174 at para 101; Beth Bilson, "The Voice from the Trenches: Administrative Tribunals and the Interpretation of the *Charter*" (2006) 69 *Saskatchewan Law Review* 3 at para 40.

221 *Citron v Zundel*, [2002] CHRD No 1.

222 *Ibid* at para 93.

223 Sullivan, above note 48 at 503.

224 Miller, above note 208 at paras 23, 25, and 31.

225 *Ibid* at paras 26–27.

ground under section 15(1) of the *Charter*, despite the fact that the legislative record reveals that the proposal to include sexual orientation as an enumerated ground was considered and rejected by the parliamentary committee.[226]

With quasi-constitutional legislation, the courts do not disregard legislative intent in the interpretive exercise, and the few cases that refer to the living tree metaphor also try to account for legislative intent. Similar to the courts' approach to primacy in the absence of an express provision, they justify the broad, liberal, and purposive interpretation of quasi-constitutional legislation by rationalizing that the intention of the legislature was to advance fundamental rights. For example, the Federal Court in *Canada (Attorney General) v Public Service Alliance of Canada* justified its interpretation of the *Canadian Human Rights Act* by stating that "[i]t is consistent with Parliament's intention that the 'living tree' of the Act should be nourished . . . "[227] The courts therefore seek to promote an interpretation that is in accordance with the fundamental character of quasi-constitutional legislation while also respecting legislative intent.

2) The Interpretation of Quasi-constitutional Legislation and Legislative Intent

Courts and tribunals often begin with the fundamental nature of rights in their approach to the interpretation of quasi-constitutional legislation, although they also commonly seek to draw more concrete links to legislative intent than merely relying on the doctrine of presumed legislative intent. Just as they cite a primacy provision when there is one, they similarly refer to a preamble, purpose statement, and interpretation act in support of a broad, liberal, and purposive interpretation of quasi-constitutional legislation. These interpretive tools provide a supportive role in the interpretation of quasi-constitutional legislation. Furthermore, just as the courts will accept an override to primacy when there is clear legislative language, they will not employ a broad, liberal, and purposive interpretation if it is contrary to the actual provisions of a statute.

As was observed in Chapter 2, the courts adopted a broad, liberal, and purposive interpretation because the preambles and purpose statements revealed the legislature's intent to advance fundamental rights. Preambles

226 *Ibid* at para 27. *Egan v Canada*, [1995] 2 SCR 513 at 536.

227 *Canada (Attorney General) v Public Service Alliance of Canada*, [2000] 1 FC 146 at para 100 (TD).

and purpose statements are viewed as establishing the principles and policy goals of the legislature; they provide "the lens through which all other provisions are viewed."[228] Accordingly, legislative intent is discerned through the aspirations of these acts of eliminating discrimination, protecting linguistic minorities, granting access to government information, and protecting personal privacy.

Second, courts and tribunals also routinely cite interpretation acts as the legislative authority for the broad, liberal, and purposive interpretation of quasi-constitutional legislation in order to demonstrate their adherence to the intentions of the legislature. The federal government and all provinces have enacted interpretation acts that deem all statutes as remedial legislation that should be interpreted broadly, liberally, and purposively. Characteristic of these provisions is section 12 of the federal *Interpretation Act*:

> Every enactment is deemed remedial, and shall be given such fair, large and liberal construction and interpretation as best ensures the attainment of its objects.[229]

All provinces and territories have interpretation acts containing similar provisions, which are routinely cited by the courts for the broad, liberal, and purposive interpretation of quasi-constitutional legislation.[230]

References to the interpretation acts by the courts do not imply that the authority for a broad, liberal, and purposive interpretation of quasi-constitutional legislation stems solely from legislative intent as expressed in these statutes, but rather demonstrates the dialogue between the courts and the legislature on an interpretive approach that can best

---

228 Sara Slinn, "Untamed Tribunal? Of Dynamic Interpretation and Purpose Clauses" (2009) 42 *University of British Columbia Law Review* 125 at para 60.

229 *Interpretation Act*, RSC 1985, c I-21, s 12.

230 *Interpretation Act*, CQLR c I-16, s 41; *Interpretation Act*, RSBC 1996, c 238, s 8; *Interpretation Act*, RSNB 1973, c I-13, s 17; *Interpretation Act*, RSNL 1990, c I-19, s 16; *Interpretation Act*, RSNS 1989, c 235, s 9(5); *Interpretation Act*, RSNWT 1988, c I-8, s 10; *Interpretation Act*, RSNWT (Nu) 1988, c I-8, s 10; *Interpretation Act*, RSO 1990, c I.11, s 10; *Interpretation Act*, RSPEI 1988, c I-8, s 9; *Interpretation Act*, RSY 2002, c 125, s 10. For references to the interpretation acts by the courts for the adoption of the broad, liberal, and purposive interpretation of quasi-constitutional legislation, see, especially, *CNR v Canada (Human Rights Commission)*, [1987] 1 SCR 1114 at para 24 [*CNR*]; *Beaulac*, above note 203 at paras 1 and 23; *Fédération Franco-Ténoise v Canada (Attorney General)*, 2008 NWTCA 6 at para 60, leave to appeal to SCC refused (*sub nom Northwest Territories (Attorney General) v Fédération Franco-Ténoise*), [2008] SCCA No 432 [*Fédération Franco-Ténoise*].

advance fundamental rights. Caselaw and the literature suggest that the intention of the legislatures in enacting these provisions in interpretation acts was to end the practice by the courts of interpreting certain statutes restrictively.[231] Interpretation acts have arguably diminished use of the strict interpretive approach by the courts.[232]

Even more important, the caselaw reveals that the courts rely on the interpretation acts as legislative support for an interpretive approach based on the fundamental nature of quasi-constitutional legislation. In *Canadian National Railway Co v Canada (Human Rights Commission)*, which is referred to as *Action Travail des Femmes*, Lamer J first emphasized the special importance of human rights legislation for the development of a proper interpretive approach, and only afterwards did he mention the interpretation act for additional justification for this interpretive approach:

> Human rights legislation is intended to give rise, amongst other things, to individual rights of vital importance, rights capable of enforcement, in the final analysis, in a court of law. I recognize that in the construction of such legislation the words of the Act must be given their plain meaning, but it is equally important that the rights enunciated be given their full recognition and effect. We should not search for ways and means to minimize those rights and to enfeeble their proper impact. Although it may seem commonplace, it may be wise to remind ourselves of the statutory guidance given by the federal *Interpretation Act* which asserts that statutes are deemed to be remedial and are thus to be given such fair, large and liberal interpretation as will best ensure that their objects are attained.[233]

This statement provides interpretation acts with a supportive rather than a determinative role in the adoption of the broad, liberal, and purposive interpretation of quasi-constitutional legislation. This supportive role was, indeed, first assigned to interpretation acts by some of the earliest decisions from the tribunal level even before the issue reached the

231 Sullivan, above note 48 at 467; *Estabrooks*, above note 143 at para 36.

232 Craik, above note 142 at 388–89.

233 *CNR*, above note 230 at para 24.

Supreme Court of Canada.[234] It continues to be the approach advanced by courts today.[235]

Reliance on these direct expressions of legislative intent helps address concerns with the legitimacy of presumed legislative intent, which has been challenged based on theories of democracy that reject substituting the view of judges for the policies of a democratically elected legislature.[236] Jeremy Waldron, for example, has argued that disagreements will persist about the status and extent of rights, as with any other area of social life, and that a representative and democratic legislature is better suited than the judiciary to determine the scope of rights because it balances disagreement and takes account of the opinions of all participants.[237]

Courts and tribunals have accordingly been cautious of not adopting an interpretation that would defeat the purpose of the legislation. In *Re Cummings and Ontario Minor Hockey Association*, Evans J, of the Ontario High Court, stated that "while I agree that the language in a statutory

---

234 In the unreported 1968 decision of *Allen v Lougheed*, which was decided almost two decades before *CNR*, above note 230, Ontario Board of Inquiry Chairman Horace Krever said the following about the *Ontario Human Rights Code*:

> The purpose of the *Code* is to bring about a state of affairs in which the recognition that every person is free and equal in dignity and rights irrespective of race or colour would find a realization in the conduct of residents of this Province. Effect could not be given to this purpose if a narrow and restrictive interpretation were placed on the language of section 3(a). In coming to this conclusion, I am mindful of the provisions of section 10 of the *Interpretation Act*, RSO 1960, c 191, which reads as follows: Every Act shall be deemed to be remedial . . . and shall accordingly receive such fair, large and liberal construction and interpretation . . .

Allen Walls v Louis Lougheed (21 August 1968), unreported, as quoted in *Bailey et al v Minister of National Revenue* (1980), 1 CHRR D/193 at 58 (CHRT).

235 The supportive role attributed to interpretation acts is found in the following cases: *University of British Columbia v Berg*, [1993] 2 SCR 353 at para 26 [*Berg*]; *Robichaud*, above note 96 at para 8; *Action Travail des Femmes*, above note 230 at para 24; *Fédération Franco-Ténoise*, above note 230 at para 60; *O-I Canada Corp v United Steelworkers of America, Local 2805 (NA Grievance)*, [2005] OLAA No 170 at para 7; *Axton v BC Transit*, [1996] BCCHRD No 25 at para 15; *Sarnia Cranes Limited*, [1999] OLRD No 1282 at para 184; *Rashead v Vereschagin*, 2005 BCHRT 426 at para 41.

236 Sullivan, above note 48 at 455.

237 Jeremy Waldron, *Law and Disagreement* (Oxford: Clarendon Press, 1999) at 12. See also Jeremy Waldron, *The Dignity of Legislation* (Cambridge: Cambridge University Press, 1999). Jeffrey Goldsworthy refers to Jeremy Waldron as "the most renowned proponent of the objection from democracy." Jeffrey Goldsworthy, "Structural Judicial Review and the Objection from Democracy" (2010) 60 *University of Toronto Law Journal* 137 at 137. For a summary of Waldron's perspective, see, especially, Jeffrey Goldsworthy, "Legislation, Interpretation, and Judicial Review" (2001) 51 *University of Toronto Law Journal* 75.

code of this nature should be given a wide and liberal interpretation, I do so with the caveat that the language should not be distorted to arrive at a conclusion which will tend to defeat the purpose for which the Ontario Human Rights Code was presumably enacted."[238]

Courts and tribunals are equally cautious in ensuring that a broad, liberal, and purposive interpretation is not based solely on the legislation's purpose at the expense of its actual provisions. As the Saskatchewan Court of Appeal described it in *Saskatchewan (Human Rights Commission) v St Paul Lutheran Home of Melville*, in some instances, "the expression of the objects of the *Code* occasionally outrun the effect of its enacting parts."[239] For this reason, the broad, liberal, and purposive interpretive approach does not provide the courts with "a license to ignore the words of the Act or to rewrite it."[240] Justice Iacobucci, who wrote for a majority Supreme Court of Canada in *Gould v Yukon Order of Pioneers*, asserted:

> On the subject of the appropriate interpretive approach for human rights statutes, the need to approach the legislation purposively, giving it a fair, large and liberal interpretation with a view to advancing its objects, is well accepted. But it is also well established that the wording of the statute is an important part of this process.[241]

Justice Abella in *New Brunswick (Human Rights Commission) v Potash Corporation of Saskatchewan Inc* similarly explained that the broad, liberal, and purposive interpretation of quasi-constitutional legislation does not "permit interpretations which are inconsistent with the wording of the legislation."[242]

In *Canada (Information Commissioner) v Canada (Minister of National Defence)*, the Supreme Court of Canada rejected the interpretation of the *Access to Information Act* proposed by the information commissioner of Canada because it avoided reference to the provision of the Act in question and instead focused solely on the purpose of the legislation:

---

238 *Re Cummings and Ontario Minor Hockey Association* (1978), 21 OR (2d) 389 (Div Ct), aff'd (1979), 26 OR (2d) 7 (CA).

239 *Saskatchewan (Human Rights Commission) v St Paul Lutheran Home of Melville*, [1993] SJ No 591 at para 10 (CA).

240 *Canada (Attorney General) v Mowat*, [2010] 4 FCR 579 at para 99 (CA), aff'd (*sub nom Canada (Canadian Human Rights Commission) v Canada (Attorney General)*), 2011 SCC 53.

241 *Gould v Yukon Order of Pioneers*, [1996] 1 SCR 571 at para 5.

242 *New Brunswick (Human Rights Commission) v Potash Corporation of Saskatchewan Inc*, 2008 SCC 45 at para 19.

> [T]he Commissioner relies heavily on the quasi-constitutional characterization of the *Access to Information Act* . . . . She argues that, as such, the purpose of the Act becomes of paramount importance in the interpretative exercise, and that the legislation should be interpreted broadly in order to best promote the principles of responsible government and democratic accountability. While I agree that the *Access to Information Act* may be considered quasi-constitutional in nature, thus highlighting its important purpose, this does not alter the general principles of statutory interpretation. The fundamental difficulty with the Commissioner's approach to the interpretation of the term "government institution" is that she avoids any direct reference to the legislative provision at issue. The Court cannot disregard the actual words chosen by Parliament and rewrite the legislation to accord with its own view of how the legislative purpose could be better promoted.[243]

Practically, this means that a broad, liberal, and purposive interpretation based on the fundamental nature of the rights contained in quasi-constitutional statutes cannot be used to effectively bypass the substantive provisions of the statute. As Décary J, of the Federal Court of Appeal, cautioned in *Forum des maires de la Péninsule acadienne v Canada (Food Inspection Agency)*: "it is not because a statute is characterized as quasi-constitutional that the courts must make it say what it does not say, especially when the statute, as in this case, has been careful not to say it."[244]

This approach is most readily observed in the interpretation of defences and exceptions contained in quasi-constitutional legislation. Even though courts are to interpret defences and exceptions in quasi-constitutional statutes narrowly and restrictively, the Supreme Court of Canada has warned that this approach should not be used to effectively read defences and exceptions out of the legislation. Chief Justice Lamer cautioned against this in *University of British Columbia v Berg*:

> This interpretive approach does not give a board or court license to ignore the words of the *Act* in order to prevent discrimination wherever it is found. While this may be a laudable goal, the legislature has stated, through the limiting words in s. 3, that some relationships will not be subject to scrutiny under human rights legislation. It is the duty of boards and courts to give s. 3 a liberal and purposive construction,

243 *Canada (Information Commissioner)*, above note 66 at para 40.

244 *Forum des maires de la Péninsule acadienne v Canada (Food Inspection Agency)*, 2004 FCA 263 at para 40, leave to appeal to SCC granted but later withdrawn, 2005 SCC 85.

> without reading the limiting words out of the *Act* or otherwise circumventing the intention of the legislature.[245]

Furthermore, in *Rubin v Canada (Minister of Transport)*, the Federal Court of Appeal explained that applying a broad, liberal, and purposive interpretation

> does not mean that the Court is to redraft the exemptions found in the Act in order to create more narrow exemptions. A court must always work within the language it has been given. If the meaning is plain, it is not for this Court, or any other court, to alter it.[246]

This idea was most succinctly explained at the tribunal level when the Manitoba Board of Adjudication under the *Human Rights Code* stated that "[t]he legislation must be given a liberal and purposive interpretation, without reading limiting words out of the statute or circumventing the intention of the legislature."[247]

What this means in practice is exemplified in the case of *Macdonell v Quebec*, which concerns a request for access to a document outlining the expenses of members of Quebec's National Assembly. Quebec's access-to-information legislation explicitly requires the consent of the members of the Legislative Assembly for access to documents that are produced for them or are held in their offices. Section 34 of the Act reads:

> No person may have access to a document from the office of a member of the National Assembly or a document produced for that member by the services of the Assembly, unless the member deems it expedient.[248]

Justice Gonthier, writing for the majority, agreed with the decision of the Commission d'accès à l'information du Québec that the document requested had been prepared for a member and thus could not be disclosed without the member's consent.[249] In doing so he explicitly rejected the minority opinion that the commission should have taken the broad purpose of the Act and the "fundamental principle that access may be had to government information" into account to limit the scope of section

---

245 *Berg*, above note 235 at para 27.

246 *Rubin v Canada (Minister of Transport)*, [1998] 2 FC 430 at para 24 (CA) [*Rubin*].

247 *Pollock v Winnipeg Condominium Corp No 30*, [2011] MHRBAD No 1 at para 61.

248 *Act respecting Access to Documents Held by Public Bodies and the Protection of Personal Information*, CQLR c A-2.1, s 34.

249 *Macdonell*, above note 67 at para 16.

34 to "documents that relate to Members' decision-making process."[250] Justice Gonthier acknowledged that exceptions to disclosure have traditionally been narrowly construed, but he stressed the point made by the Federal Court of Appeal in *Rubin*, namely, that a court is to begin with the statutory language it has been given and not redraft exceptions that are clear on their face on the basis of broad legislative purpose.[251]

Quasi-constitutionality represents the statutory and common law forms of fundamental law that are rooted in the normative elements of the Constitution. In order to ensure an expansive application of fundamental rights, the courts have endorsed both a broad, liberal, and purposive interpretation of quasi-constitutional statutes and their primacy over regular statutes. Although primacy can prevent the operation of a provision that conflicts with a quasi-constitutional right, it does not question whether the impugned provision was validly enacted; instead, primacy operates to prioritize a quasi-constitutional statute over a regular one in the interpretive exercise. Hypothetically, therefore, a statutory provision declared inoperable would be automatically restored if the quasi-constitutional statute is repealed; such repeal would, however, require clear statutory language. A quasi-constitutional statute can hold primacy even in the absence of an express primacy provision, but declarations of inoperability that purport to affect the application of a provision in another statute beyond the context of the immediate case must be based on the broad remedial authority found in human rights legislation. This requirement is indicative of the balance that the courts have achieved between the fundamental nature of rights and legislative intent with regard to both primacy and the broad, liberal, and purposive interpretation of quasi-constitutional legislation. Chapter 5 will proceed to review how quasi-constitutionality and its defining legal characteristics have developed under the six categories of quasi-constitutional law.

FURTHER READINGS

AHMED, FARRAH, & ADAM PERRY. "The Quasi-entrenchment of Constitutional Statutes" (2014) 73 *Oxford Journal of Legal Studies* 514.

---

250 *Ibid* at para 12.

251 *Ibid* at para 18; *Rubin*, above note 246.

ELLIOT, ROBIN. "Rethinking Manner and Form: From Parliamentary Supremacy to Constitutional Values" (1991) 29 *Osgoode Hall Law Journal* 215.

ELLIOTT, MARK. "Embracing 'Constitutional' Legislation: Towards Fundamental Law?" (2003) 54 *Northern Ireland Legal Quarterly* 25.

HOGG, PETER W. *Constitutional Law of Canada*, 5th ed (Toronto: Carswell, 2007) ch 12.

MACDONNELL, VANESSA. "A Theory of Quasi-constitutionality" (2016) 53 *Osgoode Hall Law Journal* 508.

MACKAY, WAYNE A. "Evolving Fundamental Principles and Merging Public Law Silos: The Reshaping of Canada's Constitutional Landscape" (2013) 61:2 *Supreme Court Law Review* (2d) 83.

MUMMÉ, CLAIRE. "At the Crossroads in Discrimination Law: How the Human Rights Codes Overtook the Charter in Canadian Government Services Cases" (2012) 9 *Journal of Law and Equality* 103.

TARNOPOLSKY, WALTER SURMA. *The Canadian Bill of Rights*, 2d rev ed (Toronto: Carswell, 1978).

TREMBLAY, LUC B. *The Rule of Law, Justice and Interpretation* (Montreal & Kingston: McGill-Queen's University Press, 1997) ch 3.

CHAPTER 5

The Development of Quasi-constitutionality

The purpose of this chapter is to explore the emergence of quasi-constitutionality and the development of its defining legal principles, including its primacy and the broad, liberal, and purposive interpretation. It will consider the development of these attributes in the six categories of quasi-constitutional law, beginning with the *Canadian Bill of Rights*, where the concept was first devised and extended to the other categories of quasi-constitutional statutes.

An account of the development of quasi-constitutionality and the gradual extension of its defining principles to all quasi-constitutional laws reveals the interconnectedness of these laws and their relationship to the Constitution. As the first quasi-constitutional statute, primacy developed under the *Canadian Bill of Rights*. The weakness with this statute, however, was the restrictive approach adopted by the courts for its interpretation, which made it rare for other statutes to run afoul of its provisions. This shortcoming, however, influenced the adoption of a broad, liberal, and purposive approach to the interpretation of human rights legislation, which ensured an expansive protection of rights, particularly when combined with primacy.

The Supreme Court of Canada initially turned to its jurisprudence under human rights legislation in developing its approach to the right to equality under section 15(1) of the *Charter*. The Court's eventual adoption of a more stringent test under section 15(1) brought into question whether a separate analytical framework should be maintained under human rights legislation when a government service established by legislation is being challenged, or whether the *Charter* analysis should apply. With silence on the issue from the Supreme Court of Canada, the framework from the Ontario Court of Appeal's 2010 decision in *Ontario (Director, Disability Support Program) v Tranchemontagne* (discussed in detail later in this chapter) is being applied.

The protection of privacy finds its roots in human rights legislation but was eventually more suitably coupled with access to information in a framework where the two rights must be balanced. Accordingly, the broad, liberal, and purposive interpretation that developed under human rights legislation was extended to privacy and access to information because of their quasi-constitutional character.

The development of language rights legislation initially outpaced the rudimentary linguistic rights originally found in the Constitution, and similar to the cross-fertilization between human rights legislation and section 15(1) of the *Charter*, constitutional and legislative language rights regimes form a dialectical relationship that inform each other in the interpretive exercise. Although the Supreme Court of Canada at one point endorsed a restrictive interpretation of language rights, it has since adopted the broad, liberal, and purposive interpretation for both legislative and constitutional language rights.

Finally, the common law protection of a person's good reputation displays both the significance of quasi-constitutional rights and their relationship to the Constitution, as this right is to be balanced with the constitutionally protected freedom of expression in the context of a defamation suit.

A. TOWARDS A BILL OF RIGHTS

The first category of quasi-constitutional legislation reflects the initial legislative efforts by Parliament and the provincial legislatures to protect civil liberties during the emergence of the human rights movement after the Second World War.[1] These statutes protect traditional civil liberties against the actions of government: they include the rights to life, liberty, security of the person, and property, as well as the freedoms of religion, speech, assembly and association, and the press. The history of protecting the traditional civil liberties in statutory form can be traced back to the

1 Christopher MacLennan, *Toward the* Charter*: Canadians and the Demand for a National Bill of Rights, 1929–1960* (Montreal & Kingston: McGill-Queen's University Press, 2003) at 3.

1947 *Saskatchewan Bill of Rights Act* and the 1960 *Canadian Bill of Rights*, which served as statutory precursors to the constitutional entrenchment of these rights in the *Charter*.[2]

Most provincial civil rights statutes were repealed or struck down before quasi-constitutionality as a concept was developed by the courts, although elements of the traditional civil liberties were incorporated into some provincial human rights statutes.[3] Alberta remains the exception with both the *Alberta Bill of Rights*, which upholds traditional civil liberties, and the *Alberta Human Rights Act*, which protects against discrimination by both government and private actors.[4] The original *Alberta Bill of Rights* from 1946 was struck down by the Judicial Committee of the Privy Council in 1947 as *ultra vires* because in addition to upholding civil liberties, it established a scheme for the issuance of credit, a federal power under the *British North America Act, 1867*.[5] The current version is almost identical to the *Canadian Bill of Rights*, and it has been referred to as quasi-constitutional by the courts.[6] As a result of the similarities between

2 *Saskatchewan Bill of Rights Act, 1947*, SS 1947, c 35; *Canadian Bill of Rights*, SC 1960, c 44; *Canadian Charter of Rights and Freedoms*, Part I of the *Constitution Act, 1982*, being Schedule B to the *Canada Act 1982* (UK), 1982, c11.

3 For example, *The Saskatchewan Bill of Rights Act* was repealed by *The Saskatchewan Human Rights Code*, SS 1979, c S-24.1, s 51, and the civil liberties that it protected were incorporated into part I of that Act. The Supreme Court of Canada referred to *The Saskatchewan Human Rights Code* as quasi-constitutional in *Battlefords and District Co-operative Ltd v Gibbs*, [1996] 3 SCR 566 at para 18 [*Battlefords*]. Some traditional civil liberties are also found in the Quebec *Charter of Human Rights and Freedoms*, CQLR c C-12, chapter I.

4 *Alberta Bill of Rights*, RSA 2000, c A-14; *Alberta Human Rights Act*, RSA 2000, c A-25.5.

5 The *Alberta Bill of Rights Act*, SA 1946, c 11; *Alberta (Attorney General) v Canada (Attorney General)*, [1947] AC 503 (JCPC). What was the *British North America Act, 1867* is now the *Constitution Act, 1867* (UK), 31 & 31 Vict, c 3, reprinted in RSC 1985, App II, No 5.

6 In *Federation of Alberta Students v University of Alberta*, [1980] AJ No 867 at para 22, the Alberta Court of Appeal observed that "[t]he language of the *Canadian Bill of Rights*, s. 1, is almost identical to that found in the Alberta statute." In *Midgley v Law Society of Alberta* (1980), 31 AR 118 at para 10, Foisy J, of the Alberta Court of Queen's Bench, stated that "I think it a fair proposition that the *Canadian Bill of Rights*, R.S.C. 1970, Appendix 3 as amended, and the *Alberta Bill of Rights* are very much the same with the former applying to federal legislation and the latter applying to Alberta provincial legislation." This case was affirmed, [1980] AJ No 712 (CA). It was referred to as quasi-constitutional by the Alberta Court of the Queen's Bench in *Alberta (Minister of Public Works, Supply and Services) v Nilsson*, 1999 ABQB 440 at para 121, aff'd on other grounds 2002 ABCA 283, leave to appeal to SCC refused, [2003] SCCA No 35. See also *Lavallee v Alberta (Securities Commission)*, 2009 ABQB 17 at para 166 [*Lavallee v Alberta*], aff'd 2010 ABCA 48 (without mention of the quasi-constitutional nature of the Act), leave to appeal to SCC refused, [2010] SCCA No 119; *Trelenberg v Alberta*

the two statutes, the interpretation of the *Alberta Bill of Rights* is influenced by the interpretation of the *Canadian Bill of Rights*.[7]

The *Canadian Bill of Rights* was a product of a larger global movement commonly viewed as the post-Second World War model of rights protection, which involved the enactment of human rights in domestic law with an increased role for the judiciary.[8] The atrocities that occurred in Europe during the Second World War and the domestic human rights abuses in Canada against Japanese Canadians and other minorities resulted in the scrutiny of Canada's common law–based rights model and led to demands for a national bill of rights.[9] The parliamentary record on the *Canadian Bill of Rights* reveals that the government at that time felt the need to enact human rights legislation in light of the international experience. On 13 May 1958, Prime Minister John Diefenbaker lamented in the House of Commons that "[a]s a matter of fact we are one of the few nations which have not done anything to implement the declaration of human rights as passed by the United Nations."[10] The *Canadian Bill*

(Minister of the Environment), [1980] AJ No 29 at para 18 (QB) [*Trelenberg v Alberta*]; *Alberta v Kingsway General Insurance Company*, [2005] AJ No 1126 at para 157 (QB).

7 In *Lavallee v Alberta*, above note 6 at para 169, Wittmann J, of the Alberta Court of Queen's Bench, stated that "[g]enerally, case law that interprets the *Canadian Bill of Rights* is very instructive with respect to the interpretation of almost identical provisions found under the *Alberta Bill of Rights*." For equality before the law, see *Moore v Edmonton*, [1997] AJ No 111 at para 30 (QB); *R v Pennington*, [1981] AJ No 658 at paras 11–14 (CA); and *Marr v Marr Estate*, [1989] AJ No 1033 (QB). For the enjoyment of property and the right not to be deprived thereof except by due process of law, see *Byron Hills Resources Ltd v Alberta (Sustainable Resource Development)*, 2009 ABQB 292 at para 78; *Trelenberg v Alberta*, above note 6 at paras 27–28; *Gonzalez v Alberta (Driver Control Board)*, 2001 ABQB 757 at paras 92–95 [*Gonzalez v Alberta*]; *Alberta (Justice and Attorney General) v Echert*, 2013 ABQB 314 at para 48; *Alberta (Driver Control Board) v Lupien*, 2001 ABQB 511; *Midgley v Law Society of Alberta*, above note 6 at paras 10–13; and *Richmac Interiors Ltd (Re)*, [1996] AJ No 132 at para 64 (QB). For the right to a fair hearing, see *R v Greckol*, [1991] AJ No 325 (QB).

8 Lorraine E Weinrib, "The Supreme Court of Canada in the Age of Rights: Constitutional Democracy, the Rule of Law and Fundamental Rights Under Canada's Constitution" (2001) 80 *Canadian Bar Review* 699; Beverley McLachlin, "Canada's Coming of Age" in Joseph Eliot Magnet et al, eds, *The Canadian Charter of Rights and Freedoms: Reflections on the* Charter *After Twenty Years* (Markham, ON: Butterworths, 2003) 353 at 365; Walter Surma Tarnopolsky, *The Canadian Bill of Rights*, 2d ed (Toronto: Carswell, 1978) at 3; MacLennan, above note 1 at 4.

9 MacLennan, *ibid* at 3–4. See also DA Schmeiser, *Civil Liberties in Canada* (Glasgow: Oxford University Press, 1964) at 23.

10 Canada, *House of Commons Debates*, 24th Parl, 1st Sess, vol 1 (13 May 1958) at 35 (Rt Hon John G Diefenbaker).

of Rights was introduced in the House of Commons two years later.[11] The choice to enact rights in statutory form rather than entrenching them in the Canadian Constitution was driven entirely by political realities that would have prevented an amendment of the Constitution at that time.[12]

1) The Adoption of a Restrictive Interpretation of the *Canadian Bill of Rights*

Two years after Laskin CJ first designated the *Canadian Bill of Rights* quasi-constitutional in the 1974 case of *Hogan v R*, he stated that it is the "duty of the Court not to whittle down the protections of the *Canadian Bill of Rights* by a narrow construction of what is a quasi-constitutional document" in *Miller and Cockriell v The Queen*.[13] Despite this statement, the Supreme Court of Canada never adopted a broad, liberal, and purposive interpretation of the *Canadian Bill of Rights*. Rather, the Court ultimately endorsed a restrictive interpretation of the *Canadian Bill of Rights* due to the declaratory nature of section 1:

> It is hereby recognized and declared that in Canada there have existed and shall continue to exist without discrimination by reason of race, national origin, colour, religion or sex, the following human rights and fundamental freedoms, namely, . . .[14]

The Court viewed this section as implying that the rights enumerated in the *Canadian Bill of Rights* were rooted in common law principles that Parliament was merely declaring to now exist in statutory form. Justice Richie expressed the view of the Court in the 1963 case of *Robertson and Rosetanni* that: "the *Canadian Bill of Rights* is not concerned with 'human rights and fundamental freedoms' in any abstract sense, but rather with such 'rights and freedoms' as they existed in Canada immediately before the statute was enacted."[15] This perception is even more apparent in the majority opinion of Martland J in the 1975 decision of *R v Burnshine*:

11 *Ibid*, vol 4 (7 July 1960) at 4638 (Rt Hon John G Diefenbaker).

12 Tarnopolsky, *The Canadian Bill of Rights*, above note 8 at 12–14; Peter W Hogg, *Constitutional Law of Canada*, 5th ed (Toronto: Carswell, 2007) at 35-1.

13 *Hogan v R*, [1975] 2 SCR 574; *Miller and Cockriell v The Queen*, [1977] 2 SCR 680 at 690.

14 *Canadian Bill of Rights*, above note 2, s 1.

15 *Robertson and Rosetanni v The Queen*, [1963] SCR 651 at 654 [*Robertson and Rosetanni*]. See also Tarnopolsky, *The Canadian Bill of Rights*, above note 8 at 143.

> Section 1 of the Bill declared that six defined human rights and freedoms "have existed" and that they should "continue to exist". All of them had existed and were protected under the common law. The Bill did not purport to define new rights and freedoms. What it did was to declare their existence in a statute, and, further, by s. 2, to protect them from infringement by any federal statute.[16]

The Court continued to interpret the rights contained in the *Canadian Bill of Rights* as they were found in their common law form by adopting what Professor Walter Tarnopolsky labelled the "frozen concept" of rights.[17] This approach was in line with traditional views of civil liberties in Canada and in other Commonwealth countries, where in the nineteenth and early twentieth centuries the common law was favoured over the enactment of abstract rights.[18]

Some of the early literature made similar observations about the declaratory nature of the *Canadian Bill of Rights*. In 1959 Louis-Philippe Pigeon wrote that "the proposed enactment purports to be declaratory of existing law . . ."[19] Douglas Schmeiser suggested that the wording of section 1 may be interpreted to imply that Parliament was approving all previous laws as being compatible with the rights enumerated in the *Canadian Bill of Rights*.[20] Even Bora Laskin, who would later be the most vocal justice on the Supreme Court of Canada in favour of a robust application of the *Canadian Bill of Rights*, viewed it as little more than a codification of existing common law principles when it was first proposed, and he stated that "[t]he Bill of Rights now proposed for Canada is not in emulation of the United States nor does it go much beyond the English position."[21] The

16 [1975] 1 SCR 693 at 702. See also *Smythe v The Queen*, [1971] SCR 680 at 686 [*Smythe*], and the dissent of Pigeon J in *R v Drybones*, [1970] SCR 282 at 305.

17 Walter Surma Tarnopolsky, "A New Bill of Rights in the Light of the Interpretation of the Present One by the Supreme Court of Canada" in Law Society of Upper Canada, ed, *The Constitution and the Future of Canada* (Toronto: R De Boo, 1978) 161 at 181–91. See also Joel Bakan et al, eds, *Canadian Constitutional Law*, 4th ed (Toronto: Emond Montgomery, 2010) at 715.

18 Leslie Zines, *Constitutional Change in the Commonwealth* (Cambridge: Cambridge University Press, 1991) at 33.

19 Louis-Philippe Pigeon, "The *Bill of Rights* and the *British North America Act*" (1959) 37 *Canadian Bar Review* 66 at 68.

20 Schmeiser, above note 9 at 38.

21 Bora Laskin, "An Inquiry into the Diefenbaker Bill of Rights" (1959) 37 *Canadian Bar Review* 77 at 77. Justice Laskin took a different course in his judgments and wrote in dissent in cases following the *Drybones* decisions where the Court adopted a frozen theory

early literature reveals that the general sense at the time of the enactment of the *Canadian Bill of Rights* was that Parliament intended to maintain the traditional approach to civil liberties.

The Supreme Court of Canada's restrictive interpretation of the *Canadian Bill of Rights* was driven entirely by the pre-existing common law status of civil liberties, even though the parliamentary record reveals that the drafting of section 1 was influenced more by the international experience and an unwillingness to relegate the theoretical basis of rights to positive law, than by a desire to indefinitely freeze rights in their 1960 common law form. The flurry of interest in rights instruments after the Second World War was followed by renewed discussions on rights in legal theory.[22] A rigorous theoretical debate ensued on whether immoral laws passed according to proper domestic procedures in a state are valid as law, or whether they are legally invalid because they breach a higher law based on moral or natural law principles.[23] This debate influenced Canadian thinking about rights arguably as much as did the international push for the creation of rights instruments.[24]

As a result, the government sought to enact legislation protecting civil liberties, but it was unwilling to suggest that these rights did not previously exist in Canada or that such rights would originate with the positive enactments of Parliament. The minister of justice expressed this view when he explained why the government chose to enact the enumerated rights in a declaratory statement:

> It is my view that one of the primary purposes of parliament — one of them — is to protect the rights and freedoms of the citizens of Canada. It seemed to me it would be a presumption, if not for parliament itself, then, certainly, for the government, to suggest that parliament should create the very rights and freedoms which it is our obligation to protect. It seems to me it would be a presumption for us to say that now, by

---

of rights. See also RJ Sharpe, "Bora Laskin and Civil Liberties" (1985) 35 *University of Toronto Law Journal* 633.

22 Michael Ignatieff, *The Rights Revolution* (Toronto: House of Anansi Press, 2000) at 47–49.

23 At the forefront of this discussion was the debate between HLA Hart and Lon Fuller. The two key articles that encapsulate the Hart–Fuller debate are HLA Hart, "Positivism and the Separation of Law and Morals" (1958) 71 *Harvard Law Review* 593; and Lon L Fuller, "Positivism and Fidelity to Law: A Reply to Professor Hart" (1958) 71 *Harvard Law Review* 630. See also HLA Hart, *The Concept of Law*, 3d ed (Oxford: Oxford University Press, 2012); and Lon Fuller, *The Morality of Law*, 2d ed (New Haven: Yale University Press, 1969).

24 MacLennan, above note 1 at 6–7.

> this bill of rights, we are creating the rights and freedoms enumerated thereunder. It seems to me, not only would it be a presumption, but I believe it would be an absurdity. These rights and freedoms have existed in Canada. They are our traditional rights and freedoms; and it was on that basis that we used the words:
>
> It is hereby recognized and declared that in Canada there have always existed and shall continue to exist the following human rights and fundamental freedoms . . .[25]

This was Parliament's attempt at dealing with what has been referred to as one of the paradoxes of human rights: rights deemed universal and inalienable require constitutional and legislative codification that is not universal or inalienable.[26]

The literature quickly began to question the Supreme Court of Canada's failure to provide a more expansive interpretation of the *Canadian Bill of Rights*, which was called "disappointing to observers who had hoped that it would approach the *Bill* sympathetically, and interpret it liberally."[27] In 1968 Professor Maxwell Cohen referred to the Court's restrictive interpretive approach as "one of the minor tragedies of the past nine years," which he described as "a kind of kiss of death . . ."[28] In 1979 Rosalie Abella lamented that "[h]opes for creative and expansive interpretation increasingly languished with each restrictive decision . . . ."[29] Berend Hovius was critical of the Court's restrictive interpretation and suggested it could have dealt with "the most important ambiguity of the *Bill*" by adopting a broad interpretation.[30] Professor Tarnopolsky similarly expressed the view that the interpretation of the *Canadian Bill of Rights* should not remain frozen in 1960, but should rather be based on the broad interpretation principles of the Canadian Constitution established

---

25 Canada, Special Committee on Human Rights and Fundamental Freedoms, *Minutes of Proceedings and Evidence*, 24th Parl, 3rd Sess, No 6 (22 July 1960) at 411–12 (Hon Edmund Davie Fulton, minister of justice).

26 Stanley Corbett, *Canadian Human Rights Law and Commentary* (Markham, ON: LexisNexis, 2007) at 46.

27 Bakan et al, eds, above note 17 at 714.

28 Maxwell Cohen, "Human Rights: Programme or Catchall? A Canadian Rationale" (1968) 46 *Canadian Bar Review* 554 at 561–62.

29 Rosalie Silberman Abella, "The Social and Legal Paradigms of Equality" (1989) 1 *Windsor Review of Legal and Social Issues* 5 at 6.

30 Berend Hovius, "The Legacy of the Supreme Court of Canada's Approach to the *Canadian Bill of Rights*: Prospects for the *Charter*" (1982–1983) 29 *McGill Law Journal* 31 at 33.

in the 1930 decision of *Edwards v Attorney General of Canada*.[31] Professor Ruth Sullivan found that "the Supreme Court of Canada's highly conservative response to the *Canadian Bill of Rights* precluded it from having a significant impact."[32] Claire Mummé suggested that "the limited role of the *Canadian Bill of Rights* in the protection of human rights had less to do with its design than with the attitudes brought to its interpretation by the Canadian judiciary of the era," and that this was due to "unease with the expanded institutional oversight role that a liberal approach to human rights interpretation seemed to demand of the courts."[33]

These accounts identify the restrictive interpretive approach adopted by the Supreme Court of Canada as the major weakness with the *Canadian Bill of Rights*, compared to concerns over its statutory rather than constitutional form.[34] Since the 1969 decision of *R v Drybones*, it is beyond question that a statute that cannot be interpreted consistently with the provisions of the *Canadian Bill of Rights* can be declared inoperable. The reason judicial review rarely occurs under the *Canadian Bill of Rights* is more a consequence of the restrictive interpretation.

---

31 Tarnopolsky, *The Canadian Bill of Rights*, above note 8 at 159; *Edwards v Attorney General of Canada*, [1930] AC 124 at 136 (JCPC).

32 Ruth Sullivan, *Sullivan on the Construction of Statutes*, 5th ed (Markham, ON: LexisNexis, 2008) at 505.

33 Claire Mummé, "At the Crossroads in Discrimination Law: How the Human Rights Codes Overtook the *Charter* in Canadian Government Services Cases" (2012) 9 *Journal of Law and Equality* 103 at para 15.

34 In contrast, Professor Hogg states that the Court's "cautious attitude stemmed in large part from the fact that the Bill was largely a statute." Hogg, *Constitutional Law of Canada*, above note 12 at 35-10 & 35-11. He also stated that "the failure to entrench the Bill of Rights by constitutional amendment meant that it could be amended or repealed at any time by the Federal Parliament, and raised the question whether it could be effective at all." (*Ibid* at 35-1–35-2.) Joel Bakan similarly holds that "[t]he *Bill of Rights* is simply a statute of Parliament, and not entrenched, like the *Constitution Act, 1982*. Two important consequences follow . . . . Second, it can be amended like any other statute — although no significant amendments have been made." See Balkan et al, eds, above note 17 at 713–14. Some commentators expressed the view that a statutory bill of rights is better than no bill of rights. For example, in 1959 WR Lederman wrote, "the proposed *Canadian Bill of Rights* is well worth doing, even though it takes the form of an ordinary federal statute — a relatively modest form for such a document." WR Lederman, "The Nature and Problems of a Bill of Rights" (1959) 37 *Canadian Bar Review* 5 at 14. Similar criticisms arose from the time the Bill was unveiled. Christopher MacLennan observed the following at the unveiling of the *Canadian Bill of Rights* at the National Conference on Human Rights in 1958: "[w]hile they praised the broad goals of the measure, speaker after speaker criticized the specific provisions of Bill C-60 as ineffective and incomplete. Most doubted the value of a bill of rights passed as a statute and not as an amendment to the constitution." See above note 1 at 128.

The government was warned prior to its enactment that the declaratory nature of section 1 could result in a restrictive application by the courts, yet the debate in the Committee on Human Rights and Fundamental Freedoms reveals that parliamentarians were far more concerned with the new role taken on by Parliament to protect fundamental rights. In his testimony before the committee, Professor Frank Scott explained that

> I do not think it will have very much effect, because I think all judges, in interpreting laws which they find coming from the federal parliament, would try to interpret them so as not to invade a right, if they could possibly do so.[35]

Unfortunately, the discussion on the possible legal effect of the *Canadian Bill of Rights* was almost completely overshadowed by the theoretical question on the source of rights. Given the unwritten and arguably vague nature of these rights in their common law form, the debate concerned whether it is accurate to say that such rights "have always existed."[36] The only concrete change that resulted from this discussion was the removal of the word "always" in the original draft of the section that previously read: "It is hereby recognized and declared that in Canada there have always existed . . ." As important as the step was for Parliament to declare itself the protector of fundamental rights through the enactment of the *Canadian Bill of Rights*, its preoccupation with the theoretical basis of rights resulted in the enactment of existing rights in what has been referred to

35 Canada, Special Committee on Human Rights and Fundamental Freedoms, *Minutes of Proceedings and Evidence*, 24th Parl, 3rd Sess, No 1 (14 July 1960) at 37 (Professor Frank Scott, McGill University).

36 This discussion at one point was sparked by a comment by Professor Frank Scott, of McGill University, that the declaration in section 1 that such rights have always existed is a "legislative lie." *Ibid* at 27 and 33. Minister of Justice Edmund Davie Fulton expressed the view that "these rights have existed previously in Canada. I recognize there is an opinion that holds that we have gone too far by the inclusion of the word 'always,' and there are those who hold it should be taken out and some other expression, or words, substituted such as the words 'heretofore' or 'hitherto.'" See above note 25 at 436. Paul Martin stated: "I agree that it should come out. We all take the view, I hope, that these rights have always existed in Canada; but as there is argument, of some persuasion, that that has not always been the case, it seems to me the more accurate thing to do." Canada, Special Committee on Human Rights and Fundamental Freedoms, *Minutes of Proceedings and Evidence*, 24th Parl, 3rd Sess, No 5 (22 July 1960) at 436 (Hon Paul Martin). Another member asked, "I wonder if it would suit the purpose if we eliminated the three words and substitute 'should have existed'?" *Ibid* at 440 (Hon Mr Aiken).

as "carelessly drafted in incredibly feeble language."[37] The Supreme Court of Canada likewise has been accused of failing to do anything "to vitalize the Bill" because it took this wording at face value and in light of the traditional view of civil liberties without considering the broader context.[38]

Ironically when the Supreme Court of Canada adopted a restrictive interpretation of the *Canadian Bill of Rights*, it was at the close of a decade that saw some of the Court's most liberal and progressive decisions on human rights, including *Saumur v City of Quebec*, *Switzman v Elbing*, and *Roncarelli v Duplessis*, which collectively became known as the implied bill of rights cases.[39] These decisions display both a liberal interpretation of the *British North America Act, 1867*, and the principles of legality and the rule of law that has been described as implying that there is a "zone of liberty into which the state must not unjustifiably enter."[40] The same approach could have been taken by the Court to further advance the *Canadian Bill of Rights*. In other words, if the Court was creative in the way that it gave effect to human rights in the implied bill of rights cases that were decided in an era before human rights instruments, it certainly did not have to adopt a narrow or restrictive interpretation of the *Canadian Bill of Rights*.

2) The *Canadian Bill of Rights* and the Interpretation of the *Charter*

Many of the rights in the *Canadian Bill of Rights* were largely replicated in the *Charter*, with the exception of the protection of property through "due process," and the guarantee to a fair hearing whenever a person's rights are to be determined. Unlike section 1(a) of the *Canadian Bill of Rights*, section 7 of the *Charter* does not protect property, but rather "life, liberty and security of the person," and the right "not to be deprived thereof except in accordance with the principles of fundamental justice." This omission is described by Professor Peter Hogg as "a striking and deliberate departure from the constitutional texts that provided the models for s. 7."[41]

---

37 Schmeiser, above note 9 at 52.

38 *Ibid.*

39 *Saumur v City of Quebec*, [1953] 2 SCR 299; *Switzman v Elbing*, [1957] SCR 285; *Roncarelli v Duplessis*, [1959] SCR 121. See also *Reference re Alberta Statutes*, [1938] SCR 100.

40 Bakan et al, eds, above note 17 at 694.

41 Hogg, *Constitutional Law of Canada*, above note 12 at 44-9; Maxime St-Hilaire, "The Codification of Human Rights in Canada" (2012) 42 *Revue de droit de l'Université de*

The Supreme Court of Canada rejected the restrictive approach it adopted for the interpretation of the *Canadian Bill of Rights* for the interpretation of the *Charter*. The Court did so by distinguishing the declaratory nature of the *Canadian Bill of Rights*, which resulted in a static interpretation of rights as they were found in 1960, from the loftier goals of the *Charter*. In *R v Big M Drug Mart*, the Supreme Court of Canada made it clear that the strict construction of the Bill is inappropriate for the *Charter*:

> The basis of the majority's interpretation in *Robertson and Rosetanni*, *supra*, is the fact that the language of the *Canadian Bill of Rights* is merely declaratory: by s. 1 of the *Canadian Bill of Rights*, certain existing freedoms are "recognized and declared", including freedom of religion. For Ritchie J. this language dramatically narrowed the possible interpretation of the rights and freedoms enunciated by the *Canadian Bill of Rights*:
>
> It is to be noted at the outset that the *Canadian Bill of Rights* is not concerned with "human rights and fundamental freedoms" in an abstract sense, but rather with such "rights and freedoms" as they existed in Canada immediately before the statute was enacted . . . . It is therefore the "religious freedom" then existing in this country that is safe-guarded by the provisions of s. 2 . . .
>
> It is not necessary to reopen the issue of the meaning of freedom of religion under the *Canadian Bill of Rights*, because whatever the situation under that document, it is certain that the *Canadian Charter of Rights and Freedoms* does not simply "recognize and declare" existing rights as they were circumscribed by legislation current at the time of the *Charter*'s entrenchment. The language of the *Charter* is imperative. It avoids any reference to existing or continuing rights but rather proclaims in the ringing terms of s. 2 that: Everyone has the following fundamental freedoms . . .[42]

The Court then proceeded to adopt a broad, liberal, and purposive interpretation of the *Charter*.

The difference between a restrictive approach under the *Canadian Bill of Rights* and a broad, liberal, and purposive interpretation under the *Charter* has resulted in different outcomes in cases involving similar facts. As Lysk J, of the British Columbia Supreme Court, explained: "[i]t is the

Sherbrooke 505 at para 85. See also *R v Banks*, [2005] OJ No 98 at para 46 (SCJ), aff'd [2007] OJ No 99 (CA), leave to appeal to SCC refused, [2007] SCCA No 139.

42 *R v Big M Drug Mart Ltd*, [1985] 1 SCR 295 at paras 114–15.

case that the meaning given to a word or words in the *Canadian Bill of Rights* will not necessarily be attributed to the same word or words appearing in the *Charter*."[43] In *R v Big M Drug Mart*, for instance, the Supreme Court of Canada concluded that legislation requiring store closures on Sunday offends freedom of religion under the *Charter*, contrary to its decision in *Robertson and Rosetanni* under the *Canadian Bill of Rights*.[44] Similarly, the word "detained," in the context of the right to counsel guaranteed by section 10(b) of the *Charter*, was given a different meaning from that given to it under section 2(c)(ii) of the *Canadian Bill of Rights*.[45]

It has even been suggested that because of the broad, liberal, and purposive interpretation of the *Charter*, the *Bill of Rights* may be of no force or effect, even though it was never formally repealed.[46] This notion was unequivocally rejected by Beetz J in *Singh v Minister of Employment and Immigration* when he said:

> the *Canadian Bill of Rights* retains all its force and effect, together with the various provincial charters of rights. Because these constitutional or quasi-constitutional instruments are drafted differently, they are susceptible of producing cumulative effects for the better protection of rights and freedoms. But this beneficial result will be lost if these instruments fall into neglect. It is particularly so where they contain provisions not to be found in the *Canadian Charter of Rights and Freedoms* and almost tailor-made for certain factual situations such as those in the cases at bar.[47]

Practically, therefore, the relevance of the *Canadian Bill of Rights* since the entrenchment of the *Charter* is largely limited to rights that were never incorporated into the *Charter*, including the right to the enjoyment of property and not to be deprived thereof except by due process of law, and the right to a fair hearing when a person's rights and obligations are to be

---

43 *Transpacific Tours Ltd (cob CP Air Holidays) v Canada (Director of Investigation and Research)*, [1985] BCJ No 551 at para 19 (SC) [*Transpacific Tours Ltd v Canada*].

44 *Robertson and Rosetanni*, above note 15.

45 *Chromiak v The Queen*, [1980] 1 SCR 471, cited in *Transpacific Tours Ltd v Canada*, above note 43 at para 19.

46 Hogg, *Constitutional Law of Canada*, above note 12 at 35-2 and n 8; Peter W Hogg, "A Comparison of the *Charter of Rights* with the *Canadian Bill of Rights*" in Gérald Beaudoin & Ed Ratushny, eds, *The Canadian Charter of Rights and Freedoms* (Toronto: Carswell, 1989) 1 at 4.

47 *Singh v Canada (Minister of Employment and Immigration)*, [1985] 1 SCR 177 at para 85.

determined. Much of the jurisprudence under the *Alberta Bill of Rights* similarly concerns the right to the enjoyment of property.[48]

In some instances the wording of the *Charter* departs from the wording of certain rights in the *Canadian Bill of Rights* as a result of a deliberate effort to avoid the outcomes reached by the courts in *Canadian Bill of Rights* jurisprudence. This is particularly the case with section 15(1) of the *Charter*. The legislative history reveals that it was consciously drafted to avoid the pitfalls with the narrow interpretation of the *Canadian Bill of Rights*.[49] The *Canadian Bill of Rights* refers to "equality before the law and the protection of the law," which the Supreme Court of Canada interpreted narrowly and as not guaranteeing equal benefit of the law. In its infamous decision of *Attorney General of Canada v Lavell*, Ritchie J, writing for the majority, reasoned that a provision of the *Indian Act* that deprives women and not men of their Indian status if they marry a non-Indian does not discriminate on the basis of sex because it was not considered discrimination under the common law that, in his view, the Bill was meant to reflect.[50] He rejected the idea that equality before the law invokes the egalitarian concept as in the 14th Amendment of the US Constitution, but instead guarantees only "equality in the administration or application of the law by the law enforcement authorities and the ordinary courts of the land."[51]

The Court followed this reasoning in *Canada (Attorney General of Canada) v Bliss*, which involved a claim by a pregnant woman that the denial of unemployment benefits to which she would have been entitled if she was not pregnant was discrimination on the basis of sex contrary to the right to equality before the law. In rejecting her argument, the Court found that that there was no discrimination on the basis of sex: the class she fell in was pregnant women, and all pregnant women were treated equally under the *Unemployment Insurance Act*.[52]

These decisions heavily influenced the wording of section 15(1) of the *Charter*, which was drafted to include equality "before and under the law,"

48 *Alberta v Kingsway General Insurance Company*, above note 6 at paras 157–58; *Gonzalez v Alberta*, above note 7 at para 93.

49 Andrea York, "The Inequality of Emerging *Charter* Jurisprudence: Supreme Court Interpretations of Section 15(1)" (1996) 54 *University of Toronto Faculty Law Review* 327 at para 4.

50 *Attorney General of Canada v Lavell*, [1974] SCR 1349 at 1365 [*Lavell*]. See also *Smythe*, above note 16 at 686.

51 *Lavell*, above note 50 at 1366–67.

52 *Bliss v Canada (Attorney General)*, [1979] 1 SCR 183.

as well as "equal protection and equal benefit of the law," in hopes that it would result in more expansive interpretation.[53] Even with these substantive differences in the wording of the provision, questions arose during the patriation process about whether such changes would, in fact, result in the adoption of a different interpretive approach. Professor Tarnopolsky, in his testimony before the Special Joint Committee of the Senate and House of Commons on the Constitution of Canada, stated: "[o]ne just does not know whether the change of the word equality before the law to something such as equality under the law will make a difference."[54]

Despite this concern, the Supreme Court of Canada acknowledged the different wording and accordingly adopted an interpretation of the right to equality under the *Charter* that differed considerably from its approach under the *Canadian Bill of Rights*. This change was recognized in *Andrews v Law Society of British Columbia*, the Court's first decision on section 15(1):

> The principle of equality before the law has long been recognized as a feature of our constitutional tradition and it found statutory recognition in the *Canadian Bill of Rights*. However, unlike the *Canadian Bill of Rights*, which spoke only of equality before the law, s. 15(1) of the *Charter* provides a much broader protection. Section 15 spells out four basic rights: (1) the right to equality before the law; (2) the right to equality under the law; (3) the right to equal protection of the law; and (4) the right to equal benefit of the law. The inclusion of these last three additional rights in s. 15 of the *Charter* was an attempt to remedy some of the shortcomings of the right to equality in the *Canadian Bill of Rights*.[55]

The Court's more expansive interpretation of equality under the *Charter* was influenced by its different wording from the *Canadian Bill of Rights*.

---

53 Dale Gibson, *The Law of the* Charter*: Equality Rights* (Toronto: Carswell, 1990) at 32; York, above note 49 at para 4.

54 Canada, Special Joint Committee of the Senate and House of Commons on the Constitution of Canada, *Minutes of Proceedings and Evidence*, 32nd Parl, 3rd Sess (17 November 1980) at 2005 (Professor Walter Tarnopolsky, president of the Canadian Civil Liberties Association). See also *ibid* at 2005 (Mr Borovoy, general counsel, Canadian Civil Liberties Association); *ibid* at 1940 (Lucie Pépin, vice-president, Canadian Advisory Council on the Status of Women); *ibid* (Doris Anderson, president, Canadian Advisory Council on the Status of Women); *ibid* (Ms M Eberts, legal counsel, Canadian Advisory Council on the Status of Women).

55 [1989] 1 SCR 143 at para 33 [*Andrews*].

Chief Justice Brian Dickson looked back at the Supreme Court of Canada's jurisprudence in the 1986 decision of *Beauregard v Canada*, and after observing that "the Court was concerned with the merely statutory status of the *Canadian Bill of Rights* and the declaratory nature of the rights it conferred," he declared that "I believe the day has passed when it might have been appropriate to re-evaluate those concerns and to reassess the direction this Court has taken in interpreting that document."[56] The Court has not departed from its restrictive interpretation, and in the 2003 decision of *Authorson v Canada*, Major J continued to stress that "[t]he *Bill of Rights* protects only rights that existed at the time of its passage in 1960."[57]

B. FROM A BILL OF RIGHTS TO HUMAN RIGHTS AND ANTI-DISCRIMINATION

The *Canadian Bill of Rights* was the focus of human rights advocates in the 1960s, but by the 1970s their attention had almost entirely shifted to human rights statutes because of the setbacks with the caselaw under the Bill.[58] The shifting of attention away from the *Canadian Bill of Rights* may have been prompted, in part, by a belief that the courts would apply a more generous interpretation of human rights legislation because there was no question that these statutes, which focus on the right not to be discriminated against, created new rights and did not merely codify the existing common law.[59] The orthodox view of parliamentary sovereignty that led the Supreme Court of Canada to a restrictive interpretation of the *Canadian Bill of Rights* because it codified existing common law rights also allowed it to recognize that Parliament and the provincial legislatures can enact legislation that advances rights beyond traditional conceptions. It was believed that human rights statutes were meant to make up for the limitations of the common law. With this experience the Supreme Court of Canada turned to its human rights jurisprudence when it began analyzing the *Charter*. The Court's eventual adoption of a more stringent test to the right of equality under section 15(1) of the *Charter*, however, has caused lingering questions about the similarities and differences of the test under the two rights regimes.

---

56 *Beauregard v Canada*, [1986] 2 SCR 56 at para 67.

57 *Authorson v Canada (Attorney General)*, 2003 SCC 39 at para 52.

58 Mummé, above note 33 at para 15.

59 Corbett, above note 26 at 24.

1) Overcoming the Limitations of the *Canadian Bill of Rights* with Human Rights Legislation

The origins of the traditional civil liberties in the *Canadian Bill of Rights* can be traced back to the constitutional principles of the English common law, while the right not to be discriminated against in human rights legislation is rooted in the reluctance on the part of the judiciary in the mid-twentieth century to develop common law protections against racial discrimination. By 1940 the jurisprudence was becoming increasingly clear that a victim of discrimination could not find redress in the courts. This issue was brought to light in the 1940 case of *Christie v York Corporation*, where a patron of a Montreal tavern brought an action in tort for not being served because of the colour of his skin. The appeal to the Supreme Court of Canada was dismissed on the basis that "any merchant is free to deal as he may choose with an individual member of the public."[60] Minor advances made under contract law when a party to an agreement refused to honour the terms based on discriminatory motives were limited to breach of contract, and there was no general common law remedy in tort for the resulting humiliation or loss of dignity from discriminatory practices.[61] Professors Frank Scott and Maxwell Cohen, of McGill University, expressed the opinion in their testimony before the Special Committee on Human Rights and Fundamental Freedoms that the *Christie* decision would not have been decided differently under the *Canadian Bill of Rights*.[62]

60 [1940] SCR 139 at 142 [*Christie*]. A similar conclusion was reached in that same year by the British Columbia Court of Appeal which stated that anyone "may conduct a business in the manner best suited to advance his own interests." *Rogers v Clarence Hotel*, [1940] BCJ No 25 at para 1 (CA). This is in line with the 1924 case of *Franklin v Evans* (1924), 55 OLR 349 (HC), where a restaurant owner refused to serve patrons because of their race and colour. See also *Loew's Montreal Theatres Ltd v Reynolds* (1919), 30 Que KB 459, where a black man was refused an orchestra seat at Loew's theatre in Montreal, but was offered a balcony seat because of a policy to restrict coloured people to balcony seats. Denise G Réaume states that "[t]he story of the Canadian courts' refusal to use their authority to create a cause of action for any form of discrimination is well-known." Denise G Réaume, "Of Pigeonholes and Principles: A Reconsideration of Discrimination Law" (2002) 40 *Osgoode Hall Law Journal* 113 at para 19.

61 In the 1899 case of *Sparrow v Johnson* (1899), 15 Que CS 104, patrons of the Montreal Academy of Music were awarded damages for breach of contract because they were restricted from taking their seats because of the colour of their skin even though they had purchased their tickets in advance. The precedential value of this case was restricted to contract law, and the principle was held not to be applicable in tort.

62 Professor Frank Scott stated, "[i]n my view, this bill would have no effect whatsoever on the decision of the courts in the *Christie* case." See above note 35 at 35. Likewise,

In contrast to the *Canadian Bill of Rights*, the human rights statutes enacted provincially were meant to directly address the type of discrimination witnessed in the *Christie* case and not captured by the common law, beginning with Ontario's *Racial Discrimination Act* in 1944.[63] This was followed in Ontario by the *Fair Employment Practices Act* and the *Fair Accommodation Practices Act*, and similar legislation was subsequently enacted in the other provinces.[64] The *Racial Discrimination Act* and the *Saskatchewan Bill of Rights Act* were quasi-criminal statutes, whereas the fair accommodation and fair employment practices acts were premised on the model first developed in New York in 1945. That model employed the process used in the labour context, which included investigation, conciliation,

---

Professor Maxwell Cohen said, "I do not think the *Christie* case would have been different if this clause was here." Canada, Special Committee on Human Rights and Fundamental Freedoms, *Minutes of Proceedings and Evidence*, 24th Parl, 3rd Sess, No 1 (21 July 1960) at 37 (Professor Maxwell Cohen, acting dean of the Faculty of Law, McGill University) at 382.

63 Ontario's *Racial Discrimination Act*, SO 1944, c 51, is credited as being the first contemporary human rights statute in Canada. Ian A Hunter, "The Development of the Ontario *Human Rights Code*: A Decade in Retrospect" (1972) 22 *University of Toronto Law Journal* 237 at 238. Hunter attributes the purpose of these statutes as combatting the "whites only" signs. See Ian A Hunter, "Human Rights Legislation in Canada: Its Origin, Development and Interpretation" (1976) 15 *University of Western Ontario Law Review* 21 at 24–25. After Ontario, Saskatchewan enacted *The Saskatchewan Bill of Rights Act*, RSS 1965, c 378, which included the traditional political liberties in addition to anti-discrimination provisions. A 1793 statute of Upper Canada which freed the children of slaves when they reached the age of twenty-five is credited as being the first Canadian anti-discrimination statute. *An Act to Prevent the Further Introduction of Slaves and to Limit the Term of Enforced Servitude Within This Province*, Statutes of Upper Canada 1793, 33 George 3, c 7. This statute became redundant when the Imperial Parliament enacted the *Emancipation Act, 1833* (UK), 3 & 4 Wm IV, c 73. See also Walter Surma Tarnopolsky, "The Iron Hand in the Velvet Glove: Administration and Enforcement of Human Rights Legislation in Canada" (1968) 46 *Canadian Bar Review* 565 at 567–68.

64 *Fair Employment Practices Act*, SO 1951, c 24. The fair accommodation practices statutes included the following: *Fair Accommodation Practices Act*, SO 1954, c 28; *Fair Accommodation Practices Act*, SNB 1959, c 6; *Fair Accommodation Practices Act*, RSS 1965, c 379; *Fair Accommodation Act*, SNS 1956, c 5; *Fair Accommodation Act*, SM 1960, c 14; *Fair Accommodation Act*, SBC 1961, c 50. There was no fair accommodation act in Quebec, although the *Hotels Act*, SQ 1963, c 40, s 8, addresses discrimination in hotels, restaurants, and campgrounds.

The fair employment practices statutes included the following: *Fair Employment Act*, SM 1953, c18; *Fair Employment Act*, SNS 1955, c 5; *Fair Employment Practices Act*, SNB 1956, c 9; *Fair Employment Practices Act*, SBC 1956, c 16; *Fair Employment Act*, SS 1956, c 68; *Canada Fair Employment Practices Act*, SC 1952-53, c 19; *Fair Practices Ordinance*, RONWT 1974, c F-2; *Fair Practices Ordinance*, ROYT 1971, c F2.

commissions, and boards of inquiry. Professor Tarnopolsky observed that "the Fair Accommodation and Fair Employment Practices Acts marked a considerable advance over the quasi-criminal approach to human rights legislation."[65] The provinces also passed equal pay legislation to prohibit discrimination in the rates of pay between men and women.[66]

Ontario was the first Canadian jurisdiction to consolidate its anti-discrimination statutes into a comprehensive *Human Rights Code* in 1962, and other provinces quickly adopted this model.[67] These comprehensive codes differed from their predecessor statutes because they addressed discrimination in several areas such as employment, services, and accommodation, and they also created a commission with a statutory duty to promote and seek compliance.[68]

Since human rights legislation was an expression of political will rather than a continuation of the common law, the courts recognized the need for a different interpretive approach. At the same time, the comprehensiveness of these codes also resulted in the Supreme Court of Canada effectively halting any further development of the common law to provide protection against discrimination. In the 1981 case of *Seneca College*

---

65 Tarnopolsky, "The Iron Hand in the Velvet Glove" above note 63 at 570.

66 *Female Employees Fair Remuneration Act*, SO 1951, c 177; *Equal Pay Act*, SBC 1953, c 6; *An Act Amending the Alberta Labour Code*, SA 1957, c 38; *Equal Pay Act*, SS 1952, c 104; *Fair Employment Practices Act*, SM 1956, c 18; *Female Employees Fair Remuneration Act*, SNB 1961, c 7; *Equal Pay Act*, SNS 1956, c 5; *Equal Pay Act*, SPEI 1959, c 11.

67 *Ontario Human Rights Code*, SO 1961-62, c 93; *Human Rights Act*, SA 1966, c 39; *Human Rights Act*, SBC 1969, c 10; *Human Rights Act*, SM 1970, c 104; *Human Rights Act*, SNB 1967, c 13; *Human Rights Code*, SPEI 1968, c 24; *Charter of Human Rights and Freedoms*, SQ 1975, c 6; *The Saskatchewan Human Rights Code*, SS 1979, c S-24.1; *Human Rights Act*, S Nfld 1969, No 75; *Human Rights Act*, SNS 1963, c 5; *Human Rights Act*, SY 1987, c 3; *Canadian Human Rights Act*, SC 1976-77, c 33; *Human Rights Act*, SNu 2003, c 12. For the development of human rights legislation, see Maxime St-Hilaire, "The Codification of Human Rights in Canada" (2012) 42 *Revue de droit de l'Université de Sherbrooke* 505; Hunter, "Human Rights Legislation in Canada," above note 63; Hunter, "The Development of the Ontario *Human Rights Code*," above note 63 at 238; Tarnopolsky, "The Iron Hand in the Velvet Glove," above note 63; Alan D Reid, "The New Brunswick *Human Rights Act*" (1968) 18 *University of Toronto Law Journal* 394; Daniel G Hill, "The Role of a Human Rights Commission: The Ontario Experience" (1969) 19 *University of Toronto Law Journal* 390.

68 Tarnopolsky, "The Iron Hand in the Velvet Glove" above note 63 at 571–72. In the case of New Brunswick's *Human Rights Act*, Alan Reid observes that "it was thrown together hurriedly. It comprises pieces of existing fair accommodation and fair employment practices legislation, as well as sections from the Ontario *Human Rights Code* and the Nova Scotia Act. Regrettably, the pieces do not fit neatly together." Reid, above note 67 at 394.

of Applied Arts and Technology v Bhadauria, the Court rejected the idea of a tort of discrimination, thereby leaving no question that the right against discrimination was based entirely on statute and not the common law.[69]

The inability of the common law to protect against discrimination was arguably more a result of judicial reluctance to develop the common law in this direction than any inherent limitations with the common law itself. When Bora Laskin was a young lawyer working on the case *Re Drummond Wren*, he believed that protections against discrimination could be advanced under the common law. This case, which was decided by Mackay J of the Ontario High Court in 1945, is an early example of how the common law had the potential to develop protections against racial discrimination.[70] Justice Mackay found that a restrictive covenant in a deed that stated that the land was "not to be sold to Jews or persons of objectionable nationality," was void and of no force and effect; it was contrary to public policy, as witnessed in Ontario's *Racial Discrimination Act*, which was enacted the previous year, and reinforced by "the wide official acceptance of international policies and declaration frowning on the type of discrimination which the covenant would seem to perpetuate."[71]

The *Re Drummond Wren* decision suggests that the common law had great potential that was never fully realized because of judicial restraint. The interplay between an early anti-discrimination statute and the common law was particularly interesting in this case. *Re Drummond Wren* therefore suggests that the common law could have had a role to play in supplementing anti-discrimination legislation, as Mackay J relied on public policy and international sources — fifteen years prior to Parliament's enactment of the *Canadian Bill of Rights*. As the late Professor Stanley Corbett explained, "Justice Mackay's reasoning in *Re Drummond Wren* captured the changing climate of global opinion at precisely the moment when the world was beginning to recognize the full implications of the Second World War."[72]

The interplay between the common law and human rights legislation first displayed in *Re Drummond Wren* may continue to have some limited application despite *Bhadauria* SCC. In the 1990 decision of *Canada Trust Co v Ontario Human Rights Commission*, the Ontario Court of Appeal held

69 *Seneca College of Applied Arts and Technology v Bhadauria*, [1981] 2 SCR 181 [*Bhadauria* SCC]. Corbett, above note 26 at 60.

70 *Re Drummond Wren*, [1945] OR 778 (HCJ).

71 *Ibid.*

72 Corbett, above note 26 at 61.

that a trust's exclusion of "all who are not Christians of the White Race" violated public policy and that the trust could survive with the deletion of the discriminatory restriction.[73] The Court of Appeal distinguished the case from *Bhadauria* SCC, which involved the Supreme Court of Canada finding that the development of the common law in the area of discrimination was not necessary because of the comprehensiveness of the *Human Rights Code*, compared to the question about the administration of a trust, over which superior courts have inherent jurisdiction.[74]

The potential of the *Re Drummond Wren* decision was recognized by the Ontario Court of Appeal in *Seneca College of Applied Arts and Technology v Bhadauria*; where Wilson JA defined a new intentional tort against discrimination in respect to employment on the ground of race or national origin.[75] Similar to the analysis in *Re Drummond Wren*, Wilson JA found that the tort arises at common law through the public policy observed in the *Human Rights Code*. Justice Wilson specifically held that "I do not regard the *Code* as in any way impeding the appropriate development of the common law in this important area."[76]

Chief Justice Laskin's approach, however, had shifted after *Re Drummond Wren* — as had the approach of the Canadian Jewish Congress he had worked for — from human rights activism through test cases to the legislative route with a goal to "supersede the courts and the common law entirely by creating statutory prohibitions on discrimination."[77] Thus, by the time Laskin J was chief justice of the Supreme Court of Canada, he believed that legislative measures to protect rights should be given a chance to work rather than developing parallel protections under the common law. In rejecting a common law ground of action for discrimination in *Bhadauria*, the chief justice stated that "[t]he reason lies in the comprehensiveness of the *Code* in its administrative and adjudicative features, the latter including a wide right of appeal to the Courts on both fact and law."[78]

---

73 *Canada Trust Co v Ontario Human Rights Commission* (1990), 74 OR (2d) 481 (CA).

74 *Ibid.* See also Alan LW D'Silva, "Giving Effect to Human Rights Legislation: A Purposive Approach" (1991) 3 *Windsor Review of Legal and Social Issues* 45 at 62–63.

75 (1979), 27 OR (2d) 142 (CA).

76 *Ibid.* See also Kate Sutherland, "Precedent, Principle and Pragmatism: Justice Wilson and the Expansion of Canadian Tort Law" (2009) 41 *Supreme Court Law Review* (2d) 131 at 136–37.

77 Philip Girard, *Bora Laskin: Bringing Law to Life* (Toronto: The Osgoode Society, 2005) at 248.

78 *Bhadauria* SCC, above note 69 at 183.

It was in this context that the Supreme Court of Canada decided *Insurance Corporation of British Columbia v Heerspink*, only a year after *Bhadauria* SCC, where Lamer J (later CJ) stressed the fundamental nature of human rights legislation. Echoing Laskin CJ from *Bhadauria* SCC on the comprehensiveness of human right codes, Lamer J referred to British Columbia's *Human Rights Code* as being a "comprehensive statement of the 'human rights' of the people living in that jurisdiction," and said that "their legislature clearly indicated that they consider that law, and the values it endeavours to buttress and protect, are, save their constitutional laws, more important than all others."[79]

The significance of Lamer J's comments in *Heerspink* cannot be overstated. They have been cited in hundreds of reported decisions, including in most of the subsequent human rights decisions from the Supreme Court of Canada.[80] A unanimous Court in *CNR v Canada (Human Rights Commission)* referred to Lamer J's comments in *Heerspink* as "[t]he

---

79 *Insurance Corporation of British Columbia v Heerspink*, [1982] 2 SCR 145 at 157–58 [*Heerspink*].

80 See, for example, *Winnipeg School Division No 1 v Craton*, [1985] 2 SCR 150 [*Craton*]; *Ontario Human Rights Commission and O'Malley v Simpsons-Sears Ltd*, [1985] 2 SCR 536 [*O'Malley*]; *Bhinder v Canadian National Railway Co*, [1985] 2 SCR 561; *Scowby v Glendinning*, [1986] 2 SCR 226; *CNR v Canada (Human Rights Commission)*, [1987] 1 SCR 1114 [*CNR*]; *Robichaud v Canada (Treasury Board)*, [1987] 2 SCR 84; *R v Mercure*, [1988] 1 SCR 234 [*Mercure*]; *Brooks v Canada Safeway Ltd*, [1989] 1 SCR 1219; *Canada (Human Rights Commission) v Taylor*, [1990] 3 SCR 892 at para 59; *Zurich Insurance Co v Ontario (Human Rights Commission)*, [1992] 2 SCR 321; *Dickason v University of Alberta*, [1992] 2 SCR 1103 [*Dickason*]; *Central Okanagan School District No 23 v Renaud*, [1992] 2 SCR 970; *Canada (Attorney General) v Mossop*, [1993] 1 SCR 554; *University of British Columbia v Berg*, [1993] 2 SCR 353; *Gould v Yukon Order of Pioneers*, [1996] 1 SCR 571; *Newfoundland Association of Public Employees v Newfoundland (Green Bay Health Care Centre)*, [1996] 2 SCR 3; *Bell v Canada (Canadian Human Rights Commission)*; *Cooper v Canada (Human Rights Commission)*, [1996] 3 SCR 854; *Béliveau St-Jacques v Fédération des employées et employés de services publics Inc*, [1996] 2 SCR 345 at para 43; *Battlefords*, above note 3; *British Columbia (Public Service Employee Relations Commission) v British Columbia Government and Service Employees' Union (BCGSEU) (Meiorin Grievance)*, [1999] 3 SCR 3; *Quebec (Commission des droits de la personne et des droits de la jeunesse) v Montréal (City)*; *Quebec (Commission des droits de la personne et des droits de la jeunesse) v Boisbriand (City)*, 2000 SCC 27 [*Boisbriand*]; *B v Ontario (Human Rights Commission)*, 2002 SCC 66; *Syndicat Northcrest v Amselem*, 2004 SCC 47; *Canada (House of Commons) v Vaid*, 2005 SCC 30; *Tranchemontagne v Ontario (Director, Disability Support Program)*, 2006 SCC 14 [*Tranchemontagne* SCC]; *New Brunswick (Human Rights Commission) v Potash Corporation of Saskatchewan Inc*, 2008 SCC 45 [*Potash*].

first comprehensive judicial statement of the correct attitude towards the interpretation of human rights legislation."[81]

The observation by Lamer J that human rights legislation is fundamental law due to its being a comprehensive statement of human rights had an important bearing on both its primacy over all other legislation, even without an express primacy provision, and the interpretive approach adopted by the Supreme Court of Canada. Justice Lamer stated that "short of that legislature speaking to the contrary in express and unequivocal language in the *Code* or in some other enactment, it is intended that the *Code* supersede all other laws when conflict arises."[82] A unanimous Court relied on *Heerspink* in the 1985 decision of *Winnipeg School Division No 1 v Craton* in support of its conclusion on the primacy of human rights legislation that could not be impliedly repealed.[83] A unanimous Court also decided *Ontario Human Rights Commission and O'Malley v Simpsons-Sears Ltd* in 1985, in which it adopted an interpretive approach in keeping with Lamer J's observations in *Heerspink* on the special nature and purpose of human rights legislation.[84]

Justice Lamer did not explicitly refer to quasi-constitutionality in *Heerspink*, yet the case is now commonly viewed as the first judicial recognition of the quasi-constitutional character of human rights statutes. Justice Cory, who wrote for the majority in the 1992 case of *Dickason v University of Alberta*, cited Lamer J's comments in *Heerspink* in support of the conclusion that

> this Court has long recognized that human rights legislation should be interpreted both broadly and purposively. Once in place, laws which seek to protect individuals from discrimination acquire a quasi-constitutional status, which gives them preeminence over ordinary legislation.[85]

In this short statement the Court both explicitly recognized the quasi-constitutional status of human rights legislation, and its two defining legal features.

---

81 *CNR*, above note 80 at para 18.

82 *Heerspink*, above note 79 at 158.

83 *Craton*, above note 80 at para 8.

84 *O'Malley*, above note 80 at para 12.

85 *Dickason*, above note 80 at para 94.

2) Human Rights Legislation and the *Charter*

To avoid the shortcomings of the interpretation of equality under the *Canadian Bill of Rights*, the Supreme Court of Canada turned to its approach for the interpretation of human rights legislation when developing the analysis for equality under section 15(1) of the *Charter*.[86] This analysis, undertaken when that provision came into effect in 1985, began with the term "discrimination." The Court found the term had to be understood in the larger context of "pre-*Charter* history" in statutory human rights legislation and through the definition it developed in *O'Malley*.[87] It relied on the understanding of discrimination developed under human rights legislation when adopting the following definition in *Andrews*:

> a distinction, whether intentional or not but based on grounds relating to personal characteristics of the individual or group, which has the effect of imposing burdens, obligations, or disadvantages on such individual or group not imposed upon others, or which withholds or limits access to opportunities, benefits, and advantages available to other members of society.[88]

Accordingly, the Court based the original test for finding a violation of section 15(1) of the *Charter* in *Andrews* on the approach to discrimination found in human rights legislation.[89]

Undeniably, this reliance on human rights jurisprudence for the development of the *Charter* highlights the esteem to which the Court held human rights as quasi-constitutional legislation. Professor Corbett suggests that the reference to the definition of discrimination under human rights legislation displays a continuing dialogue between the courts and Parliament despite the *Charter*'s constitutional nature.[90] Leslie Reaume

---

86 Leslie Reaume, "Postcards from *O'Malley*: Reinvigorating Statutory Human Rights Jurisprudence in the Age of the *Charter*" in Fay Faraday, Margaret Denike, & M Kate Stephenson, eds, *Making Equality Rights Real: Securing Substantive Equality Under the* Charter (Toronto: Irwin Law, 2006) 373 at 382; York, above note 49 at para 4.

87 *Andrews*, above note 55 at para 37.

88 *Ibid*.

89 Wayne A MacKay, "The Marriage of Human Rights Codes and Section 15 of the *Charter* in Pursuit of Equality: A Case for Greater Separation in Both Theory and Practice" (2013) 64 *University of New Brunswick Law Journal* 54 at para 23; Wayne A MacKay, "Evolving Fundamental Principles and Merging Public Law Silos: The Reshaping of Canada's Constitutional Landscape" (2013) 61 *Supreme Court Law Review* (2d) 83 at para 135.

90 Corbett, above note 26 at 64.

considers this to be the appropriate starting point because of the convergences between the *Charter* and human rights legislation as "[b]oth the *Charter* and human rights statutes share the goal of achieving substantive equality, and are driven by similar underlying principles."[91]

The 1988 case of *Canada (Attorney General) v Druken* from the Federal Court of Appeal is considered to be the last significant decision concerning the use of human rights legislation to challenge a government service established through legislation; after that, most attention switched to section 15(1) of the *Charter*.[92] Then, in 1999, within a decade of *Druken*, the Supreme Court of Canada handed down its decision on *Law v Canada (Minister of Employment and Immigration)*, which established a more onerous framework under section 15(1) of the *Charter*. Under the *Law* analysis claimants not only had to demonstrate that the distinction or differential treatment was on the basis of an enumerated or analogous ground, but also that the difference perpetuated a stereotype or impugned their human dignity.[93] The *Law* test has been summarized as three parts, with the third part involving four contextual factors:

1. Does the impugned law (a) draw a formal distinction between the claimant and others on the basis of one or more personal characteristics or (b) fail to take into account the claimant's already disadvantaged position within Canadian society resulting in substantively differential treatment between the claimant and others on the basis of one or more personal characteristics?
2. Was the differential treatment to which the claimant was subjected based on one or more of the enumerated and analogous grounds?
3. Does the differential treatment discriminate in a substantive sense, bringing into play the purpose of section 15(1) of the *Charter* in remedying such ills as prejudice, stereotyping, and historical disadvantage? The four contextual factors to consider include:
   (i) pre-existing disadvantage experienced by the individual or group;
   (ii) correspondence between the ground claimed and the claimant's actual characteristics or circumstances;
   (iii) ameliorative purpose or effects of the impugned law on a more disadvantaged person or group; and

---

91 Reaume, above note 86 at 382.

92 Mummé, above note 33 at para 35. *Canada (Attorney General) v Druken* (1988), [1989] 2 FC 24 at para 3 (CA) [*Druken*], leave to appeal to SCC refused, [1988] SCCA No 433.

93 [1999] 1 SCR 497 [*Law*].

(iv) the nature and scope of the interest affected by the impugned law.

Claire Mummé attributes the onerous framework under section 15(1) of the *Charter* adopted in *Law* as the reason for the renewed attention on the ability of courts and tribunals to declare a statute inoperable under human rights legislation "with its claimant-friendly analysis and decreased costs."[94] With this renewed interest in declarations of inoperability under human rights legislation, she explains that government lawyers began arguing in favour of applying the *Law* analysis in the human rights realm. These arguments found support in the practical similarities in outcome between declarations of inoperability under human rights legislation and orders of invalidity under the Constitution.

In the 2006 decision of *Tranchemontagne v Ontario (Director, Disability Support Program)*, Bastarache J observed the similarities in practical outcome between the invalidity and inoperability of a statutory provision. He stated that "whether there is a conflict with the *Code* or the *Constitution*, the ultimate effect is that the other provision is not followed and, for the purposes of that particular application, it is as if the legislation was never enacted."[95] As noted in Chapter 4, Bastarache J found that the theoretical differences between the two were more important than the similarities. The similarities, however, form the basis of Abella J's dissent to Bastarache J's conclusion that the Social Benefits Tribunal retained jurisdiction to apply the *Human Rights Code*. At the root of their disagreement was the provision in the *Ontario Works Act* that provides that the tribunal cannot determine "the constitutional validity of a provision of an Act or a regulation."[96] Justice Abella reasoned that since the legislature ousted the jurisdiction of the Social Benefits Tribunal to consider the constitutional validity of its enabling legislation, it logically follows that it wanted to prevent it from making any determinations that provisions of its own statute should not be applied, even under the *Human Rights Code*. In other words, Abella J believed that Bastarache J's interpretation made the provision barring the tribunal from applying the *Charter* redundant because a substantially similar result could be achieved by applying the *Human Rights Code*. In her own words: "the legislature did not want the

---

94 Mummé, above note 33 at para 49.

95 *Tranchemontagne* SCC, above note 80 at para 35.

96 *Ontario Works Act*, SO 1997, c 25, s 67(2).

SBT to be able to refuse to apply any of its enabling provisions by finding these to be inoperable, period."[97]

The cross-fertilization between human rights legislation and the *Charter* therefore began to move in the opposite direction following *Law*, where the framework under section 15(1) began to influence and, in some instances, supplant the evidentiary burden of a *prima facie* case, as first established in *O'Malley*, in cases that could be pursed under either section 15(1) of the *Charter* or human rights legislation. The case of *Gwinner v Alberta (Human Resources and Employment)* from the Alberta Court of Queen's Bench is credited as establishing this trend in favour of incorporating the constitutional analysis into the statutory human rights context, even though Greckol J only applied the first two of three parts of the *Law* test.[98] What followed was a line of decisions under human rights legislation where the *Law* test can be found on what Leslie Reaume calls a "continuum": at one end, *Law* does not dominate the analysis under human rights legislation; at the other end, there is a complete incorporation of the full application of the three-part analysis from *Law*, which also includes a consideration of the effect on the claimant's dignity.[99] Lower courts grappled with the framework.

The Supreme Court of Canada was condemned in the literature for its approach to section 15(1) of the *Charter* in *Law*, which it acknowledged in *R v Kapp*.[100] The courts were likewise criticized for their incorporation

97 *Tranchemontagne* SCC, above note 80 at para 80.

98 Mummé, above note 33 at para 60; *Gwinner v Alberta (Human Resources and Employment)*, 2002 ABQB 685 at paras 94–123 [*Gwinner*], aff'd 2004 ABCA 210, leave to appeal to SCC refused, [2004] SCCA No 342.

99 Reaume, above note 86 at 374 and 396–97.

100 2008 SCC 41 at para 22 [*Kapp*]. For academic criticism of the *Law* analysis, see, especially, Sophia Moreau, "Equality Rights and the Relevance of Comparator Groups" (2006) 5 *Journal of Law and Equality* 81; Nicole Vaz, "Equality Versus Non-discrimination: Which Are We Striving For and Which Is the Attainable Goal?" (2006) 32 *Supreme Court Law Review* (2d) 221; Reaume, above note 86; Beverley Baines, "Equality, Comparison, Discrimination, Status" in Faraday, Denike, & Stephenson, eds, *Making Equality Rights Real*, above note 86 at 73; Daphne Gilbert & Diana Majury, "Critical Comparisons: The Supreme Court of Canada Dooms Section 15" (2006) 24 *Windsor Yearbook of Access to Justice* 111; Daphne Gilbert, "Time to Regroup: Rethinking Section 15 of the *Charter*" (2003) 48 *McGill Law Journal* 627; Dianne Pothier, "Connecting Grounds of Discrimination to Real People's Real Experiences" (2001) 13 *Canadian Journal of Women and the Law* 37; Donna Greschner, "Does Law Advance the Cause of Equality?" (2001) 27 *Queen's Law Journal* 299; Margot Young, "Blissed Out: Section 15 at Twenty" in Sheila McIntyre & Sanda Rodgers, eds, *Diminishing Returns: Inequality and the* Canadian Charter of Rights and Freedoms (Markham, ON: LexisNexis, 2006) 46. For an account of *Kapp*, see, especially, Paul-Erik Veel, "A New Direction in the

of the *Law* analysis into statutory human rights claims. Unlike the earlier influence of human rights legislation over the *Charter*, which occurred because the Court relied on well-established human rights jurisprudence for the newly entrenched *Charter*, the trend towards the conformity of human rights legislation with the analysis under section 15(1) was seen as being solely for the benefit of government service providers rather than for any underlying benefit for the cause of substantive equality. Experience had shown that human dignity and the more recent requirement of proving prejudice or stereotype "has turned it into a formidable barrier for claimants" and often "the fulcrum on which many section 15 claims have turned."[101]

Direction on the appropriate framework finally came from the Ontario Court of Appeal in the 2010 *Tranchemontagne* decision. This case is both celebrated for the use of the *Human Rights Code* to successfully challenge a provision in the *Ontario Disability Support Program Act, 1997* that clearly discriminated against one group of disabled individuals, and criticized for the adoption of a framework heavily based on the approach to section 15(1) of the *Charter*, as articulated in *Kapp*. Benjamin Oliphant explained:

> The mischief in the *Tranchemontagne* decision and others that follow a similar conceptual framework is not that these cases have necessarily reached the wrong conclusions on the facts but, rather, that by modifying the procedure for establishing a successful claim they have redefined the scope of the prohibition on discrimination, either without averting to this fact or acknowledging it openly.[102]

As observed in Chapter 3, the framework adopted by the Ontario Court of Appeal asks:

1. Does the law create a distinction based on an enumerated or analogous ground?
2. Does the distinction create a disadvantage by perpetuating prejudice or stereotyping?[103]

Interpretation of Section 15(1)? A Case Comment on *R. v. Kapp*" (2008) 6 *Journal of Law and Equality* 33.

101 Bruce Ryder, "The Strange Double Life of Canadian Equality Rights" (2013) 24 *Supreme Court Law Review* (2d) 261 at para 10.

102 Benjamin Oliphant, "*Prima Facie* Discrimination: Is *Tranchemontagne* Consistent with the Supreme Court of Canada's Human Rights Code Jurisprudence?" (2012) 9 *Journal of Law and Equality* 33 at para 56.

103 *Ontario (Director, Disability Support Program) v Tranchemontagne*, 2010 ONCA 593 at para 86 [*Tranchemontagne* CA].

The logic of turning away from well-established principles under human rights legislation that had helped advance substantive equality in favour of the approach under section 15(1) of the *Charter* was justifiably questioned. Lesli Bisgould asserted that "[r]ather than improve the law, uniformity here smooths away important distinctions, with significant implications for those who seek meaningful enforcement of their human rights." [104] For this reason Professor Wayne MacKay laments that "the *Charter* has become more of a burden than a benefit to its statutory partner" and that "the importation of *Charter* equality concepts into the interpretation of human rights codes has limited the goal of substantive equality and reduced access to justice for front line victims of discrimination."[105]

Tranchemontagne CA was an opportunity to clarify the appropriate analytical framework for challenges to government programs, but the Ontario Court of Appeal created more unease over the possibility that the elements of the analysis under section 15(1) of the *Charter* would have a restrictive effect on rights claims under human rights legislation. The elevated burden on the claimant far surpasses the *prima facie* test as first articulated in *O'Malley*.[106] The *prima facie* test requires the complainant to establish the following three components apply:

1) That he or she is a member of a group protected by the *Code*;
2) That he or she was subjected to adverse treatment within one of the social areas covered by human rights legislation;
3) That one of the enumerated grounds of discrimination was a factor in the alleged adverse treatment.

Once the complainant establishes a *prima facie* case, the burden shifts to the respondent to justify the conduct or practice within the framework of the human rights statute.[107]

Lesli Bisgould points out that had the Court of Appeal applied the traditional *prima facie* test in *Tranchemontagne* CA, the exclusion of persons with addictions from the *Ontario Disabilities Support Program Act* would have been resolved without a significant evidentiary burden. It was

104 Lesli Bisgould, "Twists and Turns and Seventeen Volumes of Evidence, or How Procedural Developments Might Have Influenced Substantive Human Rights Law" (2012) 9 *Journal of Law and Equality* 1 at para 2.

105 MacKay, "The Marriage of Human Rights Codes and Section 15 of the *Charter*," above note 89 at para 2; MacKay, "Evolving Fundamental Principles and Merging Public Law Silos," above note 89 at para 130.

106 Reaume, above note 86 at 400.

107 *Moore v British Columbia (Education)*, 2012 SCC 61 at para 33 [*Moore*]; *Shaw v Phipps*, 2012 ONCA 155 at para 14; *Peel Law Association v Pieters*, 2013 ONCA 396 at para 56.

already determined that an addiction was a disability under the *Human Rights Code*, that the claimants would have been eligible for benefits but for the explicit exclusion of those with addictions, and that the distinction that the Act created was based on the claimants' disabilities — a prohibited ground under the *Code*. In these circumstances, the burden of establishing a *prima facie* case had already been met by virtue of the provision in the statute itself.[108]

Justice Abella reiterated the *prima facie* test under human rights legislation for a unanimous Supreme Court of Canada in the 2012 decision of *Moore v British Columbia (Education)*.[109] As noted in Chapter 3, that case did not involve a challenge to a government program created by legislation, but it still provided the Court with an opportunity to address the issue through the decision of the lower court and the arguments made before it. Justice Dillion, of the British Columbia Supreme Court, observed the following:

> This case is not about a constitutional challenge to government policy or programs of education in place during 1992–1995. Indeed, no such attack was made upon the legislation or policies and Moore's parents did not challenge program decisions made about their son at the time. Nonetheless, a great deal of argument was focused on whether and to what extent *Charter* cases applied in the human rights context. The jurisprudence is unclear as to the extent the formal *Charter* discrimination analysis should apply in the human rights context. While there has been an indication that *Charter* jurisprudence should be applied in cases with governmental overtones (see *Vancouver Rape Relief Society v Nixon*, 2005 BCCA 601, 262 DLR (4th) 360 at para 39, leave to appeal to S.C.C. refused, [2006] SCCA No 365), there does not appear to be any clear direction from our Court of Appeal on this issue.[110]

An account of the oral arguments before the Court in *Moore* notes that the relationship between the constitutional and statutory tests for discrimination was called "the elephant in the room in this case," and when the Court was urged to find that the test for discrimination is the same under the *Charter* and human rights legislation, Abella J stated, "we've been saying that since *Andrews*."[111] Given both the criticisms levelled against the

108 Bisgould, above note 104 at para 33.

109 *Moore*, above note 107.

110 *British Columbia (Ministry of Education) v Moore*, 2008 BCSC 264 at para 109, aff'd 2010 BCCA 478.

111 Ryder, above note 101 at para 39.

Ontario Court of Appeal's 2010 *Tranchemontagne* decision, and this direct plea from Dillion J for clear direction, the Supreme Court of Canada could have taken the opportunity to definitively resolve the issue.

With the Supreme Court of Canada's silence on the issue, the Ontario Court of Appeal's framework from *Tranchemontagne* CA is still being applied by courts and tribunals, but often in a manner that comes to terms with the criticism levelled against it. The concern was not with maintaining a degree of dialogue and overlap between section 15(1) of the *Charter* and human rights legislation, which, indeed, the literature supports, but rather the outright domination of the more onerous analysis developed under section 15(1) for human rights legislation.[112]

Leslie Reaume suggests that the challenge is "to find ways to develop analytical concepts which give life to the purposes which underlie these important instruments," and that in doing so, the goal should be to aim at "enriching equality rights jurisprudence and advancing substantive equality."[113] As vice-chair of the Human Rights Tribunal of Ontario, she articulated a solution in *Hendershott v Ontario (Ministry of Community and Social Services) v Ontario*. It was to emphasize the court's observation in *Tranchemontagne* CA that the second part of the test requiring evidence of stereotypic treatment or of perpetuating disadvantage or prejudice will, in most instances, be evident in the human rights context once "a *prima facie* case of discrimination has been established."[114] With the goal of substantive equality in mind, one can ask whether the distinction established in the first step of the test "falls within the range of human rights experiences which were intended to be captured by the *Code*."[115] In simple terms, the relevance of the second part of the test is for cases where a distinction has been made out, but questions remain about whether it is truly a human rights issue.[116] This framework can continue to be employed since the Supreme Court of Canada again declined the opportunity to provide guidance on the issue in the 2018 decision of *Canada (Canadian Human Rights Commission) v Canada (Attorney General)*, and instead left the task of determining the analytical framework to individual tribunals.[117]

112 Reaume, above note 86 at 375.

113 *Ibid* at 400.

114 *Tranchemontagne* CA, above note 103 at para 90; *Hendershott v Ontario (Ministry of Community and Social Services)*, 2011 HRTO 482 at para 40 [*Hendershott*].

115 *Ibid* at para 45.

116 *Ibid* at para 51.

117 *Canada (Canadian Human Rights Commission) v Canada (Attorney General)*, 2018 SCC 31.

Quite aside from the analytical framework, the influence of the *Charter* over human rights legislation extends to the courts reading-in grounds of discrimination through use of section 15(1) of the *Charter*. Even though the grounds of discrimination in human rights legislation appear to present a more rigid list than the concept of enumerated and analogous grounds under section 15(1) of the *Charter*, the broad, liberal, and purposive interpretation of grounds was observed in Chapter 2 as expanding the scope of protected rights. At the same time, the Supreme Court of Canada has also endorsed the reading-in of grounds of discrimination in human rights legislation through use of section 15(1) of the *Charter*. The Supreme Court of Canada has stressed that human rights legislation does not have to "mirror" the *Charter* but must be interpreted in light of *Charter* values. Particularly "when a statutory provision is open to more than one interpretation, it must be interpreted in a manner consistent with the provisions of the *Canadian Charter*."[118] With the decision of *McKinney v University of Guelph* in 1990, it was becoming clear that the requirement for human rights legislation to be read consistently with the *Charter* meant that the *Charter* could be used to challenge human rights legislation not in accordance with section 15(1).[119]

This culminated in the 1999 case of *Vriend v Alberta*, where the Supreme Court of Canada found that the exclusion of sexual orientation from Alberta's *Individual Rights Protection Act* violated section 15(1) of the *Charter*.[120] As a remedy, sexual orientation was read into the statute as a prohibited ground of discrimination.[121] The Court sought to quell concerns that extending the legislation was an undemocratic exercise. It categorized the remedy to be the least intrusive, and it underscored the availability of "parliamentary safeguards" such as the ability of the government to enact exceptions and defences in the legislation.[122] In holding that human

118 *Boisbriand*, above note 80 at para 42. See also *Potash*, above note 80 at para 69; *Slaight Communications Inc v Davidson*, [1989] 1 SCR 1038 at para 87; *Gwinner*, above note 98 at para 99; *Newfoundland and Labrador v Sparkes*, 2004 NLSCTD 16 at para 37. For the application of this principle by the Canadian Human Rights Tribunal, see *Day v Canada (Department of National Defence)*, [2002] CHRD No 31 at para 29.

119 Corbett, above note 26 at 65; *McKinney v University of Guelph*, [1990] 3 SCR 229.

120 *Vriend v Alberta*, [1998] 1 SCR 493 at para 107 [*Vriend*]. See also *Haig v Canada*, [1992] OJ No 1609 (CA).

121 *Vriend*, above note 120 at para 150.

122 *Ibid* at paras 176–77. Timothy Macklem has gone further. He suggests that the Court in *Vriend* assisted in the democratic exercise by breaking a political deadlock, and that once the decision was released, the change to the law was "broadly acceptable to the Alberta government and to the Alberta public." Timothy Macklem, "*Vriend v. Alberta*:

rights legislation does not always have to "mirror" the *Charter* in all cases, the Court stressed the need for a case-by-case contextual analysis to determine whether the exclusion of a ground of discrimination in a human rights statute that is recognized as an enumerated or analogous ground under section 15(1) of the *Charter* would be found to be in violation of the *Charter*, and whether it could be upheld under section 1. In the words of the Court: "[i]f a provincial legislature chooses to take legislative measures which do not include all of the enumerated and analogous grounds of the *Charter*, deference may be shown to this choice, so long as the tests for justification under s. 1, including rational connection, are satisfied."[123] Yet, the Court's valid point that the exclusion of sexual orientation meant that the Alberta government was effectively saying that "'all persons are equal in dignity and rights,' except gay men and lesbians," makes it difficult to conceive of a situation where the exclusion of a ground of discrimination in a provincial human rights statute that is recognized as an enumerated or analogous ground of discrimination under section 15(1) would not violate the *Charter*.[124]

C. THE QUASI-CONSTITUTIONALITY OF ACCESS TO INFORMATION AND PRIVACY

The origins of access-to-information and privacy legislation stem from the increasing role of government in the 1960s and 1970s. This active role resulted in the need for citizens to access information held by government to have meaningful democratic participation and to hold government

---

Making the Private Public," Case Comment (1999) 44 *McGill Law Journal* 197 at para 2. In contrast, Craig Bavis states that "[t]he Court's decision in *Vriend* to read sexual orientation into Alberta's human rights legislation as a prohibited ground of discrimination against the express wish of the Alberta Legislature has been praised by gay and lesbian rights activists as rectifying a fundamental injustice and at the same time scorned by others as an undemocratic and inappropriate intrusion into the legislative domain of elected government representatives." Craig D Bavis, "*Vriend v. Alberta, Law v. Canada, Ontario v. M. and H.*: The Latest Steps on the Winding Path to Substantive Equality" (1999) 37 *Alberta Law Review* 683 at para 1.

123 *Vriend*, above note 120 at para 106.

124 *Ibid* at paras 105–6. Shirish Chotalia states, "[g]iven the filial relationship between human rights laws and *Charter* laws, a violation of *Charter* rights by human rights laws cannot be upheld as a legitimate legislative exercise." See Shirish Chotalia, "The *Vriend* Decision: A Case Study in Constitutional Remedies in the Human Rights Context," Case Comment (1994) 32 *Alberta Law Review* 825.

accountable for its actions.[125] At the same time, the mass collection of personal information by government and big business, and its storage and dissemination electronically, resulted in concerns about the protection of personal information.[126]

1) The Emergence of Privacy

The first legal protections of personal privacy at the federal level were provided in the *Canadian Human Rights Act*, part IV, in 1977. The Office of the Privacy Commissioner of Canada was also established. The right to privacy did not fit well within the anti-discrimination provisions of the *Canadian Human Rights Act*, however, so this was addressed in 1983 with the enactment of both the *Privacy Act* and the *Access to Information Act*, which together formed "the complementary nature of data protection and freedom of information as critical components of a strong and healthy democracy."[127] This double enactment was followed by provincial legislation in these spheres in the 1990s.

The Supreme Court of Canada endorsed the quasi-constitutional status of privacy acts and the broad, liberal, and purposive approach to their interpretation in the 2002 decision of *Lavigne v Canada (Office of the Commissioner of Official Languages)* because of the "quasi-constitutional mission" of privacy rights, and since personal privacy was first protected at the federal level under the *Canadian Human Rights Act* prior to the enactment of the *Privacy Act*. Justice Gonthier explained for a unanimous Court:

> Until 1983, the core elements of the legal guarantees of the confidentiality of personal information were set out in Part IV of the *Canadian Human Rights Act* . . . Part IV of the *Canadian Human Rights Act* was repealed . . . and replaced by the *Privacy Act* . . . In view of the quasi-constitutional mission of that Act, the courts have recognized its special nature.[128]

---

125 Tom Onyshko, "The Federal Court and the *Access to Information Act*" (1993) 22 *Manitoba Law Journal* 73 at paras 4–5; Vincent Kazmierski, "Something to Talk About: Is There a *Charter* Right to Access Government Information?" (2008) 31 *Dalhousie Law Journal* 351.

126 Canada, Parliamentary Information and Research Service, *Canada's Federal Privacy Laws* (Ottawa: Parliamentary Information and Research Service, 2013) at 1.

127 *Ibid* at 2.

128 *Lavigne v Canada (Office of the Commissioner of Official Languages)*, 2002 SCC 53 at para 24 [*Lavigne*].

Even though the quasi-constitutional status of the *Privacy Act* was not expressly endorsed by the Supreme Court of Canada until the 2002 *Lavigne* decision, it was previously recognized by the Federal Court in the 1996 decision of *Canada (Privacy Commissioner) v Canada (Labour Relations Board)*, where Noël J stated:

> The enactment by Parliament of Part IV of the *Canadian Human Rights Act*, later replaced by the *Privacy Act*, illustrated its recognition of the importance of the protection of individual privacy. A purposive approach to the interpretation of the *Privacy Act* is thus justified by the statute's quasi-constitutional legislative roots.[129]

In 2000 Parliament enacted the *Personal Information Protection and Electronic Documents Act*, known as *PIPEDA*, to govern the collection, use, and disclosure of personal information in private sector commercial activities.[130] *PIPEDA* has been described as trying to strike a balance between the individual's right to privacy and an organization's need to collect, use, and disclose information.[131] Three provinces passed statutes displacing *PIPEDA*,[132] and four other provinces passed legislation recognized under *PIPEDA* as protecting personal health information.[133]

The Supreme Court of Canada endorsed the quasi-constitutional status of the second kind of privacy statute in the 2013 case of *Alberta (Information and Privacy Commissioner) v United Food and Commercial Workers, Local 401*, where it held that "[i]nsofar as *PIPA* [*Personal*

---

129 *Canada (Privacy Commissioner) v Canada (Labour Relations Board)*, [1996] 3 FC 609 at 652 (TD), cited by Gonthier J in *Lavigne*, above note 128 at para 24.

130 SC 2000, c 5 [*PIPEDA*].

131 *Mountain Province Diamonds Inc v De Beers Canada Inc*, 2014 ONSC 2026 at para 37 [*Mountain Province Diamonds Inc*]. See also Christopher Berzins, "Protecting Personal Information in Canada's Private Sector: The Price of Consensus Building" (2002) 27 *Queen's Law Journal* 609; Teresa Scassa, "Text and Context: Making Sense of Canada's New Personal Information Protection Legislation" (2000–2001) 32 *Ottawa Law Review* 34.

132 *Organizations in the Province of Alberta Exemption Order*, SOR/2004-219; *Personal Information Protection Act*, SA 2003, c P-6.5; *Organizations in the Province of British Columbia Exemption Order*, SOR/2004-220; *Personal Information Protection Act*, SBC 2003, c 63; *Organizations in the Province of Quebec Exemption Order*, SOR/2003-374; *An Act respecting the protection of personal information in the private sector*, CQLR c P-39.1.

133 *Personal Health Information Custodians in New Brunswick Exemption Order*, SOR/2011-265; *Personal Health Information Privacy and Access Act*, SNB 2009, c P-7.05; *Health Information Custodians in the Province of Ontario Exemption Order*, SOR/2005-399; *Personal Health Information Protection Act, 2004*, SO 2004, c 3; *Personal Health Information Custodians in Newfoundland and Labrador Exemption Order*, SI/2012-72; *Personal Health Information Act*, SNL 2008, c P-7.01.

Information Protection Act] seeks to safeguard informational privacy, it is 'quasi-constitutional' in nature."[134] It did so by extending its reasoning from its decisions in *Lavigne* and *Dagg v Canada (Minister of Finance)* on the *Privacy Act* to legislation dealing with privacy in the private sector. Even though there were earlier decisions from lower court referring to *PIPEDA* as quasi-constitutional,[135] there were lingering questions about whether this kind of privacy statute was deemed quasi-constitutional until the Supreme Court of Canada ruled on the issue. For instance, in the 2012 decision of *Pearson v Peninsula Consumer Services Cooperative*, Gaul J, of the British Columbia Supreme Court, stated: "I find myself unable to accept the respondent's submission that the *PIPA* is a quasi-constitutional statute, and therefore entitled to a special or preferential status when compared to statutes such as the *Co-op Act*."[136] Justice Gaul explicitly rejected the extension of the Supreme Court of Canada's reasoning in *Lavigne* to the second kind of privacy statute because of the distinction between privacy rights vis-à-vis government institutions and those in the private sector.[137] This distinction is not a valid reason to prevent this category of privacy legislation from being recognized as quasi-constitutional since human rights legislation applies to both government and private actors. Nonetheless, since *UFCW, Local 401*, there is no longer any question that this type of privacy legislation is quasi-constitutional.[138]

2) The Emergence of Access to Information

Proponents of access to information in Canada were inspired by the early developments in Scandinavian countries and the enactment of the *Freedom of Information Act* in the United States in 1966.[139] Access-to-information legislation was first enacted in Nova Scotia and New Brunswick in the late 1970s, and the federal *Access to Information Act* was enacted in 1983.[140]

---

134 *Alberta (Information and Privacy Commissioner) v United Food and Commercial Workers, Local 401*, 2013 SCC 62 at para 22 [*UFCW, Local 401*]. See also *Mountain Province Diamonds Inc*, above note 131 at para 37.

135 *Eastmond v Canadian Pacific Railway*, 2004 FC 852 at para 100; *Nammo v TransUnion of Canada Inc*, 2010 FC 1284 at paras 74–75.

136 *Pearson v Peninsula Consumer Services Cooperative*, 2012 BCSC 1725 at para 33.

137 *Ibid* at para 34.

138 *UFCW, Local 401*, above note 134 at para 22. See also *Mountain Province Diamonds Inc*, above note 131 at para 37.

139 *Freedom of Information Act*, 5 USC § 552.

140 Library of Parliament Research Branch, *Public Access to Federal Government Information* by David Johansen (Ottawa: Library of Parliament, 1979) at 3.

The other provinces quickly followed and enacted legislation that provides both access to information and the protection of personal privacy. These statutes entirely reversed the principle of administrative secrecy in government, and the new model was that "information should be released unless the Government can make a good case for keeping it secret."[141]

The interpretation of access-to-information legislation is linked to its close connection to privacy, and given the latter's historic link to human rights legislation, the courts have adopted the approach developed under human rights legislation. As La Forest J noted in *Dagg*: "[t]he *Access to Information Act* and the *Privacy Act* were originally considered together by Parliament as Bill C-43, and were enacted simultaneously."[142] In *Canada Post Corp v Canada*, Létourneau J, of the Federal Court of Appeal, applied the broad, liberal, and purposive interpretation to access-to-information legislation first developed under human rights legislation:

> It is, in my view, as much the duty of courts to give subsection 4(1) of the *Access to Information Act* a liberal and purposive construction, without reading in limiting words not found in the Act or otherwise circumventing the intention of the legislature as "it is the duty of boards and courts", as Chief Justice Lamer of the Supreme Court of Canada reminded us in relation to the *Canadian Human Rights Act*, "to give section 3 a liberal and purposive construction, without reading the limiting words out of the Act or otherwise circumventing the intention of the legislature."[143]

This statement was relied upon by the Federal Court of Appeal in *3430901 Canada Inc v Canada (Minister of Industry)*, where Evans JA held that "it was the duty of the courts to give the same kind of 'liberal and purposive construction' to the interpretation of the public right to access that they give to statutory rights to be free from discrimination."[144]

Despite the broad right to access government information, it has been recognized that access to information needs to be strengthened to bring it in line with more progressive regimes in the Commonwealth and the rest of the world.[145] Some have even argued in favour of outright

---

141 *Ibid.*

142 *Dagg v Canada (Minister of Finance)*, [1997] 2 SCR 403 at para 50.

143 *Canada Post Corp v Canada (Minister of Public Works)*, [1995] 2 FC 110 at para 33 (CA).

144 2001 FCA 254 at para 26, leave to appeal to SCC refused, [2001] SCCA No 537.

145 Canada, Standing Committee on Access to Information, Privacy and Ethics, *The Access to Information Act: First Steps Towards Renewal* (Ottawa: Report of the Standing Committee on Access to Information, Privacy and Ethics, 2009); Murray Rankin, The

constitutional protection of access to information in Canada.[146] The government has responded with Bill C-58, which, it claims, is the first significant revitalization of the *Access to Information Act* in its thirty-four-year history.[147] Despite this claim, the Bill has been criticized by the information commissioner of Canada, non-governmental organizations, and politicians alike.[148] The information commissioner of Canada has called it a regression rather than an advancement of rights, and said that "it allows the government to decide what information Canadians can obtain rather than letting Canadians decide for themselves."[149] The Information Commission specifically points out that the Bill imposes new obligations on requesters, adds new grounds for institutions to decline to respond to requests, introduces the possibility of fees, and, for some information, replaces the right of access and independent oversight with proactive disclosure. The Bill also failed to extend the application of the *Access to Information Act* to the Prime Minister's Office and ministers' offices, as well as administrative institutions that support Parliament and the courts, thus not empowering the information commissioner to order the release of information. The information commissioner therefore made recommendations to the government to improve Bill C-58.[150]

Access to Information Act 25 Years Later: Towards a New Generation of Access Rights in Canada (2008); Stanley L Tromp, *Fallen Behind: Canada's Access to Information Act in the World Context* (2008); Vincent Kazmierski, "Accessing with Dinosaurs: Protecting Access to Government Information in the Cretaceous Period of Canadian Democracy" (2001) 25:3 *Constitutional Forum* 57 at 62; Canadian Bar Association, Modernization of the *Access to Information Act* (Ottawa: National Privacy and Access Law Section, Canadian Bar Association, 2013).

146 Tromp, above note 145 at 56; Kazmierski, "Something to Talk About," above note 125.

147 *House of Commons Debates*, 42nd Parl, 1st Sess, Vol 148, No 204 (22 September 2017) at 1020 (Hon Scott Brison).

148 Information Commissioner of Canada, *Failing to Strike the Right Balance for Transparency: Recommendations to Improve Bill C-58: An Act to Amend the* Access to Information Act *and the* Privacy Act *and to Make Consequential Amendments to Other Acts* (Vancouver: Information Commissioner of Canada, 2017); Centre for Law and Democracy, *Canada: Note on Bill C-58 Amending the* Access to Information Act (Halifax: Centre for Law and Democracy, 2017); *House of Commons Debates*, 42nd Parl, 1st Sess, Vol 148, No 204 (22 September 2017) at 1024 (Hon Murray Rankin); *House of Commons Debates*, *ibid* at 1034 (Hon Tom Kmiec).

149 Information Commissioner of Canada, *Failing to Strike the Right Balance for Transparency*, above note 148 at 2.

150 *Ibid.*

D. THE QUASI-CONSTITUTIONALITY OF LANGUAGE RIGHTS

The only provision in the *Constitution Act, 1867* that directly addresses linguistic rights is section 133, which guarantees the use of English and French in the debates, legislation, records, and journals of the federal Parliament and the National Assembly of Quebec.[151] A similar guarantee applicable to Manitoba is found in the *Manitoba Act, 1870*, section 23.[152] As a result of the limited linguistic rights, the Supreme Court of Canada described these protections as "a rudimentary language rights scheme."[153] More specific language rights were developed through legislation both at the federal and provincial levels, which consequently influenced constitutional changes when the Constitution was patriated. The interplay between statutory language rights and rights entrenched in the *Charter* in 1982 is indicative of the quasi-constitutional status of language rights.

1) Language Rights Legislation and the Constitution

Despite the limited nature of the early constitutional protections of language rights, the courts have found that Confederation would not have occurred without the protection of linguistic minorities in the *Constitution Act, 1867*. As the Ontario Court of Appeal explained in *Lalonde v Ontario (Commission de restructuration des services de santé)*: "[t]he protections accorded linguistic and religious minorities are an essential feature of the original 1867 Constitution without which Confederation would not have occurred."[154] As a result, the Supreme Court of Canada has safeguarded these constitutional language rights when provinces have made legislative attempts to reduce them.[155]

151 (UK), 30 & 31 Vict, c 3, reprinted in RSC 1985, App II, No 5.

152 33 Vic, c 3.

153 *Solski (Tutor of) v Quebec (Attorney General)*, 2005 SCC 14 at para 4 [*Solski*].

154 [2001] OJ No 4767 at para 81 (CA) [*Lalonde*]. The court echoed Lord Sankey LC, of the Judicial Committee of the Privy Council, in *Re the Regulation and Control of Aeronautics in Canada*, [1932] AC 54 at 70 (JCPC). See also *Reference re Secession of Quebec*, [1998] 2 SCR 217 at para 79.

155 Quebec's first enactment of the *Charter of the French Language*, SQ 1977, c 5 (CQLR c C-11), was found *ultra vires* by a unanimous Supreme Court of Canada in *Quebec (Attorney General) v Blaikie (No 1)*, [1979] 2 SCR 1016 [*Blaikie (No 1)*], because it was in direct violation of s 133 of the Constitution. For a comprehensive historic account of the language rights in Quebec, see, especially, Joseph E Magnet, *Official Languages of Canada: Perspectives from Law, Policy and the Future* (Cowansville, QC: Yvon Blais, 1995); Marcel Martel & Martin Pâquet, *Speaking Up: A History of Language and Politics*

The adoption of a federal model in 1867 has been described by the Supreme Court of Canada as a direct response to the fear of assimilation by minorities as it would protect French language and culture both directly, through the adoption of French as an official language in Quebec and Canada as a whole, and indirectly by assigning legislative authority over education and "Property and Civil Rights in the Province" to the provinces.[156] The Supreme Court specifically said that

> the presence of two distinct language communities in Canada and the desire to reserve an important place for them in Canadian life constitute one of the foundations of the federal system that was created in 1867.[157]

The federal structure also ensures the protection by the federal government of French language rights outside Quebec. As the Ontario Court of Appeal observed, "implicit in the Confederation bargain" is that the French linguistic minority outside Quebec "could look to the federal government for constitutional protection."[158] This protection is provided, in part, through quasi-constitutional language rights statutes.

The federal government made great efforts to extend the application of section 133 of the *Constitution Act, 1867* to the other provinces, both at the 1971 Constitutional Conference in Victoria and during the process commenced in 1979 that resulted in the patriation of the Constitution in 1982. By 1980 federal Justice Minister Jean Chrétien was lamenting the fact that, during the Victoria conference, the federal government had secured the agreement of seven provinces to bind themselves to section 133, but by 1980, only New Brunswick remained willing to be bound.[159] When pressed on whether the federal government would allow Quebec or Manitoba to voluntarily withdraw from the requirement if they sought

---

in Canada and Quebec, trans by Patricia Dumas (Toronto: Between the Lines, 2012). The Supreme Court of Canada's decision in *Forest v Manitoba (Attorney General)*, [1979] 2 SCR 1032, was in response to Manitoba's *Act to Provide That the English Language Shall Be the Official Language of the Province of Manitoba, 1890* (Man), c 14, later RSM 1970, c O10. See also Joseph E Magnet, "Court Ordered Bilingualism" (1981) 12 *Revue générale de droit* 237.

156 *Reference re Secession of Quebec*, above note 154 at paras 38 and 79; *Lalonde*, above note 154 at para 79.

157 *Solski*, above note 153 at para 6.

158 *Lalonde*, above note 154 at para 86.

159 Canada, Special Joint Committee of the Senate and House of Commons on the Constitution of Canada, *Minutes of Proceedings and Evidence*, 32nd Parl, 3rd Sess (7 November 1980) at 1435 (Hon Jean Chrétien).

to do so, he rejected this idea because "[t]he Fathers of Confederation bound Canada, in 1867, as well as Quebec and Manitoba."[160]

Given the limited nature of the original constitutional protections of linguistic rights, and the unsuccessful attempt at extending the application of section 133 of the *Constitution Act, 1867* to other provinces, a more concerted effort was made to protect linguistic rights with legislation.[161] The earliest examples are the federal *Official Languages Act* and the *Official Languages of New Brunswick Act*, both enacted in 1969.[162] As the Supreme Court of Canada explained, "legislation that was quite broad in scope, although it did not have constitutional status, had been implemented by the federal government and by a number of provinces."[163] During the constitutional patriation process, the federal commissioner of official languages marvelled at the achievements of advancing rights through legislation:

> As one who is responsible to Parliament for the administration of the law relating to language, I have been struck personally by the extent to which legislation has made real progress in this area of fundamental rights . . . . I think our own experience here in Canada these last 11 years since the adoption of the *Official Languages Act*, has shown that it is possible to make substantial advances by means of legislation.[164]

Despite his confidence in the *Official Languages Act*, the commissioner supported the constitutional entrenchment of those rights because "neither federal nor provincial actions over the last decade or so should blind us to the historical record of neglect and suppression which has brought those communities to the precarious condition in which they find themselves."[165]

The language rights that were constitutionally protected in sections 16 and 20 of the *Charter* at the time of patriation find their origins in the 1969 federal *Official Languages Act* and the *Official Languages of New*

160 *Ibid*, (12 November 1980) at 2010 (Hon Jean Chrétien).

161 *Ibid.*

162 *Official Languages Act*, SC 1968-1969, c 53; RSC 1970, c -2; currently the *Official Languages Act*, RSC 1985, c 31 (4th Supp). *Official Languages of New Brunswick Act*, SNB 1969, c. 14; RSNB 1973, c O-1, repealed and replaced by the *Official Languages Act*, SNB 2002, c O-0.5.

163 *Solski*, above note 153 at para 4.

164 Canada, Special Joint Committee of the Senate and House of Commons on the Constitution of Canada, *Minutes of Proceedings and Evidence*, 32nd Parl, 3rd Sess (17 November 1980) at 2005 (MF Yalden, commissioner of official languages).

165 *Ibid.*

Brunswick Act. Section 16 of the *Charter* establishes English and French as the official languages of Canada and New Brunswick, and section 20 provides members of the public the right to communicate and receive services from the federal government and New Brunswick in both official languages. These provisions significantly expanded upon the constitutional language rights in section 133 of the *Constitution Act, 1867*, which does not apply to New Brunswick, does not establish the official language status of English and French, and does not provide a right to communicate and receive services in those languages. The federal commissioner of official languages, in his testimony before the Special Joint Committee of the Senate and House of Commons on the Constitution, endorsed sections 16 and 22 as "they confirm and enshrine certain basic tenets of the *Official Languages Act*."[166] The *Official Languages Act* is, therefore, a precursor of the language rights in the *Charter*.

Since the entrenchment of language rights in the *Charter* in 1982, there has been a proliferation of legislation protecting language rights that has been recognized as quasi-constitutional. The advancement of language rights through legislation is intentionally built into the *Charter*, as section 16(3) provides that "[n]othing in this *Charter* limits the authority of Parliament or a legislature to advance the equality of status or use of English and French." The Ontario Court of Appeal interpreted this provision to mean that "[t]he *Charter* contemplates the advancement of the equality of status of English and French not only by Parliament but also by the provincial legislatures."[167] In 1988 the federal government enacted a new *Official Languages Act* that the courts have said, "adopted the wording of the *Charter*, which gives it special status."[168] Language rights were also enacted in part XVII of the *Criminal Code*, comprising sections 530 and 530.1, which give accused persons the right to be tried in the official language of their choice, and to have their information or indictment translated into English or French.

There are considerable differences between the federal *Official Languages Act* and the language rights schemes from one province to the next.[169] The official status of English and French in New Brunswick, the

166 Above note 164.

167 *Lalonde*, above note 154 at para 89. The court succinctly described the expansion of language rights with the enactment of the *Charter* at paras 87–88.

168 *Doucet v Canada*, 2004 FC 1444 at para 16 [*Doucet*].

169 Vanessa Gruben, "Bilingualism and the Judicial System" in Michel Bastarache, ed, *Language Rights in Canada*, 2d ed (Cowansville, QC: Yvon Blais, 2004) 141 at 211.

only bilingual province, is established in both section 16(2) of the *Charter* and in the *Official Languages Act* of that province.[170] The three territories are officially bilingual through their language rights ordinances, which can be described as quasi-entrenched because the federal legislation enabling the territories prevents amendment or repeal of these ordinances without the concurrence of Parliament.[171] Language legislation in Ontario, Alberta, Saskatchewan, and the three territories provides for the use of English and French in the Legislative Assembly,[172] and French versions of the acts of the legislature are required in Ontario and the three territories.[173] The legislation in Alberta, Saskatchewan, and the three territories allows for the use of the French language in court proceedings to various degrees.[174] The language rights statutes in Alberta and Saskatchewan were enacted after the decisions of *R v Mercure* and *R v Paquette*, where the Supreme Court of Canada held that these provinces could unilaterally amend the language rights in the *North-West Territories Act, 1886* and the *Saskatchewan Act, 1905*.[175] Ontario and Prince Edward Island also provide a degree

---

170 For the history of language rights in New Brunswick, see Michael MacMillan, *The Practice of Language Rights in Canada* (Toronto: University of Toronto Press, 1998) ch 5.

171 *Yukon Act*, SC 2002, c 7, s 27; *Northwest Territories Act*, RSC 1985, c N-27, s 43.1; *Nunavut Act*, SC 1993, c 28, s 38. See also Michel Bastarache et al, *The Law of Bilingual Interpretation* (Markham, ON: Lexis Nexis, 2008) at 140–42.

172 *French Language Services Act*, RSO 1990, c F.32, s 3; *Languages Act*, RSA 2000, c L-6, s 5; *The Language Act*, SS 1988-89, c L-6.1, s 12; *Official Languages Act*, RSNWT 1988, c O-1, ss 4 and 6; *Official Languages Act*, RSY 2002, c 133, ss 1 and 3; *Official Languages Act*, SNu 2008, c 10, ss 3–5.

173 Ontario *French Language Services Act*, above note 172, s 4, requires all acts of the legislature since 1991 to be enacted in French, while all earlier statutes must be translated. According to s 4(3), only the regulations that the Attorney General deems appropriate have to be translated into French. The language ordinances in the three territorial governments require the records and journals to be published in English and in French. Ontario's *French Language Services Act* does not make mention of records or journals. Saskatchewan's *The Language Act*, above note 172, s 12, allows the Assembly to require the printing of records and journals in French as well. In Alberta, Acts of the Legislative Assembly and journals of the Assembly are to be in English only. *Languages Act*, RSA 2000, c L-6, ss 3 and 5.

174 Alberta *Languages Act*, *ibid*, s 4; Saskatchewan *The Language Act*, above note 172, s 12; Northwest Territories *Official Languages Act*, above note 172, s 9; Nunavut *Official Languages Act*, above note 172, s 8; Yukon *Official Languages Act*, above note 172, s 5.

175 *Mercure*, above note 80; *R v Paquette*, [1990] 2 SCR 1103; Alberta *Languages Act*, above note 172; Saskatchewan *The Language Act*, above note 172; *North-West Territories Act*, RSC 1886, c 50; and the *Saskatchewan Act*, SC 1905, c 42, s 16. See William Henkel, "A Commentary on French Language Rights in the Prosecutions of Provincial Offences in Alberta" (1989) 27 *Alberta Law Review* 302; WH McConnell, "Bilingualism on the Prairies: The Constitutional Status of French in Saskatchewan" (1989) 53 *Saskatchewan*

of bilingualism in government services.[176] In Ontario, the *French Language Services Act* establishes zones where French language services from the provincial government are required based on the number of French speakers.[177] Nova Scotia's *French-language Services Act* seeks to provide French-language services by designated government departments.[178] British Columbia and Newfoundland and Labrador do not have legislation protecting language rights.

2) The Broad, Liberal, and Purposive Interpretation of Language Rights

Language rights legislation was first declared quasi-constitutional by the Federal Court of Appeal in the 1991 decision of *Canada (Attorney General) v Viola*. Justice Décary described it as follows:

> The 1988 *Official Languages Act* is not an ordinary statute. It reflects both the Constitution of the country and the social and political compromise out of which it arose. To the extent that it is the exact reflection of the recognition of the official languages contained in subsections 16(1) and (3) of the *Canadian Charter of Rights and Freedoms*, it follows the rules of interpretation of that *Charter* as they have been defined by the Supreme Court of Canada. To the extent also that it is an extension of the rights and guarantees recognized in the *Charter*, and by virtue of its preamble, its purpose as defined in section 2 and its taking precedence over other statutes in accordance with subsection 82(1), it belongs to that privileged category of quasi-constitutional legislation which reflects "certain basic goals of our society" and must be so interpreted "as to advance the broad policy considerations underlying it."[179]

While the original 1969 version of the *Official Languages Act* was a precursor to sections 16 and 20 of the *Charter*, Décary J identified the 1988 version as a reflection and extension of the *Charter* that gives it its

---

Law Review 143; Edmund A Aunger, "Legislating Language Use in Alberta: A Century of Incidental Provisions for a Fundamental Matter" (2004) 42 *Alberta Law Review* 463; Edmund A Aunger, "The Mystery of the French Language Ordinances: An Investigation into Official Bilingualism and the Canadian North-West: 1870 to 1895" (1998) 13 *Canadian Journal of Legal Studies* 89.

176 *French Language Services Act*, SPEI 1999, c 13.

177 Ontario *French Language Services Act*, above note 172, s 5.

178 *French-language Services Act*, SNS 2004, c 26.

179 *Canada (Attorney General) v Viola*, [1991] 1 FC 373 at para 16 (CA) [*Viola*].

quasi-constitutional status. This statement was adopted by Bastarache J, who wrote for the majority of the Supreme Court of Canada in the 1999 decision of *R v Beaulac*, although the Court did not expressly endorse language legislation as quasi-constitutional until 2002 in the unanimous *Lavigne* decision.[180]

The language rights in the *Criminal Code*, which were addressed by the Court in *Beaulac*, have since been declared to be quasi-constitutional by the Federal Court.[181] Holding the language rights in the *Criminal Code* as quasi-constitutional supports the suggestion that individual provisions, or specific rights, may be designated as quasi-constitutional in addition to entire statutes.[182]

Beaulac firmly established the broad, liberal, and purposive interpretation of language rights. Justice Bastarache reviewed the judicial history of interpreting language rights broadly, liberally, and purposively, going back to a series of decisions in the 1970s that confirmed that section 133 of the *Constitution Act, 1867* provided a minimal protection that did not preclude the extension of language rights through federal or provincial legislation.[183] This interpretive approach, however, was reversed in a trilogy of cases decided by the Supreme Court of Canada in 1986, which viewed language rights as stemming from "social and political compromise," and consequently held that they should be interpreted with "restraint."[184] The fact that language rights were a product of political compromise was not a legitimate reason to adopt a restrictive interpretation as it has been recognized that "[t]he rights of linguistic and religious minorities were the only ones entrenched in the *British North America Act* that left the

---

180 *R v Beaulac*, [1999] 1 SCR 768 at para 21 [*Beaulac*]; *Lavigne*, above note 128 at para 23. See also *Doucet*, above note 168 at paras 16–17.

181 *Canada (Commissioner of Official Languages) v Canada (Department of Justice)*, 2001 FCT 239 at paras 139, 142, 182, 194, & 195. See also *Belende v Patel*, 2008 ONCA 148 at para 24.

182 See Vanessa MacDonnell, "A Theory of Quasi-constitutionality" (2016) 53 *Osgoode Hall Law Journal* 508 at 520.

183 *Beaulac*, above note 180 at para 15. The Court referred to the following decisions as first establishing the broad, liberal, and purposive interpretation of language rights: *Jones v Attorney General of New Brunswick*, [1975] 2 SCR 182; *Blaikie (No 1)*, above note 155; *Attorney General of Quebec v Blaikie (No 2)*, [1981] 1 SCR 312.

184 *Beaulac*, above note 180 at para 16; *MacDonald v City of Montreal*, [1986] 1 SCR 460; *Société des Acadiens du Nouveau-Brunswick Inc v Association of Parents for Fairness in Education*, [1986] 1 SCR 549; and *Bilodeau v Manitoba (Attorney General)*, [1986] 1 SCR 449. For an overview of the trilogy and its aftermath, see Marc Cousineau, "Survol des droits linguistiques : enfin de vrais droits linguistiques au Canada" (2000–2001) 32 *Ottawa Law Review* 117 at para 24.

usual civil liberties to the protection of common law and party politics."[185] As such, the Court should have considered the fact that some aspects of language rights were removed from the whims of politics in the constitutional arrangement of 1867, and although these rights were limited in scope, their protection was more constitutionally guaranteed than many of the traditional civil liberties.

The Supreme Court of Canada began to depart from the narrow interpretation of language rights following the 1986 trilogy, but it was not until *Beaulac* that the Court was credited with having revolutionized the interpretation of language rights to bring them in line with other categories of quasi-constitutional legislation.[186] This approach has since been confirmed and applied by the courts in numerous decisions.[187] Following *Beaulac*, the Court promptly overturned decisions that applied a restrictive approach to the interpretation of language rights.[188] This interpretive approach is often justified on the basis that language rights in quasi-constitutional statutes serve as an extension of rights contained in the *Charter*, beginning with the Federal Court of Appeal's decision in *Viola*.[189] In *Thibodeau v Air Canada*, the Federal Court stated the following about the *Official Languages Act*: "[t]he quasi-constitutional nature is clear. That is why the Act must be interpreted having regard to the

---

185 Leslie Green, "Are Language Rights Fundamental?" (1987) 25 *Osgoode Hall Law Journal* 639 at 639.

186 Cousineau, above 184 at para 2. *Beaulac*, above note 180 at para 17. The Court in *Beaulac* referred to the following cases as departing from the 1986 trilogy: *Ford v Quebec (Attorney General)*, [1988] 2 SCR 712; *Mahe v Alberta*, [1990] 1 SCR 342; *Reference re Manitoba Language Rights*, [1985] 1 SCR 721; *Reference re Public Schools Act (Man), s 79(3), (4) and (7)*, [1993] 1 SCR 839.

187 See, for example, *Arsenault-Cameron v Prince Edward Island*, 2000 SCC 1 at para 27; *Desrochers v Canada (Industry)*, 2009 SCC 8 at para 31; *R v Caron*, 2015 SCC 56 at para 35; *Lavigne*, above note 128 at para 24; *Fédération Franco-Ténoise v Canada (Attorney General)*, 2008 NWTCA 6 at para 60, leave to appeal to SCC refused (*sub nom Northwest Territories (Attorney General) v Fédération Franco-Ténoise*), [2008] SCCA No 432; *Thibodeau v Air Canada*, 2005 FC 1156 at para 45 [*Thibodeau*]; *Kilrich Industries Ltd v Halotier*, 2007 YKCA 12 at para 43; *R v Pooran*, 2011 ABPC 77 at para 17; *Lalonde*, above note 154 at para 132.

188 *Arsenault-Cameron v Prince Edward Island*, above note 187.

189 *Viola*, above note 179 at para 16. See also *R v Gaudet*, 2010 NBQB 27 at para 25, where the New Brunswick Court of Queen's Bench stated, "[t]he *Official Languages Act* has a quasi-constitutional status because the said Act flows from the authority conferred upon the legislature of New Brunswick by s. 16(3) of the *Charter*."

constitutional guarantees and must be given such broad and liberal interpretation as will best ensure that these guarantees are attained."[190]

E. THE QUASI-CONSTITUTIONALITY OF THE COMMON LAW RIGHT TO THE PROTECTION OF A PERSON'S GOOD REPUTATION

The quasi-constitutional common law right to protect a person's good reputation arises in the context of defamation suits. In *Hill v Church of Scientology of Toronto*, the Supreme Court of Canada observed that a person's good reputation "is closely related to innate worthiness and dignity of the individual," and accordingly, a democratic society "has an interest in ensuring that its members can enjoy and protect their good reputation so long as it is merited."[191]

The defendants in *Hill* argued that the common law tort of defamation unwarrantedly restricted their constitutional right to freedom of expression by placing too much emphasis on the right to the protection of a person's good reputation. The Court accordingly considered whether the common law needed to be changed to better balance the freedom of expression with the protection of a person's good reputation. The Court had previously held in *RWDSU v Dolphin Delivery Ltd* that the whole body of common law can be subject to *Charter* scrutiny, regardless of whether there is a government action.[192] Despite the fact the *Charter* does not apply in situations involving a suit under the common law between two private parties, the common law must be developed and applied in a manner consistent with the *Charter*. The Court in *Hill* referred to the *Charter* as "a restatement of the fundamental values which guide and shape our democratic society and our legal system," and as a result held that "it is appropriate for the courts to make such incremental revisions to the common law as may be necessary to have it comply with the values enunciated in the *Charter*."[193]

In considering whether the common law achieves the appropriate balance, the Court in *Hill* observed that the constitutional protection of

---

190 *Thibodeau*, above note 187 at para 46. The court referred to Pierre-André Côté, *Interpretation of Legislation in Canada*, 3d ed (Scarborough: Carswell, 2000) at 500.

191 [1995] 2 SCR 1130 at paras 107–8 [*Hill*].

192 *Retail, Wholesale and Department Store Union, Local 580 (RWDSU) v Dolphin Delivery Ltd*, [1986] 2 SCR 573 at paras 25–26.

193 *Hill*, above note 191 at 92.

the freedom of expression in section 2(b) of the *Charter* does not make it an absolute right; instead, it has to be viewed in light of its underlying basis in "the quest for truth, the promotion of individual self-development, and participation in the community."[194] Accordingly, the freedom of expression can be subject to legal restrictions for considerations of decency and public order, including obscenity and hate speech.[195] When considering these factors, the Court noted that defamatory statements are "very tenuously related to the core values which underlie s. 2(b)," and, in fact, are contrary to the search for truth, do not enhance self-development, and do not enhance participation in the community.[196]

The common law right to protect a person's good reputation is not constitutionally protected, yet the Court in *Hill* found that it "reflects the innate dignity of the individual, a concept which underlies all the *Charter* rights," and "is intimately related to the right to privacy which has been accorded constitutional protection." [197] For that reason, the Court held that it is "worthy of protection in our democratic society and must be carefully balanced against the equally important right of freedom of expression."[198] After the Court analyzed and balanced the competing principles of the freedom of expression and the protection of a person's good reputation, it concluded that there is no need to alter the common law of defamation because it complies with the underlying values of the *Charter*.[199] A unanimous Court in *Éditions Écosociété Inc v Banro Corp* looked back at the *Hill* decision and declared that "this Court has recognized that one of the primary purposes of the law of defamation is to protect the reputation of the individual, which was elevated to quasi-constitutional status."[200]

The emergence of quasi-constitutionality with the development of its defining legal characteristics displays both the interconnectedness of these laws and their relationship to the Constitution. The primacy of quasi-constitutional legislation originates in the *Canadian Bill of Rights*; however, a restrictive interpretation of its provisions limited its use, and since the entrenchment of the *Charter* its relevance is now generally

194 *Ibid* at para 104.

195 *Ibid* at paras 102–6. See also *R v Keegstra*, [1990] 3 SCR 697; *R v Butler*, [1992] 1 SCR 452.

196 *Hill*, above note 191 at para 106.

197 *Ibid* at paras 120–21.

198 *Ibid* at para 121.

199 *Ibid* at para 141.

200 *Éditions Écosociété Inc v Banro Corp*, 2012 SCC 18 at para 57.

limited to the right to property and a fair hearing in the administrative law context. Primacy gained more widespread application under human rights legislation as a result of a broad, liberal, and purposive interpretation, and this approach was extended to privacy, access-to-information, and language rights legislation. The Supreme Court of Canada has also endorsed a reciprocal interpretation of quasi-constitutional legislation with similar rights in the *Charter*, beginning with a departure from the restrictive approach that it applied to the *Canadian Bill of Rights*. The interpretation of human rights and language rights legislation has influenced the interpretation of similar rights in the *Charter* since these statutes predate the *Charter*, but the interpretation of these statutes has also been influenced by the more authoritative *Charter*. As the sole common law principle recognized as quasi-constitutional, the protection of a person's good reputation has to be balanced against the constitutionally protected freedom of expression.

FURTHER READINGS

CORBETT, STANLEY. *Canadian Human Rights Law and Commentary* (Markham, ON: LexisNexis, 2007).

COUSINEAU, MARC. "Survol des droits linguistiques: enfin de vrais droits linguistiques au Canada" (2000–2001) 32 *Ottawa Law Review* 117.

HOVIUS, BEREND. "The Legacy of the Supreme Court of Canada's Approach to the *Canadian Bill of Rights*: Prospects for the *Charter*" (1982–1983) 28 *McGill Law Journal* 31.

MACKAY, WAYNE A. "The Marriage of Human Rights Codes and Section 15 of the *Charter* in Pursuit of Equality: A Case for Greater Separation in Both Theory and Practice" (2013) 64 *University of New Brunswick Law Journal* 54.

OLIPHANT, BENJAMIN. "Prima Facie Discrimination: Is *Tranchemontagne* Consistent with the Supreme Court of Canada's Human Rights Code Jurisprudence?" (2012) 9 *Journal of Law and Equality* 33.

ONYSHKO, TOM. "The Federal Court and the *Access to Information Act*" (1993) 22 *Manitoba Law Journal* 73.

RÉAUME, DENISE G. "Of Pigeonholes and Principles: A Reconsideration of Discrimination Law" (2002) 40 *Osgoode Hall Law Journal* 113.

REAUME, LESLIE. "Postcards from *O'Malley*: Reinvigorating Statutory Human Rights Jurisprudence in the Age of the *Charter*" in Fay Faraday, Margaret Denike, & M Kate Stephenson, eds, *Making Equality Rights Real: Securing Substantive Equality Under the Charter* (Toronto: Irwin Law, 2009) 373.

ST-HILAIRE, MAXIME. "The Codification of Human Rights in Canada" (2012) 42 *Revue de droit de l'Université de Sherbrooke* 505.

CHAPTER 6

Conclusion

Quasi-constitutional laws protect a broad range of rights through methods that are distinct from the constitutionally entrenched model of the *Charter*. The type of rights protected by quasi-constitutional laws include basic civil liberties, the right against discrimination, the right to access government information, the right to privacy in both the public and private sectors, and the protection of an individual's good reputation. Many of these differ from the rights in the *Charter*. Quasi-constitutional laws also provide distinct methods of upholding rights compared to constitutional entrenchment, and they thereby strain the stark division traditionally depicted between legislation and common law on the one hand, and constitutional law on the other.

Lord Sankey's famous statement in *Edwards v Attorney General of Canada* (the *Person's* case), about the *British North America Act*, that "there are statutes and statutes," has appropriately been quoted to describe quasi-constitutional statutes, since they are interpreted and applied in a fashion that recognizes both their increased importance over regular statutes and their relationship to the Constitution.[1] This begins, at a theoretical level, with the term "fundamental law," which has been used to describe the rights upheld by both the Constitution and quasi-constitutional laws. Chapter 4 explored how the concept of fundamental law connotes a link

1 *Transpacific Tours Ltd (cob CP Air Holidays) v Canada (Director of Investigation and Research)*, [1985] BCJ No 551 at para 24 (SC); *Edwards v Attorney General of Canada*, [1930] AC 124 (JCPC).

between a right and the foundational principles of the Canadian Constitution. It revealed that the theoretical distinction between fundamental rights, whether in constitutional or quasi-constitutional form, and any other type of right, is that the former maintains a link to the foundational principles of the Constitution, while the latter is acquired through the regular statute or the common law principle in which it originates. At a more observable level, the term fundamental law has been associated with judicial review and a more onerous process for amendment and repeal than regular law, which formed the basis for the study of the practical aspects of quasi-constitutionality in Chapters 2 and 3.

Chapter 3 focused on the primacy of quasi-constitutional legislation and its effect on the interpretation of other statutes. Primacy was shown to be engaged when a quasi-constitutional statute conflicts with a regular statute, which requires courts and tribunals to depart from the conventional methods of statutory interpretation and attempt to interpret the regular statute in accordance with the quasi-constitutional one. When a conflict cannot be avoided through interpretation, a court or tribunal can declare the conflicting provision in the regular statute inoperable if the conflict is with human rights legislation or the *Canadian Bill of Rights*. Initially, there was considerable doubt that a primacy provision granted the courts authority to refrain from applying the conflicting statutory provision or to declare it inoperable. While some of the early commentators on the *Canadian Bill of Rights* suggested that it gives "the Courts some power to challenge the validity of federal legislation,"[2] others believed that primacy was restricted to a rule of statutory construction that mandated an interpretation that avoids conflict.[3] This remedy was first developed under the *Canadian Bill of Rights* and is now most frequently applied under human rights legislation. Declarations of inoperability have not been explicitly endorsed by the courts under the other categories of quasi-constitutional legislation, although it was shown that a similar outcome is often achieved through an interpretation that avoids conflict or by the courts applying the quasi-constitutional statute and refraining from applying another statute.

In addition to primacy and the influence of quasi-constitutional legislation on the interpretation of other legislation, the Supreme Court of Canada has also adopted a broad, liberal, and purposive interpretive

2 Douglas A Schmeiser, *Civil Liberties in Canada* (London & New York: Oxford University Press, 1964) at 21.

3 Peter W Hogg, *Constitutional Law of Canada*, 5th ed (Toronto: Carswell, 2007) at 35-4.

approach because "it is inappropriate to rely solely on a strictly grammatical analysis . . . [for] the interpretation of legislation which is constitutional or quasi-constitutional in nature."[4] Chapter 2 focuses on the application of the broad, liberal, and purposive interpretation of quasi-constitutional legislation, and provides a comprehensive review of the concrete results achieved by the courts through this interpretive approach and how it has expanded the rights in quasi-constitutional legislation.

The interpretation of quasi-constitutional statutes and their primacy are interrelated methods of upholding rights. Chapter 4 reveals that both are a product of an interpretive approach that aims to advance the fundamental nature of the rights contained in quasi-constitutional legislation while remaining subject to legislative supremacy. The former encompasses the interpretation of quasi-constitutional statutes, whereas the latter involves the effect that quasi-constitutional statutes have over the interpretation of other statutes. How the fundamental nature of rights translates into an interpretation and application of quasi-constitutional statutes that reflects both their legislative form and relationship to the Constitution was described by Estey J in *Law Society of Upper Canada v Skapinker*:

> The *Canadian Bill of Rights* is, of course, in form, the same as any other statute of Parliament. It was designed and adopted to perform a more fundamental role than ordinary statutes in this country. It is, however, not a part of the Constitution of the country. It stands, perhaps, somewhere between a statute and a constitutional instrument. Nevertheless, it attracted the principles of interpretation developed by the courts in the constitutional process of interpreting and applying the Constitution itself.[5]

Justice Estey looked back to Laskin CJ's decision in *R v Curr*, which he believes displays "the distinction between simple 'statutory interpretation' and 'a constitutional role'" of the *Canadian Bill of Rights*.[6]

Quasi-constitutional legislation is not subject to the more onerous amendment process in Part V of the *Constitution Act, 1982*, although because of its primacy, the Supreme Court of Canada has held "that it may not be altered, amended, or repealed, nor may exceptions be created

4 *Quebec (Commission des droits de la personne et des droits de la jeunesse) v Montréal (City); Quebec (Commission des droits de la personne et des droits de la jeunesse) v Boisbriand (City)*, 2000 SCC 27 at para 30.

5 *Law Society of Upper Canada v Skapinker*, [1984] 1 SCR 357 at para 10.

6 *Ibid; R v Curr*, [1972] SCR 889 at 889.

to its provisions, save by clear legislative pronouncement."[7] This means that quasi-constitutional legislation is not subject to implied repeal. Importantly, the primacy of quasi-constitutional legislation is recognized by the courts even in the absence of an express primacy provision because of its fundamental character. This presumption can be rebutted by the substantive provisions of the statute, although because of the fundamental nature of the rights that quasi-constitutional statutes uphold, the courts will only recognize a departure from this interpretive approach when there is clear legislative language.

The primacy of quasi-constitutional legislation has been compared to legislative "manner and form" requirements. Manner and form requirements, however, were shown to be procedural steps imposed by one Parliament on a subsequent one for legislation to be considered validly enacted, whereas primacy is an approach that prioritizes quasi-constitutional legislation over regular legislation in the interpretive process. Primacy does not speak to the validity of legislation in conflict with quasi-constitutional legislation, but rather the precedence of legislation in the interpretive exercise.

Justice Estey's recognition that the *Canadian Bill of Rights* has "attracted" the principles of interpretation developed by the courts for the interpretation of the Constitution was shown in Chapter 4 not simply to involve the wholesale adoption of the principles of constitutional interpretation for quasi-constitutional legislation. The interpretation of quasi-constitutional legislation may find its basis in the foundational principles of the Constitution, but it also remains subject to legislative supremacy. This means, first and foremost, that the courts cannot eschew the intent of the framers in the interpretive exercise. Instead, the courts balance the fundamental nature of rights with legislative intent through presumptions about the values that the legislature sought to uphold and promote when it enacted the quasi-constitutional legislation.

Chapter 3 demonstrated that quasi-constitutional legislation in Canada can be considered an example of the weak-form model of constitutionalism and judicial review as adopted for the protection of rights in other Commonwealth countries. In this respect, Canada has adopted both a stronger form of judicial review under the *Charter*, and a weaker form under quasi-constitutional legislation. The primacy of quasi-constitutional legislation begins with an interpretive approach similar to the

7 *Winnipeg School Division No 1 v Craton*, [1985] 2 SCR 150 at 156.

interpretive mandate found within the Commonwealth, although declarations of inoperability provide a remedy to the rights claimants when a statute cannot be interpreted consistently with the rights statute. A more limited remedy has been devised in the United Kingdom with the concept of the disapplication of a law when it conflicts with the *European Communities Act 1972*, but the primacy of quasi-constitutional legislation in Canada and the ability of courts to declare conflicting statutes inoperable provides the strongest form of judicial review within the weak-form model in the Commonwealth.

While quasi-constitutional statutes are an example of the weak-form model of judicial review, they should not be thought of as a less effective form of rights protection than the *Charter*, but rather as an additional layer of rights that complements the Constitution. This is most obvious with respect to the rights included in quasi-constitutional legislation that are not protected by the *Charter*. Moreover, unlike the *Charter*, some quasi-constitutional statutes apply to private actors as well as to the public sector. Towards that end, section 26 of the *Charter* holds that "[t]he guarantee in this *Charter* of certain rights and freedoms shall not be construed as denying the existence of any other rights or freedoms that exist in Canada."

There are also instances where quasi-constitutional statutes provide an effective means of rights protection when recourse to a similar right protected by the *Charter* is not available. For example, while the *Ontario Works Act* explicitly precludes the Social Benefits Tribunal of Ontario from considering the constitutional validity of a provision, the Supreme Court of Canada confirmed in the 2006 decision of *Tranchemontagne v Ontario (Director, Disability Support Program)*, that this does not prevent the tribunal from declaring a provision inoperable under the *Human Rights Code*.[8]

The case of *Ford v Quebec (Attorney General)* demonstrates how the same principle applies in situations involving the invocation of the section 33 notwithstanding clause. In that case, the Supreme Court of Canada found that a section of Quebec's *Charter of the French Language* requiring commercial advertising to be only in French could not be challenged as a contravention of the guarantee of the freedom of expression in section 2(b) of the *Charter* because the section 33 override clause had been

---

8 2006 SCC 14 at paras 30–32.

successfully invoked by Quebec's National Assembly.[9] Instead, the Court held that the provision was inoperable because it infringed the freedom of expression and the guarantee against discrimination based on language in Quebec's *Charter of Human Rights and Freedoms*.[10]

The theoretical advantage of protecting rights in legislative quasi-constitutional form rather than through constitutional entrenchment is that quasi-constitutionality cannot be criticized as usurping the democratic process, except by the most ardent adherents to the traditional view of legislative supremacy.[11] In Chapter 4, it was observed that a prevalent critique of the strong-form variety of judicial review is that it is contrary to democracy because it results in what Jeremy Waldron refers to as a "mode of final decision-making."[12] Within the Commonwealth, such concerns are typically expressed in terms of constitutional rights undermining the doctrine of legislative supremacy. The *Charter* is sometimes described as having transformed Canada from a system of legislative supremacy to one of constitutional supremacy.[13] Others have been critical of the use of the *Charter* by interest groups to obtain legislative change that could not have been achieved through the democratic process.[14] The dialogue view of the *Charter* was developed by Professor Peter Hogg to counter claims that judicial review under the *Charter* is undemocratic because section 1 allows for reasonable limits to rights, and section 33 allows Parliament and the provincial legislature to override rights.[15] While this has become the prevailing view in Canada, the combination in the *Charter* of a strong-form model of judicial review and a legislative override was examined and rejected in the UK when the *Human Rights Act* was being enacted. The Lord Chancellor at the time considered this approach to be

9 *Ford v Quebec (Attorney General)*, [1988] 2 SCR 712 at para 83.

10 *Ibid*; *Charter of Human Rights and Freedoms*, CQLR c C-12, ss 3 and 10.

11 See, for example, HWR Wade, *Administrative Law* (Oxford: Oxford University Press, 2000) at 28; HWR Wade, "Sovereignty — Evolution or Revolution?" (1996) 112 *Law Quarterly Review* 568 at 574.

12 Jeremy Waldron, "The Core of the Case Against Judicial Review" (2006) 115 *Yale Law Journal* 1346 at 1348.

13 Lorraine Weinrib, "Canada's *Charter of Rights*: Paradigm Lost?" (2001–2002) 6 *Review of Constitutional Studies* 119.

14 FL Morton & Rainer Knopff, *The Charter Revolution and the Court Party* (Peterborough, ON: Broadview Press, 2000).

15 Peter W Hogg, "The *Charter* Revolution: Is It Undemocratic?" (2001–2002) 12 *Constitutional Forum/Forum constitutionnel* 1.

contrary to the British view of parliamentary supremacy.[16] Quasi-constitutionality accounts for these critiques because it protects fundamental rights and provides a form of judicial review within the doctrine of legislative supremacy.

An area that remains to be explored is the relationship between quasi-constitutional statutes and constitutionally protected statutes. The concept of constitutionally protected statutes arose in the 2014 *Reference re Supreme Court Act, ss 5 and 6* case, in which the Supreme Court of Canada held that certain sections of the *Supreme Court Act* were constitutionally protected as a result of the references to the Court in Part V of the *Constitution Act, 1982*.[17] The Court only referred to changes to the "composition of the Supreme Court of Canada," and to "other essential features of the Court" as being protected under Part V of the *Constitution Act, 1982*. This appears to suggest that certain provisions in the *Supreme Court Act* are not constitutionally protected and thus remain in regular statutory form. It has similarly been suggested that certain aspects of a statute can be designated quasi-constitutional while others are not. Building on the Supreme Court of Canada's analysis in *R v Beaulac*, for example, the Federal Court only designated the language rights in Part XVII of the *Criminal Code* as quasi-constitutional and not the entire *Criminal Code*.[18]

If part of a statute can be held to be quasi-constitutional or constitutionally protected, while the balance of the statute remains regular, then the question arises whether a statute can contain both constitutionally protected and quasi-constitutional provisions. This may be the case with legislation implementing treaties with Indigenous peoples. As observed in Chapter 4, modern treaties with Indigenous groups, including land claims agreements and self-government agreements beginning with the 1975 *James Bay and Northern Quebec Agreement*, and the statutes that implement them, contain primacy provisions.[19] These treaties and their

16 Lord Irvine of Lairg, *Human Rights, Constitutional Law and the Development of the English Legal System: Selective Essays* (Oxford: Hart, 2003) at 98.

17 *Reference re Supreme Court Act, ss 5 and 6*, 2014 SCC 21.

18 *Canada (Commissioner of Official Languages) v Canada (Department of Justice)*, 2001 FCT 239 at paras 139, 142, 182, 194, & 195; *R v Beaulac*, [1999] 1 SCR 768 at paras 21–22; *Criminal Code*, RSC 1985, c C-46. See also *Belende v Patel*, 2008 ONCA 148 at para 24.

19 *James Bay and Northern Quebec Agreement*, 1975, s 2.5. The federal enabling legislation of the James Bay and Northern Quebec Agreement was the *James Bay and Northern Quebec Native Claims Settlement Act*, SC 1976-77, c 32, s 8 and, in Quebec, *An Act Approving the Agreement Concerning James Bay and Northern Quebec*, CQLR c C-67, s 6. See also *Eeyou Marine Region Land Claims Agreement Act*, SC 2011, c 20, s 6; *Gwich'in*

implementing legislation were never declared to be quasi-constitutional by the courts prior to becoming constitutionally protected in 1982 with the inclusion of section 35 in the *Constitution Act, 1982*. However, in the 2010 decision of *Quebec (Attorney General) v Moses*, four dissenting justices took interest in the primacy provisions despite the constitutionally protected status of these agreements, and they declared that "[t]hese provisions have never been repealed, and they continue to bind both governments."[20] The dissenting four justices also referred to the primacy provision as "an intention to elevate the Agreement to supra-legislative status."[21] This raises the question of whether these agreements and their implementing legislation had quasi-constitutional status prior to their constitutional protection in 1982.

An examination of the relationship between quasi-constitutional and constitutionally protected statutes and the primacy provisions in treaties with Indigenous peoples is beyond the scope of this work, although it is a subject that merits study. It does, however, reflect back on the overarching theme of this book that quasi-constitutionality helps reveal that the traditional tripartite division of law in Canada with sharp boundaries between the Constitution, statutory law, and the common law is far too simplistic. Quasi-constitutionality is an area of law that challenges this traditional approach and helps give rise to new perspectives that approach the relationship between the various categories of law as more malleable, dynamic, and flexible, with qualities that are both statutory and constitutional. Quasi-constitutionality should therefore no longer be overlooked because it helps provide a deeper theoretical understanding of Canadian law, and it provides an important form of rights protection in Canada with potential wider international influence for jurisdictions that have not adopted the strong-form model of rights protection.

Land Claims Settlement Act, SC 1992, c 53, s 8; *Maanulth First Nations Final Agreement Act*, SC 2009, c 18, s 5; *Nisga'a Final Agreement Act*, SC 2000, c 7, s 6; *Nunavik Inuit Land Claims Agreement Act*, SC 2008, c 2, s 6; *Nunavut Land Claims Agreement Act*, SC 1993, c 29, s 6; *Tla'amin Final Agreement Act*, SC 2014, c 11, s 5; *Tlicho Land Claims and Self-Government Act*, SC 2015, c 1, s 5; *An Act To Give Effect to the Westbank First Nation Self-Government Agreement*, SC 2004, c 17, s 5; *Western Artic (Inuvialuit) Claims Settlement Act*, SC 1984, c 24, s 4; *Yale First Nation Final Agreement Act*, SC 2013, c 25, s 5; *Yukon First Nations Land Claims Settlement Act*, SC 1994, c 34, s 13; *Yukon First Nations Self-Government Act*, SC 1994, c 35, s 3.

20 2010 SCC 17 at para 92.

21 *Ibid.*

Table of Cases

Index

About the Author

JOHN HELIS, called to the Ontario bar in 2006, has worked in the areas of law covered in this book for more than a decade. He is currently a member of the Social Benefits Tribunal, the tribunal from which originated the *Tranchemontagne* cases, some of the most significant decisions on the ability to use quasi-constitutional statutes to challenge other legislation. Before this appointment he practised law at a legal clinic in the areas of human rights and social justice. He was counsel for the City of Ottawa and Ottawa Police Services Board where he dealt with human rights, access-to-information, and privacy issues. He also worked for the Department of Indian and Northern Affairs as part of a team negotiating land claims and self-government agreements with Indigenous groups. He taught law as an instructor at Carleton University. He holds a PhD in law from Queen's University, a law degree (LLB) and an honour's degree in political science from the University of Ottawa, and a master of arts degree in legal studies from Carleton University. His writing includes an article on quasi-constitutionality, which will be part of an edited book.